N
350

Emphasis Art

A Qualitative Art Program for Elementary and Middle Schools

SIXTH EDITION

Frank Wachowiak

Robert D. Clements

University of Georgia

An imprint of Addison Wesley Longman, Inc.

New York • Reading, Massachusetts • Menlo Park, California • Harlow, England
Don Mills, Ontario • Sydney • Mexico City • Madrid • Amsterdam

Editor-in-Chief: Priscilla McGeehon
Project Coordination and Text Design: York Production Services
Cover Designer: Nancy Sabato
Cover Illustration/Photo: Baiba Kuntz, Glencoe, IL; International Collection of
    Children's Art, Illinois State University, Normal, IL; Frank Wachowiak,
    Athens, GA
Electronic Production Manager: Valerie Zaborski
Manufacturing Manager: Helene G. Landers
Electronic Page Makeup: York Production Services
Printer and Binder: R. R. Donnelley & Sons Company
Cover Printer: Phoenix Color Corp.

For permission to use copyrighted material, grateful acknowledgement is made
to the copyright holders on pp. 355–356, which are hereby made part of this
copyright page.

Library of Congress Cataloging-in Publication Data

Wachowiak, Frank.
        Emphasis art: a qualititative art program for elementary and middle
schools/Frank Wachowiak, Robert D. Clements. —6th ed.
            p.   cm.
        Includes bibliographical references and index.
        ISBN 0-673-99736-7
        1. Art—Study and teaching (Elementary) 2. Art—Study and teach-
ing (Middle school) I. Clements, Robert D. II. Title.

N350.W26   1996   96-17457
372.5'044—dc20   CIP

ISBN 0-673-99736-7

234567890-DOW-999897

To children everywhere who make the teaching of art a never-ending, forever-rewarding adventure, and to their teachers, in both elementary and middle schools, who share in the wonder and discovery. With special thanks to teachers of art around the world and to former students, now teachers and professors of art, who have been so generous in sharing the results of their teaching to help make this book a colorful treasury of child art.

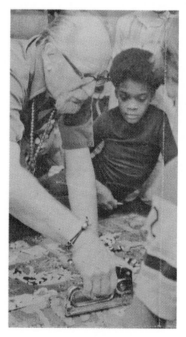

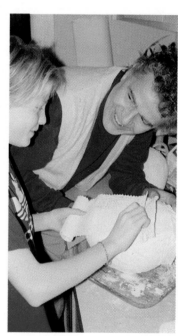

FRANK WACHOWIAK   ROBERT CLEMENTS

contents

CHAPTER 15

CHAPTER 16

part 3

Art Appreciation, Art History, Art Criticism, and Aesthetics

CHAPTER 17

CHAPTER 18

CHAPTER 19

part 4

Teaching Art Production

Preface

This sixth edition of *Emphasis Art* is based upon Frank Wachowiak's teaching of art to children, beginning with his first elementary-school art classes in rural Minnesota and continuing for the next 50 years. His passion for a life in art is shown as Frank says, "I was born in 1913, the year of the Armory Show." After receiving his M.A. degree, he did his first art teaching, but service in the Navy during the Second World War interrupted his art teaching career until after the war and after he had received his M.F.A. degree. His creative encounters with children enriched and colored his life, and he found in the happy, charged environment of children's searching, discovering, and creating that it was easy to stay young at heart. Although Frank's health nowadays precludes his hands-on involvement in this new edition, he lives nearby and I have the opportunity to visit with him. He can recall the creation of each of his illustrations as if it happened yesterday. His inspiring words, the beautiful examples of children's art, and his clear technical directions continue in this new edition. His belief in the intrinsic worth of the art-studio experience remains central. The emphasis is on art—art as an adventure; a flowering; a celebration; and a discipline with its own singular demands, unique core of learning, and incomparable rewards.

One major thrust of education in our day is the increased attention to how general elementary classroom teachers can integrate art with other subjects. To meet this need, strongly called for by this edition's reviewers, two new chapters are added, giving recommendations for integrating art learning and learning in science and social studies. Several of the illustrations and ideas for this integration were previously spread throughout the text, although most are new to this edition.

Allowing children to discover how their innate desire to react and respond verbally to their own artwork and to that of others can enrich their studio art experience. At every stage of human development, a response to art is an exploration of the self and of human nature! Art educators have identified art criticism, art history, and aesthetics as the formal disciplines that can best aid students in this exploration. These three areas, along with studio production, comprise the elements of discipline-based art education (DBAE). Strategies for incorporating DBAE will meet the needs of teachers in the increasing number of school systems, colleges, universities, and states (through state education departments policies) which mandate that art education be treated in the four areas of art criticism, art history, aesthetics, and art production.

The response of educators at all levels to the fifth edition of Emphasis Art has been gratifyingly positive. The book's clarity, structure and wealth of colorful illustrations have found enthusiastic endorsement. The art teaching strategies, motivations, techniques, and evaluative procedures described are based on actual experiences and observations of outstanding elementary- and middle-school art practices both in this country and abroad. This new edition again concerns itself with the adventures, joys, responsibilities, problems, and rewards of teaching art to children;

with the strategic, guiding role of the teacher; with projects based on perennial, universal art principles; and with the ongoing evaluation of lesson objectives in design and composition, art history, art criticism, and aesthetics. In many chapters, new illustrations have been added showing the work of students in today's schools. The craft illustrations, formerly dispersed throughout the book, have been supplemented by new illustrations and the material organized into a new chapter of crafts.

Emphasis Art is designed first and foremost for elementary- and middle-school teachers of art who want to augment and enrich their art programs. It is also proposed as a text for the college or university student in search of high-caliber elementary- and middle-school art practices. It offers a lucid description of a proven, dynamic program for those veteran teachers who seek continuing challenges, new techniques, and classroom-tested art projects for their instructional repertoire.

I wish to especially acknowledge the assistance and contributions of two teachers, both now in leadership positions at universities, who coauthored earlier editions and without whose sharing with Frank Wachowiak the book(s) would not have come into being: Theodore K. Ramsay, Professor of Art, University of Michigan, Ann Arbor, coauthor of the first and second editions of *Emphasis Art*; and David Hodge, Professor of Art and Coordinator of Graduate Studies in Art, University of Wisconsin, Oshkosh, coauthor of the now out of print *Art in Depth*. Thanks to those who taught with Frank Wachowiak in his University of Georgia children's art classes and who have continued to give permission to use artworks they and Frank had their students produce: Dr. Mary Hammond, Head of the Art Department, George Mason University, VA and Dr. Patrick Taylor, Head of the Art Department, Kennesaw College, Kennesaw, GA.

Thanks to Baiba Kuntz, Winnetka, IL and to Sharon Burns-Knutson, Iowa City Schools, IA for their many new and ongoing contributions. Special thanks to Joyce Vroon, Trinity School, Atlanta, for so many new illustrations and for critiquing the manuscript. Special thanks also to Barbara Thomas, Whitehead Elementary School, Athens, Ga and to Melody Milbrandt, Valdosta, GA for many new illustrations. Other new contributors to this edition include Jackie Ellett, Rockbridge Elementary School, Gwinnett County Schools, GA; Debby Lackey, Fulton County Schools, Atlanta; Donna Cummins, Rockview Elementary School, Atlanta; Carol Case, Cobb County Schools, GA; Alisa Hyde, Savannah, GA, and Julie Phlegar, East St. Tammany Parish School District, Slidell, LA. Thanks to ongoing contributors from Faye Brassie, Nancy Elliott, David Harvell, and Mary Lazzari, all from the Athens, GA schools. Other teachers throughout the nation have works reproduced: Shirley Lucas, Oshkosh, WI; Alice Ballard Munn, Anchorage, AL; Ted Oliver, Marietta, GA; Carolyn Shapiro, Brookline, MA; Mary E. Swanson, Nashua, NH; Lawrence Stueck, Watkinsville, GA, and Diane Turner, Laurens, SC. For assistance in selecting 77 child art pictures and researching the credits, I wish to thank Dr. Barry Moore, Curator of the International Collection of Child Art and Professor of Art Emeritus, Illinois State University, Normal, IL. The USSEA Art Collection of Dr. Anne Gregory, Los Angeles Public Schools, is represented by works of students of Barbara Bluhm, Maine, and Susan Whipple, Oregon Christian School. Colleagues at the University of Georgia have helped: W. Robert Nix, Claire B. Clements, Carole Henry, Andra Johnson, and Diane Rives.

The beauty of this book has also been made possible through the contributions of art teachers from around the world: Chen huei-Tung, Tainan, Taiwan; Jean Grant, coordinator, arts and humanities, Department of Defense Dependents' Schools (DODDS), Atlantic Region; Eric Ma Presado, Manila, Philippines; James McGrath, coordinator, arts and humanities, DODDS, Pacific Region; George Mitchell, Atlanta; Federico Moroni, Santarcangelo, Italy; Michihisa Kosugi, Saga, Japan; Norihisa Nakase, art education liaison, Tokyo, Japan; Michael F. O'Brien, American High School, Seoul, Korea, and Linda Riddle, Heidelberg, West Germany. I also want to thank the following persons for giving permission to use published material: Masachi Shimono, editor, *Nihon Bunkyo Suppan*, Osaka, Japan; and Professor Osamu Muro, executive director, *Art Education Magazine*, Tokyo, Japan. Nostell Priory, Yorkshire, England; the Boston Museum of Fine Art; and the National Gallery of Art and the Hirshhorn Museum in Washington, DC, among others, have given permission to reproduce artworks in their collections.

I would also like to thank the following reviewers for their comments and suggestions during the revision process: Victoria J. Fergus, West Virginia University; Wendy Catalano, St. Norbert College; Mary S. Hammond, George Mason University; Amelia C. Watson, Cleveland State University; Cheryl A. Grossman, University of Missouri-Kansas City; and Arthur R. Guagliumi, Southern Connecticut State University. To the members of the editorial and production staff at Addison Wesley Publishers, my grateful acknowledgment for their contributions, especially those of former executive editor Christopher Jennison, editorial assistant Nicole Mauter, assistant to the editor-in-chief Kjersti Monson, production editor Jeff Houck, and book designer Candice Carta.

Robert D. Clements

Part 1

Art, Society, and Children

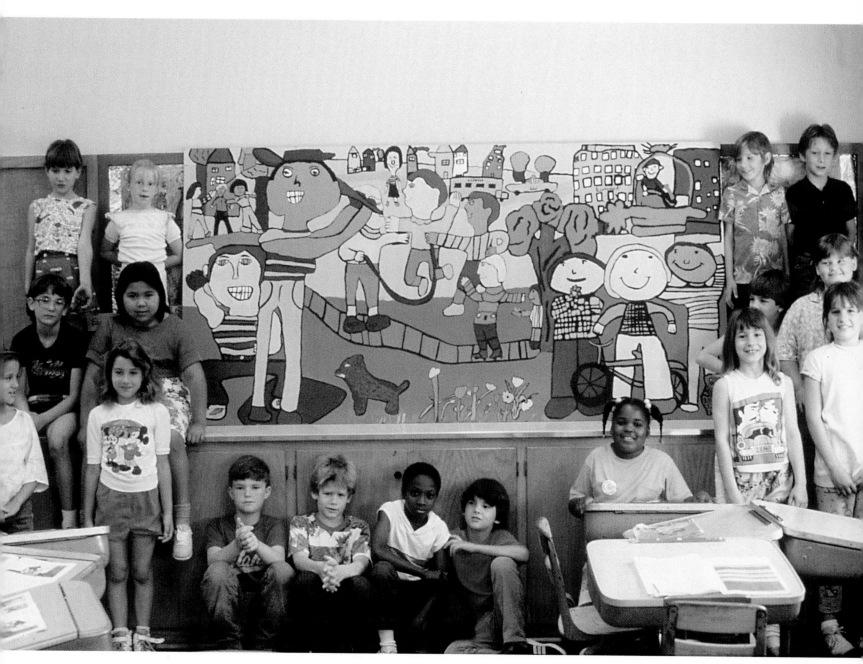

Chapter 1

The Role of Art in Society and in the Schools

Art in Society

On the one hand, art is an international language; it is universally accessible even to those with little knowledge of how it was used in a culture. Through its organization and content, it communicates something of its meaning without words. On the other hand, because it came from a specific culture, it is relative both to that culture and to the time, place, and circumstances of its creation. For the members of any cultural group, art provides a mirror, and it helps them to have a unique sense of cultural identity. Art is one of the main ways for transmitting, maintaining, and analyzing culture; it is a way for people to find out about a culture. Culture is not just a people's artistic, musical, food, holiday, and historical heritage, however. It also is the shared values, attitudes, belief systems, and cognitive styles that affect a group of people's behavior and serve to direct them in their lives and give those lives meaning. Study of the arts and humanities enriches daily life and develops a sense of community.

The arts are important to a nation's people and to their culture. More Americans go to museums than to sporting events, and over 1 million Americans from all communities and cultures call themselves artists. All communities and all cultures make art because art makes events special. When art is made to celebrate ordinary experiences, these experiences take on a special quality. By making events and things stand out from the commonplace, art transforms and reorganizes our conceptions of the world.

Multicultural Pluralism

America is becoming increasingly multicultural. More and more, both our nation in general and the specific arts in our nation address the importance of multiculturalism. For example, one of the major focuses of postmodern art (the term applied to much of our contemporary art) is the relationship of art in a particular culture to social and political issues. This renewed interest of art in things sociopolitical is a sharp departure from earlier modern movements such as abstraction and abstract expressionism, which avoided sociopolitical commentary. Art has become an agent for social change, as anyone who has visited a museum of modern art recently or seen artworks such as Nancy Spero's and Leon Golub's works about brutality, Judy Chicago's and Mary Kelly's pieces about women and motherhood, or Nam June Paik and Joseph Beuys' video about whales knows.

Not only have postmodern artists become agents for change, museums are beginning to move in a new direction as well. As one of society's major institutions dealing with the transmission of culture, the museum in America plays a major role in determining what is considered art. In this decade, art and museums have been the focus of fierce national debates over artistic freedom and censorship. Museums have now begun to mount exhibitions such as Hispanic-American artists, women artists, and Harlem's African-American artists, but multicultural progress is slow. Ninety percent of museum exhibitions in the past decade had a Euro-American focus, and cultural institutions are increasingly challenged to take into account the values, attitudes, and beliefs of minority cultures.

Just as today's artists, museums, and society in general make efforts to create a just society serving all its citizens, teachers in the schools are striving to give equitable treatment to the cultural contributions of their students' ethnic groups. As the student populations of American schools become more multicultural, it is essential that teachers of art design curricula that will promote the appreciation of diverse cultures' artistic heritages. In designing a curriculum, we must ask: Whose culture is being taught? In addition, we must ask if the culture is one in

which contributions are made both by men and by women. Female artists generally have been ignored by the museums and the art establishment.

Art curricula should recognize the students' diversity of class, race, and gender. Art is a natural area in which to combat ethnocentrism and monoculturalism, where European culture is seen as *the* central culture. Newer art programs emphasize the idea that culture is specific. The goal is not to add "multicultural" ingredients as new elements to education but to make education truly multicultural. Teachers need to be open to and nonjudgmental about diverse cultural experiences. They should use their students' preferred styles of learning to make the art curriculum more relevant to the disenfranchised groups that have suffered from prejudice. Artistic experiences that are encountered in daily life should guide development of the curriculum.

Teachers do not set out purposefully to culturally suppress a particular group. Rather, they do so unintentionally, but the effect is similar in both cases. Taking education out of the hands of a particular ethnic group and imposing the dominant society's values leads to feelings of alienation and frustration in that ethnic group. There are two ways to move beyond the approach of suppression, in which nothing of the minority culture is considered worth preserving, toward that of multiculturalism. The first, assimilation involves the cultural heritage of the minority group becoming part of the majority culture. The second involves a kind of cultural pluralism: the minority group retains its cultural traditions while it adopts practices necessary for the smooth functioning of society as a whole.

Past practices have led to inequities, omissions, and stereotyping. What content should be covered in school? There is a debate between elitists and populists concerning how much effort should be devoted to studying the classic masterpieces and how much to studying folk art, popular arts, and commercial art. Elitists say that the great art masterpieces should be studied, because they concern universal themes and have stood the test of time in meeting peoples' needs. Others say that informal art forms, such as folk art and video, are more relevant and lend themselves to increased interpretive possibilities.

Although art communicates some of its meaning across eras and cultures, its creation is relative to its culture. It helps to create a sense of cultural community and identity. **Top:** *Dropped Bowl with Scattered Slices and Peels, 1989, Claes Oldenburg and Coosje van Bruggen, Art in Public Places Program, Miami, FL.* **Middle:** *Native-American kachina.* **Bottom:** *Mola (reverse appliqué) by San Blas Indians.*

Courtesy of Alice Ballard Munn, Anchorage, AL, and Diane Rives, Athens, GA.

An appreciation of Native-American culture is brought to these second-grade children through examining the myths and art of the northwest and southwest Native-American cultures. Each second-grade class selected its own power animal. **Top left:** Wolf kachina with exciting patterns. **Bottom left:** Blue bird kachina based on southwest Native-American stories. **Top middle:** Boy with symbolic collar and headpiece. **Top right:** Black-and-white-striped doll based on Hopi clown kachina. **Bottom right:** A girl in white costume enacts the northwest Native-American myth of how the loon lost her voice.

Some examples of multicultural approaches for your classroom are: Why do the people in our community do art, as different from in other lands and other times? In our area, how does art bring about a sense of community? How are the varied cultural customs around us shown in the art of our community? How have people in our community and elsewhere, and at other times, made art to mark life transitions and other social purposes?

To draw on what is familiar to the students, begin with their own beliefs, values, and community. Appreciation should not be disseminated in a top-down manner. Strive to make the classroom a more democratic place by incorporating the neglected peer group's subculture. Form students into small groups from different cultural backgrounds, and have them explain and defend why they like the art that they do. The art program you provide your students can help them to feel pride in and connectedness to themselves and their own cultural backgrounds, to other people, and to other cultures.

Art in the School

What kind of curriculum should America's nearly 50 million school-children be taught? Where does art fit in? Americans do believe in arts education. One national survey found that almost all feel it is important for children to be exposed to the arts. A large survey of American schools by John Goodlad found that parents do not want, and never have wanted, a "back to basics" curriculum. Instead, they want a curriculum based on four areas: academic, vocational, social-civic-cultural, and personal.

In the social-civic-cultural area, the art goal (as described in the earlier material on multiculturalism) is to apply basic concepts in the fine arts and humanities to the appreciation of the aesthetic contributions by other cultures. Under the personal area, which also includes the arts, one goal is to expand a student's ability to use leisure time effectively. When surveyed, students consistently rated the arts as more interesting and enjoyable than academic subjects. However, about arts classes, Goodlad (1984) wrote:

Communities use the arts to celebrate their historic heritage and myths. Elementary school children from Tainan, Taiwan, have depicted their culture's traditional festivals and pageants. **Top and bottom:** *The Dragon Dance.* **Middle:** *The River Festival.*

Courtesy of Davis Publications, Worcester, MA.

Artist Eddie Edwards and students at Martin Luther King Elementary School, San Diego, created this mural about Reverend King's dream, "We shall overcome." It is described in Kay Wagner's article, "A Mural Worth a Million Words," School Arts Magazine, *January 1991.*

I am disappointed with the degree to which the arts classes appear to be dominated by the ambience of English, mathematics and other academic subjects. Arts classes, too, appear to be governed by characteristics which are best described as "school"—following the rules, finding the one right answer, practicing the lower cognitive processes. [The arts] did not convey the picture of individual expression and artistic creativity toward which one is led by the rhetoric of forward-looking practice in the field.

The qualitative approach for teaching art brings with it an attitude of rigor and the need for artistic creativity. Art requires a high level of abstract reasoning. The new curriculum in art criticism and aesthetics requires analysis and interpretation, and it is another way to include higher-order cognitive processes in art. America needs citizens who can think for themselves, communicate effectively, and appreciate our nation's ethnic diversity. Art education is needed to develop better-educated human beings, citizens who will value and evolve a worthy life. In the art classroom, all of the rationales for education can be addressed: academic excellence, cognitive development, social adaptation, social change, and personal growth. The goal of education is to help students develop both their intellectual capabilities and their capacity to express their thoughts and feelings. Art brings these together, and in large part, this accounts for the power of art.

Enriched and stimulated in art classes by a teacher's varied and challenging motivations, children learn to see more, sense more, and recall more. They become more aware of their changing and expanding environment, and they realize that making art is not something special done by special people. Everyone can put their imprint on a piece of art. The aesthetic state can be likened to that of the human infant: nonspecialized, nondirectional, inquisitive, imaginative, open, and creative. The art teacher in an elementary school can begin talking very early to the young child about the exciting wonders and uses of design and color. Children readily understand the ideas of using dark and light values or dull and bright colors for contrast, of creating big and little shapes for variety, of repeating a shape or color to achieve pattern, and of drawing things large to fill the composition. Children who express their ideas, responses, and reactions with honesty, sensitivity, and perceptiveness within a framework of compositional principles and design create art. For most students, this sense of design and art structure must grow from the many planned art–life experiences and happenings that are provided by the resourceful teacher.

A Qualitative Approach to Teaching Art

Everyone can engage in art-making behavior. Some people, however, think that anything a child draws, paints, or constructs is art. It may be called art, but the question remains as to whether it is a work of good or bad art. It may indeed be a child's visual statement, but it is not necessarily a quality work of art. To have quality, it must, as much as possible, be expressed in the language, structure, and form of art.

What some observers call "art" in a child's drawing very often is not art at all, but simply a visual report that relates to factual writing. Art, on the other hand, is more akin to poetry, which like all fine art comes to life when it distills the essence of an experience in highly expressive and discriminative choices. This is how the qualitative method of teaching art differs from other methods. In poetry, one discovers that the quality of the verse often depends on the choice use of an expressive word, phrase, or couplet and on effective alliteration, meter, rhythm, and sometimes rhyme. Likewise, in the most evocative, colorful art creations of children, one sees how artworks that employ art principles result in a unity and a rich design that distinguishes these works from ordinary, relatively impoverished expressions.

Where qualitative teaching differs from other methods is that it requires the teacher to go beyond initial stimulation. In general, all art

The child's knowledge of science, nature, and art come together as the child represents the natural world, which can be as near as the schoolyard. Teachers should take advantage of the immediate environment—the school playground, the cafeteria kitchen, the band room with musical instruments—as a visual motivational resource. Here, the children are employing 18- × 24-inch sections of hardboard as sketching pads for drawing.

methods emphasize the teacher's responsibility for keeping students engaged in worthwhile experiences so they have something meaningful to express, draw, paint, print, model, or construct. Often, they help the children to recall a past event or provide new visual enrichments through a field trip, model brought to class, dramatization, film, dance, musical recording, story, or poem. For qualitative teaching in art, however, this initial stimulation is not enough. The teacher also must guide the students as they express their responses from a preliminary drawing through to the finished product (see also Chapter 8).

Every time children create a work of art—painting, collage, print, sculpture—they should be encouraged to evaluate their efforts in terms of the lesson's instructional objectives, beginning with the initial sketch. If nothing is said about design, structure, composition, line, value, color, contrast, pattern, and other aspects of the artwork, it is presumptuous to assume that students will develop their aesthetic awareness and artistic potential.

Students who persevere when they make art create more fulfilling, rewarding, and exciting art if they are guided to become more fully aware of their environment. If their contact with the world, the people in it, and nature is superficial and their identification with and response to visual stimuli minimal, they are apt to be content with a hasty, casual, lazy, noncommittal, shorthand statement of an event. Stereotyped interpretations such as stick figures, lollipop trees, box houses, and two curved lines for a bird are seldom based on children's richly observed experiences of distinguishing identifying characteristics and noting differences in things. Without the teacher's help, the average child's art production, limited by abbreviated time schedules, tends to be cursory and sterile.

Teachers who see examples of children's art like those in this text often inquire how long it takes the children to complete projects of the quality illustrated. No doubt, they sense that the artworks enriching this text are not the result of a single, 45-minute lesson. In most instances, the motivation and preliminary drawing alone take one art period. A completed project may take three to four periods depending on the age or grade of the child. When art class is scheduled only once per week, some classroom teachers are concerned that should a project ex-

Oconee Elementary School. Courtesy of Mary Ruth Moore.

Second-grade children learned about poisonous and nonpoisonous snakes through creating this stitchery mural.

A qualitative artwork, such as this "pet in a garden" oil pastel, takes time to create. On 12- × 18-inch violet-colored construction paper, it took three 50-minute class periods. The preliminary drawing was made in school chalk, then reinforced with a large-sized, black felt-nib pen. Color then was applied up to, but not covering, the black lines. Instructional objectives for color were to use color imaginatively and repeat colors for unity. The animal (pet) was drawn first and the garden environment added afterward. See the child at work on this painting in the circle illustration at the right.

tend over a period of several weeks, they could not hold the children's interest. One way to deal with time constraints and still produce qualitative art is limiting the size of the paper—for example, using 9- × 12-inch surfaces instead of 12 × 18 inches for detailed compositions and 12- × 18-inch paper instead of 18 × 24 inches for expressively free tempera paintings.

Qualitative art experiences should have a regularly scheduled and undisputed place in the curriculum of elementary and middle schools. When art is not allotted sufficient time in the school week, when it plays a subordinate role to every other subject, and when it consists mainly of peripheral activities and stereotyped holiday decorations, expecting it to perform a vital role in children's creative growth is unrealistic.

Instructors faced with today's overloaded classes and limited time schedules often do well just to keep the students under control. Teachers can maintain an effective, positive, and productive atmosphere in their classes, however, when they can alert the students to an awareness of the project's instructional objectives and the satisfaction to be achieved in a purposeful art endeavor. When taught effectively, purposefully, and qualitatively, art has a body of knowledge and skills to be mastered. It has unquestionable merit as a unique avenue to mental, social, and individual growth. Artistic creativity should be recognized, lauded, and embraced as a living and learning experience in its own right. Indeed, if taught imaginatively and qualitatively so that every lesson augments and enhances the students' skills in basic learning as well as in perceiving, reading, analyzing, and building a vocabulary, then art is education.

Courtesy of the International Collection of Child Art, Illinois State University, Normal, IL.

When art is taught both purposefully and qualitatively and the instructional objectives to be mastered are made clear, beautiful work results. A St. Petersburg, Russia, scene of children skiing in the snow uses the figures of many children to fill the page, age 6.

Chapter 2

Fundamentals of Art: An Overview

A high-quality methods course, whether directed to the classroom teacher or the teacher of art, should provide students with aesthetically significant, in-depth art experiences. Art concepts based on recurring compositional principles employed in the visual arts, both past and present, should be central features of college- or university-level art education programs. The studio content should be characterized by a deliberate, continuing emphasis on sensitive and expressive drawing experiences. Preliminary sketches or drawings, evaluated in an art context, should be the rule in most studio projects. Beyond college and art course training, art teachers in our elementary and middle schools can grow both creatively and professionally if they continue to read articles on painting, sculpture, printmaking, architecture, and crafts. There, they will discover recurring references to the basic elements of art— line, shape, color, value, form, space, texture, and pattern—as well as to many of art's fundamental principles, such as balance, rhythm-repetition, variety, emphasis, domination-subordination, radiation, and unity. Art creation is a continually challenging adventure, providing few shortcuts to a successful composition. Even so, there are some constant elements that teachers can always turn to and use with confidence when instructing children in their art classes.

Line

Line in art is a human invention, a unique method of perceiving and documenting the visible world. Therefore, a primary concern of teachers of art should be an understanding and implementation of the linear image. The line drawing is the basic structural foundation of all graphic composition and pictorial design. Expressive, sensitively drawn lines vary in weight, width, and emphasis. They may be delicate, bold, static, flowing, rhythmic, ponderous, hesitant, violent, or dynamic. They are achieved through freedom and spontaneity, or through thoughtful and deliberate action. They may converge, radiate, run parallel, meander, twist, skip, and criss-cross to create confusion, flow, rhythm, order, or chaos.

An object or image usually is more exciting visually when it is delineated in a variety of expressive lines. Lines that are sensitively drawn can create and define shapes, values, and paths of motion. Teachers and students should turn to nature and select objects for limitless sources of line variety: frost, roots, spider webs, water ripples, lightning, veins in leaves, feathers, seashells and coral, grain in wood, cracks in ice and dried mud, insect wings, bridges, road maps, shopping carts, birdcages, wicker furniture, and tree bark as well as branches. Children should be provided with many opportunities to study and express their ideas through line and pattern in their myriad forms.

Shape

A study of pictorial design—of composition in painting, prints, and posters—eventually centers on the *shape* of things. The shapes created by lines merging, touching, and intersecting one another take many forms. They may be square, rectangular, round, elliptical, oval, triangular, or amorphous. They may emerge as nonobjective, figurative, or free-form. Shapes also can be created by ink or color washes, charcoal smudges, paint pourings, object printing, and paper cutouts. The achievement of varied, expressive shapes in a developing composition provides students with one of art's most stimulating challenges and rewards.

Nature is by far the richest source of inspiration for the study of variety in shapes. Natural forms and configurations such as those found in tree branches, leaves, seashells, eggs, nuts, petals, berries, and feathers

Lines depict a variety of types of fish, and the lines of the seaweed create interlocking shapes of various sizes which tie the design together.

usually are much more varied and subtle than those based on precise formulas. Perhaps that is why artists turn to aging, dilapidated buildings for their drawing inspiration instead of the coldly geometric shapes of much contemporary architecture. There is far too much reliance on for-mulas and rules of perspective in the rendition of tabletops, doors, win-dows, fences, roofs, and sidewalks. Teachers should encourage students to use artistic license to give vitality to static imagery through meaning-ful distortion, omission, exaggeration, and free-form interpretation.

The shapes of objects or figures in a composition such as trees, houses, people, animals, furniture, and vehicles generally are called *positive shapes*. The empty area around them is referred to as *negative space*, even though this space may include ground, water, and sky. Many artists keep the negative shapes in mind as much as the posi-

Courtesy of Frank Wachowiak, Athens, GA.

The curvilinear shapes of fish and crescents were paired up in the spiraling, radiating design of this upper-elementary-grade class mural.

tive shapes to achieve a strong figure/ground relationship. When the positive shapes are varied in size and shape, in many instances the negative spaces or shapes consequently will be just as varied and interesting.

Value

Value, especially the contrast produced by juxtaposing a variety of values, plays a very important role in pictorial design. Simply stated, *value* refers to the light and dark elements in a composition. Every shade (dark value) and tint (light value) of every color or hue has a place on the value scale. An attractive disposition of values in a picture is even more important than color. When repeated, values create movement in a painting, leading the viewer from one part of the composition to another. Value analyses of master paintings and prints can help students to understand and appreciate the principles employed in achieving successful light-and-dark orchestration. Compositions with sharply contrasting values generally are more dramatic and dynamic in their visual impact.

Courtesy of Baiba Kuntz, Glencoe, IL, Student KaWai Cheung, Grade 8.

The black-and-white values contrast boldly in this scratchboard. Linear patterns and textures drawn from a still life form other values.

When famous American artist Georgia O'Keeffe was studying to be an art teacher, her professor at Teacher's College of Columbia University, Arthur Wesley Dow, emphasized both in his lectures and his writings the importance of value. Many people acknowledge that the value patterns seen in O'Keeffe's paintings are one of their strongest features.

Color

Can you imagine a world without color? How dull it would be. *Color* has three properties or components: *hue*, the name of the color; *value*, the lightness or darkness of the color; and *intensity* (saturation), the brightness or dullness of the color. Unfortunately, its most amazing property often is ignored. Color has magic!

Color in painting is a continuing challenge to art students, teachers of art, and often artists. It is not uncommon to observe students performing with confidence and success when they draw or compose in line or in black-and-white values only, yet they are completely at a loss when they tackle color. Fortunately, successful strategies in color usage exist: to employ intense colors sparingly, to limit the total number of colors or use related colors, to neutralize certain colors, and to create value patterns.

Limitation definitely plays an important role in mastering color orchestration. Students sometimes may be advised to limit their palettes to black, white, and one color in all of its various tints and shades, a system which is very effective. Another suggestion is to use analogous or related colors, those adjacent to one another on the color wheel—for example, blue, blue-green, green, and yellow-green. Two or three colors usually are enough; five colors are too many. One color should dominate and set the tone for the whole color scheme.

To avoid pitfalls of clashing color or strident chromatic relationships, students should be counseled to minimize the intensity of colors in a composition. This process, sometimes referred to as *neutralization* or *dulling* of a color, involves mixing or combining a color with its complementary hue, which can be found opposite to it on the color wheel. Examples of complementary colors are red and green as well as blue and orange. Find the opposites in each; as Vincent Van Gogh wrote to his brother Theo, "While painting, I perceived for the first time how much light there was in darkness." Many colors now available in crayon, oil pastel, and tempera already are neutralized—for example, sienna, brown, umber, ochre, and chrome green.

A fraction of bright, intense color will hold its own against a more generous employment of neutralized colors. Surrounded by duller colors, brighter colors in the middle of the picture give it a sense of glowing light. Colors can be repeated to create movement and unity, but the size and shape of the repeated color should be varied for effectiveness. Dark, cool colors generally recede; bright, warm colors usually advance. Complementary colors such as red and green in their fullest intensities create vibrant contrasts when juxtaposed. Black, grey, and white can be

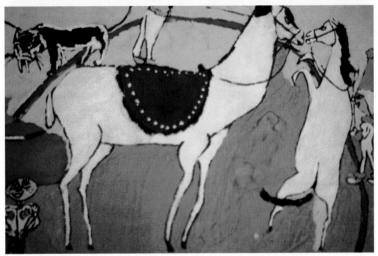

Courtesy of Shirley Lucas, Oshkosh, WI.

One color dominates each of these paintings and provides unity. Notice the mixtures of blue and violet and blue and green in the top painting and the mixed yellow-brown color in the yellow painting. Many tints and shades were mixed. Small areas of other colors provide brilliant contrast. The theme "If I ran the circus" was the motivational catalyst that prompted these two action-filled tempera paintings by fourth-grade children.

combined with any color scheme without creating harmonic conflicts. Often, as in the case of black outlining, the dark linear accent gives a contrasting sharpness and sparkle to the composition. The character, identity, and impact of a color depend a great deal on the colors that are adjacent to or surrounding it. For example, a green shape on a turquoise background may be relatively unnoticed, but intense orange against an intense blue (a complementary relationship) will vibrate and arrest the eye.

Limiting colors to greys and tans give a unifying sense of serenity to this fifth-grade student's collage of an imaginary house.

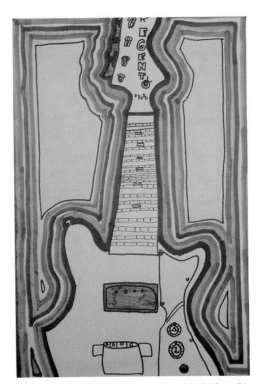

In fifth-grade student Eleanor Siegel's artwork, the yellow background shapes contrast with the guitar's light purple and green repeated outlines.

The teacher's strength in teaching about color is evident in this picture. The peacock is crayoned mainly in green and its variations, along with strong, pure accents of blue, red, and yellow. White crayon is especially effective with the dark grey crayon resist.

To make colors beautiful, we ironically must consider first not hue but value, because it is the main pattern of values or shade that give a picture its overall effect and strength. It is more important to vary the shades than to vary the hues. Contrasts of light and dark colors will make a picture bold.

The painters of the postimpressionist era, including Franz Marc, Marc Chagall, and Odilon Redon, as well as contemporary colorists such as Karel Appel, Helen Frankenthaler, Richard Anuskiewicz, and Victor Vasarely, have provided the art world with eye-opening creations in color, resulting in surprises such as blue horses and multihued people. Teachers and students also should turn for inspiration in color usage to the luminous stained-glass windows of Gothic cathedrals, the jewel-like miniatures of India and Persia, the shimmering mosaics of Byzantium, and the fascinating ukiyo-e color woodcuts of Japan.

Space

Space is an element both in pictorial composition and in abstract design that often confuses the student. In two-dimensional art expression, *space* sometimes is designated as the negative area between positive objects. This kind of space often is referred to as *decorative* or *surface* space. Another category of space to be considered is space-in-depth. Common pictorial devices for achieving the illusion of space-in-depth on a two-dimensional plane, as in a painting, are:

- Vertical placement to suggest depth
- Diminishing sizes of objects as they recede in distance
- Drawing sharp, clear details in the foreground and blurred, indistinct elements in the background
- Overlapping shapes or forms
- Drawing objects that are farther away from the observer higher on the picture plane
- Using bright, intense colors in the foreground and dulled colors in the background
- Employing perspective-creating techniques such as converging lines and horizon levels

Courtesy of Baiba Kuntz, Glencoe, IL. Student Ashley Milne.

The color spectrum forms the surreal background, the nose, and the spiraling eyes for this eighth-grade student's black, heart-shaped, abstract face done in acrylics.

Courtesy of the International Collection of Child Art, Illinois State University, Normal, IL.

Although the shoppers' heights remain constant, this market scene from Turkey shows depth through vertical placement.

In the fifth-grader's Antarctica scene, the biggest penguin is four times as large as the distant penguin. This creates an effect of space, as does their all being at different levels.

Courtesy of the International Collection of Child Art, Illinois State University, Normal, IL.

Space is shown by overlapping and diminishing sizes of the heads. This gives an effect of hundreds of dancers in the community folk-dance celebration. The painting is by an 11-year-old from Kastamonu, Turkey.

As students move into middle school, they discover other means of creating space through shading and foreshortening. Some of this expertise in space-handling comes intuitively, but most children must be guided in mastering the intricacies of perspective and space-in-depth. Rules of perspective should not be imposed on children unless they indicate a need for them. One cannot guarantee the success of a composition simply by applying the canons of perspective.

Texture and Pattern

Texture and pattern usually are considered as adorning or secondary elements that add richness and variety. However, they also can become the main feature of a design, as, for instance, in the design of floor tiles or in the repetitions of windows and columns in a work of architecture. Some names for textures are rough, smooth, actual, implied, bumpy, and jagged. Artists such as Rembrandt, Rubens, and Velasquez were virtuosos in painting the textures of hair, silk, velvet, and fur.

Third grade. Courtesy of Jackie Ellett, Fort Daniel Elementary School, GA.

Patterns of wavy bands go across the spectrums going in opposite directions of the background and fish.

Saturday Children's Classes. Courtesy of Frank Wachowiak, Athens, GA, and Mary Sayer Hammond, Fairfax, VA.

Imaginative patterns of circles, checkerboards, stripes, and diamonds grace this upper elementary child's oil pastel on pink paper. It was drawn with white chalk and inspired by a stuffed bird and photos of birds.

Courtesy of Frank Wachowiak, Athens, GA, and Mary Sayer Hammond, Fairfax, VA.

In nature, few examples of patterns are as striking as the leopard's spots. This third-grader has camouflaged the leopard in an equally exciting pattern of a triangular grass motif in a multicolor checkerboard environment.

Some types of patterns are regular, irregular, stripes (bands), zigzag (chevron), scallop (fish scale), plaid (crossband), notched (crenellated), and checkerboard (counterchange). Patterns can be created by setting up a series of parallel lines or lines that criss-cross, often at right angles. These lines can be straight, curved, wavy, or jagged.

Patterns in nature usually have a mathematical basis. For example, the arrangement of seeds in the head of a sunflower and the bumps on a pineapple are two of the many natural occurrences of the mathematical series called a *Fibonacci series*. Such seemingly random patterns as those formed by the branches of a tree or the indentations on a coastline are in fact governed by the same geometric phenomenon, *fractal geometry*.

Both pattern and texture can be created by the repetition of individual elements—for example, lines to make grass or circles to make apples on a tree. Patterns usually are made up of the repetition of one or more clearly discernible shapes. In textures, however, individual elements are merged together into the whole and are difficult to distinguish. It sometimes is hard to make a clear distinction between pattern and texture. For example, seen from a distance, apples on a tree would create a texture, but seen from up close, apples on a tree would create a

Courtesy David Hodge, Oshkosh, WI.

Clay is the supreme material for creating textures. Buttons, wire mesh, bottle caps, and kitchen tools can be helpful.

Teachers can help students to see the series of patterns and shapes in nature's leaves and seeds. These exquisite sunflower oil pastels on black paper have compositions that fill the page. Each seed, petal, and leaf and leaf vein are carefully drawn. Arranged alternately on the stem, the leaves run off the edges of the picture to create dramatic black background shapes. In the first picture, what wonderful variety is shown in the leaves. In the middle picture, a flower is drawn side view, and exciting negative shapes remain in the background. In the right picture, subtle blending of colors on the leaves and petals contrast to the bold, black patterned head of seeds. It would be wonderful if children everywhere could have the experience of studying with an art teacher who brings out the best in them, as was the case with these students.

pattern. Microscopes and telescopes can further determine whether something is seen as a texture, a pattern, or a shape.

Both pattern and texture can be used overall. On the other hand, they may take on even more importance when they are used judiciously and separated by empty, plain areas of a solid, unvaried color. When a texture changes in a progressive way, such as from distinct in front to blended together in the distance, it is called a *textural gradient*. This phenomenon can be seen in views of the ocean's waves, clouds, and fields of trees and crops.

Balance and Symmetry

Line, shape, value, color, space, texture, and pattern are the *elements* of design. Balance, symmetry, and variety are some of the *principles* of design. Both teachers and students should be familiar with the two types of compositional balance: symmetrical or formal balance, and asymmetrical or informal balance. Formal balance has gone in and out of favor as styles have changed. In general, however, a symmetrical arrangement in which objects or figures on the right balance similarly weighted components on the left makes a more rigid, static composition. Two sides being similar is called *bilateral symmetry;* all four quarters being similar is called *quadrilateral symmetry.*

A common misconception about art composition is that emphasis can be achieved by drawing something very large and placing it in the center of the picture. Size and placement by themselves do not ensure domination. The object to be noticed must exhibit other attributes as well; contrasting value, color, and detail usually will attract the viewer's attention. While there are no hard-and-fast rules, a pictorial creation often is much more interesting and attractive when the principal subject is not placed exactly in the center of the composition.

Variety, Emphasis, and Domination-Subordination

Variety in composition and design has always played a significant role. Analyses of past and present art masterpieces have revealed the artists'

Saturday Children's Classes. Courtesy of Frank Wachowiak, Athens, GA, and Mary Sayer Hammond, Fairfax, VA, student Megan Clements.

What riotous variety is shown in this primary-grade child's wonderful marker-pen harbor scene! No two cabin cruisers are alike. How delightful are the beach house architecture, the intensely colored empty spaces, and the windswept trees and hairstyles.

Cats' faces are blue, yellow, striped, and banded in the exciting variety of this animal in the garden scene.

reliance on, and constant use of, a variety of shapes and forms in their compositions. Seldom does one discover two shapes that are alike. Look at a score of multifigure paintings by recognized artists throughout the centuries and you will discover endless variety. No two heads are on the same level. No two figures are in the same position. No two figures stand on the same levels in the foreground.

In nature, examples of variety are evident in the wings of a butterfly, the stripes on a zebra, the spots on a leopard, the feathers on a bird, the scales on a fish, the web of a spider, the cracks in an ice flow, and the frost on a windowpane. No two are alike. Although humans are nature's children, they must learn to employ variety in their graphic imagery, unlike the embodiments and creations of the natural world. Variety as a vital element in pictorial design can be employed in every aspect—line, shape, value, color, pattern, texture—to give excitement and interest to a work of art, but it must be counterbalanced by a repetition of those art elements if the desired unity is to be achieved. Related to variety are the concepts of *emphasis* (that one object or motif should stand out above others) and *domination-subordination* (that equality is to be avoided in favor of one object or motif being major). Most successful compositions employ both major and minor areas of emphasis. Variety in the compositional placement of objects can be achieved by having objects:

- Change in size and shape
- Begin on different planes
- Terminate at different heights
- Touch the edges of the picture plane at different points, creating lines into the composition
- Strategically overlap one another to create even more varied shapes and negative spaces

Summary

The basic elements and principles can provide a practical design foundation on which to build a qualitative art program over the years. Art knowledge is acquired as these concepts are revisited time and again in the context of different assignments. In most instances and most classrooms, students' knowledge and application of composition and design principles, as exemplified in art masterpieces as well as the art around them and enhanced by a growing appreciation of design in nature, will prove both successful and personally rewarding. The development of a student's ability in making and thinking about art requires a continuing exposure at various developmental levels to certain core concepts, such as the basic elements and principles of composition and design.

Chapter 3

Considerations Regarding a Sequential Art Curriculum Based on Children's Development

Children from the first through eighth grades respond and grow during a program in which art fundamentals and techniques are not left to chance but are taught sequentially, purposefully, and imaginatively. This chapter provides a background for considering child development in art; the subsequent four chapters give specific recommendations.

Children's Similarities

Children everywhere have much in common. They react in similar ways to their environment. They laugh and cry, play, act, sing, and dance. They delight in seeing and manipulating bright, colorful objects and in games, machines, and vehicles. They respond to sympathetic, supportive voices and to loving, nurturing hands.

Likewise, children everywhere draw in much the same manner during their early developmental stages. Long before we learn how to respond to the world cognitively, we respond to it aesthetically: through touch, taste, smell, and sound. Preschoolers begin with random, haphazard marks and then move on to explore some of the 20 kinds of scribbles that have been classified (Kellogg, 1970). These include:

Patterns of marking in strokes
Patterns of dots
Vertical, horizontal, diagonal, circular, curved, and waving lines
Placement of patterns on the page, such as overall, quarter page, centered, in halves, along a diagonal axis, and following the shape of a two-corner arch, a one-corner fan, or a two-corner pyramidal form

Rather than thinking of these as *scribbles*, a term which has negative connotations to some people, one can think of them as presentations, in contrast to children's later *re*-presentations.

Gradually acquiring more control and the desire for representation, children move on to simple, geometric, schematic symbols. They confidently and proudly give to their drawings names and titles that might change from one minute to the next. They then progress to tadpolelike forms and semirealistic interpretations. Contrasted with later stages, in which development is much more variable, the early stages of artistic development (up to 5 to 7 years of age for children without developmental disabilities) are universally determined; they are strongly similar across different cultures and times. The young child's natural graphic responses are instinctive, spontaneous, and intuitive.

Moving beyond the scribbling stage, the young child begins to use geometric shapes to make representations. Butterflies in the Garden shows a wonderful, intuitive use of color in the multihued flower petals and cheerful use of background washes. White crayon lines are especially effective in crayon resist.

Courtesy of Melody Milbrandt, Valdosta, GA.

Simple geometric shapes are combined by this kindergartener to form people, airplanes, and building windows in rows and columns.

Children's Variability

While universal patterns of development govern the early stages of expression, forces of the specific culture and its educational and enrichment programs play greater roles as children mature. Some fortunate students may have had abundant experiences in working with art materials, whereas others may have had only limited creative opportunities. No two children are alike. Even twins, who may confuse their teachers with surface similarities, have different personalities, different feelings and reactions, and different mental and creative abilities. As anyone who has looked at children's art would attest, the complexity of children's graphic imagery varies with the stages of their mental, physical, psychological, and social development.

Because no two children are alike, it is almost impossible to categorize them by grade or by age. Students in the same class may come from different backgrounds and economic levels, and they may have had totally different day-to-day experiences. Their problems and needs are not the same. To understand and help them to grow through art, however, the teacher must be aware of those characteristics that have been identified with certain age groups by researchers in art education, educational psychology, sociology, and child study. The following detailed,

From the book, *Heidi's Horse*, by Sylvia Fein, Exelrod Press, Pleasant Hill, CA. Courtesy of the author and publisher.

These drawings illustrate increasing refinement in drawing horses made by the same girl at ages 7, 9, and 10.

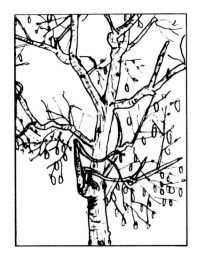  

No two children will draw the same tree in the same way. The teacher's role is to challenge them to notice trees and their varied parts. ("Describe in your art the trunk, bark, knots, branches, leaves, roots, twigs, buds, blossoms, and fruit.") Let them touch the trees, perhaps climb them, and pretend to be a tree swaying in the wind, feeling the rain, the snow, and the warm sunlight.

sequential description of children's growth and behavioral patterns as well as art learning needs should give helpful lesson-planning clues.

A word of caution is indicated here. Stage theory should be used only as a descriptive and not a prescriptive device. Stages are "external," not "internal." A person does not "have" a stage. Rather, a stage is a commonly available structure of thought. Stage theory fails to account for how cultural influences can shape development. Lowenfeld's stages (the scribbling stages; the preschematic stage [first representational attempts], 4–7 years; the schematic stage [achievement of a form concept], 7–9 years; and the gang stage [dawning realism], 9–12 years) have been criticized for these reasons. In school, the child is taught culturally approved systems of drawing and to ignore those which that culture does not approve of or value. In older children, a wider variety of graphic expressions are manifested, and development becomes less universal and more relative. Chance and choice can occur. Stages may be skipped and even reversed, and even within one drawing, indications of several stages may be found.

Art Development

Artistic expression is not a driving force that seeks improvement, nor is it an unfolding of predetermined abilities. Instead, it is bound to the time and place of its creation, and it reflects the creative options available at that time and place. It is not the case that "later is higher is better." A younger child's work may appear to show more giftedness than that of an older child. The spontaneity, beauty, and naiveté of a child's artistic expression at age 10 may never again be seen in that unique form in that child's work. Like fine art from past times, work from earlier stages in a child's life is not inferior to later work. Instead, the work from each time shows the distinctive characteristics of that time.

How and why do children draw? Do they draw what they know, or do they they draw what they see? What guides the drawing process, knowledge or vision? Perhaps it is a third element, feelings, that guides children's drawings. Or is it a fourth, their cultural context? Developmentalists have made the case for a connection between children's drawings and their intellectual growth. Perceptualists have emphasized instead the tie to children's ability to see, and especially to see differences. Still others have emphasized the emotional and psychological basis for art expression, and contextualists maintain that development does not move toward a specified end. In their view, the process is one of making choices within a given context; for example, some cultures have not been concerned with showing realism while others have.

The known and the remembered are delightfully combined in this Greek child's depiction of the terraced countryside. It shows the boat pulled up onto the beach, the houses lining the meandering road, and the sun peeking around the mountain.

Young children tend to pay little or no attention to the object and instead use a scheme, a product of individual cognition. After the primary grades, children do attempt to draw objects as they appear. In general, however, young children draw what they know, and older children in our culture tend to draw what they see. Thus, the young child's stubborn use of a consistent scheme is a feature of that child's quest to depict things as they are known. In other words, young children draw "what they know." Even so, the traits and characteristics described here are but clues to understanding children in general, and they may not necessarily apply to a particular or individual child. For a description of the characteristics of children with special needs—those with significant mental or physical handicaps and the gifted—refer to Chapters 13 and 14.

Need for Sequential Curriculum Across the Grades

For the teacher who has the chance to teach children over a span of years, the sequential teaching of art is a richly rewarding and highly ful-

filling experience. When undertaken with conviction, purpose, imagination, and love, it is a privilege, a revelation, and a joy to guide children as they create and to witness this fascinating aspect of their personalities emerge. Their designs and configurations are excitingly unpredictable. Their naiveté delights us. No wonder, then, that their spontaneous and intuitive visual expressions have influenced noted artists such as Jean Dubuffet, Juan Miro, Paul Klee, and Karel Appel.

For no other subject area taught in the elementary and middle schools is continuity of learning so misunderstood, and so neglected, as it is in art. In other subjects, most classroom teachers are familiar with the specific content to be mastered at each grade level and can help students confidently build on previous years' learning. In elementary and middle school art classes, however, it is a different story. In most instances, teachers in the upper elementary grades are unfamiliar with the content of the primary-grade art program, if in fact such a program even exists. Middle school instructors of art are often unaware of the art skills mastered during the elementary school art curriculum, and in too many

Grade 1 girl

Grade 1 boy

Grade 2 girl

Grade 2 boy

Grade 6 boy

Grade 7 boy

Children's development in art is sequential. In our culture, it moves toward showing more realistic proportion, more muscles, gender characteristics, and detail; however, there are numerous exceptions to the "typical" sequence. After leaving the scribbling stage, children at first draw tadpolelike figures, in which single, straight-line limbs protrude from the head. By first-grade, most children conceive of the head as a separate circle, from which hangs a body drawn with a triangle or square. Attached to this are straight limbs, with two sides, rather than just being a stick (grade 1 girl). Then, the phenomenon of bending limbs becomes graphically realized and curved, sausage-type limbs

Grade 3 boy

Grade 4 boy

Grade 5 girl

Grade 6 girl

Courtesy of Frank Wachowiak, Iowa City Elementary Laboratory School, except grade 1 girl courtesy of David Harvell, Athens, GA, and grade 7 girl courtesy of Baiba Kuntz, Glencoe, IL.

are drawn (grade 2 boy). Joints develop, and knees and elbows then are drawn as the locations of the bending (grade 3 and 4 boys). The limbs become progressively more fused to the body (grade 3 boy and grade 5 girl). Overlapping of limbs over the body can be seen (grade 2 and 4 boy, grade 6 girl and boy). Proportions change from the three-heads-high figure (grade 2 boy) to the five-heads-high figure (grade 6 boy). The form of the neck, arising from the torso, becomes more clearly realized. Hips and muscles become more clearly represented (grade 6 girl and boy). Foreshortening appears (grade 8 girl's writing arm), and three-quarter views may appear (grade 8 girl's face).

Grade 7 girl

Grade 8 girl

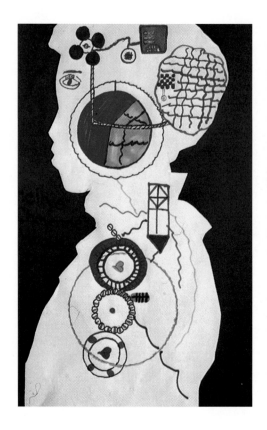
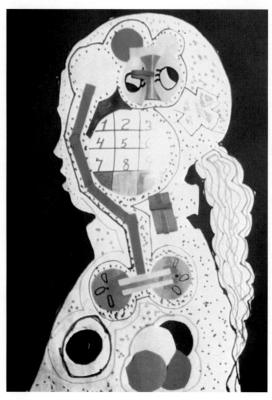
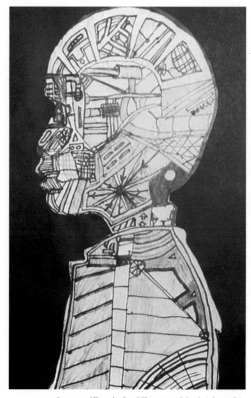

Courtesy of Timothy Road Elementary School, Athens, GA.

Fifth-grade students, whose knowledge about perception, evaluation, and aesthetics is increasing, created these X-ray silhouettes. They show how the opportunities and challenges of technology—for example, radio transistors, motors, battery watchworks, cameras, computers, and television—have affected them. Materials employed were 18- × 24-inch white construction paper, watercolor markers and crayons, wallpaper samples, scissors, pencils, and paste. A film projector lamp was used to create the student's shadow, and the silhouette was drawn by outlining the student's profile in pencil on the white paper. The completed drawings were cut out and mounted on dark-colored construction paper.

elementary schools, art projects are a medley of one-shot, spur-of-the-moment activities unrelated to one another or to the children's earlier art experiences. Often, these token art lessons are hastily concocted to fit into, but not exceed, the 30- or 45-minute period allotted to art once a week, or once every 2 weeks. Very often, they are squeezed in on a late Friday afternoon, when the children are exhausted by the long day's activities and certainly not at their creative, physical, and mental best.

Because of a paucity in the planning of sequential art experiences, children from first through eighth grades often are provided with a monotonous diet of endless crayon lessons, usually seat-work assignments, that supposedly are designed to illustrate some aspect of social studies, literature, or science. It is only natural for students to lose interest and become bored when they realize they are not growing in fundamental art skills. Too much art class time is spent on the insignificant, the peripheral, and the frivolous, on the "instant" activity. "All right, children," says the classroom teacher at the close of the art lesson, "put away your crayons now, and let's get down to something serious" (such as math, science, or language, perhaps?).

In today's art education, two forces have converged to produce a call for a clearly defined curriculum. One is competency-based education's mandates for clear instructional objectives, written in terms of what skills the student will be able to demonstrate (see Chapter 12). The other is teachers' uncertainty about how to implement the call by proponents of discipline-based art education for a more scholarly approach.

Confronted by conflicting mandates, some teachers feel that their difficult jobs would be easier if the art curriculum were clearly spelled out, but what if a systemwide curriculum proves to be too structured? To what degree should the school system direct a teacher in the goals and objectives for each grade? There is already a constraint on elementary classroom teachers, who must attempt to fit their art teaching in between meeting grade-level goals on the standardized reading and math tests. A top-down art curriculum may further hinder teachers from carrying out the specific art projects they personally would like to use. Some teachers will feel that their autonomy in directing the students' instruction has been taken away, making them feel like mere tools in the school district's hands.

Another force working against a top-down curriculum results from developments in cognitive theory that have caused a shift from the curriculum-centered instruction of the 1970s to learner-centered instruction. These new approaches engage students at their level of understanding and require them to examine their own knowledge to come up with their own solutions. Another force opposing a sequentialized curriculum in art making and criticism is the intrinsic, cumulative nature of art learning itself. Art learning follows more of a spiral course than a clearly delineated sequence.

Districtwide standards need to be balanced against the teachers' individualized differences. It is important that the content of art instruction develop from the essential strengths of the teachers themselves and their passions about art. In observing a class where art is taught purposefully, seriously, imaginatively, and knowledgeably, with an emphasis on the continuity of learning, the observer will see education at its finest, a total education of the whole child. He or she will witness students absorbed in making hundreds of decisions: sharing, evaluating, comparing, revising, growing in language skills, and adding to their development as perceptive, discriminative, and aesthetically aware human beings. Teachers who use the following sequential, developmental, quality art program will see children each year growing more confident in self-expression, verbal and visual literacy, and self-worth.

Chapter 4

A Sequential Curriculum for Grades 1 and 2

Developmental Characteristics

The left-hand column of the following table lists some of the developmental characteristics of first- and second-grade children. The right-hand column lists some implications of these characteristics for art teaching.

Developmental Characteristics of First and Second Graders	Implications for Art Teaching
Are active and easily excited.	Use most any topic as motivation.
Enjoy working with their hands.	Use hands-on art activities as vehicles for correlated learning.
Take great pride in their work.	Display work in the hall.
Exhibit strong feelings of possessiveness.	Be aware that some children may cry if work is kept for an exhibit.
Are eager to learn.	Teach them many ways to see and draw. Do not underteach.
Want to be first.	Assign special responsibilities, such as, "You may be the scissor monitor today."
Have a limited span of interest and are easily fatigued.	Give a series of objectives *throughout* the lesson rather than all at the beginning.
Have feelings that are easily hurt.	Point out several alternative ways to draw something, with each conveying different qualities, rather than just one right way. Praise when students have arrived at their "own way" of drawing something.
Are alternately cooperative and uncooperative.	Give "road signs" to foreshadow how long each phase will be, when the phase will stop, and what the next phase will be.
Usually can grasp only one idea at a time.	Give instructional objectives throughout the lesson instead of all at the beginning.
Delight in imaginative games, dances, stories, and plays.	Use psychomotor games and role-playing exercises.
Like to pretend and engage in make-believe.	Use puppet plays and made-up stories about the characters in their pictures. ("What would this character in your picture say?")
Desire the approval of classmates and teachers.	Encourage them to tell about their pictures at sharing time.
Often live in their own secret world.	Use fantasy as a motivation. ("If I were a . . . , what would I be like?")
Are interested in new things to touch and taste.	Use tactile motivations, such as rabbits, toys, turtles.
Are fascinated by moving and mechanical devices.	Arrange wind-up toys as still lifes. Use visual-perception devices such as kaleidoscopes.
Enjoy TV, illustrated books, movies, picnics, school field trips, new clothes, pets.	Ask them to do art criticism of book illustrations. Have children draw after field trips, draw pictures of pets.

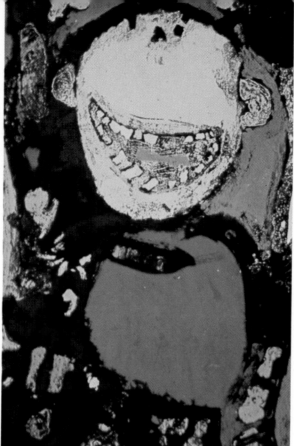

Courtesy of Frank Wachowiak and Ted Ramsay, *Emphasis Art*, Second Edition, University Elementary School, Iowa City, IA.

In these attractive, first-grade tempera and India-ink portraits can be seen the characteristic features often found in very young children's art. These include circle heads; *the figures from 2½ to 3 heads high; the bodies comprising circles, squares, and triangles; and the sausage limbs.*

This and the following chapters treat students' development at each 2-year period: primary grades 1 and 2, intermediate grades 3 and 4, upper elementary grades 5 and 6, and middle school grades 7 and 8. Each time period is discussed in three parts. First, characteristics are listed on the left side of a table, and some implications of the developmental characteristics for the teaching of art are listed on the right side. Second, children's artistic development is described in terms of their use of shape, size, color, space, shading, ways of drawing objects, the human figure, and favorite subject matter. Third, teaching procedures for the four areas of art criticism, art history, aesthetics, and art production are described.

Art Development

This next table shows how many children ages 5 through 7 employ various art elements. The left-hand column shows early development and the right-hand column later development. At these stages, enormous variability and change in children's art development occur. Although the table is written in the form of instructional objectives, it is not meant to be prescriptive. Beauty and expression can be achieved in many ways, not just one teacher-prescribed "right way." Representations consisting of scribbles can be as expressive as those depicting houses, if not more so. Later is not necessarily better.

Changing colors on the teacher's signal in a game of "Pass the Paint Please," is a good way to maintain young children's attention. A good topic for this rotating color painting is "A Flower Garden from Above."

Three strong figures overlap a big red house and fence in this first-grade student's painting in analogous colors.

A still life of flowers motivated this second-grade student's crayon and watercolor painting.

Early Art Development: Ages 5 and 6   *Subsequent Development: Ages 6 and 7*

SHAPES	Student will draw the geometric symbols of the circle, square, triangle, oval, and rectangle. Student will employ a basic symbol, such as a circle, to depict varied visual images—the sun, the head of a person or animal, a table, a flower blossom, a tree, a body, and even a room. Students will use combinations of symbols that very often are different from those of their classmates. Student will depict simplified representations and are not too concerned with details.	(Because child art develops so rapidly during this period, this column deals with the development of some 6-year-olds but especially of 7-year-olds.) Student will change slowly from geometric, symbolic interpretations to more specific characterization and delineation. Student will use more details in depictions—hair ribbons, buttons, buckles, eyeglasses, necklaces, rings, shoelaces, purses, fingernails, patterns, and wrinkles in clothes.
SIZE	Student will use emotional exaggeration of size. Students will enlarge things that are important to them and omit features that are not. For example, children may draw themselves bigger than their parents or omit arms and hands if they are not needed in their depiction. Size also may be determined by the need to fill an empty space or the desire to show a clear relationship.	Student will approximate more representative proportions, although figures still may be three heads high (the proportions of the *Peanuts* cartoon character, Charlie Brown) rather than the subsequent five heads high.
COLOR	Student will use color in a personal or emotional context without regard to its local use or identity. For example, a face may be painted blue or green.	Student will use color in a local, stereotypical way. For example, tree trunks are brown, and the sky is blue.
SPACE	Student will employ a baseline as a foundation on which to place objects such as a house, tree, or figure. The bottom of the page sometimes substitutes for the baseline. Student will draw both the outside and inside of a place, a person, or an animal as if in an X-ray or transparency. Later, student may use a second or third baseline higher on the page.	Although distant objects often are drawn the same size as closer objects, student will begin to place distant objects higher on the page. Students will use a foldover technique, turning their paper completely around as they draw, to show people on both sides of the street, diners around a table or a picnic lunch, people at a swimming pool, or players on a baseball field.
SCHEMAS FOR DRAWING OBJECTS	Students will draw things intuitively as they know them: the sky as a band of color at the top of the page, the sun that appears in part or whole in an upper corner of almost every picture, the railroad tracks that seldom converge, the leaves that are wider where they attach to the branch or stem, the tree with a very wide trunk to make it strong, the eyes high up in the head, and the mouth as a single, curved, happy line.	Students will draw objects as they know them to be rather than how they see them at the moment, such as a table with four legs when only two are visible from their vantage point or a house with three sides when only one is visible from their sketching station.
THE HUMAN FIGURE	Students will devise a variety of interpretations or schemata of the human figure, house, tree, animal, and so on, depending on their experience.	Student will begin to use characteristic apparel and detail to distinguish sexes, such as skirts and trousers, and differences in hair styles.

This busy child is not a slave to realism. Four eyes are called for, two to keep track of the hair brushing and two to keep track of the simultaneous teeth brushing. What could be more expressive! Figure schemes are energetically explored. This Picasso-like black crayon self-portrait, 12 × 18 inches, is by a first-grade girl.

Art Criticism, Art History, and Aesthetics

"Do you like this painting? Why?" This kind of art criticism can be done at this early age. For children at this time, subject matter is most important. If they like the object portrayed, they will like the picture. For example, in responding to Albrecht Dürer's drawing of a hare, the

A second-grade student uses a schematized way of drawing the human figure to show the joy of giving friends valentines. Notice the sausage-like arms, swinging leg, and the bold outlining in black after the colors are applied.

Three-dimensional Vincent van Gogh's Starry Night was the motivation for this first-grade student's cut-paper and crayon-resist version of the radiating starlight.

Courtesy of Barbara Thomas, Whit Davis School, Athens, GA.

Studying the artist William Johnson's use of enlarged body parts, third-grade student Kelisha Scott did this colored drawing of the cook skillfully using his hands to flip pizza at the school's partner Pizza Hut.

ference between appearance and reality develops gradually. For example, one first grader, needing to assure himself that he had not created a frightful lion, told the class, with some uncertainty in his voice, "It's not a real lion."

Children at this age like pictures that are clear and vivid. Clarity of perceptual cues and orderly organization of elements are very important. They look through the visual rendition; they do not see the style, the composition, or the multiple meanings. Their perceptions are limited to a single interpretation. Talking about art reproductions helps to develop their skill in drawing inferences. They can scan and take in whole scenes to figure out situations, characters, and narration. They can predict what a scene would be like if they were there and how they would feel about it. They cannot imagine the scene in an alternative way, and art inquiry thus is limited to what is shown rather than how what is shown could be changed. By the second grade, however, their preferences grow beyond like or dislike of a subject to include personal experiences as important factors.

Children between ages 5 and 7 are particularly drawn to the effects of color. From the very first day of school, begin teaching perception of the art elements, especially color awareness, with emphasis on the child's everyday surroundings: the classroom, clothes, books, artwork, and posters on display. ("If you have anything turquoise around your desk, maybe a notebook or a bracelet, hold it up.") Help them to identify the primary and secondary colors. Introduce the warm, sunny colors

Courtesy of Eastern Airlines.

A child's aesthetic awareness is at work in thinking about the patterns and pentagonal symmetry of a starfish echinoderm.

children like it because it's cute or because they like rabbits. When speaking, children do not differentiate between the world of pictures and what the pictures represent. They like pictures of things they like and reject pictures of things they dislike or fear. Understanding the dif-

such as yellow, orange, pink, and red as well as the events associated with them—the circus, county fairs, parades, Mardi Gras, autumn harvest, and shopping malls. Talk about the deep, cool colors such as green, turquoise, blue, and blue-violet and the images they evoke—the mysterious night, the ocean depths, the rain-wet jungle, and the deep, dark forest.

Take advantage of the many stimulating games, toys, and devices available for developing color awareness: the prism, paint chips, the color wheel, and the kaleidoscope. If a rainbow can be seen from the schoolroom window after a rainfall, use this natural phenomenon as the basis for a discussion of the color spectrum. Encourage color matching and sorting exercises using found materials such as scraps of art paper, wallpaper, magazine illustrations, cloth, and yarn. Store the color collection in shoe boxes, one box for each color. When the children are using paints, encourage them to create new colors by mixing colors on wet or moist paper and naming their new color inventions.

Have children explain the meaning and contribution of the following terms: color, shape, line, pattern, repeat, scribble, and texture. Encourage them to describe pattern and texture in clothing, in school surroundings, and especially in nature's bark, fur, fish scales, and plumage. Just as talking about art helps to promote their artistic creativity, artistic creation helps them to talk about art.

Teachers should exploit all means at their disposal, including the chalkboard and bulletin board, to call the child's attention to art pro-ject–related vocabulary. Children of this age should know the following basic art terms: black, blue, bright, brown, brush, cardboard, chalk, circle, clay, coil, construction paper, crayon, dark, dot, drawing, easel, eraser, fingerpaint, glue, green, grey, hammer, ink, kiln, light, manila paper, mural, nail, newsprint paper, orange, oval, overlap, paste, pastel, pen, pencil, pink, pinch pot, purple or violet, rectangle, red, ruler, scribble, shape, square, stripe, tempera paint, tissue paper, triangle, watercolor, weaving, white, and yellow.

Designing, Drawing, and Painting

> Something big, something small.
> Something short, something tall,
> Something dark, something light,
> Helps to make your drawing right.

This rhymed stanza helps to remind young children to add variety to their compositions. In most instances, the *more* images, shapes, or ideas the students incorporate in their compositions, the more unified their drawings become. Say to them, "Who else was there? What else might have been on the ground?"

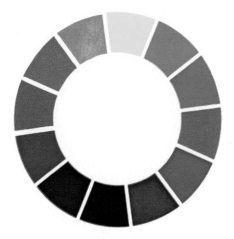

Complementary colors are those opposite each other on the color wheel; analogous colors are those side by side.

Courtesy of Barbara Thomas, Whit Davis School, Athens, GA.

Various techniques were used in kindergartener Derek Looney's illustration of the story, "The Rainbow Fish." An initial pencil drawing then was outlined in permanent marker, after which watercolor washes and a touch of sparkle were applied.

A first-grade youngster uses the circle-square figure schema in her drawing of Pets and Friends. Figures are shown with no elbows and no shoulders, which would distract from the figures' crosslike forms, but the cat has well-defined elbows and shoulders. Pattern in clothing is depicted by stripes, plaids, and even a floral design. The multi- *color crayon engraving technique requires considerable patience. Because it calls for the application of several layers of crayon, use a small size of heavy oaktag. Begin with a light hue, such as yellow or pink, and build layer on layer through darker colors to a final brown, dark blue, or black. Lakewood Elementary School, Ann Arbor, MI.*

As children join the community of picture makers, they begin to understand the demands of representation. They like to paint simple images, using themes such as a favorite toy or "What I like to do when it rains." For children who have developed beyond the scribbling stage, discourage their rushing to finish or scribbling haphazardly. Children love to use their pictures to tell stories, and both pictures and stories can change from time to time. Children often make several representa- tions of the same subject—for example, the family's new baby. Some can write their own titles and stories; in other cases, help is needed.

Introduce your students to various tools for making linear images. These include pencil, ballpoint and felt-nib pens, crayon, oil and chalk pastel, brushes, school chalk, a nail for crayon-engraving projects, or fingers for finger painting. Praise their discovery of various line pat- terns: stripes, plaids, circles, stars, spirals, radiating lines, and zigzags.

Children this age like their pictures to show clear relationships. One good way to achieve this is to use large brushes; ¼-inch, ½-inch, or larger. Another way to show clarity is to draw objects against an empty background. Passing the paint containers every few minutes works well at this age. During this period, floating objects will gradually diminish, replaced by figures on a stand line or a baseline. Later, the children may move to the use of multiple stand lines. At this time, however, it is too early to introduce overlapping.

Some children will make the delightfully charming foldover drawings. They will show figures arranged in a circle or on both sides of the street and upside down on one of the sides. Games such as ring-around-the-rosy can be used to stimulate these charming representations. For the children, foldover is a quite satisfactory method of design representation, because it tells very clearly what is occurring.

Another pleasing representational device that appears in some drawings is X-ray drawing or transparency—seeing the figure through the clothes or seeing through the walls to what is inside the house. As children grow older, this way of representation diminishes; children say they do not do it that way anymore. Transparency does not mean that children think clothes are transparent; instead, it comes about because they draw the figure first and then dress it, just like using paper dolls. The representational device is used in some other cultures, such as Australian aboriginal art, which can be used as motivational materials.

Introduce the children to line drawing, variety of shades, light and dark value, color, and pattern. Encourage drawing based on personal experiences and observations, but welcome and praise imaginative expression as well. Provide many opportunities for them to draw from real objects. These might be plants in and around the school, pets brought to class, flower arrangements, toys and dolls, classmates as figure-drawing models, self-portraits, depictions of the family in various settings, community helpers, and subject matter observed on field

Here, the walking figures and cabin cruiser are seen as if from the side, while the rowboats and sidewalk are seen as if from the top. Showing both the top and side views in one scene is called mixed-plan-and-elevation drawing. This and foldover drawings, which show the events upside down on the other side of the street, are charming ways by which artists represent what is known rather than what is seen. Conception and perception work together in this Taiwanese primary-grade child's telling about events at the water's edge.

Courtesy of Joyce Vroon, Trinity School, Atlanta, GA.

The outside shape and inside rooms of the child's house, from basement to attic, are shown in Millie Rhodes' X-ray or cross section view.

Courtesy of Sharon Burns-Knutson, Iowa City, IA.

This remarkable self-portrait is a contour drawing. A second-grade child from Iowa City patiently delineated what she observed. Guide children to look carefully and see freckles, collar stitchery, and patterns in the hair. This portrait reveals once again what drawing skills youngsters are capable of when they are encouraged to become aware, observe details, and draw slowly and deliberately.

trips. Give large-size paper or newsprint so that details they consider to be important can be shown. In figure drawing, the size of the drawn head often determines the size of the body. Encourage the children to fill the page.

Collage (Cut and Paste)

Encourage students in their scissors-cutting skills. Invite them to create simple, basically geometric shapes out of construction paper. Make sure to have scissors available designed that are especially for left-handed children. Provide opportunities that involve pasting little shapes onto big shapes. Point out how contrast is achieved by pasting a light-col-

Courtesy of Joyce Vroon, Trinity School, Atlanta, GA.

Using mirrors, these primary grade students draw and paint themselves in fancy hats. Art by third-grade student Natalie Long.

Courtesy of Frank Wachowiak and Ted Ramsay, *Emphasis Art*, First Edition, University Elementary School, Iowa City, IA.

"On our street" was the subject of this colorful colored construction paper collage by a first-grade child. The class first discussed shapes of houses, garages, churches, syna-gogues, and stores, then trees, bushes, hedges, fences, sidewalks, telephone poles, traffic signs, billboards, mailboxes, pets, cars, and trucks.

ored shape over a dark-colored shape and vice versa. Demonstrate how to use paste and glue economically and effectively. A felt board can be employed to introduce children to the countless possibilities of cut-out shapes and how they can be juxtaposed. Cooperative murals employing

the cut-and-paste technique in which each child contributes one or more parts to the whole are very satisfying projects (see Chapter 20). Almost any theme lends itself beautifully to collage making at this stage: flowers in a garden, animals in the jungle, fish in the sea, birds in a tree, and butterflies in flight.

Printmaking

Simple repeat prints will result in colorful, all-over patterns. These can be made using vegetables, found objects, clay pieces, erasers,

Saturday Children's Classes. Courtesy of Frank Wachowiak, Athens, GA.

For primary-grade children, delightful prints can be created by using discarded plastic foam meat trays as the printing plates. Trim off the curved part of the tray. A prelimi-nary drawing with a felt-nib pen or soft-lead pencil is recommended. Make the impres-sion by pressing a blunt-pointed pencil into the tray. Water-base black printing ink, rolled out on the engraved tray with a brayer may be used.

cellulose scraps, and hands and fingers. In most instances, colored construction paper is recommended for the background printing surface. Other possibilities are colored tissue paper, newsprint, wallpaper samples, brown wrapping paper, and fabric remnants. Printmaking activities at this age are somewhat limited, because young children do not possess the necessary skills for complicated techniques. Emphasize space filling when trying plastic foam meat-tray prints with incised relief created by pencil pressure. Monoprints are wonderful at this age.

Ceramics

Sufficient clay must be available; a ball of clay about the size of a grapefruit is recommended for every child. The clay must be of the proper malleable plasticity; if too sticky, let it dry a while. Allow the children to discover clay's potential. Encourage squeezing, pinching, poking, and stretching the clay. Show them how to make coils and form the clay into small balls or pellets. Guide the children in the creation of simple, familiar forms. Suggest they hold the ball or lump of clay in their hands as they manipulate it into the desired shape. This procedure discourages the tendency of some children to pound the clay flat on their desks. Primary-grade children can control the relatively simple sculptural forms of an elephant, hippo, cow, horse, rabbit, turtle, pig, dog, cat, whale, or resting bird. They enjoy manipulating the clay in either an additive or a subtractive way. Teachers prefer the subtractive (pulling features out) way, because it results in a form less likely to fall apart.

Construct simple pinch pots from a lump of clay the size of an orange, and bisque-fire the pots if a kiln is available. Ask them to hold the clay ball in the palm of one hand and insert the thumb of the other into the middle of the clay, about half-way down. As the children rotate the clay, they should push and pinch their thumb and fingers along the inside and outside of the ball in overlapping pinches. Caution them not to make the wall or bottom of the pot too thin. Because the marks of their fingers and thumb often add an attractive texture, discourage the use of water to smooth their clay.

Suggested Subjects or Themes

The following topics are suitable for children of ages 5, 6, and 7 (grades 1 and 2):

An animal with a figure or with its young is a popular ceramic theme. Additively constructed pieces can come apart in drying and jostling. Therefore, emphasize heavy legs, firmly attached with roughening and smearing of the clay at the points of attachment. Japan.

Courtesy of Melody Milbrandt, Valdosta, GA.

This first-grade student painted her fantasy wish to be able to fly like a bird.

Playground games
Fun in the snow
Fun in the fall leaves
A flower garden with insects
My pet and me
Stuffed animals
Animals in the zoo or jungle
Farm animals
Noah's ark
What I like to do when it rains
What my parent and I like to do together
My make-believe wish
Skipping rope
Our community helpers
Butterflies in a garden
Fish in the sea
Land of make-believe
My favorite toy
Clowns (for pattern)
Kings and queens

Courtesy of Melody Milbrandt, Valdosta, GA.

In this first-grade student's painting of a clown, an initial crayon drawing was then gone over with watercolor.

A Sequential Curriculum for Grades 3 and 4

Although children's art at all developmental stages has a unique beauty, some people refer to that grades 3 and 4 as the "golden age of child art." Just as roses are most beautiful at the moment halfway between bud and full flowering, children at this time create art that reflects the charm of newly discovered representational concepts along with signs of a move toward realism. Abstraction and realism are in a state of happy coalescence, and children's belief in their expressive powers is not disturbed by the anxiety about "not looking right" that comes later. By this time, most children have developed methods of drawing that satisfactorily communicate their meaning to adults. Their schemes may be based partly on concepts and partly on perception. Early forms such as a lollipop tree, which once

seemed okay, yield under increasing perceptual input to become more novel, fresh forms. Beneath the surface, however, the conceptual model still has an influence, but the child who uses a conceptual scheme should not be made to feel inadequate. This child's vision may be driven more by intuitive design decisions. Rather than settling for stereotypes, the teacher should instead encourage students putting visual discoveries into representational forms. The teacher might say, "Does anyone see anything around the mouth that we could draw? Juan says he sees half-circle lines at the edge of the mouth. How can we draw these?"

Developmental Characteristics

The left-hand column of the next table lists some of the developmental characteristics of third- and fourth-grade children. The right-hand column lists one or more related art instructional objectives for each characteristic.

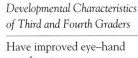

Courtesy of Sharon Burns-Knutson, Cedar Rapids, IA, students Elizabeth Browning, Caleb Rucker, and Jenna Lindberg.

These fourth-grade students were encouraged to observe details in their oil pastel self-portraits.

Developmental Characteristics of Third and Fourth Graders	Some Related Art Instructional Objectives
Have improved eye–hand coordination.	Students will draw from peers posing as models.
Have better command of small muscles.	Students will draw details of clothing and features.
Are becoming aware of differences in people.	Students will show differences among figures and objects in their artwork.
Are gradually learning to become responsible, orderly, and cooperative.	Students will share, distribute, and collect art material.
Begin to form separate-sex groups.	Give art motivations for both boys' and girls' interests.

May start to join gangs and cliques.

Students will depict their friends in their art. The teacher can use peer approval to modify behavior.

Enjoy comic books.

Students will create their own comic characters and superheroes.

Are growing in critical skills, self-evaluation, and evaluation of others.

Students will use instructional objectives to evaluate their work.

Are now able to concentrate for a longer period.

Projects may span more than one period if new objectives are brought forth.

Are developing an interest in travel.

Students will describe how historical artworks relate to a culture.

Are interested in the life processes of plants and animals.

Students will draw from life, taxidermy models, and pictures of flora and fauna, and they will describe how their drawings show the specific features of plants or animals.

Are developing a sense of humor.

Students will discuss aesthetic issues raised by art cartoons.

Are becoming avid hobby fans and collectors.

Students will discuss their collections in terms of art criticism. "The picture shows his batting strength."

An intermediate-elementary-grade boy, who incidentally was in need of braces, did this fantasy oil pastel resist of an imaginary creature; part animal, part bird, part fish, and part insect. The white shapes of the head and ears are repeated in the spirals of the tail and hind legs. Star, flower, and leaf forms fill the background.

A major developmental issue at this time is whether the child develops feelings of competence or inferiority. While regular classroom activities develop children's skills in reading and math, children may develop feelings of inferiority about their drawing ability if they are not instructed.

Art Development

Once again, later is not better. The stages described in this section are descriptive and not prescriptive.

Shapes	Students will draw and compose with more conscious, deliberate planning, and they will show more naturalistic and realistic proportions.
	Students will select and arrange objects to satisfy their compositional design needs.
Color	Students will mix and experiment with an expanded range of colors, including tints and shades.
	Students will discuss the mood and effects of warm and cool colors, both within a painting and in the environment.
	Students will use related colors (those adjacent to one another on the color wheel).
	Students will neutralize (dull a color) by mixing it with the complementary hue (opposites on the color wheel).
	Students will describe the effect of subdued colors next to bright, intense colors.
Space	Students will create space and depth by employing vertical placement, diminishing size, and overlapping shapes.
	Students will describe how the horizon line can be used to show distant space.
Objects	Students will select and arrange objects to satisfy their compositional design needs.
The Human Figure	Students will show action in their drawings of people and animals. Students will draw with more naturalistic and realistic proportions; more will use the five-heads-high figure.

Art Criticism, Art History, and Aesthetics

This is the stage of beauty and realism—the golden age of child art. The child believes the purpose of art is to represent something. The children yearn to make objects look real, and they strive for clarity and good de-

Courtesy of David Hodge, Oshkosh, WI.

Third-grade youngsters show their individuality in these large (12 × 24 inches) tempera self-portraits. Notice especially the spirit and wonderful complementary and analogous colors in the self-portrait with orange and purple eyes, purple and green fingernails, and green lips and eyelashes! Beautiful! Here again, qualitative, in-depth teaching strategies are the key to such successful artworks. These strategies include mixing a varied range of tempera hues, making sure the children devote time to doing preliminary sketches and encouraging the imaginative use of color.

finition. The more real and clear the artworks, the better the artworks are liked. In responding to realistic art, children comment, "I wish I could draw like this." In fact, this hankering after realism is so strong that when confronted by abstract artworks, the children try to find a specific image in it.

By this time, children are beginning to try to figure out what an artwork is about, to make their first interpretive efforts. They take a longer time to look at art. Children now have the linguistic skills to express the concept that artworks are different from the thing itself. ("It is a picture of a rabbit" rather than "It is a rabbit.") Students can identify events depicted in artworks, and they can describe both likenesses and differences between pictures. They can accept their peers' differing representations as being valid art expressions. They can recognize style in each other's works. They can tell about the colors, shapes, lines, and textures in an artwork. Children this age can recognize different media and techniques in different works of art. They can identify the forms of artwork, such as sculptures, ceramics, landscape, portrait, and architecture. They can describe some criteria for art, and they can plan an art exhibition.

The following words can be added to the children's growing art vocabulary: background, balsawood, batik, brayer, cellophane, ceramics, collage, collograph, color wheel, complementary colors, composition, cone, contrast, contour line, crafts, cube, cylinder, engraving, foreground, form, found material, hue, India ink, inking slab, intensity, landscape, linoleum, linoprint, masking tape, monoprint, mosaic, negative shape, papier mâché, plaster, plywood, positive shape, poster, pyramid, radiation, rasp, scoring of clay and paper, shade, sketch, slab, slip, spiral, staple, still life, stitchery, tie-dyeing, tint, unity, value.

Courtesy of Joyce Vroon, Trinity School, Atlanta, GA.

Third-grade students studied Mondrian's paintings as a motivation for making their designs.

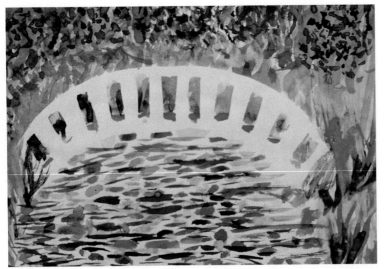

Studying Monet's paintings of his water lily garden at Giverney, fourth-grade students first cut a stencil for their bridges before doing their Impressionistic painting.

Fourth-grade students learned about overlapping, perspective, and pattern in architecture as they drew projected city scenes.

Drawing, Designing, and Painting

Children like to depict clothing—their favorite outfit or occupational clothing, like a police uniform. Group projects comprised of students' individual works can demonstrate the power of working together to create projects of large size and scope. Continue to call attention to the immediate and visually stimulating subject or image for drawing. On sketching excursions, scout for the unusual site, the pictorially exciting vista with multifaceted structures, interesting towers and spires, and varied foreground and background breakup. In representing distance and overlapping, children often change color and size to show space, and they like to show the vastness of space. Suggest new directions in design such as:

- Overlapping shapes
- Achieving distance through diminishing sizes and placement of objects higher on the page
- Creating pattern and textural effects contrasted with quiet or plain areas
- Drawing the lines with varied weights and in varied ways

At this stage, and by the fourth grade certainly, children can be introduced to observational drawing and basic contour-drawing techniques. For an immediate visual stimulus, begin with simple, easily recognizable, everyday objects: a fruit, vegetable, shoe, glove, helmet, cap, cowboy hat, baseball mitt, football, or water pitcher. When the students' skill and confidence in contour drawing increase, introduce a combined arrangement of several objects in which the items overlap. Guide the children to look carefully and intently at the object and to draw it very slowly and deliberately.

Explain about inner contour lines. For example, with a flower, suggest they begin in the middle with the core, adding one petal at a time, rather than with a hasty and general outline of the entire flower. In other instances, such as with a banana or okra, begin with the outer contour line and then add inner contour lines to clarify the form. A few children can even draw oblique planes and use overlapping.

A soft lead pencil is best for contour drawing. Kindergarten pencils are recommended. Erasures should be discouraged; a second, corrective line more carefully observed is suggested. The students may stop at critical junctures, reposition the drawing tool, and then continue drawing.

Direct the children's attention to the environment, to nature and its variety of lines, shapes, textures, colors, patterns, rhythms, and contrasts, and help them to see examples of radiation, emphasis, and unity in natural forms. Urge students to bring interesting natural objects

Courtesy of Barbara Thomas, Whit Davis School, Athens, GA.

Pattern was the focus of this third-grade student's cat drawing. Interest is created by the bold black and white diamonds in the floor, the patterns in the cat's fur and the wall moldings, and, for a finishing touch, the background three-dimensional dot pattern using t-shirt paint.

(taxidermy specimens, roots, weeds, fossils, honeycombs, bird's nests, pods, pinecones, seashells, and coral) into class to be used in discussions about artistic perception and for inspirational still lifes.

Color Awareness

Introduce art projects that demand multiple color choices. These include:

- Making collages using colored construction paper, colored tissue paper, wallpaper samples, paint chips, and assorted color fabrics and felts
- Weaving with colored papers
- Coloring with crayon or oil pastel on colored construction paper
- Making mosaics with colored tesserae on a colored or black background
- Creating a color environment or happening in the classroom, combining, for example, crepe paper, balloons, beach towels, hula hoops, fans, colored cellophane, ribbons, scarves, umbrellas, posters, and fabrics

Courtesy of Sharon Burns-Knutson, Cedar Rapids, IA, student Caleb Rucker.

This fourth-grade student shows a keen observation of nature, the changes in the size and direction of the leapard's spots, on this decorative plate employing a marker drawing.

Courtesy of Joyce Vroon, Trinity School, Atlanta, GA.

For her stuffed animals' still life, Christy Kelly plans to use many premixed containers of paint in a variety of tints and shades.

Encourage students to mix and experiment with an expanded range of colors, including tints and shades. Discuss the mood and effect that warm and cool colors give within a painting and in the environment. Call attention to the related colors (those adjacent to one another on the color wheel). Students often now are ready to tackle the intricacies of color neutralization (dulling a color) by mixing a color with its complementary hue (opposites on the color wheel). They also can appreciate the subtle contrast of subdued colors next to bright, intense colors.

Collage

Introduce cut, tear, and paste projects that require the creation of texture and low-relief effects. These can be accomplished by folding, crimping, pleating, fringing, weaving, braiding, and curling the paper. Direct the children's attention to positive and negative shapes. Suggest how the positive shape, obtained by cutting a motif (star, leaf, heart, cross, diamond) from a piece of paper, and the negative shape, the paper that remains after the shape is cut out, can be juxtaposed in a collage design. Introduce colored tissue paper, either cut or torn, as a collage medium. Urge the use of light-colored tissues first and only later build up to the sparing use of darker colors as accents. Encourage color discovery by suggesting that students build several tissue layers. Collage projects in tissue lend themselves beautifully to nonobjective designs

and depictions of dreams and moods. Children also can make collages interpreting sounds: whisper, shout, swish, rattle, squeak, roar, and thunderclap.

Courtesy of Barbara Thomas, Whit Davis School, Athens, GA, student Amy Wallace.

Studying Henri Matisse's paper cut out pictures, fourth-grade student Amy Wallace made this joyous collage.

Printmaking

The vegetable, clay stamp, and found-object print media, introduced in the primary grades, now can be augmented with oil pastel as a final, rich embellishment. A variety of printmaking processes, which are explained fully in Chapter 24, now are manageable. These include the glue-line print, the collograph or cardboard relief print, and the string or cord print, in which string is glued to a cardboard plate, inked, and printed. An excellent medium for greeting-card designs is the plastic foam meat-tray print, in which lines are indented into the tray with a pencil and the plate inked and printed so that lines will appear white in the completed print. In the monoprint technique, a sheet of plastic laminate or of glass (its edges taped) is inked with a brayer. The composition then is created by scratching through the paint with a stick, Q-tip, edge of a cardboard piece, eraser end of a pencil, or a wood chopstick. Then, a sheet of paper is placed over the inked surface, pressed down, and pulled off carefully.

Ceramics

At this stage, review the knowledge that children have gained in earlier school years about clay: where it comes from; its properties, such as plasticity; its possibilities; and its limitations. Describe the importance of ceramics in the everyday life of both ancient and contemporary cultures. An exploratory session in clay manipulation is again recommended to help students recall that:

- Hardening clay is difficult to model.
- Clay that is too moist sags if the supports of clay or rolled paper, or the "fifth leg" under the stomach of an animal, are not sturdy enough.
- Appendages break off when the clay piece dries unless they are securely joined to the main structure with clay-scoring or slip-cementing.
- Textures, patterns, and details can be made in clay with fingers, pencils, and assorted found objects.
- Solid clay pieces over a $\frac{1}{2}$-inch thick may explode in the firing kiln unless openings are made through which the air inside can escape.

In pottery making, children can make the basic, simple pinch pot into a larger container or an animal's body by joining with clay-slip two pinch pots of the same size. Cut out openings, and add feet and spouts for more complex pots.

Courtesy of Joyce Vroon and Marlee Puskar, Trinity School, Atlanta, GA.

A collage display is made from third-grade students' brass fastener action puppets.

Suggested Subjects or Themes

These topics are suitable for children of ages 7, 8, and 9 (grades 3 and 4):

Inside me (imaginative X-ray)	Totem poles
Fun on the jungle gym	Action poses
Sports poses and stillifes	
The circus parade	A tree house
The merry-go-round	Tree of life
The house where I live	Imaginary animals
Rare birds	Prehistoric animals
Animals and their young	Teddy bears
Flowers from above	The insect world
Autumn leaves and trees	Playing a musical instrument
The pet show or pet store	Still life of interesting objects
A magic forest	Flower market or fruit market
The wedding	The toy store or Santa's workshop
Western objects	
Here comes the clowns!	The circus in action
Washing the family car	Space voyage
Food we like to eat	Self portraits
Boarding the school bus	Sunken treasure
A quiet activity at home	A special place to go
Design in nature: radiation	

If I were a balloon seller, a juggler, a tightrope walker, a ballerina, a scarecrow, a skydiver, an astronaut, a clown.

Chapter 6

A Sequential Curriculum for Grades 5 and 6

After the powerful beginning in the primary and middle elementary grades, when almost all children feel they can do art, a period of plateau or decline may occur during the upper elementary grades. It is not known whether self-doubt about drawing is the cause of this decline, or whether the decline is the result of self-doubt. To be sure, the best art, whether realistic or abstract or primitive, is characterized by assuredness and verve, and this confidence seems to be shaken in the upper elementary grades. Children's criteria of what is good in art outrace their abilities. They come to feel that their drawings are "not good enough," and they decide they are "no good in art." These attitudes underscore the importance of discussions of aesthetics, on what makes quality in art, and whether realism is the only goal.

We believe that the guidance and encouragement of a sympathetic, knowledgeable teacher can prevent students from lagging on the same creative plateau for years. Without a teacher's guidance and encouragement, children's cognitive and affective growth in art, employment of visual resources, command of the vocabulary and language of art, and use of formal elements may remain static or even retrogress. This eventually may lead to discouragement, frustration, and apathy. If children are not taught art skills and are left to their own devices, many develop into adults who feel limited in their ability to make and discuss art.

On the other hand, under the guidance of a teacher who helps them to create and appreciate the beauty they create and who gives them good reasons to try, children will grow in their ability to be careful

Fifth- and sixth-grade youngsters created these sophisticated self-portraits with an animal or bird. The drawing was first done in gold or silver crayon on black construction paper. Then, oil pastel was used to create the complementary and analogous color areas. Notice the perceptive and sensitive handling of the eyes, eyelids, hair, and face planes.

Iowa City Schools. Courtesy of Baiba Kuntz, Glencoe, IL.

50

delineators, to represent overlapping and receding spatial planes, and to use these concepts in their contour drawings, drawings of buildings in nature, and imaginative drawings of the fantastic. Another approach that is especially suited for those who doubt their art ability is to use art topics in which students express themselves and their values through symbols, dreams, and metaphors—in other words, art that expresses their uniqueness as people.

Developmental Characteristics

The left-hand column of the next table lists some of the developmental characteristics of fifth- and sixth-grade children. The right-hand column lists one or more related art instructional objectives for each characteristic.

Developmental Characteristics of Fifth and Sixth Graders	Some Related Art Instructional Objectives
Begin to concentrate more on individual interests.	Students will depict their individual collections, their clothes for special occasions—for example, baseball uniforms, ballet costumes, scout uniforms.
Are now interested in activities that relate to their gender.	Students will use methods of art criticism to describe and interpret art works showing preadolescents.
Vary in maturity, with girls more developed physically and emotionally than boys.	
Are becoming more dependable, responsible, self-critical, and reasonable.	Students will use their own evaluation of their artwork—describing both strengths and weaknesses—as a guide toward making changes in it.

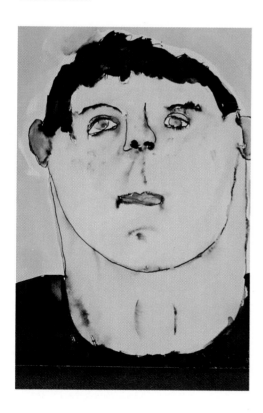  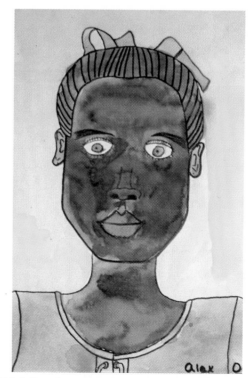

Courtesy of Melody Milbrandt, Valdosta, GA; Baiba Kuntz, Glencoe, IL; and Joyce Vroon, Trinity School, Atlanta, GA.

Left, self-portrait of a fifth-grade boy was done in ink and watercolor. Middle, fifth-grade student J. Ryan Lapatka did his self-portrait in conté crayon on grey paper.

Right, fifth-grade student Alex Owen used permanent marker and watercolor for his portrait of a classmate.

Developmental Characteristics of Fifth and Sixth Graders	Some Related Art Instructional Objectives
Are interested in doing and making things "right"; try to conform to ideals of "good" behavior.	Students will explore using the methods of realistically showing deep space. Students will be able to conform to their group's behavior policies.
Develop interests outside of home and school—in their community and the world at large.	Students will describe how the arts are incorporated into their community.
Begin to criticize grownups and anyone in authority.	Students will debate the art judgments of experts.
Are undergoing critical emotional and physical changes.	Students will depict their physical appearance and emotions in their art and writing.
Become more involved in hobbies and collections.	Students will create an art display or representation of a hobby.
Begin a phase of hero and heroine worship.	Using examples from art history, students will describe a favorite artist's life.
Often enjoy being by themselves, away from adult interference.	Students will create a personal art notebook/diary showing one's inner life.
Enjoy working on group projects.	Students will cooperative with a group of peers in planning and executing a group project.
Are developing a sense of values, a sense of right and wrong.	Students will debate issues in art ethics. ("Who should own and display Native American art, big city museums or tribal museums?")
Are increasing their interest and work span.	Students will work on an art project for three or more hours.
Tend to form separate gangs or cliques according to their interests, sex, ethnicity, neighborhoods, and family status.	Students will identify and interpret historical art exemplars representing groups with which they identify.

The principal developmental focus coming into play around this time is of identity versus role confusion. Can the child find a meaningful place in the world and in the world of work? Promote the development of a sense of identity through group art projects that focus

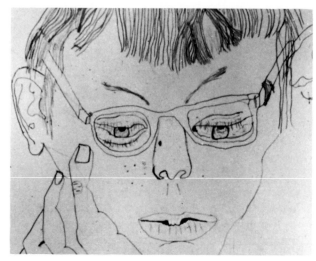

Courtesy of Suzy McNeil, Iowa City, IA.

The self-portrait of this upper-elementary-grade boy is a contour drawing, patiently delineated.

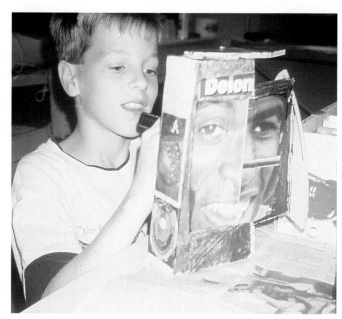

Courtesy of Joyce Vroon, Trinity School, Atlanta, GA.

Fifth-grade student Brian Davis uses a piece of wood as a foundation for a Marisol-like collage sculpture of his sports hero, Deion.

Courtesy of the International Collection of Child Art, Illinois State University, Normal, IL.

The perspective lines (lines receding into depth) of tables, trucks, and buildings in this 11-year-old student's drawing of the Bilecik, Turkey, market do not go to one vanishing point. Instead, the lines head to a general area in the upper right corner, in a method called isometric perspective. *The technique in which the perspective lines diverge as they go back in space is called* inverse perspective; *it also appears in this drawing and much Near Eastern art.*

on community occupational roles, including the many occupations artists have.

Art Development

The level of mastery that individuals achieve when developing expertise is largely intertwined with the effectiveness of instruction. Without a teacher's guidance, children's growth and interest in art and the use of formal elements, in the way they perceive artistically, and in how they discuss art may remain static. Some unique abilities do appear at this stage of development, however, to which the illustrations throughout this chapter attest.

The following table gives some general, stage-related descriptions of children's art development at this age.

Art Development	Instructional Objective
Become increasingly critical of their drawing ability and often are so discouraged with their efforts they lose interest in art class unless they are wisely and sympathetically motivated and guided.	Students will describe well-drawn and expressively drawn parts in each others' artwork. Students will describe and use design principles in creative crafts items. Students will show more interest in art history.
Develop a growing curiosity to experiment with new and varied materials, tools, and techniques.	Students will use specialized tools and techniques, such as linoleum-cutting tools, plaster carving, weaving, and stitchery.
Experiment more with value contrasts, neutralized colors, patterns, and textual effects.	Students will neutralize colors and create both pattern and texture effects.
Begin to use rudimentary perspective principles in drawing landscapes, buildings, streets, train tracks, fences, roads, and interiors.	Students will use vanishing area perspective as well as appreciate other ways to create depth.
Become more interested in their environment as a source for their drawings and paintings.	Students will draw scenes of historical interest and natural beauty in their community.

Art Criticism

At this age, students can identify the major compositional features of an artwork. They can suggest alternative ways that something could be made and make critical judgments about artworks. For example, one student said, "It needs to have a black dog in the painting." They will be able to compare and contrast works in terms of both form and expressive meaning. They can describe how the elements work together to convey the ideas, and they can learn to see beyond the subject matter and use terminology to identify the style and mood. They can describe what things are like in art, although they do not use metaphors (e.g., "icy person") until later. They can identify symbols used in artworks. They can describe artists in their community, and they have a growing multicultural awareness in that they can analyze works from a wide variety of cultures.

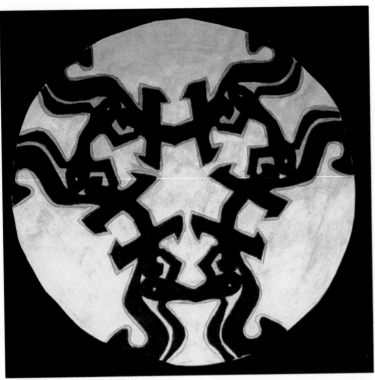

Courtesy of Fay Brassie, Hilsman Middle School, Athens, GA.

From a linear design of the student's initials, an attractive design using trilateral symmetry developed.

Children also like to know about illustrators' tricks of the trade, such as zoom lines and ways of depicting muscles, and they are interested in studying how artists and illustrators use such conventions. For example, students might brainstorm about what is necessary to make a good depiction of a villain or a princess. A bulletin board, onto which students pin up examples they bring in, can show symbols for power, violence, speed, and motion.

Students should be able to use art terms such as the following in discussing artworks:

Design: harmony, motif, gradation, symmetry, asymmetry, emphasis, balance, composition, repetition, rhythm, simplicity, unity, variety

Shape: concave, convex, conical, pyramidal, exaggerated, geometric, biomorphic

Representation: foreshortening, proportion, symbol

Color: analogous, monochromatic, shading, harmony, spectrum, neutralization, transparent, opaque, translucent

Eye movement in a picture: circular, straight, spiral

Size: microscopic, telescopic

Space: narrow, wide, horizon line, perspective, vanishing point, vanishing area

Texture: granular, pebbled, regular, irregular

Courtesy of Deborah Lackey, Fulton County Schools, Atlanta, GA.

Frank Stella's artwork motivated four students who worked together on this cut paper collage with craypas.

Art History and Aesthetics

In art history, students will be able to identify major figures and masterworks. They can explain how two styles of art differ and arrange examples of historic styles into chronological sequence. Encourage them to think more deeply about experiences, about the motives that underlie behavior. For example, ask "Why did the artist do it that way?" They will be able to explain different art criteria, those based on aesthetics and those based on nonaesthetic criteria, such as money or subject matter. Because students of this age tend to value things according to size, expense, complexity, and power, the teacher can present reproductions of artworks that are especially large, costly, complex, or that depict powerful individuals.

Courtesy of Barbara Thomas, Whit Davis School, Athens, GA.

Studying Egyptian tomb figurines, fifth-grade student Kristin French first rolled a slab of clay around a tube. Clay was added for the arms and legs and the tube's top covered, a clay ball of clay added for the head, and a draped covering and hieroglyphics added. The piece then was painted with green acrylic green paint, a black wash applied, and the figure glued to a scrap of wood.

Courtesy of Jackie Ellett, Fort Daniel Elementary School, GA.

From a study of Nigerian art, fifth-grade students used the counter repoussee metal working process.

The art preference of these children is for "super" realism and realism, a preference that peaks at age 11. In response to realistic artworks, students will say, "I wish I could draw like that." They are puzzled by pictures showing objects as they are not, or as they "should not" be. They call these depictions "weird" or "ugly." They feel that the things in pictures should be recognizable and valuable, neat, and interesting. At the same time, they are beginning to comprehend on an intellectual level (although often not on an emotional level) why an artist might show something other than a realistic rendering. They can and do use visual and verbal metaphors.

Students at this age are sensitive to the idea of "system," of a right way to do things. They try to adopt the rules and the codes necessary to survive in society. They want to know the right ways to do counting, reading, and math; the proper ways to play and to work; the codes of

Drawing, Designing, and Painting

Students now can be careful, expressive, and observational delineators. They begin to include shadows and receding planes in paintings. Scout out challenging sites to draw, such as nearby building construction and demolition sites, Victorian-style homes, and gardens. As it often is difficult to leave the school grounds, find interesting locations around the school; the lockers, halls, gym, entrance, kitchen, or playground. Students can be guided to create variety, space, and movement in their compositions by the imaginative placement of images, objects, or motifs within the picture plane. Encourage them to put figures or buildings on different foreground levels and to terminate them at varying heights in the background. Shapes can be juxtaposed or overlapped to create unity and space-in-depth.

Courtesy of Sharon Burns-Knutson, Cedar Rapids, IA.

Nigerian art also motivated this project in aluminum tooling by fifth- and sixth-grade students. Bold geometric designs have been used and stain applied to bring out the relief.

right and wrong. Because of the firmness of their convictions and their awareness of rules concerning the way things are supposed to be, their language contains many "shoulds." ("That's not what a good drawing of a car should look like.") The teacher of aesthetics can use these "shoulds" to raise contested issues about the nature of art. ("Should good art take a lot of time to make?") Encourage students to come up with questions about meanings and values. Ask them to clarify their statements, to give reasons to support them, and then to examine the reasons given.

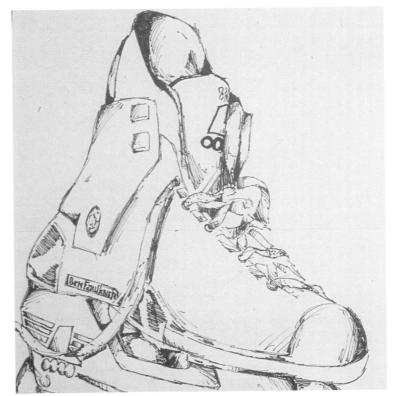

Courtesy of Joyce Vroon, Trinity School, Atlanta, GA.

Fifth-grade student Ben Faulkner's pen drawing of a roller blade shows the careful delineation of rounded forms turning away out of view.

Courtesy of Joyce Vroon, Trinity School, Atlanta, GA.

Metaphors present a way to share one's feelings. Art class can provide a venue for the expression of things one usually does not talk about, wearing a false face (by Michael Selik), an intricate maze (by Grant Arnold), and a nest of snakes in a jungle of vines (by Matthew Parker). Fifth-grade.

loneliness and despair. They can use metaphors in their designs for record album covers and billboards. Lead the students to discover the many different ways they can use line as pattern to enrich surfaces and vitalize backgrounds. Students become absorbed in the tricks of the trade; they like learning the conventions of comic book illustration, such as thought bubbles, clearly defined muscles, and stars and steam to depict violence.

When painting with color, reinforce learning about complementary, monochromatic, and analogous color harmonies. Discuss tints and shades, the directions for neutralizing colors, the color spectrum, and the color wheel. Continue to build color awareness by calling the students' attention to color usage in their everyday world: billboards, magazine and recording covers, athletic uniforms, storefronts, and automobiles. Use mood music as a background for free, expressive painting.

Collage

Recapitulate previous learnings, such as the use of positive and negative shapes. Recommend using partially three-dimensional effects through paper folding, fringing, pleating, spiraling, and curling. Introduce paper scoring to students who are ready for more skillful challenges. Demonstrate the scoring technique: placing paper to be scored on a thick pad of newspapers; using the blunt point of scissors, the pointed end of a wooden popsicle stick, or a similar tool to indent the curved line into the paper; and then carefully folding along the indented line. To enrich students' collages, encourage them to scout for found objects such as wallpaper and rug samples, fabric and ribbon remnants, yarn, old greeting cards, and discarded building materials.

Printmaking

Although the various printmaking processes introduced in previous grades—vegetable and found-object print, collograph, glue-line-relief print, polystyrene print, monoprint—can be repeated successfully at this age, the maturing students now will respond to more complex and challenging techniques. Linoleum printing is a favorite because of the opportunity to use a variety of gouges. Because more tools, materials, equipment, and time are required for advanced printmaking, see Chapter 24 for guidelines on inking, printing, and using cleanup stations.

Hilsman Middle School. Courtesy of Carole Henry, Athens, GA.

Many students are highly impressed by the ability of cartoon superhero artists to depict an exaggerated play of light and dark, revealing exaggerated muscles.

Sadly, inability to achieve satisfactory realistic results leads some children mistakenly to conclude, "I am no good at art." Challenge this now. Continue practice in contour drawing, but introduce new approaches such as fantasy, nonobjective, and optical-art themes. Interest in the surreal shows up in the use of macabre and bloody images. Children can use metaphoric images—for example, an isolated tree for

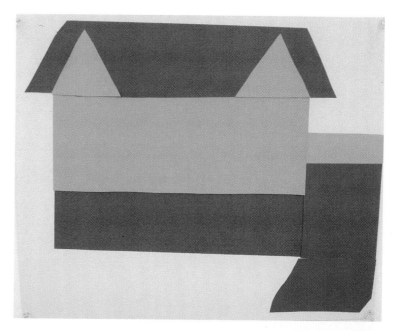

Fifth and sixth grade. Courtesy of Baiba Kuntz, Glencoe, IL.

From a preliminary drawing, an attractive disposition of the basic shapes of an imaginary house are glued down, then architectural details and landscaping added.

Courtesy of Baiba Kuntz, Glencoe, IL.

Mirrors help students to achieve success with projects like these life-sized clay-relief self-portraits. Upper-elementary-grade students are concerned with realistic portrayals showing correct proportions and details.

Ceramics, Crafts, and New Media

Ceramic homes in clay relief are very successful at this age. Popular themes include animals and their young, animals in combat, portraits and self-portraits, clowns, acrobats, and mother and child. Students now place strong emphasis on realistic portrayals and the achievement of correct proportions and characteristic detail. Toward these ends, the teacher must be prepared to offer sympathetic and supportive guidance when called on. In most instances, recalled images alone will not supply the child with sufficient visual data. Direct students to the original, inspirational source of the subject matter—to the figure or animal itself or to photographic resources. Build a library of photographs and slides showing exemplars of ceramic art through the centuries. Neither overpraise the purely realistic approach they admire nor harshly criticize it; instead, introduce students to a variety of styles and interpretations.

Many crafts are popular at this age. Simple jewelry is a favorite activity. Photography also is a popular new medium to introduce at this age. Students love to take Polaroids of the environment, city, and signs.

Suggested Subjects or Themes

These project suggestions are suitable for children of ages 9, 10, and 11 (grades 5 and 6):

At the gas station
A view from a plane
Bicycle race
Horse show
Warriors in armor
Undersea marine life
At the swimming pool
Dreams
Values
Cartoons
Winter carnival
Cities in outer space
Self-portraits
Portraits of classmates

This woodblock print of a child model playing a recorder is by an upper-elementary-grade student in Japan. It shows carefully delineated fingers, as well as lines around the mouth to indicate the blowing. Removing the background created an attractive texture. Japan.

Traffic jam
Landscape, cityscape, or seascape
Nature study
The marching band
Ball game, track meet, or scout jamboree
Amusement park
The shopping mall
Disneyland, Six Flags
Motorcycles
Renowned sports figures
Still life of musical instruments or sports equipment
Crowds at the county fair and 4-H competitions

Still lifes of watches, hair bows, typewriters, telephones, old tools, and old objects
Still life of beach paraphernalia, scuba-diving equipment, or roller blades
Bags and packaging from fast-food restaurant lunches

Courtesy of the International Collection of Child Art, Illinois State University, Normal, IL.

Maori chief by a New Zealand student, age 10.

Courtesy of Joyce Vroon, Trinity School, Atlanta, GA.

Courtesy of Joyce Vroon, Trinity School, Atlanta, GA.

Courtesy of Joyce Vroon, Trinity School, Atlanta, GA.

Sixth-grade students captured the texture of a billboard's multilayered torn surface, the diagonal pattern of sunlight and shadows falling across a colonnaded and trellised entry, and the expressive surface of a grafitti covered wall. Students Ashley Wagner, Catherine Overend, and Devon McClure.

Chapter 7

A Sequential Curriculum for Grades 7 and 8

Middle school students move into a changed academic world. For the first time, they may have a different teacher for each subject they take. If they come from the typical elementary school situation where the classroom teacher taught art, it will be their first contact with a specialist art teacher. In American schools, just a little over half of the students this age participate in visual arts classes. In some schools, students involved in band or orchestra programs cannot take art. Also regrettable is that, in general, students draw less as they grow older. For a fair number of adolescents, however, a new synthesis occurs. Their newly developed technical facility is joined to their vision of what needs to be expressed.

Middle school students are experiencing a renaissance of intellectual inquisitiveness that in some ways may never be matched again. They are less inhibited than upper-elementary-grade children, but they still are highly critical of their own performance. They are more willing to tackle new processes and new materials. They are technically more proficient. Their ability to capitalize on suggestions is heightened, and they can enter into critical discussions on art design and structure with a keener sensitivity and sharper argumentative skills. They are highly impressionable. Their cultural horizons are expanding, and they may carry with them for the rest of their lives the preferences and prejudices regarding art that they develop in these middle school years.

This middle school student is intent on his ceramic creation. For many youngsters, there is no greater satisfaction than hand building structures out of clay. The simple, basic pinch-pot form has been enriched by the addition of a foot, neck, handles, and an embellishing relief pattern.

Courtesy of David Hodge, Oshkosh, WI.

Developmental Characteristics

Developmental Characteristics of Seventh and Eighth Graders	Implications for Art Teaching
Want to be accepted by their peers. This acceptance often is more important to them than the teacher's approval.	Students will work in small groups to plan and carry out group projects.
Often are more inclined to daydream, to watch rather than to perform.	From a study of art history books, students will describe an imaginary day in the life of an artist.
Begin to place a new emphasis on their appearance, grooming, and popularity.	Students will create a clay head in three dimensions of themselves or of a classmate.
Are becoming more self-conscious regarding their changing physical characteristics.	Students will be able to draw caricatures of their prominent features.
Are fascinated with their names	Do name or initial designs as prints or collage
Possess varying degrees of physiological and sexual maturity.	Students will interpret artwork showing persons of this age.
Are in constant communication with their friends about dates, parties, TV shows, movies, recordings, classmates' doings, and teachers' and parents' foibles.	From a personal record of phone doodles, students will describe the design variations and use these ideas as the basis for a t-shirt design.
Frequently model their behavior and appearance after sports stars, television personalities, rappers, recording artists, and movie stars.	Students will be able to draw from photos persons whom they admire.
Are developing their interest in sports, music, or other arts.	Draw their own collections of souvenirs and mementos.
Often are unusually sensitive to other people's problems but do not know how to help.	Students will create a work of art to share with another person and give emphatic feedback to another student about art.
Are trying to develop a code or sense of values.	Students will interpret a work of art in terms of the moral dilemmas for the persons represented.
Form status groups and cliques, using "accepted," "tolerated," and "rejected" categories.	Students will interpret artworks by diverse groups, and looking at pictures of alienation, explain what the artists were trying to communicate.

Painting a design for a record cover may reveal that middle school students' opinions about the quality of rap music are different from the teacher's. Nevertheless, the teacher can lead them to consider how the artistic solutions of artists such Wassily Kandinsky and Peter Max may be applicable to their own designs.

Developmental Characteristics of Seventh and Eighth Graders	Implications for Art Teaching
Have a growing desire for new and exciting experiences.	Students will be able to depict exciting, imaginary adventures through art.
Fluctuate between childhood and adulthood in their interests, insights, abilities, and judgments.	Students will describe art careers in the community.

Emotional Vulnerability

Young adolescents have tender feelings, and direct criticism of students' artwork in front of their classmates can be humiliating. Avoid sarcasm and belittling remarks at all costs. Writing as an adult, Georgia O'Keeffe recalled the painful humiliation she felt when at age 13, her art teacher criticized her in front of her classmates for drawing a plaster figure's hand too small. "At the time I thought she scolded me terribly. I was so embarrassed that it was difficult not to cry" (O'Keeffe, 1988). Teachers may also embarrass students by praising their work too

Courtesy of D. Hodge and F. Wachowiak, University of Wisconsin Oshkosh Campus Laboratory School
University High, Iowa City, IA.

From "Middle School Expressions," by Teddy Oliver and Robert Clements, *School Arts Magazine*, September, 1983.
Courtesy of Davis Publications and Teddy Oliver, Marietta, GA.

A 12-year-old has expressed pain and humiliation in this oil pastel, My Mother Just Spanked Me.

Circle self-portraits in oil pastel on colored construction paper by middle school students. By using a circle format and emphasizing imaginative use of color and form, the teacher created a new artistic design challenge. Flags, flowers, camouflage, and birds serve as auxiliary ways the artists have conveyed their interests.

During middle school, teachers really begin to see the personalities and idiosyncrasies of the students reflected in their behavior and their art. While students can be conformists, they also can be fiercely independent. Roles are tried out: the extrovert, the loner, the risk taker, the methodical planner, the procrastinator, the idol seeker, the plodder, the perfectionist, the maverick, the dreamer, the braggart, the idealist, and the quiz whiz. One week one role is tried; the next week, a different role is tried. Personalities depicted throughout art history (such as Albrecht Dürer's knight on a horse and Renaissance depictions of David and Hercules) can be related to some students' fantasy interests. Rites of passage are acted out in real fights, mock fights, and challenges to authority. This is a time of increased awareness and self-consciousness, sensitivity to the differences in others, identification with the peer group, and heightened emotional responses. Possibly as a means of self-searching, preadolescents like to draw portraits and capture their changing self-image.

Red Barn, Lake George, New York, 1921, (oil on canvas, 14 ¼ × 16¼ inches), Georgia Museum of Art, Eva Underhill Holbrook Memorial, Gift of Alfred Holbrook.

Georgia O'Keeffe distastefully remembered for decades when her middle school teacher publicly rebuked the realism of her figure drawing in front of her classmates. Her paintings are acclaimed for their bold shape patterns.

lavishly in front of their peers. To avoid public embarrassment whether correcting or praising students, give individual, in-process critiques.

Emotional swings and moodiness in children are not unusual, and some students may reject their own excellent artwork. Drawings of teenage clothing, sneakers, and hairstyles considered as contrary to the adult culture's norms can express adolescents' need to be separate from that dominant adult culture. Especially if their art experiences in elementary school were limited, unsatisfying, or unrewarding, middle school students may be apathetic or cool in their response to art. Once they become caught up in the excitement of a creative, productive, and qualitative art program, however, they become enthusiastic converts to art's adventures, challenges, and personally satisfying rewards.

Courtesy of Fay Brassie, Athens, GA.

In a design for a jacket, this middle school student has expressed yearnings for love, joy, and the banning of rules.

Courtesy of Joyce Vroon, Trinity School, Atlanta, GA.

Painting "A Dream," may be a way to gain insight into the messages from one's unconscious mind. Fifth-grade student Pierce Lowrey.

Going steady, having crushes, engaging in sexual activity, and being subjected to physical and sexual harassment and abuse are emotionally charged situations in which some older students may find themselves. Other events fraught with the potential for creating feelings of guilt are the divorce of parents, an abortion, or the death of a loved one. Feelings of worthlessness, incompetence, ugliness, anger, guilt, and complicity interfere with the development of students' positive self-concepts. Teachers used to say that the schools' biggest problems were talking in class, chewing gum, making noise, running in the halls, and getting out of turn in lines. Today, more serious problems are endemic. By being a friend to the student and expressing personal concern, you may play a pivotal role in the student's life at a critical time, and the art program may provide a vehicle for the student to express his or her conflicts or develop positive responses.

When students are going through emotionally trying situations, you may see a decline in their ability to concentrate on art expression. In their behavior, you may see a shortness of temper or a lack of affect. Art expression may serve as a warning beacon, announcing that a person is in trouble. Students' verbalizations during art criticism and art interpretation often provide a forum for other students to speak out about what is on their minds. Very general and wide-open art topics, such as "crying" or "oppression," may provide a way to express, through art, what formerly seemed to be unmentionable. The teacher of art may be able to help the young person cope with problems, not by being a psychologist but by being a friend, someone with whom significant events may be shared. Through the school counselor, the art teacher also may be able to help individuals or their parents get in contact with agencies that are skilled in dealing with serious problems.

The emotional side of middle school art is shown in this soft firebrick sculpture and this driftwood sculpture. Here are seen the creators' sensitivity to others, their forming of significant relationships with others, their heightened emotional responses, and their self-searching.

Not only can art announce to the sensitive perceiver an individual's distress, it can play a major role in restoring a person's balance after a traumatic situation. Art creation as well as discussions about art can help students to feel better about themselves. Problem solving through art provides an opportunity for the "person within" to emerge. Applying the principles of good design—balance, proportion, variation—seems to foster those same qualities in the individual creator. During art creation, the individual may find help through being able to share visually, at whatever level is comfortable, the event that needs expression. Likewise, through talking about the art of others, the individual may be able to give voice to personal feelings and break out of his or her aloneness and grief. A student's art accomplishment can help others to see that person as an individual of worth. In turn, the achieve-

ment helps that individual to acquire a sense of pride and self-worth despite whatever outrageous blows that fortune has inflicted.

Art Criticism

A new and genuinely different way of thinking about art now comes into being at this level. The criterion of realism is replaced by those of intention and message. Given artwork containing expressive themes, students will talk about the expressive qualities of the artwork. They can recognize style and contrast the treatment of theme in two or more artworks. They understand metaphor and mystery, and they can identify multiple meanings in represented objects.

Accompanying the rapid changes in their bodies and their own search for identity is a shift in understanding. Students now can understand that expression of the experiences of others and of one's self is subjective. Expression characterizes this stage. Reassure students that they need not share their own personal artworks publicly unless they so desire. There is less concern about realism and the beauty of a subject. Pictures now can be seen as metaphors for ideas and emotions and valued for their ability to inspire feelings. Social commentary art, such as George Tookers, helps them to express feelings of justice. Students can speculate on the artist's mood. They can imagine alternatives to what the picture shows and speculate on different scenarios. This allows them to feel an identification with accepted, mature artists.

Students will be able to discuss the aesthetic quality of an artwork or a utilitarian object. For example, students can judge the effectiveness of the designs of athletic shoes, t-shirts, and motorcycles as well as analyze how these objects suggest ideas and feelings.

Art History and Aesthetics

Adolescents' ability to think abstractly and reason about ideas increases dramatically at this time. They can consider the logical possibilities in a problem. They make guesses about what might be going on behind the depicted scene, and they can discuss symbolism, deeper meanings, and double meanings.

Students now have the ability to conduct inquiry from several vantage points. They can role play different parts, such as art critic, artist, disgruntled client, or government official. Both individually or in small groups, students can report on artists' careers. They can stage mock debates between artists, pointing up contested issues in art, such as

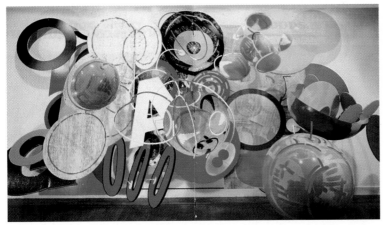

Courtesy Holly Solomon Gallery, New York.

Exciting color projects to stimulate color awareness can be motivated by showing the work of Judy Pfaff, such as her 1986 Apples and Oranges. Mixed media, 113 × 72 inches.

whether paintings should show realism or emotion. Some terms to discuss are expressivism, realism, aesthetics, anatomy, judgment, value, art critic, censorship, metaphor, spontaneity, craftsmanship.

During this new stage of aesthetic response, students can investigate questions of content and social significance. Because art is an expression of its creator, ask them to discuss how the artist uses color and design to show emotion. Students also are able to consider more abstract aspects, such as style and composition, and they understand that other students' perspectives can be different from their own.

To tap their interest in expressive works of art, expose them to Van Gogh's life and letters. Show them works about the suffering of women and children during wartime by Kaethe Kollwitz, Francisco Goya, and Max Beckman. Expand their knowledge and appreciation of master drawings and paintings by artists such as Leonardo da Vinci, Albrecht Dürer, Rembrandt Van Rijn, Rosa Bonheur, Paul Klee, Henri Matisse, Pablo Picasso, Louise Nevelson, Andy Warhol, Katsushika Hokusai, Georgia O'Keeffe, William Hogarth, Romare Bearden, Peter Breughel, and Mary Cassatt. Students love the artworks of Red Grooms and Grant Wood.

Call their attention to the cave drawings at Altamira and Font du Gaume as well, to Benin bronzes, and to the tribal-huntsmen renditions of African and Australian native cultures. Show them the sumi-e ink drawings of China and Japan and the expressive graphics of the Eskimos and Native Americans.

Courtesy of David Hodge, Oshkosh, WI.

Through drawing classmates modeling, students can express indirectly something of their own nature. Here, a middle school youth captures in a contour-line drawing a quality of openness and searching. The drawing also conveys an understanding of the human form, the chair, and folds of clothing.

Middle school students, coming as they often do from different elementary schools, will bring varied backgrounds in art vocabulary. Students should be able to match artworks to styles. One appropriate task is to identify the artwork that does not belong in a group. Vocabulary words that have been suggested in previous grades should be reviewed and new words added as they are introduced:

Art history and criticism: expressionism, neo-expressionism, op art, pop art, African sculptures from Yoruba, Benin bronzes, Zaire nail art, Chi Wara antelope sculptures, surrealism, cubism, Renaissance art, impressionism, symbolism, double meaning

Drawing and painting: conte crayon, sienna, spectrum, stipple, umber, montage, ochre, watercolor wash, distortion, encaustic, fixative, foreshortening, gesture drawing, hatching, converging lines, cross-hatch, caricature

Printmaking: baren, bench hook, burnish, etching, intaglio, printing press, proof, relief print

Photography, film, and video: negative, fixer, plate, tone, daguerreotype, cibachrome, playback, wipe, fade, establishing shot, zoom shot, soft focus, montage, slow disclosure, low-angle shot, freeze frame, long shot, pan, superimposition

Sculpture: armature, assemblage, bas relief, solder, sandcore, sepia, stabile, incised relief, repoussé, patina

Art Development

Art Development	Instructional Objective
Choose subject matter for their art expression that relates to human-interest activities, community and worldwide events, and current projects in ecology, medical research, space, and undersea exploration.	Students will use current events as the setting for their art expression. Students will explain the art principles they used in depicting the sociological, artistic, or scientific event.
Attempt shading and cross-hatch techniques to make their drawn forms appear solid, cylindrical, and believably realistic. Experiment with perspective drawing.	Students will use shading and cross-hatching to create the appearance of three-dimensional form. Students will be able to apply some perspective concepts.
Are self-conscious and self-critical about their drawing ability. Supportive instruction as well as contour and gesture drawing help them to become increasingly skillful in figure and animal drawing.	Students will use gesture and contour drawing to capture the feeling and dynamics of the posed human figure.

Art Development	Instructional Objective
Are ready to interpret complex compositions, such as richly orchestrated still lifes and multifigured events and celebrations.	Students will apply design principles of repetition and variation to draw an organized composition from a complex still life or from many figures in action.
Are mature and skillful enough to handle a variety of challenging crafts: photography, glazed ceramics, repoussé, plaster reliefs, sculpture in hard materials, and woodblock printmaking.	Students will use craft processes for personal art expression.

Drawing, Designing, and Painting

Students like their work to have expressive content—to convey a mood and have a message. They are interested in finding a powerful means to convey an experience or an idea. Whereas younger students showed scenes, adolescents now use scenic natural forms to communicate their attitudes toward life. They can study symbols and work motifs for peace, freedom, evil, or envy into their designs.

Most students at this age have a love–hate relationship with drawing; they seek realism but often are frustrated by their inability to attain it. Elaborate still-life setups with a model in expressive apparel stimulate their interest and, hence, their desire to accurately represent the model's positions and clothing. Line drawings of cartoon characters, mythical animals, and sports events are popular, as are cartoon portraits. Using shading, stippling, hatching, cross-hatching, and washes, they can begin to comprehend and depict the effect of spotlights on models. They will need guidance and reassurance, however, in handling color values and using cast shadows and reflections.

Students interested in creating depth in their pictures will begin to realize the importance of creating avenues into the composition. This is done by using lines and shapes that terminate at the boundaries or borders of the paper and lead the viewer into the picture. A bonus is that the more avenues are created, the more opportunities the student has to employ a variety of colors, values, and pattern in the resulting shapes. Perspective may be introduced as just one of many ways that artists create the illusion of depth; however, only a tiny fraction of students can work out realistic perspective showing space and depth. Thus, unless a student specifically requests help, it is wise not to introduce regimented perspective rules or foreshortening techniques at this stage.

Perspective is shown in this 10-year-old girl's street scene from Tehran, Iran. Diminishing sizes are seen in the street vanishing around the bend, its dotted centerline, the curved fence, and the street-side buildings.

Inverted perspective sometimes now appears, and the beauty of this method should be pointed out—for example, as in Persian art. Some students will want their drawings to "look right" and will request specific assistance in making their toppling, meandering fences stand straight. They want their sidewalks to lie flat and their roads to disappear believably over a distant rise or hill. To help them achieve these effects, show them that fence posts are drawn parallel to the sides of the page, division lines in sidewalks are drawn at angles directed to a distant vanishing point, and roads or highways diminish in width as they move away toward the horizon.

Older middle school students often are enchanted by the mechanical, mathematical aspects of perspective drawing. The illusion of space gives some students, especially those who do not like to draw, a feeling that they have done something of note. Their enthusiasm should not be dampened, but the teacher should enlighten them regarding the compositional limitations of a rigid reliance on perspective. Similarly, it is all right for students to strive for "right" proportions in their figures, but the instructor must help them to realize that drawing something "realistically right" does not necessarily make it "artistically right." Especially now, when the expression of feelings is so important, students can be shown that many artists throughout time who either did not know of or ignored the rules of perspective and proportion still produced art of great impact and beauty.

Middle school students are mature enough to respond to the many subtleties and complexities of color harmonization. Review the processes for making tints and shades and the techniques for neutralizing colors. Challenge the students to use color principles in designing album covers, monograms, posters, logos, book jackets, store-window displays, room decor, and stage designs. Call attention to how color is used in artworks for conveying emotion. Discuss the psychological effect of color on people, the colors emphasized in packaging and advertising, and the colors of ceremonies, celebrations, rituals, and rites of passage. Analyze how various countries and cultures use differing symbolic color meanings.

Taking ideas from contemporary color and light shows, students can be encouraged to construct their own color "happenings." They can use found materials such as ribbons, yarn, wrapping paper, kites, cellophane, balloons, hula hoops, confetti, crepe and tissue paper in assorted colors, giant paper flowers, fabric samples, and beach towels. Other exciting projects to stimulate color awareness can be motivated by examining such artists as Victor Vasarely, Richard Anuskiewicz, Marc Chagall, and Judy Pfaff. For example, students can construct toothpick-

and-box sculptures painted in bold tempera or fluorescent colors and make miniature stained-glass windows using scrap colored glass, colored tissue paper, or stage gels.

Printmaking

The simple prints that children enjoyed in earlier grades—vegetable and found-object prints, glue-line-relief prints, collographs, monoprints, linoleum prints—can be done with satisfaction and success during middle school. More complex subject matter and themes also now can be employed in a variety of printmaking processes. As always, the organization and monitoring of inking, printing, and cleanup are of special importance. At this grade level, sophisticated printmaking techniques such as woodblocks can be undertaken if teachers are experienced in supervising advanced printmaking techniques. Use nontoxic, water-based inks rather than oil-based inks.

Ceramics and Sculpture

Because students may come to middle school with varying backgrounds in clay experimentation and creation, provide for several sessions to re-

Larger-than-life clay portraits from Japan capture the human figure's expressive potential. Observe the heavy supporting neck and the freely applied dabs of clay to create the form.

view clay exploration. Discuss the importance of clay to the lives of people in other cultures.

Discuss art visuals of ceramic pottery and sculpture from ancient as well as contemporary cultures. Include Greek vases of the Hellenic period, Chinese Tang figurines, the outstanding life-size ceramic warriors and horses unearthed at Xian, Japanese Haniwa creations, and clay vessels in the form of human figures from Mexico and Peru. Library copies of *Ceramic Monthly* can bring the students up to date on the newest developments in the field of ceramic pottery and sculpture. Put up a "potter of the week" display on the artroom bulletin board so that students will become familiar with pioneers and innovators such as Shoji Hamada, Dan Lucero, and Peter Voulkos.

Students now can engage in more complex and challenging clay construction and modeling. If glazes and adequate kiln facilities are provided, students can experiment with safe ceramic glazes to give their works glowing color. A very popular sculpture activity begins with wire armatures that are attached to a block of wood for a base and covered with plaster-of-Paris strips to form expressive figures in motion: rock musicians, surfers, and sports figures.

Crafts

Crafts such as weaving, stitchery, hooked rugs, papier-mache, puppetry, and simple jewelry are especially popular at this level (see Chapter 28). All of these hands-on activities should be included in a qualitative, progressive, elementary and middle school art program. For example, weaving can progress from simple paper weaving in the primary grades to sophisticated, hanging woven panels in the middle school. The story quilts of Faith Ringgold and of Harriet Powers can motivate exciting sewn applique banners and quilts. Mask construction, simple puppets, and stitchery can be offered at all levels. Papiermache, paper sculpture, leather and metal tooling, marionettes, and jewelry are best reserved for upper elementary grades and middle school. Then, many students also are ready for challenging subtractive sculpture projects in soap, balsa wood, sandcore, leather-hard clay molds, plaster-of-Paris blocks, and soft firebrick. They will enjoy additive sculpture employing toothpicks, wood scraps, wire, metal, driftwood, and found objects. Specialized craft vocabulary terms such as the following should be taught: glaze, gouge, greenware, grog, leather-hard clay, mat, mat knife, mixed media, mold, raffia, reed, tesserae.

Courtesy of Claire Clements, Athens, GA.

Hooking a rug can bring pride and satisfaction to middle school students.

Collage

The collage process—with its related family of montage, frottage, mosaic, collograph, and assemblage—provides middle school students a host of opportunities to use the principles of art. These include variety in shapes, contrast in values and color, and overlapping to create unity. Collage allows students to express through art their personal concerns about attractiveness and intimacy as well as their social concerns about world problems such as ecology, hunger, drugs, and war.

Review with students the fundamentals of the collage process: how to identify and exploit positive and negative shapes, and how to create subtle space through overlapping. Show them how to achieve three-dimensional effects through paper folding, scoring, pleating, fringing, and curling. Preliminary drawings or sketches are recommended for collages when the subject matter deals with landscapes, figure studies, or still lifes. In themes from the imagination or in purely nonobjective interpretations, the direct cutting, tearing, and application of the shapes to the background may be encouraged. In both approaches, however, the pasting or permanent adhering of materials should be delayed until the students, with the teacher's guidance, can make those compositional changes—additions, subtractions, and revisions—necessary to enhance their creations.

Vehicles are a popular topic with middle school youths. Students created collages from detailed drawings of an open-doored van parked on the school's premises. Gas pumps and logos were added to enhance the compositions.

Both new and found materials have expanded the range of collage creation immensely. Explore the possibilities of colored tissue on white or colored cardboard, colored sections from magazine ads, wallpaper samples, and fabric remnants. Incorporate nature's store of colored and textured wonders: bark, leaves, seaweed, sand, feathers, butterfly wings, dried flowers, seeds, and snake skins. The collage is an excellent first project of the year for middle school art classes. It does not put as much pressure on the students as an assignment in drawing or painting, and it is not stressful to cut out elements and put them together to make a whole design. Every student in class can succeed in making a collage.

Suggested Subjects or Themes

These project suggestions are suitable for children of ages 12, 13, and 14. Visual resources are absolutely necessary. For additional ideas, refer to the themes recommended earlier for grades 5 and 6, which can be adapted to the middle school. Middle schools may be composed of grades 6 to 8, or even 5 to 8, and this variation will affect the suitability of topics. Some themes, such as a bouquet of flowers, self-portraits, and animal pets, can be recommended without reservation for all grades, 1 through 8.

Environmental problems and solutions
The Olympics
I wish
Great moments in music or ballet
Great moments in theater, literature, or science
Great moments in sports
I would like/I would not like
Customs and costumes of the world
The weather's mood
Sadness in the world
Legendary heroes and heroines
Helicopters, planes, or air balloon races
Bicycles or dune buggies
Landscapes
Illustrations of selected stories and poems
Dream cars, motorcycles, and boats
Historical costumes
Flying trapeze act
The electronic-game arcade
String quartet
Fashion show
Wrestling match

Part 2

Teachers and Teaching

Previous page: *A positive, cheerful personality should show in the teacher's face, actions, and words. The teacher should establish genuine rapport with the students. Most important is to respect them as artists.*

Chapter 8

The Role of
the Dedicated Teacher

Wherever art programs of quality and promise exist, whether in elementary or middle schools, in crowded cities or quiet farm communities, in the United States or abroad, one always discovers in the wings an enthusiastic, resourceful, knowledgeable, imaginative, and gifted teacher. The teacher of the successful, productive art class invariably is a planner, an organizer, an expediter, a counselor, a dreamer, a goal setter, and most of all, a lover of children, life, and especially art.

Without a well-prepared, creative, and dedicated teacher at the helm, an art program can founder in a sea of hasty, last-minute decisions; in trite, stereotyped activities; or in chaotic, pseudotherapeutic play sessions. The school that boasts a modern physical plant, generous budget, and administration sympathetic to art is fortunate, but if it does not attract teachers who are prepared to teach art confidently, enthusiastically, developmentally, and qualitatively, it has little chance of establishing and implementing an art program of excellence and stature.

Dedication is, and always will be, a vital teaching strength in a democratic society. It transcends teaching expertise. Nothing is written in a teaching contract about dedication, nor is there anything explicit about the requisites of love, patience, and sympathetic support that go hand-in-hand with good teaching. Unselfish dedication and enthusiastic involvement are freewill gifts of a devoted teacher, and they cannot be measured except in terms of the inner fulfillment and satisfaction that they bring.

The best teachers of art, whether classroom teachers or special art instructors, believe wholeheartedly in art's unique, spirit-enhancing, and rejuvenating power. In every project, they seek to perfect the critically important motivations, the technical intricacies, and the evaluative strategies. They organize materials, tools, space, and time schedules to produce exemplary working conditions. They search for inspirational art stimuli to renew children's interest in a project whenever the initial excitement wanes. In their enthusiasm, which they display openly and generously, teachers encourage students to open their eyes to the design, color, form, rhythm, texture, and pattern in the world around them, and they believe in art's power to give students a language with which to communicate and express their feelings. They identify with their students and are elated when one makes a discovery or masters a skill. Conversely, they are genuinely concerned when students encounter difficulties that defy resolution. A creative, confident, enthusiastic teacher with a love for children and understanding of art fundamentals is the prime catalyst in a productive and qualitative art program. The successful teacher is responsible for constant planning, organizing, experimenting, motivating, evaluating, and resource building, yet the privilege of sharing the contagious, exuberant, magical world of students as they explore, discover, and invent compensates beyond measure for the extra effort that is required.

Who Teaches Art and in What Kinds of Situations?

Some teachers feel handicapped by a limited background in art fundamentals. One reason for this inadequacy is the minimal art experiences that these teachers had during their own elementary, middle, and secondary school years. Another may be the lack of an art education course during their college preparation and in-service work.

Who teaches art, regular elementary classroom teachers or specialized art teachers? Most teaching of art is done by elementary classroom teachers. Three-quarters of these teachers either teach all or part of the art that their students receive in school. The classroom teacher has flexibility in scheduling and can have small groups of students work on certain phases of art projects while others engage in different subjects. Because only one group of students is involved, storage of materials is

Top row and middle row right: courtesy of Frank Wachowiak, Athens, GA; *Middle row left and center:* courtesy of David Hodge, Oshkosh, WI; *Bottom row:* courtesy of W. Robert Nix, Athens, GA.

The ever-renewing cycle of life is all around us in exquisite and radiating forms. Teachers of art should turn to design in nature for constant motivational inspiration. Be alert for opportunities to guide students to notice the subtle variations in the leaves and petals of a flower or the feathers of birds. Lead them to examine the interstices of a spider's web and the scales of a fish.

not a major problem, and there is little chance that elaborate still-life materials will be stolen.

A second situation is when art is taught by an itinerant art teacher. The nickname *à la carte,* misappropriated from the restaurant industry, often is used by those who do this mobile type of teaching. Usually, such teachers see 500 to 800 students per week, in 20 different classrooms, in two to five different schools. Supplies—and what passes for an office—are in a closet. While the regular classroom teachers may or may not be supposed to remain in the room, the art teacher in practice usually is left alone to handle discipline. The art teacher often has little opportunity to know how the regular teacher handles disruptive incidents.

The third type of situation is when art is taught by an art teacher with an art room. More elaborate facilities, such as hot plates, looms, and sinks, are possible in the specialized art room. Elaborate still lifes can be constructed. While this situation prevails in the middle school, only in a fraction of elementary schools is this the case. The middle school teacher usually sees 125 students a day. The elementary art teacher with an art room sees 500 to 800 students each week. This teacher has one 45-minute art period in which to motivate the students, distribute supplies, monitor the lesson, clean up, evaluate the lesson, and store artwork if the project is to go on for a second week.

Need to Guide Students to Create and to Appreciate

To appreciate their students' developmental possibilities and limitations, teachers must have a basic understanding of the kinds of art that children do naturally. The qualitative art program espoused by this book, however, demands more of students than what they do naturally. Some students do perceive, draw, and compose sensitively, but most require guidance and motivation. Because the teacher is the prime catalyst, it is the teacher's responsibility to establish a positive learning climate in which inquiry, creativity, and individuality thrive. Teachers of art may ask their students to set higher standards of performance for themselves or demand greater effort than the children have been accustomed to making. In most instances, the best art is the result of perseverance—of purposeful, consistent, and time-consuming effort. The results are not accidental, or the product of undemanding, trivial, or thoughtless activity. To teach that art is undemanding is to create a false impression.

Experienced teachers do not assign a new, untried technique to their classes. The teachers' confidence and effectiveness are heightened

Courtesy of International Collection of Child Art, Illinois State University, Normal, IL.

The St. Petersburg, Russia, teacher of this student was well rewarded for the planning and motivation done when this 10-year-old's story illustration showed such a sophisticated use of analogous colors and spatial divisions.

immeasurably if they have explored ahead of time the materials and tools that are available to their students and have created successfully with those tools.

Students should be guided toward a fuller aesthetic awareness of their environment—for example, to see such things as droplets of morning dew glistening in a moisture-laden spider's web. Students are highly impressionable and susceptible to visual influences over which teachers and parents have little control. Television and MTV, movies, video games, musical recordings, makeup, magazine illustrations, recording covers, posters, cars, clothes, and package design clamor for their attention, shape their developing taste, and help to shape their cultural values. While students' discriminative choices often differ from those of adults, the teacher can help guide students to consider aesthetic choices. In teaching art criticism, art history, and aesthetics, top-notch teachers of art use as many audiovisual aids as possible. These include original works of art, reproductions, films, photographs, slides, video recordings, magazine articles, colorfully illustrated art books, and examples of student work. (Chapter 10 discusses still-life arrangements, and Appendix D lists some audiovisual sources.)

Illustrations from Frank Wachowiak's university classes.

College and university students preparing to teach art should explore varied art materials and techniques. The knowledge they gain will build the confidence they need to guide children's art endeavors. **Top row:** *Oil pastel, plaster relief, tempera batik.* **Bottom row:** *Oil pastel, yarn collage, crayon engraving.*

The Teacher's Positive Personality, Rapport, and Respect

A positive, cheerful, and outgoing personality is a major asset for teachers of art. Teachers must learn in sometimes difficult and trying situations to be patient, calm, and resolute. Children want to believe in their teachers. They need the security of a teacher's abiding confidence in the worth of the subject being taught. Students come to rely on their teachers for help with important choices in resolving perplexing problems, and they become skeptical of those who confuse them with vague generalizations or place all the responsibility for decision making in their hands.

Teachers of art should learn to listen to children's descriptions of their experiences, both real and imaginary, with sympathetic interest. They should avoid a desultory, keep-your-distance approach. Instead, their commitment, concern, and excitement for the project must be evident in their actions, words, and faces. Veteran teachers learn to cultivate a ready sense of humor, which can help to alleviate many tension-fraught situations. Teachers who really care about children do not talk down to them; neither do they underestimate their potential to excel.

Saturday Children's Classes. Courtesy of Frank Wachowiak, Athens, GA, and Mary Sayer Hammond, Fairfax, VA.

Qualitative art learning is evident in the seriousness, deliberation, and confidence shown in this sixth-grade girl's oil pastel on red paper. Notice how well the hues of blue, red, and yellow-orange are carried throughout the composition.

A teacher's success in the art class is often based on the empathic rapport that can develop between instructor and students. Getting to know the students is especially important because of the one-to-one relationship demanded in a creative atmosphere. Name tags and a seating chart (with movable tabs to expedite changes) will hasten memorizing the students' names. Once teachers establish a climate of cooperation and mutual understanding, their ability to challenge their charges becomes the cutting edge of their teaching strength.

One can immediately sense the electric involvement, purposefulness of endeavor, and genuine rapport that exists between students and a teacher when visiting a classroom where qualitative art learning is taking place. The special quality that distinguishes high-quality teachers of art from average instructors is their ability to respond intelligently, sympathetically, and purposefully to the children's creative efforts. They can communicate with the students both knowledgeably and honestly regarding their progress in art. The best teachers evaluate their students' work seriously and objectively; their critical attention gives the work importance and significance in the students' eyes. These teachers show sincere respect for what the individuals are trying to do as they strive to give form to their ideas. Most important, they take the students seriously as artists.

Chapter 9

Teaching Strategies

The Art Room During the First Week of School

The first week of school, first art class, first art project, and first motivation are especially important in establishing a qualitative art program. The appearance of the classroom or art room is especially critical, reflecting as it does the teacher's art convictions and his or her awareness of design as a vital environmental influence and conditioner. Indeed, the room's impact on students during the opening day of school is, for all purposes, the teacher's first art lesson. The classroom should be orderly yet inviting and, above all, visually stimulating. Artwork by children, attractively mounted, should brighten the walls. Hanging mobiles of fish, shells, birds, or butterflies created by preceding classes add a surprising element of color in motion. The creative teacher relies on a variety of eye-catching resources, including attractive bulletin-board exhibits, found-object displays, living plants, animals, or birds, art-book displays, hobby collections, antiques, and selected original works of art and craft. These make the room into a perpetually changing world of wonders.

A word about maintaining a productive atmosphere in the art class: Experienced teachers know there is no single solution to the varied behavioral problems with which they must cope. Veteran instructors of art generally find it expedient to begin classes with a serious, organized approach, which can be modified later if the situation warrants. This is better than allowing so much uninhibited freedom that it is impossible to bring the class under control when necessary. If students suspect that the teacher is unconcerned when they waste time with idle chatter or horseplay, they will develop a self-defeating, laissez-faire attitude in art class.

Using Nonverbal Instructions

The best teachers do not rely on verbal instructions alone. The teacher's spoken, personal interaction with each student should be reinforced by the written and display materials. For example, teachers of art can enhance their instructional effectiveness by using the chalkboard or white marker board to emphasize their motivational presentation and outline the specific objectives of a project. Students entering class can read the instructions on the board and proceed to their work without wasting time. The board can be used to identify and clarify the various possibilities and steps of the project. Evaluative criteria in the form of questions posted on the board allow students to make their own evaluations of their in-progress work (see Chapter 13). Using the board minimizes students' dependence on their instructor and discourages the refrain of "Am I finished?"

Planning the Distribution, Collection, and Organization of Materials

Crucial to an art project's ultimate success is housekeeping. The teacher must organize the classroom or art-room facilities so there will be adequate working space, a sufficient supply of materials and tools, varied storage facilities for both projects in progress and those retained for exhibition, a diversity of display spaces, and effective cleanup facilities (see Appendix A).

The distribution of student work in progress, art supplies, and tools should be planned carefully before the class begins so that valuable time is not wasted. To expedite the return of artwork, have students put their names on their work at an early stage. To avoid the bottleneck of students waiting for their turn at the paper cutter, paper should be cut to size before class begins. Materials can best be distributed either through a student-monitor system or by having students come up by tables or rows to a central supply area. Because disciplinary problems can arise when supplies run short and students have time on their hands, the

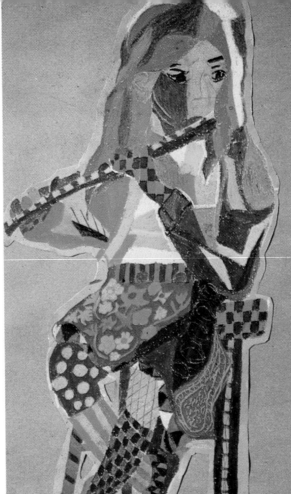

The art room was decorated with these colorful figures to stimulate other classes (see page 83). They were drawn from class models on large 24- × 36-inch colored construction paper and colored with oil pastels. Then, they were cut out and mounted on a sheet of construction paper of a complementary color. Two eighth-grade students cooperated on the coloring of each figure.

teacher must ensure that the supply of materials and tools is adequate for the project at hand.

Beginning the Lesson: Getting Attention and Keeping the Motivation Brief

Getting the class session off to a good start is a major step in creating a productive studio atmosphere. When students come to an art room at the beginning of the period, the teacher should meet them at the door. A positive, cheerful greeting by the teacher can start off the class in the right mood. If some of the incoming students are boisterous, the problem can be resolved before it gets out of hand. Experienced teachers usually wait until they have the attention of all before they provide motivational material or give demonstrations.

In striving to make sure the students understand the project's objectives, sometimes the motivational session is mistakenly too prolonged. The teacher must be alert for those unmistakable signs of disinterest: the shuffle of chairs, the tapping of pencils, the whispered conspiracies, and the far-away looks. Teachers must learn to stop before students reach their response-fatigue point. Students need information, but they also want to get into their work. Perceptive teachers can de-

Courtesy of Baiba Kuntz, Glencoe, IL.

Attractive bulletin board displays help stimulate students' achievement. The color chart over the board is used to suggest why certain colors go together. It shows the beauty of related colors combined with accents of others. Some of the most sophisticated color usage reproduced in this book was done in view of such a display.

tect when students are only half-listening or more intent on some distracting gadget they possess than on the teacher's remarks. When expert teachers spot wandering prodigals, they may bring them back with a pointed question, reprimand, or simply a pause and a meaningful look in the offender's direction. When holding a discussion before studio activity, it is recommended that materials and tools not be distributed until the discussion is over, because students naturally are tempted to explore the materials at hand instead of giving their full attention to the teacher's presentation.

Getting the Design off to a Good Start

The first few minutes of creative work are critical. Here, the parameters of a successful work are laid down and the main compositional features are put into place. Just as a push is needed to set objects into physical motion, an extra push may be needed at the initiation of the working period. The first 3 minutes immediately following the motivation,

when students pick up their art media for the first time, is crucial. While most students will be eager to do art, some may be overcome by uncertainty or fear. Students who are insecure about their own creativity may not be able to self-start. Some may sit perplexed, overcome by waves of confusion, self-doubt, and inadequacy. One way to spur such students into creative action is to give them one specific task to do. For example, the teacher may say to a student who requires direction, "To begin, place a line for the head at the top edge of the paper and a line for the feet at the bottom edge." Guided-drawing techniques at the start can get students working—for example, drawing goggles for a subsequent undersea picture or drawing roller-coaster curves and then turning these into an amusement park.

Another task is to prevent bad starts. Left to themselves, some students, perhaps those who daydreamed while instructions were given, will get off to a poor beginning and make mistakes that threaten their ultimate success. For example, some will draw tiny, tiny figures that cannot be painted or cut out. Instead of getting the over-

"Make the clown's hat touch the top of the page and his feet touch the bottom edge." This statement helped the children to create a composition that effectively filled the page, one with sufficient room to show important details. Making the figures large helps to eliminate the problem of filling up empty background space. Crayon encaustic then was used for the paintings.

all picture put into place, others will use too much time and worry in drawing one small part. They will insist on erasing one small object repeatedly, trying to "get it right." Still others may set an unrealistically high goal. Try to forestall such problems by giving instructions or materials that will prevent their occurrence. To prevent fussing with and erasing timid pencil lines, have the students draw bold outlines with chalk. Instead of criticizing the negative, focus on the positive. On seeing a problem, hold up as a model a student's artwork that avoids the mistake.

Nurturing Creativity During the Working Period

During class, the teacher should not only keep students focused by calling attention to the instructional objectives but also look for creative uniqueness. Look for work that shows imagination, elaboration, and new variations. Use these exemplars to stimulate others to arrive at their own individual solutions. Holding up a student's work, call the class's attention to the particular creative inventiveness in evidence. "Look at how this composition fills up the paper. Four dancing figures are repeated, and the arms and skirts of several touch the sides of the paper, here, here, and here, to give the design a feeling of unity. I wonder in what ways other artists are giving their designs unity?" Two words of caution are in order, however. The teacher should be careful not to embarrass the student who is singled out. Also, while the class is working seriously, the teacher should not constantly interrupt with calls to "look at this." Even so, when attention flags, then the teacher can use students' exemplars, as well as reproductions, to rekindle the fires of motivation. (See Chapter 14 for additional ways to stimulate the creativity of students.)

Strategies for Fostering Perseverance

Perseverance, which probably contributes as much as anything to a successful artwork, is central to the qualitative method. Too many students race through assignments in their desire for instant gratification, and their art reveals a lack of sustained effort. It is a mistake to equate speed of execution with freedom of expression, because a genuinely spontaneous and sparkling quality in a work of art is not achieved easily.

One major problem that an art teacher must face is lagging student interest once the initial excitement of a new project or technique has waned. Almost every class contains students who are satisfied with only a superficial effort, who do not develop a real concern for the subject matter involved, or who find it difficult to persevere. They insist they are finished with their work sooner than the others. They feel that they have exhausted the possibilities of the project while their classmates still are busily involved. Here, the challenge for a teacher is to find the right balance between what the children may be willing to settle for and what they are capable of if given sensitive teacher guidance.

If, at the outset of a project the teacher in collaboration with the students stimulates their interest in setting and reaching objectives in both expression and design, children will be less likely to rush through their work. Perseverance is reinforced when students are internally motivated. For example, when students want to express something that is personally meaningful, they will work for a long time. This is why developing instructional objectives that encourage the expression of feelings is so important. For upper elementary and middle school students, posting the process and evaluative criteria on the board allows the teacher to function effectively as both a classroom manager and a facilitator for individual students. When questions arise, the teacher can

Perseverance contributes much to the quality of an artwork. Students too often stop short, when extra effort could make the difference. Here, in contemporary artist William Sapp's 1992 piece Dogpack, *approximately 8 × 10 feet, are not just a few clay figures but a thousand.*

Courtesy of the USSEA art collection of Dr. Anne Gregory, Los Angeles School District.

This student has persevered in richly coloring every inch of the surface of this picture with markers. Student Siobhan McDermott, Teacher Susan Whipple, Grace Christian School, Medford, Oregon.

clarify and resolve them for the entire class by referring to the posted criteria rather than by repeating those criteria to each student in a time-consuming procedure.

Encourage the students to go further, to "weave in" the figures in their pictures, to tuck some objects behind others, to create rhythm. Encourage them to make their pictures swing, to have rhythm through repeating forms. One way to encourage a child to go further is to combine praise with suggestion. For example, a teacher may say, "Now Mandy is starting to put in the children; I wonder how many are in the line at noon?" Mandy likely will respond to the teacher's expressed faith by putting in many figures.

A suggestion offered to one student often will trigger fresh ideas for others who may have reached a creative impasse. Using students' work

in progress, call attention to compositional requirements as well as variations in expression. To the child who says "I spoiled mine," reply that "the only way a picture is spoiled is not to do it in your own, personal way." Another method to stimulate extra effort is to have students anticipate a special show of their work. For example, ask the kindergarten teacher if she would let your class come in for a few minutes to show their artworks.

At the upper elementary and middle school levels, the practice of writing brief, constructive remarks on the back of a student's work or on slips of paper attached to that work will promote perseverance. Although time-consuming, this strategy for evaluation can help the conscientious teacher to give individualized instruction. It gives the teacher a chance to evaluate studio performance during a time that is relatively free of distractions and other responsibilities. It strengthens the possibility that every student in class will receive specific, individual help at some point during the project, and provides students with a definite working direction for the ensuing studio period.

Courtesy of Joyce Vroon, Trinity School, Atlanta, GA.

Relating art projects to the students' personal interests and values increases their perseverance and sense of personal investment in the artwork. Fifth-grade student Sarah Nix.

Cleanup and Evaluation

Cleanup procedures should be planned in advance to ensure that enough time has been allotted and the process will occur in an orderly fashion. Because cleanup comes at the end of the lesson, when students are ready to do something else, and often requires several students to be out of their seats at once, planning is necessary to avoid problems. For example, confusion and possible disruptive behavior at the sink can be prevented by sending only students from one row or table at a time to that facility.

If time remains after cleanup, the teacher should use it to good purpose and not let the period end with idle chatter. The after-cleanup period can be used for a summing-up or an evaluation session. This is a time to come full circle and demonstrate how the instructional objectives have taken form in the students' work and produced positive results.

Saturday Children's Classes, courtesy of Frank Wachowiak, Athens, GA.

The teacher encouraged these students to go further and add more figures. Then, students were encouraged to break up the empty background space in inventive, beautiful ways. Illustrations on this page are by upper-elementary-grade children. They took turns modeling with sports equipment and musical instruments in the center of the room.

Courtesy of Barbara Thomas, Whit Davis School, Athens, GA.

Well planned out procedures for distributing and collecting supplies will facilitate both the production of artwork and cleanup, as shown by the basket and tray for materials.

Courtesy of David Harvell, Fourth St. School, Athens, GA.

In this elementary classroom are posted five rules: (1) Listen. (2) Respect others. (3) Be polite and helpful. (4) Follow directions. (5) Take care of the room and materials. The first offense results in a warning; the second and third offenses result in varying lengths of time out.

Classroom Management

A common complaint of students is that teachers have eyes in the backs of their heads. It is vitally important, however, that the teacher be aware of what is going on in the room and be at strategic stations at critical times. During materials distribution, the teacher should be near the supply area. When lecturing, the teacher should avoid facing the chalkboard or standing in front of the glaring light of a window. Effective instructors move among the students during a studio activity rather than staying at their own desk. Experienced teachers do not let themselves get beleaguered by demands from a bevy of questioning students when they should be monitoring the class as a whole, especially during the opening minutes of class or at cleanup time. Let the students know that they will be advised one student at a time, and remind them to take turns when conferences are necessary.

The quality of art expression diminishes as the amount of talking and socializing increases. Unless they are given permission by the

Courtesy of Melody Milbrandt, Valdosta, GA.

The intense working shown here has been facilitated by the containers, such as cigar boxes, full of crayons which afford each student a wide choice in colors as they enrich their watercolor paintings.

teacher to move about, children ordinarily should remain in their assigned seats during class. In large classes, students should take turns obtaining and returning materials and tools, either by tables or by rows. Excessive talking, laughing, whistling, running, throwing things, gum chewing, propping of feet on desks, table hopping, and crowding at sinks should not be tolerated. Students eager to test their power will act out in mock fighting, challenges to authority, and subversive tactics. Problems of student apathy, disinterest, and errant behavior are heightened by insufficient lesson planning, meager motivational material, too little visual stimulation, insufficient knowledge of the technique, weak rapport between teacher and student, and a lack of conviction by both regarding the worth of the art experience.

Explore all possible avenues of motivation and persuasion, of reasoning and strategic reconciliation, before resorting to chastisement of any sort, whether it involves moving students to other seats or sending them to the principal. As a rule, do not act hastily when disciplining students. Never mete out punishment during the heat of a crisis. Admonish the errant students, and tell them that you will discuss the infraction with them after class. Once you have stipulated a punishment, put it into effect. Students learn to take advantage of an instructor who makes idle threats and fails to carry them out.

Teachers realize that students have a need to communicate. Talking in class can be a common, natural occurrence, especially during studio activities: however, when the talking becomes so loud and disruptive that it prevents concentration on the project, teachers must take action. If they shout "Quiet!" or "Settle down!" or rap a desk with a ruler, ring a bell, or clap their hands, they may be successful in calming the class for a few minutes. Experienced teachers use positive, constructive approaches such as redirection and positive reinforcement. Calling the class to attention, they emphasize some aspect of the project that needs amplification. They also might hold up a student's work in process and point out specifically creative solutions that were achieved. Prepare and photocopy in advance some remarks and rewards to clip to students' artworks ahead of class time. By using positive strategy, teachers maintain motivation and order while they avoid being seen as martinets in the eyes of their students.

During art sessions in which the teacher builds respect for serious endeavor and excessive, boisterous socializing is minimized, students' performances are of a consistently higher caliber than those of students in highly permissive situations. A class is less likely to be bored or cause disturbance when it has been guided to see the many possibilities of the project and been richly motivated. Motivation is the subject of the next chapter.

Chapter 10

Art Motivation

Most children need some form of stimulating motivation, either visual or verbal, to achieve high-quality results in their studio-art endeavors. Students must have something to say if they are to give it visual form. The introductory phase of an art lesson should kindle the spark that ignites curiosity and piques interest. It is unfair to expect students to be challenged or excited by a teacher saying "Draw what you want today" or "Paint the way you feel." The many successful ways to begin an art project include:

- Showing visual materials on the theme selected
- Viewing examples of previous work
- Guiding a class discussion in recalling a past experience
- Conducting a field trip to enrich the students' knowledge of the subject selected
- Playing recordings or tapes to create the mood of the particular visual theme
- Demonstrating the technical process with student participation
- Calling attention to a bulletin board or chalkboard presentation prepared for the project
- Having a guest speak, perform, or model for the students
- Using poems, stories, songs, and music as motivational enrichment

Inspiration for children's art expression comes from many sources. It may spring from their experiences at school and at home, from their playground activities, or from their visits to special places. It may come from nature and science or from topics in social studies; these are the subjects of the following two chapters. No matter how rich the experience, however, the responsibility for reactivating motivational experiences and giving them the immediacy to stimulate students into art expression is primarily the teacher's. With motivational procedures planned in advance, students can experience art class as a time of purposeful significance and excitement, a unique and rewarding period of the school day.

Personal Experience

The most vital and successful art-project motivations usually result from vivid and meaningful personal experiences. The teacher's role is to help the students graphically clarify the significant aspects of the experience. There are two main types of personal experiences that can be used for art-lesson motivations: recalled experience, and direct perception.

Recalled Experience

In recalled experiences, children do not actually see the objects before their eyes; rather, they recall them. Teachers must activate the children's store of knowledge and help them to tap into their recall powers. Perhaps students have visited some special place, such as an aquarium or a farm, or have seen a circus, carnival, parade, dog or cat show, or sporting event. Perhaps they have read an exciting story. Perhaps it is an experience they regularly have, such as playing a sport or a video game.

Because some children are not able to recall enough specific attributes of an event or an object, they may complain that they do not know how to draw it. Then, the teacher must help them to recall their experiences by asking questions such as *Who? What? How? Where? When?* and *Why?*

The "what" is the overall experience that the child is being asked to recall—for example, a scary dream. To revive the "what" and "how" in students' minds, ask the children to physically act out the experience, using their bodies to recreate what was frightening in the dream, such as spiders or ghosts.

Campus School, University of Wisconsin, Oshkosh. Courtesy of David Hodge, Oshkosh, WI.

The everyday interests of young adolescents give them motivation to create art. These include sports, bicycling, rock celebrities, TV and movie idols, electronic games, and dancing. In the mixed-media collage by a middle school youngster, notice how the rider fills the space and the wheel motif is repeated in the background to create unity. Areas of analogous color comprise the background, and a feeling of motion is created by the bent back of the cyclist and the flowing scarf.

The purpose of *Where?* and *When?* is to make passive knowledge active. To continue the dream example, ask the child to describe the room and the setting, its location in the house, who uses the adjoining rooms, the time of day or night, what else can be seen in the room, and the feeling the experience gave. The purpose of asking *Who?* is to give the child an opportunity to express self-identity and relationships with others. For example, a child may say, "I am in bed with my teddy bear in my arms, and Momma has tucked me in."

The "why" question is for the teacher. Teachers should ask themselves why this particular theme is considered to be important enough to warrant being done. In the scary-dream example, the hope is that by representing and sharing the frightening event with the group, the individual will gain a feeling of personal control over its scariness. A theme of playing on the playground may be chosen to promote an individual's feelings of group belongingness, or a lesson topic might be chosen to stimulate a certain type of artistic representation. For example, depicting "my street" and "ring-around-the-rosy" would stimulate the use of foldover drawings, and depicting "what's inside my body" (or "inside my house") would stimulate the representation of transparency or X-ray images.

The power and charm of designs that young children create based on their personal experiences is nowhere better illustrated than in Weissa Wasse's project, Weaving by Hands (see page 95). Young children in a small Egyptian town (Hourranie, near Cairo) created beautiful designs and transformed them into utilitarian and aesthetically satisfying weavings of significant economic value.

Direct Perception

Recalled experience is one kind of motivation, another is direct perception. Long before we are cognitive beings, we are aesthetic beings, responding to the world through touch, taste, smell, sound, and sight. One of the teacher's greatest challenges is to turn students into *noticers*—avid observers of color, structure, and design in their environment. The teacher can enrich students' lives forever by helping them to become aware of the pattern, beauty, and variety in nature. Children who note the unique cornice on a door, the intricate latch on a cabinet, the subtle patina on an aged sculpture, the moving reflections in water, the varied cracks in dry mud banks, the shadow of a tree on the snow, and the veins in a leaf or dragonfly's wing can bring deeper insights to their art expression. Help students to delight in nature's colors, textures, and patterns by saying, "What else does it remind you of?" Nothing

Courtesy of the USSEA art collection of Dr. Anne Gregory, Los Angeles School District.

"My Bedroom" is an excellent topic for recalling significant things in a student's life. Here, student Catie Trezise very thoughtfully shows herself, her three cats, her wall decorations and furniture. Rather than just solid colors, teacher Barbara Bluhm of Maine taught the students to make graduated, blended colors with oil pastel.

ing replaces the actually perceived object, the direct contact, or the immediate observation for eliciting a detailed, richly expressive response. Teachers should avoid "draw-anything-you-want" assignments and instead emphasize drawing experiences based on things that can be perceived directly. Lead your students to look intently at everyday things, to see the unusual in the usual, and they will become inquisitive explorers for the rest of their lives.

Combining Recalled Experience and Direct Perception

A general tendency is to use recalled experiences more often in the primary grades and direct perception from still lifes, nature, and models more often in the later grades; however, both methods effectively supplement each other. Students can be encouraged to add things from their memories or their imaginations to the background of a picture derived from direct perception. Mature artists often blend the two methods. Artists doing a scene from memory often turn to the use of real ob-

A Philippine child recalls a favorite game, "jumping over the stick." She used her schema for profile and frontal views to depict the figures in this joyful watercolor of an important *activity. The figures up front are drawn larger and those in the background smaller. In the small figures in the lower corners, realistic requirements yield to decorative requirements.*

jects or photos to acquire supplemental information. The French painter Marc Chagall did still-life paintings from bouquets of flowers and then, from his memory, added simply drawn human figures to the background.

Still Lifes as Artistic Arrangements

The elementary classroom or the art room can be the child's first, and often most enduring, art lesson. Stimulating, eye-catching, still-

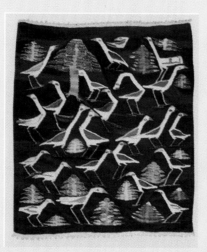

Children near Cairo, Egypt, create weavings directly from memory. They use no prior drawings and often weave with the image sideways. Weissa Wassef's world-famous experiment in creativity has brought wealth to the villagers. **Left:** *An 8- × 10-inch weaving of village animals, trees, and bird by Amal, age 11.* **Middle:** *At age 16, Amal created this sophisticated 12- × 14-inch design of ibis and trees.* **Right:** *Rowhia Ali, who had been considered the most talented of the child weavers, is now 55 years of age. She recently created the 42- × 66-inch* Bedouins Entering the Village at Night.

life arrangements should be on view for sketching purposes. Students should be encouraged to contribute to the store of found objects and nature's treasures in the classroom. The teacher's organizational ability, however, usually is needed to create a source of beauty and stimulation; what may be a source of exciting motivation to one person may be just a source of clutter to another. Whereas the next two chapters point out ways that still lifes can be integrated with other school subjects, still lifes can be arranged solely as sources for artistic, eye-catching motivation to promote students' perceptual skills.

Different kinds of fabric, both plain and patterned, and large, colorful quilts and bedspreads can be draped and pinned against a cork bulletin board. Pin the material to create bunches of fabric balanced by draped swags. Pin up an array of colorful hats against the drapery. Invite students who are willing to remove their shoes to stack them up for a still-life arrangement. Lunchboxes, bookbags, raincoats, and umbrellas usually are readily available. For late Spring, a still life pertaining to pleasant Summer activities (beachballs, floats, thermos, and picnic sup-

plies) will pique interest. Boots, shoes, shoulder pads, hats, caps, helmets, and gloves provide interesting organic shapes for drawing. A Western theme of boots, saddle, and harness brings to mind exciting associations. Objects associated with fun and pleasure, such as plastic toys and teddy bears, are good choices to hold interest. Still lifes can be made of colorful desserts, a la Wayne Thibaud. Sports equipment pertaining to skiing or skating can be combined with students taking turns modeling within the still life while draped in colorful cloths or costumes. When nothing else is available for a still-life arrangement, stack several chairs or stools one atop another, with some sticking out at different angles, and weave some drapery or beach towels in and out of the openings. In middle school, following a contour drawing of the setup, you might suggest that the students paint the negative shapes instead of the positive ones.

Have students participate in building a color environment as a motivation for painting in tempera and watercolor. Make it a class "happening," and incorporate colored tissue paper, crepe paper, fabrics, beach towels, ribbons, colored streamers, fans, banners, balloons,

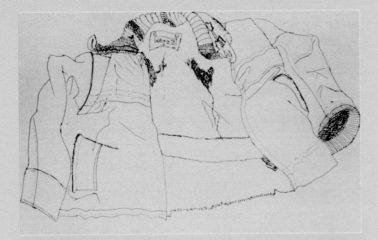

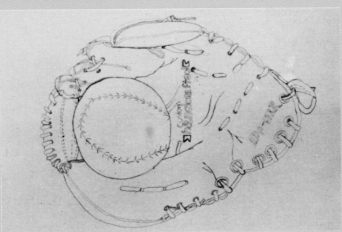

posters, party hats, beach balls, and Day-Glo materials. If the arrangement is near a window, incorporate colored cellophane for a stained-glass effect. Teachers will find many occasions during the year to use the following resources in still-life arrangements to enrich their art programs:

Fluorescent paint and papers
Fish netting and glass buoys
Window-display mannequins
Wallpaper sample books
Theater costumes and make-up
Tissue paper in assorted colors
Full-length mirror, face mirrors
Sports equipment
Contemporary posters
Duck decoys
Model cars and airplanes
Plastic-foam wig holders
Old fashioned hats, shoes, and purses
Texture table, felt board
Spotlights for illuminating still lifes
Bicycles, motorcycles, and helmets
Stained glass
Acetate or acrylic plastic in varied colors

Bulletin Boards and Art History

Plan exhibits and bulletin-board displays that relate to the art objectives. Have the students participate in designing and mounting displays and exhibits to make the classroom colorfully stimulating. Bulletin boards and displays should be changed often, allowing students to appreciate completed projects and whet their interest in further art endeavors.

Bulletin boards, videotapes, and reproductions of paintings, sculpture, prints, and crafts illuminate and intensify the objectives of the les-

---

The most common everyday object is a likely subject for drawing. Objects with special significance, like the warm fur-lined jacket, the sturdy hiking boot, and the professional baseball mitt and ball, stimulate even greater interest. Items which specifically relate to or fit the human body possess unique, lifelike qualities and natural contours that lend themselves most beautifully to dynamic, effective drawing.

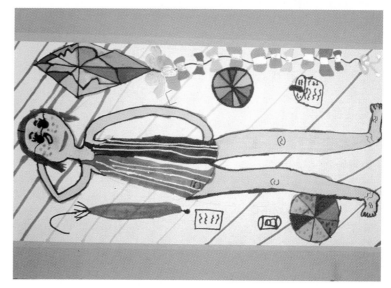

What student in May would not be stimulated by anticipation of pleasant summer days, foreshadowed and recalled by this still life of beach balls, sand buckets and shov- *els, Frisbees, kites, scuba diving goggles, figures, and scenes? Second-grade student Gregory Paulus.*

son. Color slides of art, crafts, and architecture; of design elements in nature and in constructed objects; of creative work by children worldwide; of examples illustrating the technical stages in a project; of people in active work, in sports, and in costume; and of animals, birds, fish, in-

sects, and flowers can be strong motivations. Books (stories, plays, poems, and biographies) and periodicals that can lead to a project's richer interpretation. (See Part III for an in-depth discussion on incorporating art history, art criticism, and aesthetics.)

Fourth-grade student Jenny Guilllaume. Courtesy of Joyce Vroon, Trinity School, Atlanta, GA.

Cowboy boots, hats, jackets, and riding equipment bring to mind the mystique of the Wild West.

The Art Medium

The materials, tools, and techniques of the various art projects can themselves be the special catalyst that fires students' efforts. The teacher's demonstration of a technique can challenge the students. In the primary grades, introduction of new, vibrant colors in oil pastel, tempera paint, watercolor felt-nib markers, crayon, and construction paper elicits enthusiastic response. Colorful tissue paper delights upper elementary children working in collage when they discover new colors through overlapping. In the upper grades, the teacher can stimulate students' interest by introducing them to melted crayon for encaustic painting, discarded tiles for mosaics, waxes and dyes for batiks, plaster for carving sculpture and bas reliefs, glazes for ceramics, and wire, plastic, wood, and boxes for construction projects (see Part 4).

Critics of art-education practices have recently called attention to the proliferation of media and techniques in school art programs, citing their deleterious effects. Although some of this criticism is justified, it usually is not the new materials and techniques per se that are to blame. Instead, the fault lies in how the materials are used: as the sole motivation and purpose of the lesson. The solution is to teach for qualitative

art excellence and incorporate a range of valid lesson objectives (see Chapter 14). Any teacher can testify that a poorly motivated student, equipped with the newest and most expensive art materials, may produce a careless, nonartistic monstrosity, whereas another individual, using only discarded remnants from a scrap pile, may create an object of singular beauty.

Amount and Timing of Motivation

Because most children can absorb and retain only a few ideas at a time, avoid overwhelming them with an avalanche of suggestions. Motivations should be provided in small doses. Rather than swamp the students at one session with a plethora of ideas, introduce, if possible, a new and exciting attention-getter each time the art class meets or when interest flags. Rather than read an entire story for motivation, read a brief passage. Timing is of utmost importance in suc-

Teacher Susan Whipple, Grace Christian School, Medford, Oregon. USSEA art collection of Dr. Anne Gregory, Los Angeles School District.

Watercolor felt tip markers are richly and beautifully used by student Sarah Dody in this scene of a home by the snowcapped mountains.

Courtesy of Joyce Vroon, Trinity School, Atlanta, GA.

New materials such as plaster-of-Paris strips over a wire armature will motivate upper-grade students, eager to depict their interests. Here is fifth-grade student Natalie Bennett's piece, California Beach or Bust, Surf or Die.

cessful motivations. The teacher must sense when students have reached a fatigue point and need richer incentives to ensure progress in their work. Because students are most receptive at the beginning of a period, this usually is the best time to introduce new motivations, materials, and techniques; teachers should not interrupt a busily engaged class to point out something that could have been handled at the outset. Time alloted for motivational sessions should be budgeted so that children will not feel cheated out of their studio or activity period. Plan the entire time sequence of motivation, discussion, demonstration, studio time, and evaluation both imaginatively and economically.

Exhibitions

Having one's work put on exhibition is exciting! As teachers, we can introduce students to this important aspect of the art world: exhibiting. Exhibition criteria should be based on both aesthetic grounds and students' educational growth and motivation. One principle is that the further away from the classroom, the more selective the exhibit needs to be. In the self-contained classroom, every student's work might be exhibited. Each student might assume ownership of a designated place, identified by the child's large name label. Even high places and very low places can be assigned. In the school hallway, only the most significant works of a child need be exhibited.

At some time during the term, every child should have his or her artwork on exhibit. Some teachers save each student's work in a folder, from which they select pieces for exhibition. Then, they send all of the works home at special times of the year, such as Mother's Day or the winter holiday.

To display group projects, one good way is to bring a fairly large, dead tree branch into the classroom. Mount it against a light-colored area of wall or a bulletin board. It not only provides unmatched subject

Fourth-grade. Courtesy of Joyce Vroon, Trinity School, Atlanta, GA.

The many colors of colored pencils were put to good use in a still life drawing of jelly beans and their glass containers.

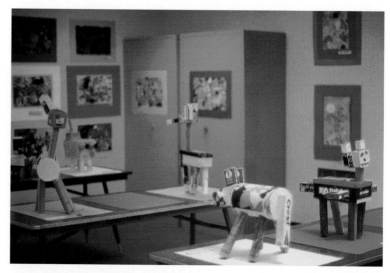

Top left: courtesy of David Hodge, Oshkosh, WI. *Top right:* courtesy of Frank Wachowiak, Athens, GA. *Bottom:* courtesy of Baiba Kuntz, Glencoe, IL.

Sharing students' artwork with the community and the larger public provides valuable social interaction. Teachers of art can help children to develop such interests, which can provide life-long leisure satisfaction. **Top left and right:** *Middle school art exhibit at annual Art Education Conference, University of Iowa, Iowa City.*

Left: *Notice the colored mats and aligned arrangements in this art display.* **Bottom:** *Observe the high degree of artistic organization in this elementary school art bulletin board. It contains sunflowers by grades 3 and 4 and sunflower paintings by grades 5 and 6.*

This display of "Stars" paintings by third-graders was made interactive by it being necessary to lift the papers to uncover the celebrity's name.

Alternating columns and rows of underwater pictures, origami, and stained glass pictures make a stunning, varied, and colorful hallway display.

inspiration for contour- and line-drawing projects, it is ideal for displaying paper sculpture or papier-mache birds, butterflies, painted eggs, fish.

Multiarts exhibits can combine an art display with students' musical or dramatic performances; students demonstrate special art skills in the hall or foyer. School arts festivals can be made more special by having students wear costumes, bring special theme-related food to be served at the opening, or by having a joint exhibition of parent and child art.

To avoid displays that look disorganized, align the pieces horizontally or vertically. Traditionally, artworks are mounted with a border that is 3- to 4-inches wide on three sides and about a $\frac{1}{2}$-inch larger on the bottom. Check with school administrators for school policies on how work is to be hung on the walls. Can tape be used, which might pull off the paint during removal, or are tacks or staples preferred, which will leave tiny holes? Another consideration is the audience. Should the work be hung at the eye level of the teachers and adult visitors or of the students?

Although a permanently installed hanging strip limits the level at which the work is hung, any type of fastener can be used in it. Another solution is permanent display panels of composition board. Tacks and staples

Displays can be made both more exciting and communicative by adding related three-dimensional objects to the display's background. Here, egg containers and straw enrich this display of third-grade students' rooster paintings.

can be freely used in these, although excess use of any flammable boards may violate fire codes. A few 4- × 8-foot, foam-core display boards can be attached together along the edge with duct tape to make a lightweight, temporary folding display area that is suitable for school open houses.

Move out into the community for even greater motivational power. Tell the students that some of their work from a project will be exhibited at a store, branch bank, or a parent's restaurant. Children's art is charming when displayed in the local post office at holiday time. Attention-catching exhibitions can be hung in unusual places. Works can be displayed in the windows of an unused store, or murals can be painted on fences or walls.

Although commercial exhibitors usually pay a fee, school art often can be exhibited for free at community events such as fall festivals, county fairs, and arts and crafts exhibits. Middle school students can take part in the local museum's exhibitions by serving as junior docents for children's tours. A hospital may underwrite the production costs for a full-color calendar of children's artwork advertising the hospital's departments. A newspaper can have a design-an-ad contest at Halloween. Sponsoring businesses also might pay to have students' artwork framed.

The following two chapters deal with science/art integration and social studies/art integration. Both science and social studies can be effective ways to motivate learning in art, and the reverse is just as true, that art can motivate learning in science and social studies. Integration can provide a synergistic effect, wherein the whole is greater than the sum of its parts.

Chapter 11

Science and Art Integrated in Direct Perception of Still Lifes

By helping students to become aware of the principles that underlie nature, we teach both art and science. Both science and art are ways of knowing, both provide students with a grasp of new similarities and contrasts, and both go beyond traditional categories to yield new visions about our world. Science and art also share many of the same goals: development of curiosity; a knowledge base; skills for investigating, fantasizing, and combining objects and ideas in new ways; and visualizing mental images. Both are reinforced through still-life drawing, emphasizing description and interpretation. John Dewey wrote that "Art—the mode of activity that is charged with meanings capable of immediately enjoyed possession—is the complete culmination of nature and 'science' is properly a handmaiden that conducts natural events to this happy issue" (1934). Dewey not only reverses the traditional hierarchy that places science over art, he also denies any rigid di-

Courtesy of Barbara Thomas, Whit Davis School, Athens, GA.

On a large sheet of paper and over a very light pencil drawing of every petal of a flower, fifth-grade students Anneke Heile and Renée Davis used watercolor to capture the overlaapping forms, in the style of Georgia O'Keeffe.

103

Art and science are two complementary approaches to understanding nature. Here, a Japanese upper-elementary-grade child envisions the famous French entomologist Jean-Henri Fabre as a boy pursuing his hobby.

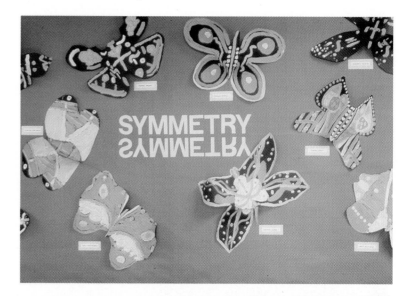

Top, courtesy of Joyce Vroon and Marlee Puskar, Trinity School, Atlanta, GA. Bottom, courtesy of Barbara Thomas, Whit Davis School, Athens, GA.

chotomy between them. Include drawing in as many aspects of the science lesson as possible—drawing specimens, mapping, charting, and illustrating experiments. Help children to sense what these fields have in common by calling attention to both the design structure and the scientific explanations of nature's phenomena.

Symmetry is an important principle of growth in nature, and it can be studied by using a small hand mirror to draw one side of a butterfly or petalled flower. Then, folding over the half-drawing and tracing or monoprinting brings out the bilateral symmetry. Some other patterns often found in nature are radial patterns (as in flower heads), spiral patterns (as in sea shells and the arrangement of a series of leaves along a stalk), fractal patterns (as in branching trees and meandering rivers), and Fibonacci series (as in the seed arrangements in sunflower heads). Relate nature's structures to those found in architecture. Discuss the mathematical background of such forms as tetrahedra and icosahedra. Groups of students can describe the geometric shapes in art reproductions, such as of domed architecture and pentagon shapes in Islamic architecture.

Help students to see analogies between things. Ask, "What does it remind you of?" Our perceived experience of what we see is extended by meanings drawn from what is remembered. Our immediate visual experience is supplemented by what our imagination brings to mind. Urge

Few natural objects surpass butterflies as an instrument for the study of bilateral symmetry. **Top:** *second-grade students' art is shown in an attractive display on symmetry using butterflies painted on black paper, with the lettering mirrored.* **Bottom:** *second-grade student Nikki Foster used a paper folded diagonally and the shapes transferred from one side to the other, then diligent application of oil pastel.*

A brown and white hamster brought to class in a cage afforded second-grade student George Sheerer a live nature drawing experience.

In drawing from nature, try a change of art medium; this perky bluebird was rendered in stitchery.

careful observation in creating the artwork. Tactfully discourage students' dependence on visual stereotypes. Let the their vivid imaginations help them to see, feel, and represent their own reality, sparked by the phenomena before their eyes.

To show art/science integration in action, this chapter covers many of the concepts taught in the elementary school science curriculum, and suggestions for art/science integration are given. For recommendations on how to teach specific art media, see the chapters in the

Courtesy of Joyce Vroon, Trinity School, Atlanta, GA.

A chalk-like artists' material, conté crayon, was used by third-grade student Quincy Smith for his animal drawing done on grey paper, a favorite drawing technique of Rennaissance artists. Second-grade student Bingham Jamison drew in pastel this delightful trio of sand birds.

last half of the book, especially the sections in Chapter 20 on still lifes and animals.

Animal Life

Enthusiastic artistic responses can be evoked by bringing to class live animals as well as terrariums and aquariums with coral and seashells. Bleached animal skulls and skeletal bones that students find make excellent studies for line drawings as well as vehicles to promote an understanding of anatomy. When studying vertebrates and invertebrates, classify and draw a wide variety of animals both with and without backbones, such as crickets, butterflies, snails, and earthworms. Draw birds' nests, birds in cages, and mounted birds, fish, and animals. Bring from the students' homes, or keep as pets in the room, turtles, rabbits, and guinea pigs, and draw these in a variety of art media. Include drawings of the animals and birds along with nature studies of bird's nests, feathers, and making casts of animal tracks. Ecology, camouflage, and types of claws and beaks can be studied by drawing animals and plants in their native environments In connection with a study of weaving, try to weave a bird's nest or other container. Use puppets to engage in artistic and fantasy extensions of science and to illustrate concepts such as predators, commensalism, and mutualism among animals. Sketch the life stages of the brine shrimp, frog, or salamander, and include sketches of the plants and animals that are found around a pond. Before or after a lesson of drawing animals or living things, an art/science card game can be played wherein small groups of students, using art reproductions, categorize the art reproductions (depicting, for example, spiders, fish, mammals, microorganisms) into the taxonomic categories of the animal and vegetable kingdoms—as well as into the various art styles.

Astronomy; Our Solar System

Using a pattern of the star points in the Big Dipper and North Star or other constellations (on black paper and using chalk), students will draw their own superheroes or objects in the sky as might be imagined from the star-point locations. Have students draw views of the Earth and Moon in space, imagining they are inside or outside space-travel vehicles and confronting interplanetary life.

Climate

Have students draw their family as if they were people from different climates, in native dress and in their homes. In artworks, show the climate through such features as the northern lights and wavy convection currents above a fire; ask "Where was it? What else can be seen? How does it feel?" Study the art of people from hot and cold climates—for example, African and Eskimo art.

Foods and Nutrition

Have students draw themselves gardening or harvesting favorite foods and berries. Make charts of the different kinds of food that we eat in a week. On a large cardboard pyramid assembled from a cast-off refrigerator carton, students can add their illustrations of favorite foods in each group of the food pyramid. Draw from a still life of fruits, vegetables, nuts, and grains.

Courtesy of Baiba Kuntz, Glencoe, IL.

In this multisession art lesson, fifth-grade students drew and watercolored themselves in their winter coats. **Left:** *Sarah Wampler added her cat and dog, a squirrel in a nest in a white snow-covered tree, and white marshmallows floating in hot chocolate.* **Right:** *Betsy Ure captured the sheen of her jacket, her multitasseled cap, and her love of basketball.*

Courtesy of Joyce Vroon, Trinity School, Atlanta, GA.

Second-grade student Juliana Ramus studied and drew cross sections of fruits and vegetables along with the patterned table cloth, and the background was given a unifying resist coat of light green. After studying Dutch still lifes of fruits and vegetables, students developed their ability with chiaroscuro (light and shade).

Geology

Take a sketching trip, perhaps to a nearby eroded gully, to draw unusual earth and rock formations. Point out the color and surface textures of sedimentary and igneous rocks as well as the effects of water and wind erosion or past glacial activity. From photos, draw cave interiors with

Courtesy of the International Collection of Child Art, Illinois State University, Normal, IL.

Through using a straw to blow paint, student David Williams vividly depicts his geological knowledge of earth's molten interior magma layer.

Courtesy of Jackie Ellett, Fort Daniel Elementary School, GA.

Pictographic systems of representing figures used by prehistoric people in their cave art are studied by third-grade students in their recreated, crumpled paper cave.

stalactites and stalagmites, and imagine an exciting "Tom Sawyer-like" story of students in a cave, finding prehistoric cave art such as that found under cliffs and on rocks throughout the world. From small still-life arrangements, draw the textures, patterns, and colors of rocks and minerals. Discuss the chemical elements that make up pigments—iron red, chrome green and yellow, cobalt blue, lead white, cadmium orange. In connection with a study of fossils, make plaster bas-relief casts of everyday objects.

Human Body, Anatomy, and Growth

After seeing anatomical drawings by DaVinci and Vesalius and making a figure drawing, then have students, using tracing paper enabling them to see through to the original drawing below, first imagine, draw, and label the muscles' locations. Then, on another sheet of tracing paper, have them locate and draw the (real and imaginary) organs inside one's body. Insights into human growth can be gained by drawing oneself from baby pictures or from imagination, doing the good and bad things

that the students did that age. Also have students draw an imaginary view of themselves when they are old and doing some favorite activity.

Insects

Create an imaginary, three-dimensional insect using a variety of materials, then write a description of the creature, describing the physical features that it uses to find food and to defend itself. Draw ant farms and insect and butterfly collections. Using tempera resist or on a dark paper, draw pictures of oneself catching fireflies at dusk, of an expedition collecting nature specimens or of yourself in a butterfly garden.

Light and Perception

Just as telescopes and magnifying lens opened many of nature's secrets for analysis, such perception-enhancing devices likewise can foster science/art integration. Assorted equipment to help expand the stu-

Courtesy of Jackie Ellett, Fort Daniel Elementary School, GA.

Earth pigments of iron oxide, charcoal, and kaolin clay, with white glue added, are used in this fifth-grader's study of cave art animal representations.

Saturday Children's Classes. Courtesy of Frank Wachowiak, Athens, GA, and Mary Sayer Hammond, Fairfax, VA.

The millions of varieties of insects have unlimited possibilities, as illustrated in this crayon engraving by an intermediate-elementary-grade youngster. It was enhanced in the final stage by an application of oil pastels on the background areas. Bordering lines of black should be preserved to unify the composition.

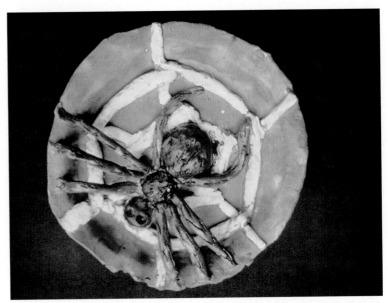

Courtesy of Julie Daniell Phlegar, East St. Tammany Parish School District, Slidell, LA.

A second-grade student constructed of white clay and painted a plaque showing a spider on its web.

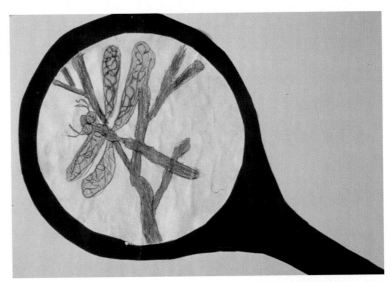

Courtesy of Joyce Vroon, Trinity School, Atlanta, GA.

Magnifying lens are useful for drawing insects. Here, the lens itself also is shown. Second-grade.

dents' awareness and visual horizons include microscopes, prisms, kaleidoscopes, touch-me kinetics, magnifiers, liquid-light lamps, telescopes, microscopic projectors, computers, mirrors, and black lights. A study of reflections and shadows can be tied in with a study of Monet's water-lily pond paintings and Impressionism as well as Seurat's Pointillism.

To promote interest in the properties of light, arrange bottles of different colored glass on window sills or against a light source, and fill some with dried flowers or branches, some clear ones with colored water, and others with strips of aluminum foil. Painting plaid stripes (with the paint still wet) is useful for studying color mixing. Study spectrums in nature by painting rainbows. The concept of mirror images can be tied in with a unit on printmaking, in which the images are reversed. A clasmate can draw one's shadow while outside on the asphalt playground or concrete on a sunny day, and this distorted image can be decorated. Perceptual distortion and the convex lens can be studied using narrow olive jars, clear glass marbles, or magnifying glasses. Students can draw the distortion seen in chrome hubcaps, shiny bowls, and other polished, convex surfaces. Study distant perception by making drawings

of objects that recede into the distance. Pinhole cameras and shadow-puppet plays also are useful for studying light.

Magnetism

To illustrate magnetism in connection with a study of photograms and light, make photograms of iron filings. Along with an explanation of the photochemical phenomena of photograms, the edges of objects such as fern leaves and lacy objects also can be discussed.

Molecules

Using Styrofoam and toothpicks, make models of the elements. Also make models of human figures, and relate this to the study of modern sculptures.

Plants and Botany

Still lifes of plant specimens can be used to call attention to the ecological devastation faced by plants and animals—for example, the fact that 250,000 of today's plant species will vanish by the year 2000. Especially in rooms with few windows, large potted plants of assorted foliage brighten up a classroom. Show vascular plants' reproductive parts, a flower's pistil, stamen, and anther. Have students draw their favorite tree (maybe their backyard treehouse), and then draw and label its visible and underground parts. Make a close-up sketch of its leaf. Using a fast-growing plant like a sweet potato, draw its stages of growth each week. The unusual shapes of sweet-potato vines and other tuberous roots are a challenge. Properties of leaves, leaf edges, and shapes can be studied by sorting and identifying those with different edges and shapes and then making a composite drawing to show this variety. Along with a discussion of the concept of photosynthesis, both live and dried flowers and plants, such as Indian corn, decorative gourds, locust pods, and Fall weeds make a wonderful autumnal still life for drawing.

Simple Machines

Arrange still-life setups of antique Americana hand tools and farm implements, such as corn shuckers, cotton gins, and cherry pitters, along

Courtesy of Joyce Vroon, Trinity School, Atlanta, GA.

Through using cameras, sixth-grade students Hadley Hughes and Alex Davis were able to study the effects of sunlight and shadow on textured and patterned surfaces.

Courtesy of Frank Wachowiak, Athens, GA, and Mary Sayer Hammond, Fairfax, VA.

with objects such as bottles, lanterns, lamps, clocks, and musical instruments. While studying machines and how they work, have students use hand tools for craft and sculpture projects. For a study of balance, fulcrums, and levers, draw children on a teeter-totter. While studying axles, draw or make toy vehicles. While studying energy-creating machines, make pinwheels, and study or draw windmills and waterwheels.

Sound

Draw a still life or students modeling with musical instruments. Make and decorate homemade musical instruments, such as drums and bottle xylophones. Play recordings of music, dramatizations, poetry, sounds of geographic regions (city and country, nature's forces, forest and jungle), and sounds of machines, planes, ships, trains, circuses, and amusement centers to enhance art/science lesson motivations.

Technology and Energy

When viewing and discussing the artistic merit of outstanding computer art, have students use computers to create art (see Chapters 25 and 19). Use videotaping to record scientific phenomena, such as pollution in the neighborhood. Make drawings of facilities and equipment associated with energy, such as power plants and solar collectors.

Water

View Paul Klee's paintings of underwater life, and make artistic charts of the ocean food chain using a combination of real objects (such as

---

A science perception objective might be: "Students will observe and be able to draw a variety of leaves." Leaf terms might be "opposite and alternate, simple and compound, with margins, entire, serrate, or dentate." Children gathered a variety of leaves and drew them in crayon using a bold contour-line technique, emphasizing the veins but not coloring in the spaces solidly. They filled up the white paper in an allover design, the leaves turning in all directions, some touching and some overlapping. Then, using their watercolors and brushes, they applied the transparent colors over and between the leaves.

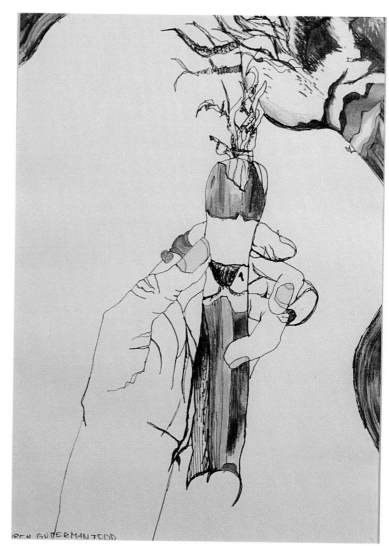

Top left, courtesy of Jackie Ellett, Fort Daniel Elementary School, GA, bottom left, Barbara Thomas, Whit Davis School, Athens, GA, and right, Baiba Kuntz, Glencoe, IL.

Over a freely painted background of delicate tints and shades, the camellia's leaf veins and petals, stamen, and anthers are drawn in pastel. Third-grade student Kristin Dudley drew this riotously energetic picture of leaves accompanied by butterflies.

Eighth-grade student Laura Gutterman drew her own hand with amarylis bulbs.

preserved dried fish) and photos of microscopic life, large fish, and mammals. Draw from a still life of sea creatures and objects that float on or in the water or are found on the beach (coral, seaweed and seashells), then add figures and other sea life and paint the sea in the background.

Using crayon resist, draw a *20,000 Leagues Under the Sea* picture of what can be viewed from an underwater-exploration vehicle. When studying water evaporation, make watercolor paintings while outdoors on a sunny day. In relation to topics of water pollution, oil spills, and

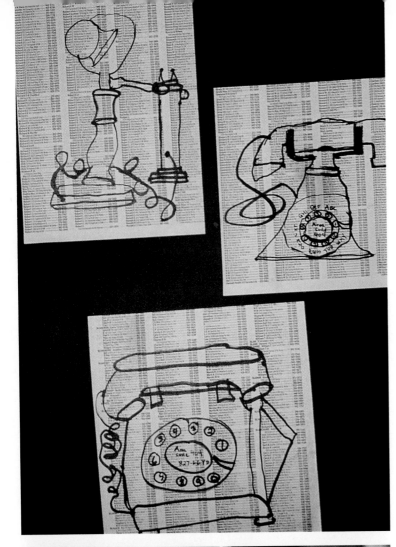

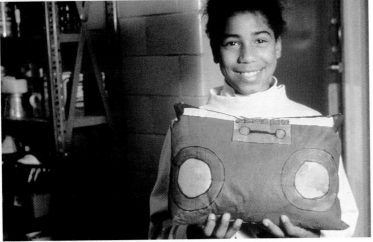

Courtesy of Joyce Vroon, Trinity School, Atlanta, GA.

After studying Ben Shahn's contour line drawings, fourth-grade student Drew Powers emphasized thick and thin lines in this drawing of old-fashioned telephones shown where else but on telephone book pages. Sixth-grade student Kristie Stephens drew a portable cassette player and headset on a musical sheet. Lower left, after discussing Claes Oldenberg's sculptures, Sahra Robinson made a soft sculpture of a boom box radio cassete player.

Saturday Children's Classes, courtesy of Frank Wachowiak, Athens, GA, and Mary Sayer Hammond, Fairfax, VA.

A seated student model holding a baritone horn is depicted in a highly original way, especially the challenge of showing foreshortened legs.

Brownian motion, students can make marbelized papers that later can be used in other art projects.

Weather

After showing Leonardo DaVinci's drawings and Turner watercolors of clouds and storms, draw a storm and/or cumulus, stratus, and nim-

Courtesy of Joyce Vroon, Trinity School, Atlanta, GA.

Toxic waste is the subject of fourth-grade student Eliot Brusman's modern day adaptation of Grant Wood's American Gothic.

Wave action on the surface of water, as well as the effects of sunset reflections, are depicted in sixth-grade student Elizabeth Leaque's Impressionistic painting in complementary tints and shades of orange and blue.

bus cloud formations and weather forecasting equipment. Draw the snow plows, road-clearing equipment, and sandbagging used to ameliorate the effects of adverse weather. Include in these drawings activities that children do under adverse and pleasant weather conditions. Along with discussing artworks showing umbrellas in use, make a still life by hanging a variety of colorful and overlapping umbrellas and raincoats from the ceiling and walls. Umbrellas from the Far East are especially attractive. (*Caution:* Don't hang anything from light fixtures.)

Imaginative underwater themes, a la Jules Verne, intrigued the Japanese children who painted these rich interpretations of oceanic exploration and adventure. When youngsters are capable of producing such rich visual statements, why allow them to settle for stereotyped, minimal results?

Courtesy of Joyce Vroon, Trinity School, Atlanta, GA.

Courtesy of Jackie Ellett, Fort Daniel Elementary School, GA.

Courtesy of Joyce Vroon, Trinity School, Atlanta, GA.

Left, the interactions of water and wind, light and shadow, object and reflection are poetically shown in sixth-grade student Mary Margaret Murphy's photograph. After looking at Currier and Ives winter scenes, this snowy scene of the student and friend ice skating on a frozen pond was painted.

Right, cloud formations, shown in Virginia Simm's photo of a figure silhouetted against the heavy clouds, are one of the most visible manifestations of wind and air. The wrath of Hurricane Hugo and its effects on beach surfaces and structures are captured in sixth-grade student Kempton Mooney's series of photos.

Wind and Air

Display Japanese, Chinese, Indian, and Indonesian kites, balloons, and banners. After a study of the principles of flight, have students decorate, make, and fly paper airplanes, parachutes, and kites. After a study of early American weathervane designs, make windvane designs (perhaps of animals, such as cats or dogs). Pieces can be cut from oak tag and attached to both ends of a soda straw, which is then pinned, through a bead that can revolve, to an upright dowel rod (or the eraser of a pencil, sunk in a spool glued to cardboard).

Just as nature and scientific phenoma have been of interest to many artists throughout time, most artists likewise have been interested, in some way, with human beings' interactions with each other and their cultures. This is the subject of the following chapter; the integration of art and social studies.

Courtesy of David Hodge, Oshkosh, WI.

By using imagination, wind can be shown indoors where there is little; on a table, three girls pose as if holding kites. (Notice also the beautifully organized, stimulating classroom environment.)

Chapter 12

Social Studies, Cultural Understanding, and Art

Culture is the common possession of a body of people who share the same traditions. It is that complex whole that includes knowledge, beliefs, art, morals, law, and customs. One of the main ways for transmitting, maintaining, and analyzing any culture is through art; hence, art plays an important role in social studies education. One current social studies text contains 600 reproductions of artworks, showing how the new methods in teaching social studies emphasize the interconnectedness of political, social, economic, and artistic issues. Art can be inte-

grated with the teaching of social studies concepts such as self-determination, location, and human/environment interactions. And, vice versa, topics from social studies can be used as vehicles for learning about light and dark, texture and color, dominance and subordinance, carrying through a motif and varying a theme, diligent workmanship, and ingenious imagination.

Social Studies Curriculum Across the Grades

Before going into art/social studies integration, what is studied in social studies should be reviewed. While this chapter as a whole is written mainly for the elementary classroom teacher who wishes to integrate art's motivational power with social studies learning, this section is written to give the art specialist an overview of the content covered in social studies. Abstract concepts such as power and status, personality and motivation, conflict and cooperation, dependency on others and the environment, freedom, diversity and equality, property, change, social behavior and roles, human needs, justice, scarcity, and truth are all taught. The general movement in the social studies curriculum across grades is from the family and neighborhood to the community to the state and nation and, finally, to the world. Ethnocentrism is a danger in this approach, however, so usually curricula intermix the study of other cultures. The Task Force on Social Studies for the Young Learner of the National Council for the Social Studies recommends the following sequence:

Kindergarten; socialization is the main goal, along with the names of one's community, state, region, nation, the basic time elements, the meaning of basic symbols, and classroom rules.

Courtesy of Melody Milbrandt, Valdosta, GA.

Third- and fourth-grade students painted this mural showing their understanding of Native-American styles of dress, artifacts, housing, and decoration.

Fourth St. Elementary School. Courtesy of David Harvel, Athens, GA.

Charlotte Country Day School. Courtesy of Alice Ballard Munn, Anchorage, AL, and Diane Rives, Athens, GA.

When art considerations are serious, integrated art and culture lessons are of value for learning in both areas. The study of ancient Egyptian culture comes alive through art expression. **Top left:** *Life-sized paintings of mummy sarcophagi create a display of grandeur and majesty in the elementary school's entrance hall.* **Above:** *A first-grade student's painting of Nut, the star-studded deity of the night.* **Lower left:** *Glazed ceramic sculpture of the Egyptian ibis-headed scribe deity, Thoth.*

Courtesy of Jackie Ellett, Fort Daniel Elementary School, GA.

In primary grades, socializaton is an important social studies goal. What better way to foster this goal than creating side by side?

First grade; school and family life, rural/urban, working cooperatively in groups, contributions of different family members to the family as a whole, working together to solve problems, and seasonal changes in the local environment.

Second grade; the neighborhood, communications, major kinds of transportation, consumption of goods and services, and how groups work to solve problems.

Third grade; the community, its history and its problems, a person's responsibility to the community, and contributions of various ethnic and cultural groups to it.

Fourth grade; the regional/world geographies are studied, using the home state as an example; land forms and characteristics of the home state are compared with other regions.

Fifth grade; close neighboring regions, the Western hemisphere, basic rights of citizens, major American historical events.

Seventh grade; a global view of the changing world, especially outside the Western hemisphere.

Eighth grade; American economic and social history, and especially its effects on ordinary people.

Courtesy of the International Collection of Child Art, Illinois State University, Normal, IL.

A Cape Town, South Africa, scene of a farmer plowing his fields has clear areas of glowing color.

Courtesy of Deborah Lackey, Atlanta, GA.

Through drawing a still life of artifacts from the Soutwest Native-American culture, fifth-grade students' learning about styles of decoration can be integrated with their knowledge of the culture's customs.

Courtesy of Joyce Vroon, Trinity School, Atlanta, GA.

Oriental watercolor landscape painting is studied along with the use of the fan in Oriental culture.

Courtesy of Joyce Vroon, Trinity School, Atlanta, GA.

A discussion of the last century's attitudes toward death, its sentimentality, and its love of Classical culture might be sparked by sixth-grade student Billy Welsh's photograph.

Multicultural Understanding Through Making Art

These suggested social studies/art integrated activities are not intended to supplant the regular art instruction period but to supplement it. The National Art Education Association recommends that in addition to 100 minutes a week for art, additional time should be devoted to art that is related to other subjects.

An important caveat: both bad art instruction and bad social studies instruction can easily result from art/social studies integration. Unthought-out stereotypes and procedures in both art and social studies regrettably are too often used. The results may be execrable, look-a-like exercises such as sketchily colored-in outlines of one's palm and fingers for a Thanksgiving turkey. If no art instruction is provided, little or no art learning will occur; art materials will just be used up. Do not use art exercises as a way to fill an unplanned 15 minutes. It goes without saying to eschew stereotyped, impersonal activities, such as dittoed patterns of pilgrims and presidents' profiles, wherein the art method (uncreatively coloring dittoed patterns) violates the social studies goal (assimilating into oneself something about the personal, creative initiative of the subjects studied).

On the other hand, art/social studies learning experiences in which the teacher sets higher standards than what students will do naturally, and which often takes hours, can just as easily result in students' most memorable experiences. In such projects, students sense the unity of thought, personal feeling, and expressive action that results from an aesthetic experience. Hence, the following suggestions for social studies/art integration are intended to be taught in tandem with the qualitative art instruction principles and methods given throughout this book for the student's serious involvement under the teacher's rigorous, steadfast guidance.

Because social studies/art integration projects often center around some other person or some remote event, always seek to motivate the student's *personal* response. "If you had been there, how would you look, how would you solve it, who would be with you, what objects would you take with you?" Seek the rapid involvement of both thought and feeling. As art often deals with the expression of personal feelings, urge students to put themselves and their daily activities into their representation of the earlier culture's figures.

Creative, hands-on art activity can promote multicultural understanding in many ways. Students can make paintings of cultural cele-

Courtesy of Sharon Burns-Knutson, Cedar Rapids, IA, and Barbara Thomas, Whit Davis School, Athens, GA.

African culture is examined through these projects: a metal embossed mask harkens to the art of the Benin kingdom, and a papier-mache constructed mask is decorated with beans and broomsedge.

Courtesy of Barbara Thomas, Whit Davis School, Athens, GA.

brations and discuss diverse customs. Provide opportunities for students to manipulate ideas through art construction—to draw their conceptions of things, to cut out labels and paste them onto drawings, to construct models and dioramas. Puppet plays and dioramas can illustrate clearly what students know about other cultures. These can be models of artifacts, buildings and communities, land forms, coal mines, offshore oil-drilling rigs, open-pit mines, sewing, soap carving, paper-bag dolls, a television set with a paper-roll program, baskets, jewelry, holiday decorations, pottery, playhouses, tie-dying, block printing, bulletin boards, posters, knitting, stitchery, quilting, and basketry. Photography, sculpting, construction of two- and three-dimensions, and representations by coloring, modeling clay, and cutting out and pasting papers together also can be valuable. The art activity must be done in depth,

however, following art instructional objectives such as those found on in Chapter 14. For example, a poster should be done in conjunction with a serious study of poster design; that is to say, the overall design and lettering must be bold and the background interesting, as in the World War II posters of Ben Shahn.

Doing an artwork in the style of another culture can teach one about that culture's way of looking at phenomena. When doing a con-

Multicultural understandings are acquired as these students from many lands work together, side by side, on a mural.

An individual's values can be given visual form through a ceramic sculpture.

temporary version of an earlier culture's style, however, be sure to discuss the sociopolitical issues of that culture. The teacher and students should bring out what they already know or can research or surmise about the culture. Just making a kachina doll will not necessarily result in multicultural understanding; without discussing the culture, such an activity may be considered a mere pastiche of surface appearances.

Drawing a Still-Life Arrangement

The study of a culture can be the focus of a still-life arrangement that you and your students put together. To give a feeling about the design motifs and indigenous art materials used in other cultures, artifacts from particular countries and regions can be collected for display or borrowed from a museum or curriculum materials center. Perhaps students' parents have masks, wood carvings, costumes, textiles, ceramics, toys, dolls, fans, puppets, and kites to loan for the still life. Travel agencies may be able to provide large, colorful posters. Teachers can help to bring out more fully the nature of a culture by having students not merely draw an object from another culture but also discuss how the

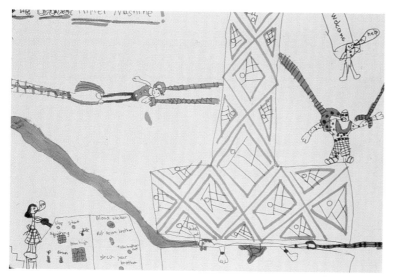

Courtesy of Joyce Vroon, Trinity School, Atlanta, GA.

One's feelings of frustration toward one's siblings have been expressed in this work called "A Brother Killer Machine," which may derive from an examination of torture machines used throughout the ages.

culture treated groups such as children, women, captives, and the elderly and from whence its wealth came.

Early Americana can be studied through travel posters of cities' historic buildings as well as through large, colorful bedspreads or quilts hung against a wall or on a counter for still-life backgrounds. Use costumes such as leather jackets and fancy dresses for student models who sit or recline in the still-life arrangements, and add picturesque farm implements for historic interest. Still lifes could be constructed around other themes such as the following:

Central American pottery
Colorful paper umbrellas from Japan
Kites, fans, and bells from the Orient
Masks: African, Indian, Malaysian, Indonesian, Mexican, Chinese opera, Mardi Gras, clown, Japanese Noh or Bugaku, Greek drama
Eskimo sculpture in soapstone or whalebone
Indian kachina and Japanese kokeshi dolls
Navaho rugs and San Blas Indian molas
Musical instruments from around the world
Puppets, toys, dolls, and wood carvings from around the world

Use of Models and Speakers

When studying a certain region of the world, invite guests to come and pose and talk while wearing ethnic costumes and to share the cultural artifacts from their collections. While drawing the visitor in costume, students can ask about the country's customs and feelings on immigrating. Also invite guests and parents with interesting occupations and hobbies to model while they chat with the students. If living near a major city, the country's embassy might be able to put you in touch with people who have objects they would be willing to loan for school use, and such an individual might be willing to come and talk while modeling either for, or with, the students in costume. The students themselves can take turns wearing special hats or clothing, such as Indian and African tie-dyed shirts, and take turns serving as models posed in a still-life arrangement dealing with the social studies material being studied. (See drawing from a model in Chapter 20).

Sketching Trips

Resource and sketching trips, which are wonderful art motivations in themselves, also may be related to social studies learning. (See the section on outdoor sketching on Chapter 20 for art principles and methods.) Students can gain insight into the relation of art and design to issues of historic preservation, trade balances, technological innovation, and community growth. Of course, it is prudent to visit the sketching site before class to check on hazards and procedures and to secure field-trip approval from authorities. Before or while there, discuss with the class sociopolitical issues as well as the site's aesthetic qualities and how to create an attractive drawing. Possible sites include:

Natural history museums
Construction sites
Manufacturing facilities
Fair or arts festivals
Bus and train stations
Shopping malls
Local art studios
Fire stations
Historic buildings
Historic monuments or statues
Art museums
Bridge sites
Boat marinas or wharves

Courtesy of David Hodge, Oshkosh, WI.

Help your students to develop a feeling for their cultural heritage through drawing a still-life arrangement incorporating Americana. When children sensitively capture in their drawings an old coffee grinder, railroad lantern, kerosene lamp, mantle clock, antique sewing machine, steam iron, architectural gingerbread, and assorted old musical instruments, these objects take on new meaning. Widen your students' cultural horizons by introducing them to a host of exciting artifacts from many cultures as subject matter for their art expression.

A student model coyly poses wearing a richly patterned silk kimono, with fan and umbrella and pussy willow flowers.

A study of figure drawing is combined with a study of 19th Century dress as fifth-grade girls took turns modeling, a half period at a turn.

Art Criticism and Art Reproductions

Art criticism *per se* is discussed in Chapter 19; here its use in connection with a social studies unit is examined. Artworks can be discussed in regard to themes about values, such as loyalty, conflict, equality, tolerance, and control (and/or these themes in conflict with one another). One might ask, "How does the artist convey who is in control? What conflicts might be on the characters' minds?" In artworks discussed in class, show a willingness to address issues of racism, sexism, and inequity. When showing the materials from diverse cultures to the class, tell students what you know about the artist's life, class, and ethnic origin, and have the students hypothesize on how issues such as life circumstances, gender, and ethnicity might have affected his or her art.

Hypothesizing, evaluation, and synthesis are skills at the top of Bloom's Taxonomy of Educational Objectives, and they can be readily practiced using art reproductions. "What happened before? What will happen afterward? Can you explain the meaning of this in terms of whether it's good for the society? Why or why not is this a good picture?"

Real objects are superior to reproductions, and they should be acquired whenever possible. For example, a real object as simple as a pair of chopsticks can stimulate a study of the Orient. Reproductions are easier to handle and store, however, and they are more often used. With postcards of artworks, photographs, or other reproductions, the learners can sort the artworks into the region or society from which they originated. Then, they can describe the overall stylistic concepts that a group of cards from one culture have in common. They might describe something that they know about that culture. Learning about the art style of a particular region or time can be facilitated by sets of art-reproduction cards made for playing an artistic version of Old Maids. "Find all the artworks made, for example, in the Orient, or during the Industrial Revolution, or in this century."

Interpreting artworks allows each person to reflect his or her understanding and sensibilities toward life. With no one feeling too personally threatened, social interaction can easily occur while talking about art. With teams of students from diverse backgrounds, discuss how the values of other cultures are shown in the artworks, and com-

Courtesy of Baiba Kuntz, Glencoe, IL.

Fifth-grade student Laura Richart captured with eight colors of Sharpie markers every fold pattern and ruffle of this 19th century dress.

Courtesy of David Hodge, in the collection of the Neville Museum, Green Bay, WI.

Take the students on sketching trips to where different cultures may be studied. Here, Amish wagons are captured by art professor David Hodge.

pare these values to those of the students' own culture. A game of picture detective can be played with pairs of students; one explains something about the picture in a sentence or two, the second interjects related points, and then they switch. A Go-Fish format also can be used; students must remember the physical location of works that go together and try to acquire sets. Such games can be played by pairs of students, in classroom learning activity centers, or by those who have finished an assigned activity early.

Multicultural understanding also can be fostered by having groups of students from diverse cultures work together arranging art reproductions about a culture into a bulletin-board display. Still another way to promote multicultural education is through exchanges of child art between schools here and in other countries. The following sections examine art/social studies integration for the elementary school as it relates to each of the social studies disciplines. Art study and expression can give insights into the methods and issues of anthropologists, economists, geographers, historians, political scientists, psychologists, and sociologists.

Egyptian artifacts and wallpaper design accompany the students' Egyptian paste jewelry in this display.

Anthropology

Anthropology is the study of a people's symbols. Cultural anthropology analyzes cultural traits and artifacts. From examining and making drawings of artifacts, students can imagine what life was like in another country. When studying objects, ask, "Of what were the artifacts made? For what purpose? How well do you think they met the need?" From students' drawings of schooling or coming-of-age rituals in some place or time, and in our own country, make comparisons. The activities that people perform and the objects used at times of the day and in different seasons can be illustrated. For example, concepts of time can be reinforced in early primary grades through a display showing the students' illustrations of their activities at different times of the day. In kindergarten, students can sort sets of artwork reproductions into time categories: now/then, first/second/third, nighttime/daytime, summer/fall/winter/spring, before/after, or in the morning/at noon/in the evening. Make drawings of today's artifacts, such as the fancy sports shoes, and generalize about our society from the artifacts that are drawn.

Patterns of crosses, thunderbolts, stripes, dots and a parade of animals and birds make this full-size replica of a Plains Indian teepee by fifth and sixth-grade students in acrylic paint an object of wonder and beauty.

A study of Southwest Native-American architecture was combined with a study of pastel, complementary colors, and use of chiaroscuro to create an illusion of roundedness in this third-grade students' work.

Third-grade students, studying Anasazi Native-American culture, created these ceramic pieces decorated with black-marker Native-American designs.

Economics

Economics deals with the structures that exist to provide jobs and services and with the distribution of wealth. Some suggestions for art integration are to illustrate an individual plan of economic action—draw or make a collage of what you would invest in "if you won $20,000." An understanding of concepts of money can be gained through discussion following children drawing make-believe choices after an imaginary motivation of being given an amount of money to buy presents.

A still life for drawing could be made of objects of scarcity, exchange, and consumption. Advertising can be analyzed for how art is used to motivate buyers. A sketching trip to a local business or construction site can show types of resources: natural resources, capital resources, and human resources. Drawings and diagrams can be made to show how rail lines, highways, airports, industrial complexes, and geographic factors interact. Drawing on top of the classified ads, fold the paper into fourths, draw four career choices of which you are aware, and then categorize these drawings of careers into those of persons who make things, fix things, create, and work with ideas.

Geography and Map Reading

Making maps helps students to learn content as well as map interpretation skills. Students' motivation for reading maps can be enhanced when they design their own map symbols. A group of students living near each other can make neighborhood maps using their own symbols for houses, streets, trees, government buildings, fun places to go, fast food restaurants, and playgrounds. To reinforce symbolization, students can match their symbols with photographs of the buildings or objects. Students also can draw a map from their homes to a favorite location and decorate it with personally significant details of what they see along the way. In the intermediate grades, make maps of regions and transportation arteries around one's city; use out-of-the-ordinary art materials, such as cut yarn pieces or cardboard relief, to encourage a different

Courtesy of Joyce Vroon, Trinity School, Atlanta, GA.

Top left: *Advertising art graces the highways and night sky in this sixth-grade student's Postmodern work showing an economy of consumption rather than production.* **Bottom left:** *Even animals are commodities in third-grade student Edgar Crossett's representation of a pet store with checkout counter.* **Right:** *Testimony to advertising's power is fourth-grade student Ross Baird's memory drawing which recalls the details of the advertising as clearly as the sports action.*

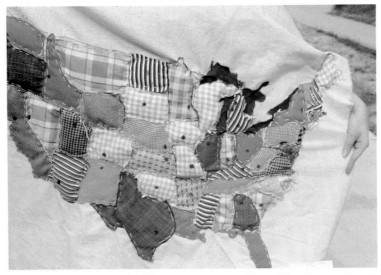

Courtesy of Claire Clements, Athens, GA.

Working in a group, students sewed and quilted their individual states together to make E Pluribus Unum.

type of artistic thinking. With these regional maps, encourage students to wonder about how major rivers, landforms, and highways affect the development of the area.

The study of transportation can be integrated by having students sketch vintage automobiles in the school parking lot and bicycles brought into the classroom, with a student modeling as the driver and backgrounds drawn from photographic views of bridges, modern cloverleaf intersections, and historic photos of downtown roads. For a very large map, students working in small groups in an out-of-the-way corner of the room can use a mixture of sawdust, glue, vermiculite, plaster of Paris, and water on a large piece of cardboard or plywood to make a raised relief map of a part of the world. To make comparisons between geographic areas, students can draw differences in climate, transportation, foods, customs, and home architecture in two areas of a paper. After studying the street names in the area, students can draw imaginary portraits of the individuals (see "Drawing Faces" on pages 214–16). Creatively illustrate the name of a famous place to show something about it. Students can sort artworks into those showing such concepts as settlement, village, town, city, suburb, metropolis, and megalopolis. Art reproductions can be examined regarding the land forms, people's

clothing, tools, homes, the weather, roads, and transportation that are shown.

History

There are many ways for art projects to make history vivid in students' minds. To foster creative thinking about peoples' motivations at a certain time in history, such as prehistoric peoples' cave art, have students hypothesize about the prehistoric artists' intent while reenacting the painting in the dim light inside a cast-off refrigerator carton. Students can draw scenes showing themselves in historical events and add their own captions. Using these pictures or art reproductions, have students sort them into chronological order and interpret what is happening in the picture. Draw and describe public buildings in the community, sort them into chronological order, and discuss the values conveyed by the architecture. In two clay figures or on two halves of a sheet of paper, contrast your life with that of a person from a historical period. Illustrate a problematic situation, such as a slave's dilemma to run away or not, or an immigrant's dilemma, or an army general's dilemma, and draw your own personal solution. Illustrate famous people's names in creative ways. Use pictograms to recount historical events. Put on a puppet play showing two varying scenarios of how an event may have taken place, and enact contrasting feelings toward the event. Make applehead dolls, with yarn hair added and dressed to represent historical figures, and add an accompanying illustration of an event in that famous individual's life. Illustrate what you may have been doing, in reality or in fantasy, when a great event occurred. Make a mural depicting historic events, and tell another class about it. Illustrated time lines can show the development of tools, inventions, and the arts. Illustrated grids can be made, such as with names of cultures down one side and concepts of house, headdress, and food across the top. Of course, models of ancient monuments, castles, cathedrals, kon-tiki rafts, dioramas and displays, masks, embroidery, engravings, and making costumes for role playing are useful for stimulating students' imaginations, especially when personalizing occurs and art principles are emphasized.

Law-Related Education and Political Science

Law-related education deals with concepts such as equality, fairness, honesty, justice, power, property, responsibility, and tolerance. It deals

Students related Medieval life to their own concerns and to the art of metalworking in these metal repoussées showing a closed-up castle with a dead knight and Claire Turner's showing a knight in shining armor astride his decorated horse.

with issues such as family law, consumer law (e.g. shoplifting), and community-safety law (e.g. bike helmets). Political science is concerned with examining rules, both good and bad, and taking the rights of others into account.

Students can illustrate examples from their lives of their own legal awareness, from raw power to group values to a belief in principles. Students can do figure drawings from a police officer who models while talking about community law problems, or from a uniformed member of

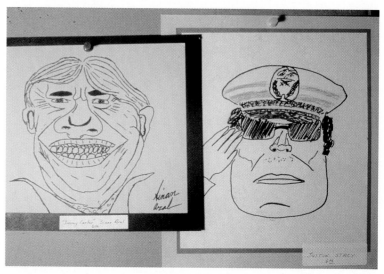

Sixth-grade students practiced the art of characterization in their drawings of President Jimmy Carter and a general.

Medieval life also is shown in these artworks. A maiden awaits her knight outside her well-protected fortress. Note the limited palette used in this third-grade student's painting of fighting knights.

the military who talks about issues of international law. Puppets can be made and used in law-related education during the primary grades, enacting issues in classroom rules, such as raising one's hand to speak, and in trials conducted on law-related issues, such as a trial of Goldilocks vs. the Three Bears. Draw and discuss how people on the playground show that they do not approve of certain behavior. Young students can illustrate rules for safety on the swings, and older students can make posters illustrating the pros and cons of community issues, such as gun control and airport or city dump relocation. After examining the symbols and stereotypes in political cartoons, older students can draw their own cartoons of politicians and world leaders.

Psychology

Psychology is concerned with how an individual perceives the world or behaves based on those perceptions. Social roles (such as leadership, followership, aggression, and submission) and personal social needs (such as acceptance and belonging) can be brought out through students making artworks on topics such as the following:

Courtesy of Joyce Vroon, Trinity School, Atlanta, GA.

Combining a study of Stuart Davis' art and the showing of a personal goal or favorite activity, a student produced this exuberant soccer design. Recalling a vivid dream, Michael Selik drew himself rapidly proceeding through an endless hall of mirrors. Illustrating "A metaphor for my life," this student wrote: I am walking through the checkerboard of life's moods and feelings, stepping through the red of happiness and the black of sadness." Studying Marisol's sculpture, Zibby Stokes did this "Celebrity Sculpture" of an Olympic runner.

during the motivation period—for example, "What (*about siblings, about food, about the playground*) makes me feel happy, sad, or mad?" Self-expression as a goal can be brought out through the teacher's eliciting and praising unique expression. "Because you are a unique individual, yours should not look like anyone else's. Make it your own way." One goal of social studies education is for students to have respect for others. To have such respect, it is first necessary to respect oneself, and creative expression in the arts is an excellent way to build self-respect and a positive self-concept.

Individuals' differences can be brought out through self-portraits that show personal interests, values, likes, and dislikes (see the sec-

Courtesy of Sharon Burns-Knutson, Cedar Rapids, IA.

Using a hand-mirror and oil pastels for her self-portrait, fourth-grade student Johanna Siska expresively delineates her purple turtleneck and her red-orange glass frames and long straight hair which dramatically goes over one eye and on the other side pulled back to show her ear and pearl earrings.

What I do to please my parents
Relationships with my siblings (or peer)
Relationships with peers on the bus

Topics such as "I am happiest when I–" "How I feel inside," and "The things I value" may be too broad and require narrowing and focus

Student Lindsey Dole, Teacher Susan Whipple, Grace Christian School, Medford, Oregon. USSEA art collection of Dr. Anne Gregory, Los Angeles School District.

In this 12- × 18-inch marker drawing, a little blue bird flies skyward under a blue patterned angel's watch, as Liberty looms large but vine-encrusted, behind the fortress-like institutions, church, state and home.

Courtesy of Barbara Thomas, Whit Davis School, Athens, GA.

First-grade students studied life in an American town in the 1800s. Richard Fisher's houses show three-dimensional form and their overlapping creates depth.

Sociology

Sociology is the study of how people function in groups. In early grades, draw the family and what it does on special days. In middle grades, illustrate the contributions of the people who live in our city or state. Or, divide the class in half, and from shoe boxes and cartons, have one group make an urban community and another make a rural community (see the section on box sculpture on Chapter 26). In upper grades, encourage thinking about concepts such as norms, society, values, competition, status, and change. For example, students might draw "If I could change this school in some way?" or "If I were the teacher?" To study abstract concepts such as status, first examine artworks showing it, then have students make their own drawings showing the concept. As a variant of drawing from an object or picture, try illustrating a concept or an event, working only from a verbal description, such as of the urbanization of an area, child labor, or the making of steel. A group of students can each draw one event in a sequence, and the whole can be pasted together. Then, students can label the drawings with explanatory sentences and take turns explaining them. Illustrations can be made of the outstanding contributions of immigrants from a particular country or

tion of self-portraits on pages 214–16). Students with certain aesthetic values can debate those with other values. Psychology exercises on peer understanding, such as "to find out three things about your partner" or "what would he or she do if given $300," can easily be integrated with the art task of drawing one's classmate (see drawing portraits in Chapter 20). When making masks, illustrate an appeal to pity or to force or to snob appeal. Have students illustrate endings to case-study situations of value conflict, such as individual freedom vs. the common good. Motivate thinking about value-based problems by having one student draw a problem situation on half of a folded paper, then have another student draw the solution on the other half. The relativity of perception can be shown by asking for different interpretations of art reproductions. "Does anyone think it means something different?" The psychology exercise of brainstorming alternate solutions to a problem also can be used for art teaching—for example, "How can we make our designs attractive and eye catching?" The values that are implicit in each solution can be analyzed later by discussing issues of aesthetics (see Chapter 19).

Courtesy of Jackie Ellett, Fort Daniel Elementary School, Gwinnett County Schools, GA.

This city drawing shows the high population density and a smog-filled sky obscuring the sun.

In A Birthday Party at the Skate Palace, *this kindergartener's crayon drawing shows the delightful social interactions and clowning around.*

region. To bring out the idea of multiple group memberships (recreational, social, religious), have the students make drawings of themselves doing an activity in their different groups, and combine the resulting artworks into a large display. Wonderful pictures that provoke thinking about careers can be made of police officers; firefighters; nurses; performers such as clowns, dancers, pantomimists and musicians with their instruments; scuba divers, air-line personnel, and athletes in uniform.

The polling methods used in sociological studies can be integrated with art inquiry. Students can conduct interviews among friends and family that investigate art-related issues and do polling research in their neighborhoods on the merits of a design for a new playscape, public sculpture, or community recreation center. Current events can be studied through an art-news bulletin board for discussion to bring out interrelated concepts in the social sciences and art. Have students write or give oral reports on a family member, relative, or neighbor engaged in the arts. This can relate language arts, social studies, and art, and the class as a whole can discuss the importance of the art in the creator's life. Also, photography and videotaping can be used to document individual interviews with artists as well as the community's eyesores and attractive sights.

Both social studies and art have much in common; they share a common interest in perceiving the distinctive attributes and amounts of things, in grouping things by shared properties, and in generalizing. Keep in mind the larger goals, even beyond learning specifically about art and social studies. The study of the arts and humanities enriches daily life, helps one to understand oneself, helps maintain civility, and develops a sense of community. The art/social studies program that you provide your students can help them to feel pride in and connectedness to both themselves and their own cultural backgrounds, as well as to other people and other cultures.

Chapter 13

Evaluation

This chapter describes evaluation in three ways. The major part deals with how the teacher, through in-process evaluation, can help students in their thinking about how to achieve a qualitative result. (Student project evaluation using instructional objectives, the topic of the following chapter, also is introduced here.) The second part discusses evaluating student performance for grades and arriving at an overall evaluation of the art program's effectiveness. The third and final part discusses tests and performance assessments that are used to evaluate the teacher.

Courtesy of Joyce Vroon, Trinity School, Atlanta, GA.

Students can be helped through in-process evaluation to assess if they have attained their goals. Here, sixth-grade student Zibby Stokes deliberates on her next course of action for her Celebrity Collage Sculpture.

In-Process Evaluation of Student Work

Among the many questions that teachers of art seek to answer, the most commonly repeated is: "How can I help those students who rush through their projects, who so often exclaim, 'I'm finished!' when they have barely begun to tap their expressive potential?" No doubt the quality and promise of a school's art program depend in great measure on how teachers meet this particular challenge. There is no miracle formula, no surefire panacea, for dealing with those students with a short interest span, deficient school preparation in art, and minimal self-motivation. Every teaching strategy and stimulative approach will meet with varying success, depending on the students' backgrounds, personalities, and readiness. Some students simply need personal encouragement, some demand specific help, and others require only a clue. All students, however, are entitled to more than vague generalizations. They are entitled to assessment of their learning. The best evaluative criticism provides the students with guidance they can understand, store, and use over and over in later art projects.

Evaluative strategies are most vital during the studio phase and the final stages of a project. One highly productive procedure is for the teacher to sit down with a student individually and discuss the student's work at various stages, perhaps using a framing mat to set off the work.

The most positive evaluations always take into consideration the personalities of the children themselves. Children at all stages have individual styles in art expression and diverse imaginative and inventive capacities. Thus, the teacher might say that one rambunctious student's piece shows his or her "energetic personality through the dynamic shapes and way the colors fly out of the shape borders." The teacher may comment on a contrasting piece by a quiet, calm student by saying that the work shows "a calm, determined, and thoughtful way of working by the way each shape is carefully drawn all the way around."

Here, in these works by intermediate-elementary-grade children, the human figure is interpreted through crayon, collage, and paint. The teacher can help students to evaluate their work in terms of the lesson's instructional objectives. The instructional objectives for the painting of the girl may have been use of analogous and complementary color. Her green lips and orange and purple eyes are inspired.

The subtle strategies of high-caliber teaching are evident in the words, action, sincerity, and confidence that teachers exhibit when they help students to evaluate their art efforts. What instructors say, how they say it, how much they say, and what they leave unsaid are vitally important.

If the students are engaged in a multilesson, crayon-engraving project, for example, the following self-evaluative questions, either written on the chalkboard or as a mimeographed handout, will provide working criteria for each stage:

1. Did I use enough pressure in applying the crayon so that the paper is completely and solidly covered? With padding under my paper, did I apply the crayon heavily and smoothly? Did I vary the sizes and shapes of the many crayoned areas?

2. After coating the drawing with black paint and transferring the sketch to it, ask: Does my preliminary line-drawing composition for my engraving fill the space effectively? Have I employed a variety of lines, shapes, and sizes? Have I emphasized detail, pattern, and textures that are especially effective in the engraving process?

3. During the engraving process (the main part of the lesson) ask: Did I engrave the basic outlines of the shapes in my composition first? Did I make variations of lines—thick, wavy, jagged? Did I take time to engrave details, vary patterns, and create textural effects as contrasts against plain black areas? Did I create some bold contrasts by scratching away solid areas of black to reveal the crayoned surface underneath? Have I used all three methods fully: engraved line only; detailed and patterned areas; and scraped-out, solid crayon shapes?

4. During the subsequent enrichment lesson, ask: Did I enrich the composition by applying oil pastel over some of the remaining black areas and repeat the oil pastel colors in different parts of my composition to achieve unity? Did I engrave lines, details, or patterns through the oil pastelled areas for even more subtle embellishment?

Evaluative questioning can be effectively employed in every art project to give purpose, direction, and continuity to the students' efforts. Although the specific instructional objectives vary with different projects and at different age levels, the important, recurring design criteria are echoed in project after project. In any one session, however, choose only one, or at most only a very few, to emphasize.

Composition and Design

Ask one or more of these questions to evaluate design and composition:

Are the sizes and shapes of objects (people, buildings, cars, trees, and so on) varied?

Do they produce interesting negative spaces?

Is informal balance employed (as opposed to formal balance) to create a varied, more flexible composition?

Are the shapes or objects drawn at different levels to create varied space breakup in the foreground and background?

Do objects or shapes overlap each other to create unity and depth?

Do some lines converge to create space-in-depth?

Do some lines or shapes touch or intersect the borders of the picture plane to create movement in depth into the composition?

Is contrast achieved by juxtaposing light areas next to dark ones, and patterned or detailed areas next to plain ones?

Color

Depending on the students' ages, one or more of the following criteria may be used in a evaluation of color use:

Are colors repeated throughout to achieve movement and unity?

Has pressure been used in coloring to achieve rich, glowing colors?

Does the picture lack excitement because of too rigid a dependence on the use of local color?

Are bright, high-intensity colors employed for emphasis wherever such emphasis is needed?

Are the intensities of the colors varied for diversity and subtlety?

Is the color scheme limited or monochromatic to achieve unity?

Are the tints and shades of the colors varied for interest and contrast?

Is the color employed based on one of the color-wheel schemes: complementary, split-complementary, analogous, or triad?

Are the neutralized colors in the palette (umber, ochre, sienna, and so on) employed for their special, subtle effects?

Are colors used to achieve a feeling or mood: warm and cool colors, colors with psychological impact?

Line Drawing

Another important area for evaluation is line drawing, and three criteria are used. To introduce the subject of instructional objectives, which

These colored-tissue-paper collages show several criteria put into practice: varied shapes, informal balance, multilevels, and border touching. **Top:** *This tissue collage by a first-grade student is given movement and unity by colors moving from a red area in the upper left corner to white in the lower right corner.* **Middle and bottom:** *A fifth-grade youngster applies colored tissue onto an 18- × 24-inch white construction paper drawing.*

Saturday Children's Classes. Courtesy of Frank Wachowiak, Athens, GA, and Mary Sayer Hammond, Fairfax, VA.

Courtesy of Barbara Thomas, Whit Davis School, Athens, GA.

A student intently paints the sunflower petals observed in the still life.

Courtesy of Barbara Thomas, Whit Davis School, Athens, GA.

This third-grade boy's gesture appears to indicate that he believes he has met the criteria of dividing the space.

is the topic of the next chapter, a chart showing the three criteria and the instructional objectives derived from them is presented here. As shown, the questions that are spoken or written on the chalkboard for students to apply in judging their own artwork can be just as easily written as lesson-plan instructional objectives.

Evaluational Questions to Be Asked or Written on Chalkboard	*Instructional Objectives from Lesson Plan*
Are the lines varied from thick to thin to create interesting linear movement and subtle space-in-depth?	Students will draw lines varied from thick to thin to create interesting linear movement and space-in-depth.
Is the line on opposite sides of a shape or object (body, tree, vase, fruit, and so on) drawn more heavily on one side and lighter on the other to create tension and space?	Students will draw lines on opposite sides of a shape or object more heavily on one side and lighter on the other to create tension and space.
Do the lines drawn complete a shape instead of floating in space?	Students will draw lines to complete a shape instead of floating in space.

Grading and Summative Evaluation

The second focus of evaluation is on grading and summative evaluation. One of the most difficult evaluative tasks any teacher must perform is the periodic grading of students. In a content field such as art, which is so subjective, colored by expressive diversity, and in which many varied interpretations are acceptable, the problem is compounded. Reporting of students' art progress varies from school to school, from primary and intermediate through upper elementary to the middle school grades. Some institutions employ separate evaluations for behavior and subject mastery; some simply indicate that the student has performed satisfactorily or unsatisfactorily. Most report cards in the middle school use the letter-grade system.

In some elementary schools, teachers write a report in the form of a letter to the parents or guardians that describes the child's growth in art. They take into account improvement in art abilities as well as behavioral factors. When letter or numerical grades for art are given, teachers often take into account the students' classroom working habits and behavior as a factor in their evaluation. This procedure sometimes has been questioned. If students have been forewarned that their behavior and conduct will affect their grades, however, such an action is defensible, because in almost every instance, the student's prudent use of class time will result in higher-quality work.

The grading of a variety of art projects should not prove to be difficult if students are advised in advance about the specific instructional objectives. In the approach recommended by this book, the teacher and students discuss the project's several criteria. For greater emphasis, the teacher writes the criteria on the chalkboard, on a specially prepared chart, or may even ask the students to take notes.

Summative evaluation is used to diagnose, to revise curricula, and to determine if objectives have been met. It summarizes both the students' learning and the teacher's effectiveness. Save the students' work in portfolios, and periodically go over them to determine if your goals are being met. Through photos and video, document three-dimensional work and exciting art events. Older students might keep journals to document what they are learning. One good time to have the students help you, either through questionnaires or class discussion, to do a summative evaluation is when the portfolios are handed back to be taken home. Is the program leading students to understand art? Are the students finding satisfaction in the process? Is the language the students use in discussing aesthetics and writing about art becoming more advanced?

Some evaluative questions the students can answer are:

Did you learn any new words or art ideas this year? What?

What was good about art this year?

What was not so good about it this year?

If anything did not work out for you, how would you handle it in the future?

What did you learn this year about how to make art?

Did we do anything in art that helped you to learn about science or social studies or other subjects? What?

How is art different from other subjects?

How could the teacher be better to the students?

When you are older, how will you ever use anything like what you did in art this year?

How would you change what we did this year?

Do you have any ideas about how we could make art more real and not just like school?

How did you like it when the class talked about art and thought together about art?

Outside of school and on your own, did you do any things that were like art? What was it? Did you do it by yourself or with someone?

Outside of school, did you talk with anybody about art ideas? What was the discussion about?

Courtesy of Baiba Kuntz, Glencoe, IL.

To achieve a chromatic unity, the color scheme is limited to analogous colors, yellow through green. What concentration the fifth-grade girl displays as she colors her sunflowers! She is using oil pastel on black construction paper. A preliminary sketch was made in silver.

Do you have any ideas for ways to make art class better?

Did anything good about art happen in the community that you knew about?

Why do you you think students should study art in school?

From the following list of what we did in art this year, mark those activities that you really liked or from which you learned a lot. Write if there was anything special about it that made it especially good.

Evaluation of the Teacher's Knowledge and Performance

Evaluation is not just a procedure that you use to plan and assess your students' work. It also is a procedure that at some time may be per-

Courtesy of Jackie Ellett, Fort Daniel Elementary School, Gwinnett County Schools, GA.

Four kindergartners prepare to discuss their paintings. The two students in the rear probably can tell stories about the shapes they have created; the two students in the front appear to have achieved a concept of a girl figure and an animal.

formed by your principal, department head, supervisor, or state education department assessors to measure your teaching effectiveness. While doing student teaching, preservice teachers are assessed by college field supervisors and their critic teachers. In many states, first-year teachers also are assessed by the local school system or state evaluators, and in some states, even experienced teachers are periodically assessed when they apply for a more advanced level of certification. The first way that your ability to teach art may be assessed is through a standardized test about art-education knowledge, such as the National Teacher Exam, its art-education component, or a similar state-developed test. For individuals seeking regular elementary school classroom teaching certification, almost a third of the states have certification tests that include art items. For individuals seeking art certification, more than a third of the states require a test in art education.

Sixth-grade student Ali Schier did this multiperiod marker drawing from a posed model, capturing the turning of the hat's every straw strand and the myriad patterned and folded cloth designs. Laura Towbin added a background, envisioning the sophisticated individual sitting on a balcony in a big city. The teacher laminated the drawings to prevent the marker color's fading. Nine 20- × 48-inch frames were grouped in this four-way hallway intersection to create a wonderful display.

Courtesy of Baiba Kuntz, Glencoe, IL.

The second type of teacher evaluation consists of assessors' judging your lesson plans and/or actually watching and scoring your teaching performance. Several states already have performance assessment as part of their requirements for beginning teachers, and many others are testing or plan to use competency-based tests of teaching performance. Fortunately, most school systems view these assessment procedures less as "weeding out" and more as diagnosing and remediating weaknesses. Teachers usually are given repeated opportunities to retake the exam or assessment.

Some suggestions for doing well in the on-site evaluation are:

Develop your lesson plans using a variety of instructional objectives. Each time the lessons are repeated, seek to make the plans and lessons richer.

Be able to show how your lesson plans meet both your goals and school-system goals.

Be alert to the art needs of your school, such as its needs for displays and public presentations such as pageant backdrop designs.

Be alert to the art needs of your school district, and network with other art teachers through district curriculum-development committees.

Be alert to how your art program can interface with the community. Involve the community, such as through displays of your students' works at banks and libraries and the dedications of new community buildings.

To maintain evidence of your overall teaching ability, write down any laudatory comments that you receive from peer teachers, supervisors, and parents. Seek out ways for your students to be recognized, and keep good records of their achievements and the publicity you may have to generate to have those achievements recognized. Through the previously discussed summative evaluation as well as photos and videotapes, document your program's effectiveness and the quality of the art that is produced. Be active in your state and local education and art-education associations, and share what you have done through their newsletters. The teacher who has done these things, and done a good job of planning lessons with valid instructional objectives, will do well, and the program cannot help but be evaluated favorably.

Courtesy of David Harvell, Fourth Street School, Athens, GA.

What evaluator would not be impressed by the art program of the teacher who so ingeniously combined children's works into such a fine display? This display of God's eyes also quietly conveys another lesson. The lesson is that through cooperation we can achieve greater goals than anyone can achieve individually.

Chapter 14

Writing Instructional Objectives for Lesson Planning

Need for and Form of Instructional Objectives

Clarity of education is greatly promoted when instructional objectives are clearly spelled out both in the teacher's own mind and for students, who gain satisfaction when they know what they are expected to do. In education, the principle of *expectancy* emphasizes the need to inform the learners in advance about the objectives of any task they are to perform (Gagné, 1975). Using instructional objectives can help novice teachers of art to incorporate their ideas about teaching into the competencies that students are expected to demonstrate. To do well in the critical first year of teaching, to keep their enthusiasm and dedication high, new teachers must acquire a growing confidence and pride in their work. Being fully prepared for each class helps to develop this necessary confidence.

The best art teachers plan their motivation, demonstration, and evaluation sessions well in advance. They do not rely on last-minute inspiration. They prepare a written outline of their objectives, and they refer to it during the class session, knowing that otherwise they may forget to emphasize critically important aspects. They are continually aware of the long-range objectives of the project. Experienced teachers plan the motivating question-and-answer session, the preliminary show-and-tell segment, and the discussion period with special care and attention.

Being able to write lesson plans in terms of instructional objectives is a skill that is absolutely necessary to graduate from many teacher-education programs and to receive teacher certification in an increasing number of states. Concerns about both the quality of education and teacher accountability have motivated proponents of the *competency-based* education movement to mandate teachers' writing clearly defined instructional objectives. State or local systems using a competency-based system usually set broad goals, then let the individual teacher focus on the specific instructional objectives that will allow students to achieve those goals. For example, a system-mandated goal might be: "Students will appreciate the art of diverse cultures." One of the instructional objectives through which a teacher believes a class can attain this goal might be: "Students will identify pre-Columbian, Mississippian Nature-American, and Greek Cycladic sculptures." By directly setting clear, attainable objectives, teachers can readily evaluate the overall success in meeting broad goals.

Indicative of this same trend toward accountability, two thirds of our nation's school districts with elementary schools have art-curriculum guides that specify instructional goals and student outcomes. Sets of required or recommended textbooks, often written in instructional objectives, are used in over a third of elementary-level art programs.

Writing instructional objectives differs from stating goals in terms of what you, the teacher, will do. Instead, you must carefully examine each goal and determine what specific competencies students will demonstrate as evidence of mastery. One widely accepted way of writing instructional objectives has four features: subject, verb, conditions, and standards of quantity or quality (Mager, 1975). Another way to remember these four features is the acronym *ABCD*, which stands for Audience, Behavior, Conditions, and Degree. In more detail:

1. The *subject* of the sentence is the student or the learner or audience. It is not what the teacher will do.
2. The *verb* should indicate some demonstrable behavior, such as to identify, list, match, or depict. It should not be a broad, vague, or difficult-to-assess goal, such as "to understand" or "to appreciate." Goals typically cover a whole curriculum or course, whereas instructional objectives deal with one lesson.
3. *Conditions* are the supplies and motivational resources available and the time allotted for each phase of an art project.

Instructional objectives to break up the space into small areas, to leave the space of the chalk line unpainted between forms, and to imaginatively use colors helped *the sixth-grade artist of this tempera-India ink resist to create this "bouquet with owl."*

4. *Standards* of quantity or degree of quality should be spelled out. (Some examples are: "Must meet at least four out of the eight criteria listed on the chalkboard." "Must bump the edges of the paper." "Must show several very large objects and many very small objects.")

An example of these four features in an objective is:

The student (or students) will sketch the main shapes of the model in the still life, using chalk on colored paper in 20 minutes, showing

Stress only a few objectives each lesson. During the first lesson in this Japanese classroom, line was used to delineate every part of the bicycle. Filling the picture plane also was stressed. Later lessons focused on using color to set off the bicycle and background.

1. Art production
2. Artistic perception
3. Art criticism
4. Aesthetics
5. Art history
6. Affective
7. Cognitive and interdisciplinary
8. Psychomotor and multisensory

Remember that these categories are not totally separate entities. Instead, like ingredients in a well-cooked stew, they blend into one another. When writing an objective, you must determine which of the several categories into which it may fit should be the focus.

With many objectives planned to convey to your students the importance and purpose of the art activity, you can pick and choose among them to meet individual students' needs. Students with differing ability levels and learning modes, as well as students with developmental disabilities, will require your emphasis to be on different objectives. Gifted students very well may already know the concept, and some stu-

the floor plane, the ceiling plane, the figure's general shape, and background's spatial breakup.

The subject is "the student"; the verb is "will sketch"; the conditions are "using chalk on colored paper in 20 minutes"; and the standards are "showing the floor plane, the ceiling plane, the figure's general shape, and the background's spatial breakup."

Eight Categories of Instructional Objectives

Just as there are many ways to teach, there are many different types of lesson objectives. From these several kinds of objectives, teachers select those which they believe should be emphasized. Major factors affecting which are appropriate for you are your own teaching style and beliefs as well as the ages, ability levels, and learning styles of your students. School administrators and supervisors, however, may require that certain types of objectives, perhaps in a certain order, be used in plans to be submitted to the school's central office. To keep art itself the central focus, five types of art objectives are discussed here first, then three other types of objectives that are widely used in schools. Together, these categories are:

Courtesy of Jackie Ellett, Fort Daniel Elementary School, Gwinnett County Schools, GA.

Using a brayer to ink the surface of a fish and then making a print is a psychomotor, perceptual, and multisensory experience, both tactile and olfactory.

dents with significant mental challenges might never fully master it. The experienced art teacher has the insight to know what specific skills are within the general grasp of a given class of students and can customize the general objectives to address individuals' special needs. By using several categories of objectives, you will create powerful motivations that will sustain the learning activity of all your students. It is better to have extra plans, which might be carried out if time permits or perhaps only with a few of the students, than to exhaust the plans for a lesson early and "try to fill up time."

Art Production Objectives

As art teachers, we must teach first about art. In too many instances, we find art teachers apologizing for making suggestions to children, initiating projects, and emphasizing art fundamentals. Let the truth be known! Where promising, sequential, imaginative, and qualitative elementary and middle school art programs exist, the classroom or special art teacher is on the job organizing, coaching, motivating, questioning, demonstrating, evaluating, approving, and advising—in other words, teaching. The importance of actively helping students learn to apply art concepts in their creation of art cannot be overemphasized.

Instructional objectives must be specific. It is not enough simply to write, "Students will draw the still life" or "Students will use colors with good design." The vagueness of these statements helps neither the teacher nor the students toward a specific goal. Without specific standards, the verbs "draw" and "use" are too general. A better phrasing would be "Students will draw the table plane, suggesting depth by overlapping and creating avenues in depth," or "Show how at least seven objects and forms overlap," or "Compose the design so at least three of the objects go off the edges."

In carrying out a project, stress only a few art objectives each class period. Do not confuse students with too many directions at once. In a drawing project, for example, emphasize the quality of line and the full use of the picture plane during the first session. During the second session, guide the students in identifying and evaluating the variety of shapes and overlapping planes in their drawing. During the third session, challenge the students to enrich their drawings with detail, texture, and pattern.

Artistic Perception Objectives

Artistic perception helps students to identify art elements in their daily lives. If teachers can bring children to notice something they have

Courtesy of Barbara Thomas, Whit Davis School, Athens, GA.

After studying Matisse's paper cut-outs, kindergartners cut out the shapes of fish, seaweed, bubbles, and water.

never noticed before, to see with the inner eye, they will have started them on an endless, exciting, and rewarding journey toward a thousand discoveries. Three sources for perceptual objectives are: the classroom, artworks, and the students' daily life experiences.

Examples of perceptual objectives based on what can be seen in the classroom are: "The student will identify at least three triangular shapes in the classroom" or "The student will describe analogous color schemes from among the colors seen in classmates' shirts."

An example of a perceptual objective based on what can be seen in artworks presented and created is: "From the artwork of a group of classmates, the student will be able to point out instances demonstrating (1) exaggeration and (2) swinging design." (Note that this particular kind of perception usually now is considered to be an art criticism objective.)

Perceptual objectives also can be based on what the students have seen outside the classroom. ("The students will be able to recall the order of the colors in a rainbow." "The students will be able to describe and depict the design of insects' homes that they have seen.") Perceptual objectives about nature state that the students "will describe verbally" or "show in their artwork" that they have perceived such natural or scientific phenomena as:

- The intricate pattern of a spider's web
- The variety of cracked shapes in mudflats, ice, and cement walks
- The blue shadows on fallen snow
- The variety of grain pattern in wood
- The varieties of green in summer foliage
- The varied textures and patterns of tree bark
- The shadows of tree branches on building walls
- The lines and patterns of bridge girders and cables
- The filigree pattern in leaf veins and insect wings
- The pattern of frost on a windowpane
- The changing formations of clouds
- The dew on early morning flowers and leaves
- The undulation of reflections in water
- The moody, misty colors of a foggy or rainy day
- The flashing colors of stoplights, neon signs, and beacons

- The glowing colors of stained-glass windows
- The tracks of animals in the snow
- The linear grace of a jet's stream
- The deterioration of paint on aging doors and old metal

Art Criticism Objectives

Objectives in art history, criticism, and aesthetics are described in Chapters 18 and 19. Here, one form in which these objectives can be written is shown. One way to state an art criticism instructional objective is: "Students will use the language of art to describe qualities in each others' artwork." In the area of feelings, or affect, an example is: "Students will describe how peers have used artistic devices to show different kinds of feelings." In a lesson about depth, an objective might be:

Courtesy of W. Robert Nix, Athens, GA.

Perceptual objectives deal with focusing attention to see vividly and aesthetically the forms around us in daily life. For example, through study of these photos, the viewer is led to appreciate how beautifully the calyx shelters the flower.

Courtesy of Joyce Vroon, Trinity School, Atlanta, GA.

The objective of artistic perception is met in sixth-grade student Michael Selik's photo of the fractal branching of tree limbs creating dramatic silhouettes against the heavy Winter sky.

"Using classmates' artworks, students will describe seven ways to indicate that an object appears to go back in space." In a design lesson using art reproductions, an objective might be: "From famous artworks, students will cite instances where an artwork's power might be attributed to the elaboration and variation of a motif."

Objectives in Aesthetics

Aesthetics is about ideas of beauty or the nature of art. Examples of aesthetics objectives are: "Students will discuss varying ideas of what makes a good picture," "Students will debate whether art that does not realistically represent objects and figures can be considered good art," "Students will debate whether ugly subject matter can make good art." (See Chapter 19.)

Art historical objectives are to be able to describe the paintings of Jackson Pollock and Abstract Expressionism; aesthetic objectives are to discuss the merits of control vs. accident in regard to whether an object is art; and artistic production and psychomotor objectives are to make a painting using this technique. (It is recommended that this activity be done outdoors and in old clothes.)

Courtesy of Joyce Vroon, Trinity School, Atlanta, GA.

What vivid feelings "A visit to a doctor" must have aroused in this young Japanese child. One can sense the anxiety by seeing how much was remembered and recorded in this watercolor painting.

Art History Objectives

Objectives also can focus on many of the important educational roles of art history, which are described in more detail in Chapter 18. These include:

Study of art history concepts: "Students will identify different art styles."

Analysis of famous historical artworks to gain a perspective into the overall development of culture and history: "Students will describe why a theme has been shown differently throughout several centuries."

Use of historic artworks to give students ideas for their own art: "From examples of Persian and medieval art, students will analyze and apply the concept of overlapping to their own artwork."

Use of artworks from different cultures to develop multicultural understanding and ethnic pride: "Students will discuss how African-Americans have been depicted in art."

Affective, Cognitive, and Psychomotor Objectives

The last three types of objectives deal with feelings, knowledge, and body movement. The affective, cognitive, and psychomotor domains, as they are called, comprise the three major categories of a system called Bloom's Taxonomy of Educational Objectives. These divisions are widely used in many schools that require written lesson plans. The affective domain deals with emotional factors in learning. The cognitive domain deals with the factual information that students learn in school, as well as with higher-level skills such as analysis and synthesis. The psychomotor domain deals with how the movement of the body is involved in learning.

Each domain can be considered as having several levels, ranging from basic to advanced. For example, in the affective domain, the steps are, from lower to higher: receiving, awareness, responding, valuing, and organizing values. In the cognitive domain, the stages are knowing, comprehending, applying, analyzing, synthesizing, and evaluating. When education critics say that too many "low-level objectives" are used and not enough "high-level objectives," they are referring to Bloom's Taxonomy.

Affective Objectives

Why bother with feelings in a book about teaching art? For many artists, aesthetic experience is rooted in concerns of life and death, nature and living beings, and the expression of feelings. Feelings often motivate art and sustain it's production over the long periods necessary for creation. Art gives a voice to our inner needs and desires. It gives shape to our hopes, fears, and ideals, and to our very sense of self (see section on Psychology in Chapter 12). If something is important in an emotional sense, then the creation of art becomes a way of taking action to share the importance of the experience.

Several variations of affective objectives are described in this section to show the wide variety of affective sources that a teacher can draw on to stimulate art learning. The following table gives six affective objectives together with an example for each of a representative statement that teachers or students could make about the particular area.

Affective Objectives in Art Lessons	Representative Statements by Teacher or Students
Students will express personal feelings in their art production.	The feeling I'd like to put in my mask is one of super power.
Students will express feelings common to their age.	Fear of scary things in the closet was something I felt strongly about when I was your age.
Students will show feelings about external events in their art.	Mary's being in the hospital makes me want to do something to try to make her feel a little better.
Students will express their personal feelings indirectly via art criticism.	The people in the picture look like they are afraid of the storm that's approaching, like bad things are going to happen to them.

Courtesy of Joyce Vroon, Trinity School, Atlanta, GA.

In sixth-grade student Paul Freschi's dream picture, the dreamer confronts devils, flames, a dead end, and a maze of high yellow walls.

Affective Objectives in Art Lessons	*Representative Statements by Teacher or Students*
Students will indirectly share personal feelings by peers' interpreting their artwork and through art history examples.	Does anyone get a different feeling from the way the trees and clouds are painted in Bernardo's picture?
Students will express feelings about sharing art as gifts.	What will you say when you give your art to someone special to you? What do you think that person might say back to you?

Personal Emotions

An affective objective might concern one's present, personal emotions—one's feelings in school, at home, with one's peers, and with one's family. ("Students will share the feelings of pleasure, fear, and courage they have while playing Red Rover.") Sharing such content usually gives the creator added emotional power to make the art piece. Of course, students should only share what they feel comfortable with sharing, whether in discussion or through their artwork.

Developmental Emotional Needs

Each developmental stage presents special emotional challenges (see Chapters 3 to 7). Some instructional objectives related to students' developmental stages are: "Student will be able to depict feelings . . . about relating to other persons and things. . . , of group belongingness. . . , of pride in accomplishment. . . , of emotionally reaching out to another person to give help or receive nurturance."

Affect Surrounding Events

The affect surrounding events refers to the feelings that are generated by world and community events—for example, one's emotions precipitated by some natural event (a storm), a war, a civil disturbance, an approaching holiday, or a classmate or family member who has had an accident. ("Through an artistic expression, students will show empathy for a hospitalized peer.")

Interpreting Affect in Peers' Work

A different venue for affective sharing is knowing that one's feelings can be communicated through art to others. ("Students will

Courtesy of the Art Education Archives, School of Art, University of Georgia, Athens, GA.

The wedding of an older sibling made an emotional impression on this upper-elementary grade child, who then captured the ceremony's sacred feeling in her tempera painting.

describe the affect shown in peers' works.") Of course, the teacher should not tolerate unkind remarks, and he or she needs to model the type of response desired. For example, the teacher might say, "This figure's expression shows eagerness to join the group playing Red Rover."

Sharing Art

It is motivating to make an art object to give to or share with another person, yet holiday art is notorious for reflecting a nonartistic, nonqualitative approach that involves trite, uncreative, "craftsy" gim-

Courtesy of Baiba Kuntz, Glencoe, IL.

Mathematical objectives integrated with art objectives can be explored through making patterns. Here, patterns are made from clay-coated Chroma paper, pasted to 13- × 13-inch stiff paper ruled into a 1-inch grid.

micks. Nevertheless, cards or craft gifts can be appropriate when they are pursued both with art concepts foremost in mind and by a teacher insisting that students push themselves beyond what they do naturally. Decorating a jean jacket for a significant friend can motivate an older student. ("Students will indicate affect through their choice of a gift recipient.")

Hex design by fourth-grade student Katherine Vickers.

Cognitive Objectives Correlated to Other Areas of Study

The topic of correlating art to the cognitive learning found in other subject areas can be anathema to art teachers in school systems where art learning is considered to be far less important than social studies, reading, math, or science. Friction also can occur when scarce art supplies, and scarcer student art-learning time, are used solely for another purpose. With the current integrated-curriculum approach, however, there is a strong movement to make art "part and parcel" of every school subject.

One example of an instructional objective that correlates science with art is: "Students will create a design, employing repetition of pattern, based on three different kinds of insects." When the art considerations are serious and fused to the theme, significant art can result. Teachers of art have succeeded in actually gaining art-learning time and qualitative art experiences for students by doing correlated art projects. Some teachers welcome correlation so long as that activity is not a substitute for formal art instruction.

Making the case that art is an area that should be part of a common, general education designed for the future nonspecialist citizen, the National Art Education Association (NAEA) recommends that there be "one hundred minutes of art class time a week in the elementary school with art taught as a subject in itself." In addition, the NAEA says that "time, space and materials should be provided for supplementary independent and individual art experiences in the regular classroom."

Mathematics, as an example, can be integrated with art through a study of tesselation as related to Escher prints, Fibonacci series to drawing sunflower heads, and hexagons and octagons to paper sculpture, snowflakes, beehive cells, Chinese lattices, and Moorish mosque tile designs from the Alhambra. Integrating academic subjects and art helps to sustain students' interest and makes their learning more enjoyable. It lets the holistic power of art knowledge permeate other areas of study. A new form of art today called *conceptual art*, or *systems art*, also does this. Two examples of art used to give insights into nature are the artist Christo's pink plastic floating islands in Miami Bay and Robert Smithson's spiral jetty in the Great Salt Lake.

One successful correlational project, Learning to Read Through the Arts, sponsored by the Guggenheim Museum and New York City Board of Education, helped students to recall with all of their senses. It involved art criticism, art production, and field trips, and it helped students to improve reading scores by 1 or 2 months for each month of involvement in the program (Kinder, 1987; O'Brien, 1978).

Another form of cognitive objective helps to focus thinking about economic ideas, such as making a living. Occupational value and economic value become of increasing concern to older students as they approach the time when they will begin to consider career options. An example of such an objective is: "Students will describe occupations that use the skills found in this lesson [for example, measuring, designing, color choices]." Examples of occupation-related discourse the teacher might encourage are: "These cards are more colorful than ones I saw at the card shop selling for over a dollar" or "Many people make their livings by being designers of items like racing automobiles and

Courtesy of Jessica Crosby, Reading for Life Project, Claiborne County, MS,
and the Mississippi Cultural Crossroads, Port Gibson, MS.

*Reading and art can augment each other. Famous quilter Hystercine Rankin passes on
quilting skills to students as they participate in the Reading for Life Literacy Program,
illustrating in quilt form their own stories inspired by the books of African-American
authors. From a theme in the book, children develop their own story, with the teacher
asking questions such as "Who, What, When, and Where."*

A first-grade student paints an illustration to a story about a dog-boy and chickens.

In this project, "Word Processing," after making a careful line drawing of an old Corona typewriter, student Eleanor Siegel then wrote a story for the background.

fashion." (See Chapters 12 and 13 for Science and Social Studies Integration ideas.)

Psychomotor and Multisensory Objectives

Moving our bodies and using other senses can stimulate art production and art criticism activities. Psychomotor and multisensory approaches also can be used for aesthetic experiences in and of themselves. Acting out a picture is one way in which kinesthetic awareness can trigger artistic awareness. One objective is that by using their bodies, students will be able to stimulate awareness of what they have perceived, such as a cat. ("How do they clean their bodies? How can we show this tongue licking the paw in our drawing?") Olfactory awareness of aromas can be a strong motivator as well. ("Sniffing a can of cinnamon, students will show in their artwork the events of which the smell of cinnamon reminds them. Show how the figures looked as they mixed ingredients, did the baking, and ate the baked goods.") A popular auditory stimulation is painting to music. ("Painting to the rhythm of *The Nutcracker Suite*, students will represent the music's measured regularity and variation in their paintings of figures in motion.") In fact, some art teachers make calm, classical music a staple feature during working periods.

Progressive children's programs at museums often use psychomotor methods to arouse interest in artworks. They have children respond nonverbally to the artworks, using their bodies and creative movement. ("Place yourself in the landscape. Move like the people shown are moving. Intuit the smells.") In the classroom, after viewing an exhibit or an art reproduction, you can have your students represent what they have seen through sounds, impromptu drama, human sculpture, and free movement. ("Students will be able to take the exact pose and facial expression of Dr. Gachet, and tell the class something that he might be thinking.")

A Sample Lesson Plan

As the art teacher uses many of the categories discussed in this chapter while writing lesson plans, students with a wide variety of learning styles, emotional needs, and life needs will become aware of the importance of serious involvement in producing quality artwork. Their spirits will be reached. A sample lesson plan containing several types of instructional objectives is presented here:

Courtesy of Yung Fu Elementary School, Tainan, Taiwan. Courtesy of Frank Wachowiak and Ted Ramsay, University Elementary School, Iowa City, IA.

Psychomotor reenactment of catching frogs may have preceded the making of this delightful watercolor painting. One color, blue, predominates. Many tints and shades of green, from blue to yellow, are used for the carefully observed leaves and frogs. The child is fortunate to have an art teacher who appreciates what children can accomplish by striving for design excellence.

Clay Dinosaurs, Primary Grades

1. Art production (specific art skills to be learned)	Students will pull head and leg forms from a ball of clay to construct a dinosaur. Students will form eyes, ears, mouths, and tails.
2. Artistic perception (where we see specific art elements in daily life)	Students will describe similar structural forms in nature, such as other animals, tree branches, tables, and post-and-lintel construction.
3. Art history (interpretation of similar artworks by artists of other times)	Students will describe animal forms shown in reproductions of Aztec pottery, tell how the legs were made, and describe the animal's expression.
4. Art criticism (discussion and interpretations of students' works)	Students will describe differences in each other's creations, identifying those which look delicate, ferocious, or strong.
5. Aesthetics (discussing ideas about art)	Students will discuss whether scary and ugly things can be art, even though some people think art should be only about what is beautiful.
6. Affective (dealing with emotional needs)	Students will describe their dinosaur's personality, how it interacts with friends or enemies that try to hurt it, whether it has any children, and what they are like.
7. Cognitive and functional (correlated to important knowledge about our world and our functioning in it)	Students will be able to match their dinosaur to photos of actual dinosaurs. Students will be able to describe how their dinosaur's diet and defense mechanisms relate to those the students use themselves.
8. Psychomotor and multisensory (dance, music, vocalization, role playing, taste, smell, hearing)	Students will mimic the sounds and movements of their dinosaur, then use these motifs to organize a dinosaur dance.

Open Objectives

Open questioning can supplement the use of instructional objectives in evaluation. Rather than focusing exclusively on the instructional objectives given at the beginning of the lesson, the teacher can help students to evaluate problems in their artwork and arrive at their own so-

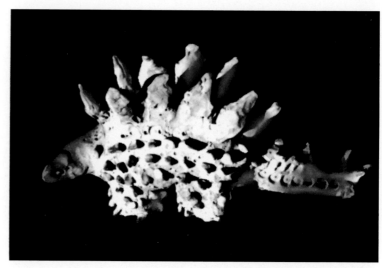

Courtesy of *Emphasis Art*, Second Edition, University Elementary School. Iowa City, IA.

Clay dinosaur, Grade 3.

lutions. For example, ask students questions like; "How do you like your picture?" "Is there some part of your picture you like best?" "Is there something that bothers you about it?" "What could you do to fix the part you don't like?"

A different type of openness also has been advocated. Instructional objective approaches have been criticized as having a hidden attitude of control and domination, and for emphasizing performing rather than thinking. Uncomfortable with the degree of specificity demanded in instructional objectives, especially when it results in describing the artistic outcomes of studio activities, Elliot Eisner (1968) has called for a more open-ended type of objective in art, which he calls *expressive objectives*. For example, "The student will use wire and wood to construct a three-dimensional form" does not specify learning outcomes or standards, only the encounter between student, materials, and goal.

Today, many school systems require clearly stated, unambiguous, sequential educational objectives along with clearly spelled-out standards for evaluation. Nevertheless, as teachers of art, which is a personal, poetic subject filled with wonder and uncertainty, we also must value and leave room for that which is open, indeterminant, and imaginative.

One example of a teacher's statement identifying and reinforcing imagination and poetic interpretation is: "Makeela's picture has a sense of mystery in it—an exciting feeling that we can't quite tell what is going to happen when the figures meet." People learn about art through continually coming back to main concepts in a holistic, contextually sensitive way. Proponents of one-dimensional curriculum goals may need to be reminded of that process.

Much quality art production by artists of all ages occurs in a state of nondirectional "play." It appears as if the artist is fiddling around, that the objective is unclear even to the creator. Allow for this "water gazing." Art education has been criticized for trying to force onto students a curriculum with predetermined contents and goals. Thus, even though school systems may require goals and instructional objectives to be spelled out, where, if not in art class, will encouragement be given for the irrational and the quirky? Where else will the mysterious, the subversive, and the unexpected be nurtured, the very elements which are necessary for our society's continuing renewal?

From Robert Clements and Lawrence Stueck, "Earthworks: A Two-Hundred Ton Art Media," *Art Education*, July 1983.

Artistic activity can occur in a state of openness, when the objective is unclear even to the creator. Allow for meditation. A mound of loose clay can provide an exciting medium for the unplanned, the unexpected, and that which is full of wonder.

Chapter 15

Art for Students Experiencing Significant Mental or Physical Disabilities

Seven Concepts

Approximately 12 percent of students in American public education are in special education programs, and they are entitled by law to art as well as other content areas of instruction. Those with mental and physical disabilities (in learning, hearing, and vision, and mobility) as well as those who use mental health services now are integrated into classrooms of children without disabilities. Every public school classroom and art teacher will deal increasingly with youths who have disabilities. Seven important concepts in the area of special education are: inclusion, people-first language, developmental disability, normalization, age-appropriateness, partial participation, and empowerment.

Inclusion

Since the passage in 1975 of Public Law 94-142, the Education for All Handicapped Children Act, *inclusion* is increasingly being implemented in regular elementary and art classrooms. The law mandates testing, individualized educational plans, parental consent, confidentiality, least restrictive environment, and educational programming for youths with developmental disabilities. Students must be served within the regular classroom unless specific social or physical barriers interfere with the child's learning. Inclusion is being implemented to the fullest extent possible. For example, in New York City, 40 percent of students facing significant mental and physical disabilities are taught in regular classes with nondisabled students.

People-First Language

In your speech, use *people-first* language. Do not say "*the* blind" or "*the* retarded," thus implying that these individuals belong in a class that is set apart; use the more respectful term, "*persons with* disabilities in seeing or learning." As another example, "persons who use a wheelchair for mobility" is more respectful than "crippled people." Do not focus on what someone cannot do, such as a child who "can't draw." Instead, focus on capability, such as a child who can "vocalize about the patterns he or she draws." Negative language continues old attitudes of exclusion and a "them vs. us" perspective. Positive language promotes positive attitudes and helps to promote independence, self-help, and community integration. Terminology changes rapidly, but at this time, the term *with disabilities* usually is preferred to *exceptional, challenged,* or *handicapped.* Even more important than terminology is attitude, such as having an attitude of acceptance and faith in the individual.

Developmental Disability

A *developmental disability* is a severe, chronic disability of a person that:

- Is attributable to a mental or physical impairment or combination thereof
- Is manifested before age 22
- Is likely to continue indefinitely
- Results in limitations in three or more areas of life activity: self-care, language, learning, mobility, self-direction, capacity for independent living, and economic self-sufficiency
- Reflects the need for long-duration, individually planned treatments.

*Facing page: Drawings depict children in a variety of art activities that build self-worth. **Left to right, top:** Construction with wood scraps from lumber yard, costumes and hats designed for a parade; paper masks. **Left to right, bottom:** Simple cardboard-and-string mobile; train engines and trucks constructed from discarded grocery cartons.*

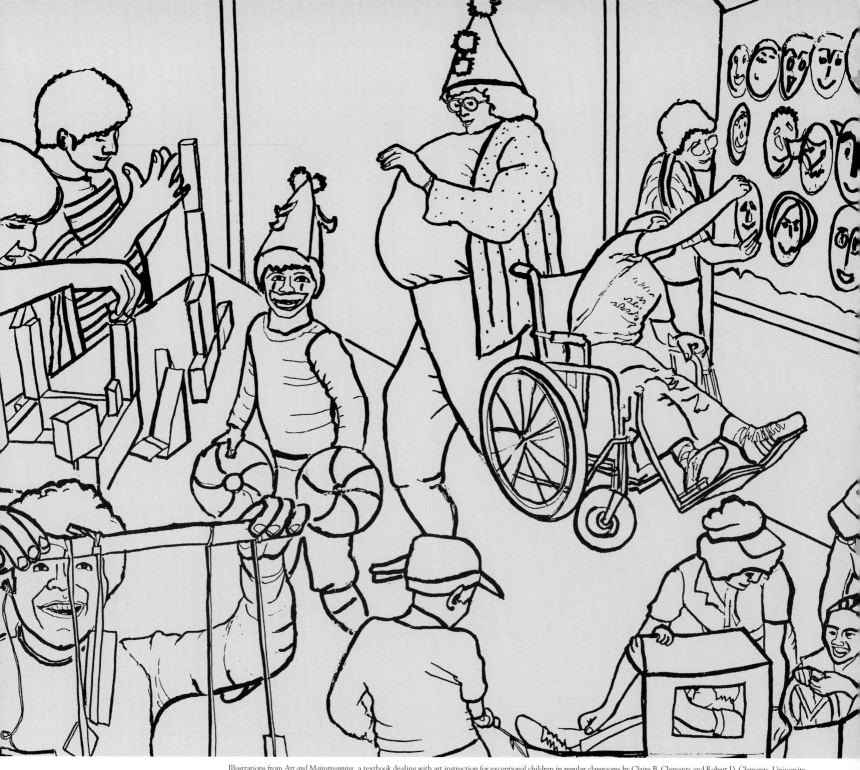

Illustrations from *Art and Mainstreaming*, a textbook dealing with art instruction for exceptional children in regular classrooms by Claire B. Clements and Robert D. Clements, University of Georgia, Athens, GA. Courtesy of Charles C Thomas Publishers, Springfield, IL.

Normalization

Normalization is the use of means as culturally normative as possible to establish personal behaviors that are as normative as possible. It does not mean that all people should be the same. It does mean that all people in a society should have, as far as possible, equal opportunity to live, work, and play. It means that students with disabilities in your art class should be treated as much like all other students as possible.

Age-Appropriateness

A concept related to normalization is *age-appropriateness*. Teachers of art frequently have been criticized for having older special education students do activities that are deemed to be "babyish." Strive to keep your choice of topics and media age-appropriate. For example, do not have older students do pudding painting; instead, use an adult material such as paper pulp. Test whether an activity is too childlike by asking yourself whether nonhandicapped persons of the same age would want to do it. When using art materials such as crayons, which some people may associate with primary school, emphasize how they have been used by famous artists, such as Picasso. (This is a good strategy even for persons without disabilities.)

Partial Participation

Keep in mind the principle of *partial participation*. Is there some way in which the student with a disability could participate in the lesson? Perhaps a student without language could hold up the art reproduction that the class discusses. A student without sight could work with another child in cleaning the paintbrushes with soap. Even if a student cannot do all of the steps in a process, you or another student can arrange for the individual to do those that he or she can. The child may need longer to do a certain step, however, so the sequence may need to be changed.

Empowerment

Another concept is that of *empowerment*. It is very easy for helpers to "overdo" for individuals with disabilities. In fact, many children both with and without disabilities are masters at geting extra services from adults, using the familiar refrain of "You draw it for me." By thus disempowering students, teachers do not help them. To foster independent achievement, the less teacher assistance, the better.

Printing designs and shapes with potatoes, sponges, and erasers provides an unusual experience in aesthetic discrimination and fine-motor coordination. In addition, the decorative patterns that result can then be used for gift wrap, for greeting cards, and for covering boxes.

Teaching Approaches

For most children in elementary and middle school, the guidelines for teaching art proposed in this book should prove to be adaptable and effective. For children with special needs, however, other teaching strategies may be needed. This chapter provides some practical approaches to help teachers meet the challenge. First, the good news: the art class or studio atmosphere is the best of all possible environments in which to work with children having developmental disabilities. Each child is accepted, and his or her potential is respected. Each child can excel in some way, and every child can be an achiever.

The importance of the teacher and his or her role cannot be stressed enough in the context of teaching children with special needs. All attributes of the dedicated teacher that we have spelled out so far—sympathy, knowledge, tact, confidence, resourcefulness, understanding, equanimity, and patience—are doubly important in the successful management of a classroom that includes students with disabilities. Precedence, if any, must be given to the qualities of understanding and patience.

General Strategies

Some general strategies for teachers who are experiencing inclusion for the first time are:

1. Accept the children as they are.
2. Familiarize yourself with the handicaps of special children assigned to your class. Use the student's out-of-school interests as guides for suitable activities.
3. Ascertain if a progress chart has been recorded on the students by a previous teacher. Note the art experiences and projects with which they have been successful.
4. Help the parents to promote the child's life-enriching recreation and leisure skills by communicating with them what art materials the child enjoys using. Suggest art and hobby materials they might acquire for use in the home, as well as community arts class offerings.
5. If teacher aides are assigned to help you with the special students in your class, involve them appropriately. Do not let the aide sit idle, but more importantly, do not let an oversolicitous aide do the project for the individuals.
6. Keep your own progress report on every child with disabilities. In a few school systems, the art teacher must write and implement individualized educational plans (IEPs) for each student with developmental disabilities.
7. Consider carefully your teaching procedures for special students. Will you use free-choice projects, in which children choose their own subject matter, materials, and time limits? Will you employ the unit or project method, in which the same art activity is planned for students both with and without disabilities? The latter usually calls for individual adjustments to meet the needs and abilities of the student with disabilities.
8. Ask the child if there is something that could be done to facilitate his or her participation in the activity. ("How can we make it easier for you to do the project?")
9. Enlist the aid of students without disabilities in the class, especially those with proven abilities and stable, pleasant personalities, to help their classmates with disabilities.
10. Above all, do not permit the children to participate in copying or tracing artwork. Help them to create their own imagery, even though this imagery may differ from that of the students without disabilities. Even when children's graphic expression consists of scribbles, they have feeling for the patterns their marks make. They have made something that did not exist before in the world.

Knox Wilkinson, *an artist with mild mental challenge, has successfully shown his work in museums throughout the nation and world. He is involved in efforts to help others achieve through art, and his design of two birds here is an announcement for a Very Special Art Exhibition.*

Specific Classroom Strategies

Here are some specific teaching strategies and tactics to follow in working with students who have developmental disabilities. Keep in mind that even if the students with disabilities have above-average IQs, they probably will require some nontraditional teaching strategies and adaptation of materials.

Learning Disorders or Hyperactivity

Try to create a calm, ordered environment. Limit opportunities for choice, and keep materials few. Deemphasize group activities. Give immediate reinforcement. Heed when the child may get close to losing control, and change the situation before that point is reached. Working with a quiet, mature student or in a carrel may help the child to concentrate. Try to create seating arrangements and projects that encourage staying in the seat—for example, looking at art history books while seated in a beanbag chair.

At all times proceed deliberately, methodically, and calmly. Give directions or instructions slowly and clearly, using simple language at a

Projects that may be undertaken successfully with children with some kinds of special needs. **Top:** *Three-dimensional animals constructed with folded and cut tagboard.* **Bottom:** *Stabile constructed out of found materials.*

rate that the children can assimilate. Make sure, if possible, that you have the child's attention when explaining something.

Make eye contact as you address the students. Sit on a chair or stool so that your face will be nearer to the child's eye level. Do not address the class while facing the chalkboard or standing in the glare from a window.

Demonstrate more, and talk less. Employ visual symbols and models. Speak in a modulated tone of voice. For youths with attention deficits, make the teaching materials colorful.

Prepare lessons to meet specific needs—hand-eye coordination, fine or gross motor-skills improvement—and to meet identifiable objectives such as color or shape naming.

Vision Deficiencies
Employ media that help them to achieve success. For example, for those who supplement vision with touch, use large, contrasting (black-and-white) sheets of paper. Some students will prefer tinted paper, which minimizes glare. Broad-line markers of vivid colors and brightly colored crayons are preferable to markers and crayons of more subdued values. Some media, such as glue-line prints, will leave a raised line that can be felt. Black paint can be added to white glue for drawing on white paper, and a raised line will be left when dry. Other techniques, such as printing on plastic-foam meat trays and drawing on heavy aluminum foil with a dull pencil, will leave a recessed line. Art media that make noise, such as squeaky brayers and markers, or that smell, such as scented markers and paste, can add interest. Figures sculptures of pipe cleaners or clay can be used to emphasize good posture. Topics such as "a call for help" can foster the expression of feelings, and making texture maps and box sculptures can foster the individual's concept of oneself as a person capable of moving around the home and community. Consistently keeping supplies in the same place helps students with vision deficiencies to easily find what they need. For students with partial vision, light shows can use colored gels and projectors.

Neurological and Orthopedic Disabilities
Borders, boundaries, and holding devices may help. Plastic meat trays can serve to contain clay and small objects, and cafeteria trays can be clamped with a C-clamp to a wheelchair work surface. Masking or duct tape can be used to tape down water containers and to tape brushes to hands. Individuals with severe limitations in movement can pull a string to move a mobile and make patterns in salt, sugar, or millet on a colorful tray. Carving blocks of balsa wood with a rasp can provide both exercise and an art experience. Papier maché can be pressed into a greased mold to create sculptural forms.

Hearing Disabilities
Emphasize projects to help overcome self-consciousness (self-portraits) and insecurity (working with a buddy on a joint project). Encourage their use of residual hearing (sitting on a wooden floor and banging on

a drum, painting to music) and development of language (staging plays with puppets, masks, and model grocery stores).

Mental Disabilities

Strive for projects that are both age-appropriate and ability-appropriate. Repeat instructions and procedures over and over again. In a word, overteach! Plan projects that may be broken down into sequential, manageable, and explainable steps. For example, there are four stages in creating a collage: the drawing stage, the cutting or tearing stage, the pasting stage, and the matting stage. Allow sufficient time for the completion of each stage, and do not begin a new one until the previous stage has been completed.

Behavioral Disorders

Art media should offer active resistance (linocuts, carving). The project should imply monetary value (glazed ceramics, leather work, crafts), and tools should be manual arts tools (hammers, gouges). The project should have three dimensions. Use unexpected rewards, such as displaying artwork outside the principal's office. Let the child arrange a bulletin board, pronounce the art vocabulary words, or sketch a tray of toy figures. Emphasize experiences that deal with kinesthetic manipulation and multisensory stimulation.

Emphasize the fundamentals of art as critical guideposts in visual expression; for example, identify basic shapes and colors. Also, emphasize the awareness of environment and space.

Be aware of the difficulty for students with disabilities to tolerate changes in routines, that some are easily distracted and have short attention spans, and that many will require constant praise and support. Brief, one-session projects demanding minimum memory recall may be suitable for some students. Also, remember that like all students, those with disabilities respond more enthusiastically when their art experiences are successful.

Using Art for Community and School Integration

Persons with disabilities are not a separate group from the community at large. They are citizens with the rights of all citizens. Congress has passed the Americans with Disabilities Act, guaranteeing these individuals rights to equity in employment, housing, and community services. Some ways the art program can promote positive community attitudes are:

Photo: William Bengston

From "The Problem with Martin Ramirez," *Clarion*, Winter 1986. Collection of Gladys Nillson and Jim Nutt.

Famous Hispanic-American artist Martin Ramirez hid his artwork behind the radiators in the mental institution where he spent his adult life, until the artistic power and rhythm of his works were discovered by an art teacher.

Encourage these students to participation in community activities so that they may see themselves as, and be seen by others as, active members of the community. Especially involve them in activities about their own cultural heritage.

Be alert to opportunities such as art exhibitions for persons with disabilities. A Pilot Club or similar civic organization in your community or state may sponsor activities in which your students could receive recognition. Make arrangements for these students to go on trips to community art openings and art festivals.

If a Very Special Arts Festival is held in your community, be sure that your students with special needs can participate, either by just attending or exhibiting their work or, even better, by putting on an activity. For information on starting such a festival in your community, talk to your school system's special education coordinator, or write to that organization at the Kennedy Center in Washington, D.C.

Display the students' work attractively to show your approval and elicit supporting response from their peers. Remember that their projects, which may differ in appearance of the art of students without disabilities, can bring pride to the school, delight to parents and visitors, and an enhanced sense of self-worth to the participating students.

Ascertain if the student, parents, or caregivers are being served by community organizations whose purpose is to provide support for them. For example, perhaps there is a support group in your community for young people requiring mental health services. Many communities have a quasi-governmental, centralized resource with a name like "Help Line" or "Community Connection" that puts people in touch with social service agencies and support groups. Certain community service organizations may provide special equipment as well. (For example, the Lions Club offers services to people with vision difficulties.)

Be an active advocate for accessibility. When setting up art exhibitions, have certain pieces designated for touching. Have labels for individuals who need large-print formats at the proper height. Be aware of alternative forms of communication, such as braille and Blissboards (boards with pictures to which a person points to communicate). Art teachers have helped children without speech to draw their own "talking books."

Experiences That May Appeal to Students Facing Physical or Mental Disabilities

Painting
Cutting
Pasting
Beach balls
Opening packages
Printmaking (with vegetables and found objects)
Big cardboard cartons to hide and play in and transform into vehicles
Toys
Construction (wood, boxes, found objects)
Meat-tray boats
Weaving
Balloons
Fingerpainting
"Keep-a-secret" progressive figure drawing
Pets and animals
Flowers and trees
Dressing up, costumes, and uniforms
Kinesthetic activities
Decorating the classroom
Puppets
Piñatas
Fanciful hats
Marching and parading
Fish in aquariums
Clowns
Making music with assorted concocted instruments
Bright colors in paper, cloth, yarn, cellophane, and ribbons
Noisemakers and horns
Modeling mixtures
Singing
Masks
Face make-up
Drums
Pantomime
Painting to music
Use of mirrors
Mobiles
Kaleidoscopes
Kites

Materials

Be aware of the many specialized devices, tools, and materials now used in art classes by children with significant physical disabilities. The school's special education coordinator may be able to help you in requisitioning materials for your students such as:

Four-holed scissors that both student and teacher can manipulate simultaneously

Fat-handled brushes (1- or 2-inches wide) or brushes that have handles wrapped with masking or surgical tape to provide a better grip.

Giant color crayons, felt-nib markers (water-based); kindergarten-size pencils with soft lead

Glue sticks (which may be easier to use than squeeze bottles of white glue)

Painting stretchers assembled together and placed on desk around the perimeter of the in-process projects so that students can judge their work's boundaries; other possibilities are plastic meat trays and cafeteria trays

C-clamps and duct or masking tape to hold artwork onto wheelchair trays; specially designed art boards for wheelchairs

Duct tape for taping brushes to hands

Forehead pointers

Mouth wands or rubber spatulas with brushes or markers taped to them

Posters and instructional signs with giant-size letters and numerals

Cameras and computers adapted for special use by those with disabilities in vision, movement, and coordination

Touch table, touch box

Flannel boards and pegboards

Building blocks in assorted shapes and sizes

Magnifying glasses and colored gelatins

Wood or plastic colored beads and sticks in assorted sizes

For additional found or recycled materials useful in art classes, see Appendix A.

Chapter 16

Giftedness and Its Art Implications for All Students

Giftedness and Art Thinking

This chapter discusses giftedness in general, relates general-intelligence approaches to artistic giftedness, gives strategies for the teacher, and offers suggestions for outreach into the school, home, and community. Admission into a school's gifted programs often requires a score on the Stanford Binet Intelligence Test of 120 to 130 points as well as teacher recommendations, high grades, and acceptance by a review committee. Some experts feel the intelligence test is overly weighted toward skills in math and reading comprehension, with areas such as art ability going unmeasured.

One alternative to the IQ test is the Torrance Test of Creative Thinking, which considers four aspects of creativity: fluency, flexibility, elaboration, and originality. For all children, these desirable characteristics can be nurtured through talking with them as they create their pictures. Examples include:

Fluency: "How many can you show?"
Flexibility: "Can you think of another way to look at it?"
Elaboration: "Can we tell about this in more detail?"
Originality: "Make it your *own* way, and show the special idea that you have."

Another way to look at intelligence comes from Harvard psychologist Howard Gardner, who does not believe that there is one, monolithic kind of intelligence. Instead, he describes seven distinct forms of intelligence or ways of "information processing" (1990):

- Language
- Logical and mathematical
- Interpersonal (knowledge about other people)
- Musical
- Spatial
- Bodily-kinesthetic
- Intrapersonal (information about oneself)

Gardner does not consider artistic thinking to be a separate form of intelligence. Instead, any of the seven forms can be directed to artistic or nonartistic ends. For example, language ability can be used by a poet or a lawyer. Kinesthetic ability can be used by a dancer or a surgeon. Spatial ability can be used by a sculptor or a sailor. You can bring these concepts into your classroom for all students in the following ways:

- Language intelligence can be related to art through discussions of art criticism, art history, and aesthetics. Encourage students to give their artwork a title and to write about it.
- Knowledge of one's own feelings (intrapersonal knowledge) can be given expression by discussing the meaning of one's own art, or of masterpieces, and by considering questions of aesthetics.
- Knowledge of other people (interpersonal knowledge) can be shown by empathetically discussing the art of others. Students can give encouragement to peers for their art and depict interpersonal relationships in their own.
- Mathematical intelligence can be related to art through the study of geometric forms such as icosahedra in three-dimensional constructions, fractal geometry in computer art, linear perspective, and topological surfaces in mapmaking and Escher prints.
- Musical intelligence can be related to art through painting while listening to music, creating music to accompany a certain painting, (such as Moussorgsky's "Paintings at an Exhibition") and studying how various cultures have expressed themselves through music and art.

Courtesy of Baiba Kuntz, Glencoe, IL.

Fifth-grade student Kristen Richardson paints her imaginary bird. A branch in bud and one bird are silhouetted against the full moon while another watches after a nest of eggs and a hatchling. School has ended for the year; everyone has gone home for the summer, and two gifted students paint on, intent on finishing their tempera birds. Pride can be taken in the finished artwork.

Sky and Water, 1938, woodcut, M. C. Escher, (1898-1972). National Gallery of Art, Washington, D.C., Cornelius Van S. Roosevelt Collection.

In this M. C. Escher print, the dark bird shape is transformed into water. The white fish changes into sky. Although Escher was a poor math student, his prints showing transformations from two- to three-dimensions have been hailed as having much significance, especially for mathematicians. Today, students in math classes often create their own similar transformation designs.

- Spatial intelligence is the area that is related most closely to visual art. It can be cultivated by ways of creating and analyzing space in art, especially in architecture and sculpture, but also in all art ideas dealing with space—for example, perspective.

Characteristics of Students Gifted in Art

In the qualitative approach to art, all students are encouraged to develop many of the characteristics possessed by persons talented in art. Talented students have greater persistence and are able to work both longer and with greater concentration. Pleasure is sought by encountering problems, which stimulate these individuals. They can become absorbed for hours in a medium, and they derive deep, personal satisfaction from their involvement in art. Some or all of the following characteristics are true of people gifted in art. These students:

- First reveal giftedness through their very early drawings, and may develop a personal style of representation early in their school years.
- Use a greater amount of detail, pattern, and texture in their artwork than most children. Some of this elaboration is observed and some imagined.
- Possess a richer store of images and ideas from which to draw, heightened by their acute observation.
- Often possess a photographic mind, with vivid recall of events engaged in or observed that distinguishes their efforts, which are characterized by a richness of details.
- Master certain technical aspects of drawing—perspective, foreshortening, volume, shading, overlapping, spatial handling, movement—much sooner than their peers.
- May choose subjects of fantasy, with complex themes involving intricate structures and a host of participants, for their art compositions.
- Are receptive to new media, techniques, and tools.
- Show great interest in the art world and the lives of contemporary artists and craftspeople. They often visit art museums on a regular basis and sometimes carry a sketchbook to record their impressions.
- Rather than merely reacting to occurrences in the world, their creativity leads them to take a proactive stance toward it.
- Learn quickly to employ the vocabulary of art both effectively and confidently and to criticize and evaluate their art production for design.
- Usually prefer drawing, painting, printmaking, and collage to step-by-step craftwork.
- Use color imaginatively, making up their own palette by combining the hues provided to the class.
- Are oblivious to distractions when engaged in their art, and often resent interference.
- Generally are highly self-motivated and engage in art on their own—after school, at home, and even during other classes.

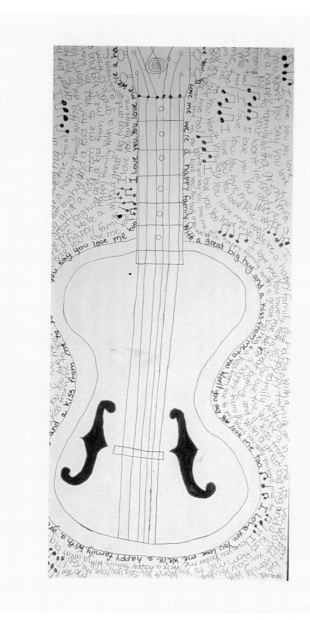

Courtesy of Joyce Vroon, Trinity School, Atlanta, GA.

Left: One way that musical ability and interests can be integrated with art is by drawing musical instruments. Fifth-grade student Courtney Clinkscales carefully draws an electric guitar and then outlines it in bands of alternating, vibrating colors. **Right:** After drawing a guitar, Tyler Grubb adds his own song lyrics, written around the guitar's outline in successive rows.

Courtesy of Baiba Kuntz, Glencoe, IL.

Seventh-grade student Beth Savitsky rendered this abstract face and figure in acrylic paints after studying Miro's use of fantasy. Note the secondary colors and the graduated purple background.

Saga Prefecture, Kyushu Island, Japan.

These fish drawings are by primary-grade children. What imaginations these youngsters possess to invent and elaborate so skillfully.

Teaching Strategies

The teacher can encourage gifted students by providing a supportive environment. Students feel this is more important than any instruction they receive. Overpraise is to be avoided, however, because it can lead to peer resentment.

A good approach is the minimal one of letting the student alone to follow his or her special direction—in effect, *underteaching*. The teacher

Collection of Frank Wachowiak.

A superb pen-and-ink drawing of lush foliage by a gifted sixth-grade Japanese girl.

can provide challenges through multimedia techniques and subject-matter assignments that demand imaginative solutions and interpretations. For example, an assignment might be to depict a famous person, when young, experiencing the first intimations of her or his future role in life. While teachers should provide challenges, on no account should the gifted child be rushed into advanced forms of expression.

Letting the child pursue his or her own endeavors may pose problems for the teacher who uses the project method, in which all students in class engage in the same subject-matter assignment using the same technique. To allow gifted children the special privilege of working on their own subject choice, at their own pace, while their classmates are required to stay with the assigned project is not recom-

Gifted students can stretch the possibilities of the assigned project to the fullest. A middle school student did this colorful simulated mosaic employing cut and torn colored paper for the tesserae. Note the gradations of blue in the harbor's water. The subject is Sakura-jima Park, with a view of an erupting volcano on a nearby island. Kagoshima, Japan.

mended. A wiser procedure is to challenge gifted children to stretch the possibilities of the assigned project or theme to the fullest. Remind gifted students there are many moments outside of class when they can soar creatively and imaginatively in subjects of their own choosing, and encourage them to share with you some of those outside efforts.

Extending into the School, Home, and Community

The teacher can foster students' creative growth not only in the art class but also in the school at large, the home, and the community. Find ways to extend art activities into the community and the individual's ongoing daily life. Community integration may be especially helpful to creative students because of their tendency to be more socially reserved, aloof, and distanced. They also are more questioning, skeptical, and opinionated. People may express negative attitudes to them, and both peers and adults may think of some as silly and perceive them as smart alecks.

To foster the creative and social growth of talented students, consider forming a club or an organization for your gifted students, who might find kindred spirits in such a group. Together, they can discuss and share their artwork and go to special events, such as museum openings. They can contribute artistically to the school's special functions, perhaps by painting a set for an assembly program. Middle school youths can be organized into a chapter of the National Art Education Association's National Junior Art Honor Society. Provide gifted students with role models from diverse cultural backgrounds and both genders, because males *and* females need role models with whom to identify. Do not enter elementary and middle school children's art into competitions, however, because such external competitions can undermine creative interest and performance. For the one child who is reinforced by a prize, 10 or 100 children will have confidence in their nascent ability undermined. Especially shun coloring contests of pictures drawn by adults.

The home environment is extremely important in encouraging creativity. At a parent conference, share with the child's parents your notice of his or her special giftedness. Direct parents' awareness toward community children's art-enrichment programs. An art specialist with hundreds of students each year might use a letter to parents to give notice of artistic giftedness and offer suggestions for how to nurture it. An example of such a letter would be:

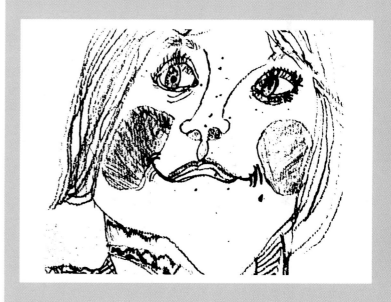

Courtesy of Sharon Burns-Knutson, Cedar Rapids, IA.

The teacher of art should call parents' attention to gifted students' abilities so that the children may receive enrichment instruction and the gift be nurtured. Gifted first-grade children have produced these detailed contour-line drawings. They reveal once again what youngsters are capable of achieving in drawing skills when they are encouraged to become aware. First-grade children can notice jewelry details, barrettes, freckles, eyeglass hinges, creases of skin around the eyes and at the mouth's sides, even the oval on the upper lip below the nose and the wrinkles in the lips.

To the Parents or Guardians of _____ :

Teaching at Anniston and Mayberry Elementary Schools for the past 2 years, I have had the opportunity to observe the art achievement of over a thousand students. You probably are already aware of your child's giftedness in art; however, I felt it to be my professional responsibility to bring to your attention my notice of and appreciation for the quality work your child does in art. As a general trait, artistic giftedness in children is shown by their being able to concentrate longer, having a lot of ideas to express, and including a lot of detail to make their drawings more elaborate. They are more self-directed, draw more realistically earlier than other children, and use art materials more creatively.

Some talented children have profited from several art-enrichment programs in our community. Although as a school employee I cannot endorse any one program, I wanted to bring their existence to your attention if you wish to look into their suitability in meeting your child's needs:

Mayberry Recreation Department, Lyndon House Art Center, classes for children ages 4–12, Tuesdays and Thursdays, 3:30 to 5:30 PM, 10 sessions, cost of $20 a term. The YMCA has art classes for members, Saturday, 10–12 AM. Alachua County Junior College has a gifted program on Saturday mornings that sometimes has classes focusing on the arts (546-9990). Private art teachers of whom I am aware in the community are Martha Menendez, 546-7783, and James Jackson, 543-3454. In addition, there are probably more programs of which I am unaware.

Please call me at school at 543-9087 (between 2:30 and 3:30 PM is best) or at home at 548-4543 (between 7 and 8 PM) if I can be of help to you about how we might work together to further your child's artistic creativity.

Art Teacher, Anniston and Mayberry Elementary Schools

Teachers who discover talented children are fortunate. They witness what children can do in art when they extend themselves to their fullest potential. Teachers can derive clues from the creative solutions that gifted children employ to help them motivate other classmates. What teachers see and learn from the characteristics and working habits of talented children is what they emphasize in a qualitative art program. They see keen, sensitive observation; rich imagination; persistence, patience, and concentration; and above all, art that is engaged in by the child both seriously and purposefully.

Part 3

Art Appreciation, Art History, Art Criticism, and Aesthetics

Previous page: *Almost all young people can identify with the dilemma represented in this painting; that choices must be made about which of our personal interests will receive uppermost attention. Painted in 1794, Angelica Kaufmann's* Self-portrait Hesitating between the Arts of Music and Painting *shows a young woman whose body seems to want to go in one direction and whose head seems to want to go toward the conflicting direction. The Muse of Music and the young accomplished musician tenderly hold hands, while her other hand seeks the palette and the Muse of Painting points to a higher calling.*

Chapter 17

New Approaches to Art Appreciation

Today, children have infinitely more opportunities to see and appreciate art than ever before. Our burgeoning museums and art centers open their doors to all, and colorful murals now enliven countless urban walls. Municipal buildings, subways, and airports display a variety of commissioned art, and magazines feature articles on art. Many colorfully illustrated books on art are published. Reproductions of art also are available at fairly reasonable prices. School textbooks in social studies and literature often are filled with colorful, correlative art visuals, and art councils in the 50 states promote art festivals, exhibits, and "artists-in-the-schools" programs.

Despite the opportunities to appreciate art that abound in the world about them, many children receive minimal training in learning how to do, think about, and talk about art. They leave school programs intimidated by museums and art galleries. They feel that serious discussions of art ideas are something in which they have no business participating. They think that the study of art criticism, art history, and aesthetics is something reserved for those going on for higher education. They have not grasped that art is not merely a way *to respond* to the world; it is a way of investigating the world and its meanings and values.

Our nation cannot afford to cut off so many of our citizens from art appreciation. *Toward Civilization*, an influential report of the National Endowment for the Arts (1988), described this situation:

> The arts are in triple jeopardy: they are not viewed as serious; knowledge . . . is not viewed as a prime objective; and those who determine school curricula do not agree on what arts education is.

Some educators believe that the activities of thinking and talking about art can give a new intellectual dimension to art appreciation, and they believe that fully implementing these activities would allow art to be accorded a higher place in the school curriculum.

Art Appreciation in the Schools: From Picture Study to Discipline-Based Art Education

The idea that students should study art masterworks and be given instruction in art appreciation is not new. In the midnineteenth century, the art historian Winkelman advised artists to dip their brushes in intellect. At that time in America, a new and distinctly American art was being advocated, one that would be pure, moral, and earnest—an alliance of art, religion, and nature. Educating the child's artistic eye was considered to be an integral part of moral and social education. At the end of that century, the "schoolroom decoration movement" worked to accomplish this by bringing plaster casts of antique sculptures into classrooms. Sepia art reproductions with a patriotic, religious, and moralistic orientation came into the public schools through the "picture study movement." From 1910 to 1920, this movement brought art prints into the schools. These pictures were filled with literary associations on which students could speculate. Works by artists such as Rosa Bonheur, Jean-François Millet, Raphael, and Winslow Homer were deemed to be suitable for young, impressionable minds, and some of these prints, such as E. G. Leutze's *Washington Crossing the Delaware*, still hang in school hallways today.

During the 1920s, formal design elements gained more attention. This was spurred by interest in art movements such as cubism, Roger Fry's writings in aesthetics, and Arthur Wesley Dow's art education writings, which focused on the elements of line, value, and color. During the mid-1950s, four-color printing of large-size art reproductions and 35-mm slides and slide projectors made it possible for masterpieces to be shown in the classroom.

Federal educational legislation also helped. The U.S. Office of Education, through its Arts and Humanities Program, sponsored programs and conferences on how to improve art education. Funds from a booming "Great Society" economy and federal educational enrichment programs (such as the Elementary and Secondary Education Act of 1965) purchased prints and slides for school libraries, social studies classes, art classes, and elementary classrooms. Innovative librarians, teachers, and administrators who sought enrichment sources realized the educational power of such reproductions. Major art museums throughout the nation printed inexpensive reproductions, and the National Gallery of Art made available a lending program to public schools for art slides, reproductions, filmstrips, and films.

Parallel with the development of printing technology and school enrichment programs was that in the nation's colleges and universities of the disciplines of art history, art criticism, and aesthetics. Art educators looked at their own discipline and analyzed the elements in its structure. Some argued that art history and criticism were disciplines equally as valid as the actual creation of art. Hence, since the 1950s, national art education conference programs have addressed the question of how to incorporate art history and criticism into school art programs. University-level art texts made the case that art education's primary goal is to help students see art's role in giving meaning to human endeavor and in meeting daily living needs. Aesthetic education's goal was not only to teach students how to experience the arts for their inherent values and delight but contribute to the students' general store of perceptions and concepts. The older term *art appreciation* came to be looked on merely as implying peripheral knowledge. Newer terms, such as *art criticism, aesthetics,* and *aesthetic education,* began to be used more widely.

Foundations took an interest in fostering school programs emphasizing a cognitive approach to art through art criticism, art history, and aesthetics. In 1982, the Getty Center for Education in the Arts was created to investigate the feasibility of having nonspecialist teachers and art teachers, in general classroom settings, teach students skills in the areas of art criticism, art history, and aesthetics side by side with the teaching of art creation. The director of the Getty Center wrote: "If art education is to become a meaningful part of the curriculum, its content must be broadened and its requirements made more rigorous." In 1984, Dwaine Greer gave this movement the label *discipline-based art education (DBAE),* by which it has come to be known. Its proponents stressed the need for balance among the four subdisciplines: art history, art criticism, aesthetics, and art production. The curriculum guides of several states have spelled out the content of art in a similar way.

While many art educators from the mid-1960s and after agreed on the importance of these endeavors, concern was also voiced regarding if, how, when, and to what degree such activities should supplant or supplement studio activities. Some worried that DBAE could have the effect of suffocating students' artistic creativity, because it emphasizes academic disciplines in which students might have little or no interest without a foundation of experience with art production. Others believed that DBAE did not account for many important functions of art, such as for healing, celebration, social protest, personal transformation, spiritual growth, exploration of the subconscious, and sheer play. Still others objected to the tacit assumption of DBAE that other approaches were fragmented and broken.

Over the past 30 years, this textbook, *Emphasis Art,* has been a strong voice emphasizing the importance of serious, qualitative studio involvement. We believe that studio involvement—thinking and problem-solving in the media themselves—is primary and central. The view of children as innate artists seeking expression, communication, and self-discovery and having confidence in their own creativity and inventiveness can be threatened by overemphasizing academic study.

During the early years of this century, the "father of child art," Franz Cizek, taught that a child understands and enjoys art only to the extent that the child has acquired that understanding through personal efforts. Many art educators today believe that studio art is fundamental to the other disciplines, which are derivative. They believe that studio art production represents the idea of the artist in general education and that it should precede academic training in disciplines such as art history and criticism.

Thus, there continues to be a healthy professional debate on topics and emphasis in art education. This text offers the following sequential approach for aesthetic activities over the years:

- In the early grades, the students should take delight in the aesthetic qualities of objects made by humans and in nature.
- In grades 4 to 6, academic learning should center on the perception of artworks.
- In grades 7 to 9, academic learning should center on the acquisition of knowledge of art history.

Below 10 years of age, production activities should always be central. This should be a time when children have hands-on involvement with the media. Especially during these early years, it is helpful to keep in mind this balance: do not give more to the mind than to the hand. When students are doing perceptual, critical, and historical activities, they should be closely related to, and whenever possible emerge from, the students' artwork.

Talking about pictures can develop thinking about art and life. The painting Road to Eternity is by America's most famous folk artist, Reverend Howard Finster. Why do you think he painted the mountains with sad expressions? Why do you think the artist put pyramids in the background? Is writing all over a picture okay for an artist to do? How can we put the ideas in which we believe into our art?

General Methods for Art Discussions

Socratic Questioning

In leading discussions about art, a preferred method is the Socratic, because it promotes the birth of ideas. The Socratic method consists of asking questions to make people think, and then contesting the answers. It prompts them to give reasons for their statements, asks them to disprove alternative explanations, and encourages them to generalize about their ideas. The interpretation of an artwork or thoughts about an aesthetic concept are, and always will be, issues that should be contested in this way. One good way to promote discussion is by asking students "What's wrong with this picture?" This question facilitates students' putting forth their criteria, which then can be debated. Avoid questions that get one-word answers, such as "This is an impressionistic painting, isn't it?" Instead, ask open questions, such as "Why do you think this is an impressionistic painting?" Encourage the students to make inferences, generalize, analyze, and synthesize.

Besides Socratic questioning, some other discussion strategies are:

- Arranging the room for discussions
- Leading discussions
- Focusing discussions
- Keeping discussions concise
- Relating to the students' conceptual stage
- Choosing topics that relate to children's developmental preferences
- Promoting confidence in thinking and talking about art

Arranging the Room for Art Discussions

The environment—the climate for viewing the artwork—can help or hinder discussions. If possible, arrange the seating to provide each child with an up-front advantage. To see the reproduction up close, rearrange the chairs into a circle, or seat the children on the floor. Invite the children to come up to the displayed art object and point out the area or detail they wish to discuss. A shy child might be asked to come up front to stand and hold the reproduction. A spotlight on the reproduction can focus students' attention. Avoid reproductions that are too small for class viewing purposes; instead, these can be used for small group discussions.

Leading Discussions

Discussion-leading skill is essential to elicit contributions by many students. Leading discussions can be difficult, especially in large classes and those containing students with behavioral problems. Some will want to monopolize the discussion, interrupting each other and talking over each other. Others will talk so quietly they cannot be heard and, by the softness and slowness of their speech, invite interruptions. We must keep in check those verbose, verbally domineering students who by monopolizing a discussion prevent participation by quiet, shy students. It sometimes is necessary to respond to, or even to interrupt, a monopolizer by saying, "John is saying . . . and we'll discuss this aspect later, but now I'd like to know what some of the people who haven't yet shared their ideas have been thinking about the idea of . . . [whether muscles need to be drawn to make a good figure drawing]." Through both planned and extemporaneous questioning, you can make art discussions truly exciting and rewarding for every child in your class. Make it a time not just to contemplate but to interact dynamically with classmates and the art object.

Focusing Discussions

A discussion can go awry if it is not kept clearly focused. Most children enjoy talking avidly about their experiences and reactions. There is no difficulty in getting them to express themselves vocally about the art that you to show them; the main problem is to keep them on the subject, or "on track." If the discussion appears unfocused to the students, too wide-ranging to be helpful to their thinking and acting, they will tune it out. Use your statements to keep the discussion on one central issue. Try not to let it diverge. For example, you might say, "This is a related idea, and an important one for us to discuss another day, but for today let's see if we can focus on the question of. . . "

Be sure, however, to be open to the idea that curricula need not be imposed from above but can arise spontaneously from the students. Avoid overdetermining the lesson. It builds students' autonomy and feelings of empowerment when they are allowed to take control of some situations.

Keeping Discussions Concise

Another goal is to keep the discussion concise. Stimulate the raising of issues, but stop the discussion before interest dissipates. Conciseness is important, because so little time is allowed for art in the school schedule. Some students in art classes think of art time as "a time when they get to make things" and resent other activities that seem to be tangential. Keep your art discussions from being long-winded and boring. There are exceptional teachers, however, who can keep large audiences of students vitally engrossed for over an hour analyzing and talking about just one reproduction.

Relating to the Students' Conceptual Stage

In motivating artistic expression, make sure that some of the historical artworks presented are appropriate for the children's conceptual and developmental stage (see Chapters 4 to 7). This does not mean that only pictures of scribbles should be shown to scribblers; however, it does mean that artworks in a range that the child is comfortable with should be presented. In this way, you do not frighten the students into feeling inadequate, raising in their minds fears that their artwork will be woefully weak. Students should not feel that the teacher's expectations are unattainable. Using artworks that are visually and conceptually accessible can assist the student in seeing alternative and attainable solutions that they can implement.

Artistic activity is a universal human attribute. Nothing in our society more effectively subverts and extinguishes artistic activity than the notion that the artistic product should be a copy of reality or someone else's version of reality. For this reason, it often is best to show historical examples as reinforcement *after* a student has reached a new conceptual and visual stage.

Choosing Topics That Relate to Children's Developmental Preferences

When choosing reproductions and slides for study and appreciation, consider the natural preferences of the children. Paintings with realistic subject matter to which students can relate usually are more popular with upper elementary children. Subject matter is the primary factor in young children's preferences, and there are strong differences between boys' and girls' preferences. Negative attitudes are expressed toward abstract works and those showing objects they do not like, such as still lifes of dead fish and birds. Young children prefer single subjects; older children can think in terms of more complex groups.

After subject matter, the next most important factor is color. Works that abound in color and contrast are more appealing to primary grade children. Older children prefer more tints and shades and subtle combinations. Middle school students will respond to more complex art themes—to moody, muted colors and abstract, nonobjective compositions. Whereas showing just one or a few pictures is better for elementary students, a variety of examples usually will be more effective for middle school students, because this multiple approach provides an opportunity to analyze contrasting styles and imagery.

Note that purposefully choosing nonpreferred artworks can evoke strong responses, which may lead to heated and stimulating discussions.

Cat and Kittens, ca. 1872 (11 ¾- × 13¼-inches), anonymous, American. National Gallery of Art, Washington, D.C. Gift of Edgar William and Bernice Chrysler Garbisch.

Consider the children's natural preferences for picture study subjects. "What's wrong with this picture? Why is one kitten mad? In how many places do you see stripes? What does this picture tell us about what life was like over a century ago?"

Promoting Confidence in Thinking and Talking about Art

Students should not be put on the defensive and made to feel that their verbalizations and artistic representations are incorrect. One goal of discussion is to give those students who have not yet grasped a concept—for example, realism—the "permission" to continue in their own intuitive way of artistic conceiving. ("How would you describe this 'different' quality that Marta's drawing has, and how did her sun help give that feeling?")

Art discussions should serve to broaden rather than restrict to a "one right way" system. Discussion should be a bridge between thinking and acting. It should help to promote in the young artist a sense of integration and a feeling of self-worth as an artist. Bounce the discussion back and forth from "what we see" to "how we can make it." In this way, the discussion can reciprocally stimulate both intellectual thought and artistic creativity.

Gamelike Educational Activities

While discussion is the major way to bring about art learning, a second way is through gamelike educational activities. Although research shows games to be no more or less effective than traditional methods, students enjoy educational games as a change from the usual classroom routine. The game aspect should be easy and students should do a practice round first. Games may require working together in small groups or pairs, serving as a welcome relief to the usual lecture and discussion and individual seat-work routines. Students must understand the educational purposes behind the gamelike format, however, lest they feel they are wasting their time or "just playing." Following up with a discussion or "debriefing session" is critical if students are to understand the new material.

Most art games use printed reproductions. A principal source is postcards from art museums and galleries, and the sorting and matching of these can be done even on a small desktop. Also, the National Art Education Association has published a series of inexpensive art reproductions. Magazine page–sized reproductions can be gotten from used copies of many popular and art magazines, such as *Artnews* and *Art in America*. Commercial firms specializing in art reproductions and museums have large-size reproductions (approximately 20 × 30 inches) that may be purchased on stiff paper, stiff cardboard or framed (see Appendix D).

Sets of art postcards can be used to meet art objectives in the following ways:

Art history: Two types of art history objectives are those requiring sorting and those requiring matching. Working in small groups, students will sort the cards into chronological order or match or group together those of one art style, such as impressionism.

Aesthetics: Students working in small groups will decide on which one artwork they might theoretically acquire for the school. The underlying instructional objective is that the students will discuss the differences between artistic and societal values in selecting artworks.

Art criticism: Students will describe the similarities and differences between artworks depicted and describe overall concepts that a group of cards have in common. Using cards that are sorted into prearranged sets, the learners will describe why one of the sets does not belong. This can lead into a discussion of categories, themes, and art elements.

Art criticism: Students will hypothesize about the artist's intent. As the students enter the room, the teacher gives each a card with an artist's name on it. The students then must find the reproduction done by "their" artist and tell the class "why" the artist painted the picture.

Art criticism: Students identify and describe works by master artists.

Courtesy of Barbara Thomas, Whit Davis School, Athens, GA.

Teacher-prepared educational materials such as "Art Bingo" and discussing solutions in small groups present these upper-elementary grade students with a change of pace from the usual methods of learning about art.

Turtle: courtesy of Frank Wachowiak, Athens, GA; photo by W. Robert Nix, Athens, GA.

Mexican figure: courtesy of Museum of Primitive Art, New York City, NY.

Pictures of a mother and child or animal with young can motivate children's creative writing about their family experiences with the birth of a sibling or a pet giving birth.

Commercial sets of art reproductions are available for playing an artistic version of Old Maids; alternatively, sets can be made up by the teacher. The task is for the student, through playing the game, to learn about an artist's personal style. ("Find all the Hokusais, the Romare Beardens, the pre-Columbian pieces, and the Georgia O'Keeffes.") Because such games can be played by students in pairs, they fit easily into use in self-contained classrooms as changes of activity. They promote friendships, provide activities for students who have self-directed time, and can be used in classroom learning activity centers.

Furthermore, with the students working in small groups, sets of art postcards can be used for integration with other subjects. In creative writing, groups of students can make up a story using all of the cards in one set. Individual students will tell or write the parts of the story going on with each reproduction. In mathemetics, students can describe the geometric shapes shown in the art reproductions—for example, of domed architecture, pentagon shapes in Islamic architecture, and sculptures containing icosahedra. (See Chapters 11 and 12 for science and social studies suggestions.)

In both discussions and games, keep in mind the level of the instructional objective. Is mere identification the desired goal? A higher level of objective—synthesis—can be attained by students subsequently explaining in their own words what makes up an artist's special style. Always try to set some tasks in the upper levels. The order, from lower to upper, is:

1. *Knowledge:* recall facts
2. *Comprehension:* participate in a discussion
3. *Application:* apply abstract information in practical situations
4. *Analysis:* separate an entity into its parts
5. *Synthesis:* create a new whole from many parts, as in developing a complex work of art
6. *Evaluation:* make judgments based on criteria

This chapter has overviewed the history and issues of art appreciation, described general strategies for leading art discussions, and listed some gamelike activities that promote talking and learning about art. We proceed in the next two chapters to think about specific ways to teach art history, art criticism, and aesthetics.

Chapter 18

Teaching Art History

Conducting Art History Discussions

Art history as discussed here refers not only to the discussion of artworks by masters and ancient civilizations but also broadly to objects that cultures recognize as having value and art expression by artists of one's own time and in one's community. Some examples of instructional objectives in art history are:

- Compare the way you have depicted something, perhaps the design of clothing or a vehicle, with the way that two other artists in history depicted it. Have you used or shown something that did not appear among artworks in certain past eras?
- Describe works from art history and the humanities where the portrayal of a theme has changed or remained the same. For example, tell about different versions of the Tarzan, Superman, mad scientist, werewolf, vampire, or brute theme. Find examples of how women have been shown as Eve or Cinderella, beautiful and innocent maidens, or witches.
- Describe how symbolism has been used. For example, why was the ruler usually shown on his horse? What ideas does the theme of the dragon express?
- Describe how different artists have given different meanings to the same themes.
- Discuss how representations of a group of people, such as Native Americans, have been shown in art.
- Describe why you think one artwork style was replaced by a different style. Describe world events that may have contributed to such changes in artistic representation. How does the art of an age say something about its character?
- Describe changing and constant elements in an artist's work, and relate this to changing and constant elements in your own art style.

When children talk about art, they grow not only in vocabulary describing visual phenomena but also in verbal sophistication. Students are weaned away from relying solely on their ordinary speech and are helped to form a new art language. New words and phrases such as those in the following list become part of their expanding vocabulary:

Action painting	Dadaism	Magic realism
African classical art	Earthworks	Mobile
Art nouveau	Encaustic	Naive art
Assemblage	Feminist art movement	Op art
Bauhaus	Folk art	Painter's style
Caricature	Gallery installation	Painterly
Critic	Genre	Patron
Critique	Happening	Pop art
Cubism	Impressionism	Postmodern art

Art History Teaching Methods

Perhaps you just visited a museum or watched a television program about an artist and want to share your excitement with the students. This is the simplest way to make art history material both interesting and relevant—to be interested in the material yourself. Then, your interest will be infectious. There are certain other specific strategies that teachers have found to be useful for adding interest.

Presentations on an Artist's Life

One method, especially suitable for middle school students who are beginning to look for adult role models, is to have students select an artist to research and role play. Pretending to be the artist, and perhaps even

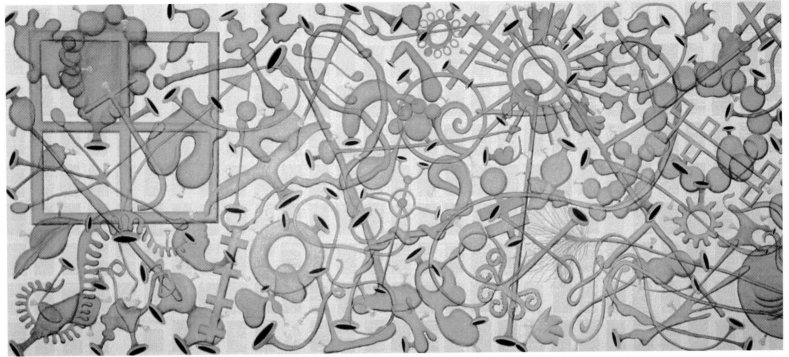

Tim Rollins and K.O.S. (Kids of Survival). Amerika, Land of the Free. A former public school art teacher, Rollins has created a student art workshop in one of New York City's roughest neighborhoods. The collaborative artworks that he and his students create grace major museums throughout the world. A beautiful overall pattern is created by the mysterious abstract forms. They remind one of boxing gloves, trumpets, gears, and windows. What do the forms suggest to you?

dressing up like the artist, the student tells the class the artist's life story. Then, the class asks the actor questions about what the artist did. What was the artist's personality like? What was the culture like? Where did the artist live? How did people of the time treat the artist? What was the artist's intention in making the art? These presentations can be videotaped and shared with other classes or at a PTO open house. Another situation can be an interview show of a small group of these artist-actors at a supposed exhibition opening or panel discussion. One student acts as the emcee and interviews the participants; other students role play critics and critique the artist's works.

Correlating Art History and Studio Projects

Art making and criticism, art history, and aesthetics are most successful and most meaningful when they complement each other in an orchestrated, coordinated endeavor. Children's intense, purposeful studio in-volvement should be related to richly planned art motivations that include art history examples. Then, their critical faculties in both appreciating and creating art are mutually enhanced.

Teachers have added to children's insights regarding African and Native-American art motifs through studio projects in mask-making. Others have coordinated the study of Egyptian tomb friezes with the making of group murals. Every phase of world art through the centuries can be given immediacy in an art-studio environment. It can be the mosaics of Ravenna in Italy, the Tang ceramics of China, the illuminated manuscripts of medieval Europe, the Benin bronzes from Africa, the marble sculptures from Greece, the ukiyo-e woodblock prints of Japan, or the wood sculptures of Louise Nevelson. Many teachers have imaginatively combined studio and art history to provide children with a growing treasury of knowledge about art, artists, art styles, and the permeating influence of art in our everyday lives.

Students took the idea of Grant Wood's American Gothic *of a couple working at their goals, and related it to showing their own interests for their lives. Here Virginia Simms shows a young couple pursuing their goals: sailing, surfing, sunning, beach volleyball, and Frisbee throwing.*

It is best if the teacher has access to color reproductions, filmstrips, and color slides. If this is not possible, most public libraries have folio-size "coffee table" art books that contain pictures large enough to show to groups. Sets of large reproductions can be ordered through the school librarian for use by the entire faculty. Some commercial sources of art visual aids are listed in Appendix D; resourceful teachers have collected and organized their own extensive picture and color-slide files. The following table lists some familiar art-education studio projects along with the names of a few artists whose works might serve as exemplars.

Suggested Art Project	Correlative Art Appreciation
Drawing-painting Helping at home or school	Genre paintings of Benny Andrews, Thomas Hart Benton, Jean Chardin, Carmen Lomas Garza, Winslow

Suggested Art Project	Correlative Art Appreciation
Drawing-painting Helping at home or school	Homer, Jacob Lawrence, Grandma Moses, Horace Pippin, Norman Rockwell, Lily Martin Spencer, Susanne Valadon, Jan Vermeer, Laura Wheeler Waring, Grant Wood, and Andrew Wyeth.
Portraits and self-portraits	Portraits by Luis Cruz Azaceta, Mary Cassatt, Chuck Close, Domenico Ghirlandaio, Hans Holbein, Leon Golub, Amos Ferguson, Lois Mailou Jones, Margo Machida, Alice Neel, Nick Quijan, John Valadez, Elizabeth Vigee-Lebrun, Leonardo da Vinci, Andy Warhol, Hale Woodruff, and Andrew Wyeth. Self-portraits by Max Beckman, Paul Gauguin, Frida Kahlo, Rembrandt van Rijn, and Vincent van Gogh.
Objects on a table, chair, or bench	Still lifes by Georges Braque, Bernard Buffet, Paul Cézanne, Jean Chardin, Janet Fish, Audrey Flack, Juan Gris, William Harnett, Margaret Angelica Peale, Pablo Picasso, and Odilon Redon.
The landscape or cityscape	Pieter Breughel, Roger Brown, Paul Cézanne, John Constable, Raoul Dufy, Robert Duncanson, Richard Estes, Paul Gauguin, Vincent van Gogh, Edward Hopper, George Inness, Dong Kingman, Gabrielle Münter, John Marin, Georgia O'Keeffe, Mattie Lou O'Kelley, Maurice Utrillo, and Grant Wood.
Fauna	John James Audubon, Rosa Bonheur, Cave paintings at Lascaux and Altamira, Chinese and Japanese animal drawings, Albrecht Dürer, Jean Louis Gericault, Franz Marc, Indian Moghul, Rembrandt van Rijn, Henri Rousseau, and Nellie Mae Rowe.
Flora	Rudy Fernandez, Roberto Juarez, Patricia Gonzales, Maria Sibylle Merian, Lowell Nesbit, Georgia O'Keeffee, and Leonardo da Vinci.

Suggested Art Project	*Correlative Art Appreciation*
Figure composition	Benny Andrews, Paula Modersohn-Becker, George Bellows, Rolando Briseño, Pieter Brueghel, Mary Cassatt, Robert Colescott, Edgar Degas, Paul Gauguin, Francisco Goya, Gronk, Robert Gwathmey, Keith Haring, Joseph Hirsch, Clementine Hunter, Angelica Kauffman, Käthe Kollwitz, Marie Laurencin, Jacob Lawrence, Henri Matisse, Edvard Munch, Alice Neal, Bill Taylor, John Valadez, Diego Velasquez, and Elizabeth Vigee-Lebrun.
The abstract, the nonobjective, the surreal, op, pop, and fantasy	Joseph Albers, Hieronymous Bosch, Marc Chagall, Georgio de Chirico, Salvador Dali, Sonia Terk-Delaunay, Arthur G. Dove, M. C. Escher, Minnie Evans, Helen Frankenthaler, Paul Jenkins, Frieda Kahlo, Wassily Kandinsky, George Longfish, Rene Magritte, Joan Miró, Piet Mondrian, Georgia O'Keeffe, Jackson Pollock, Martin Ramirez, Ad Reinhart, Bridget Riley, Tim Rollins and Kids of Survival, Mark Rothko, Frank Stella, Sophie Taueber-Arp, Mark Tobey, and Victor Vasarely.
Printmaking: collograph, plastic meat-tray print, linoleum block, glue-line-relief print, monoprint	Albrecht Dürer, Leonard Baskin, William Blake, Mauricio Lasansky, Robert Colescott, William Hayter, Gabor Peterdi, Japanese ukiyo-e artists, Ando Hiroshige Katsushika Hokusai, Rembrandt van Rijn, and Kitagawa Utamaro
Mask design and construction	African ritual masks; masks of Northern Pacific Indians; masks from Melanesia, Malaysia, Mexico, Indonesia; Japanese Noh play and Bugaku masks; Chinese opera, Greek drama, and Mardi Gras masks
Photographs	Ansel Adams, Tomie Arai, Margaret Bourke-White, Matthew Brady, Dorothea Lange, Sherry Levine, Yong Soon Min, Eadweard Muybridge, Gordon Parks, Adrian Piper, Cindy Sherman, and Edward Weston.

Courtesy of Joyce Vroon, Trinity School, Atlanta, GA.

An attractive display, along with three-dimensional objects suggestive of Native-American culture, is made of students' paintings seeking to emulate the empathy with which George Catlin captured the Native-Americans in their raiment.

Suggested Art Project	*Correlative Art Appreciation*
Three-dimensional construction, earthworks and use of found materials	Alice Aycock, Joseph Beuys Lee Bontecou, Beverly Buchanan, Alexander Calder, Christo Bessie Harvey, David Hammons, Nancy Holt, Louise Nevelson, Judy Pfaff, Pablo Picasso, David Smith, and Robert Smithson.
Abstract sculpture in plastic block, soapstone, firebrick, balsa wood	Jean Arp, Constantin Brancusi, Easter Island sculpture, Greek Cycladic figures, Judy Chicago, Nancy Graves, Barbara Hepwrth, Henry Moore, Juan Bautista Moroles, Isamu Noguchi, Northern Pacific Indian totem poles, and Martin Puryear.

A study of Georgia O'Keeffe's floral paintings with their dramatic value patterns and abstraction was central to the students' making these cut tissue paper floral close-ups in many tints and shades.

Suggested Art Project	Correlative Art Appreciation
Figurative sculpture	Magdalena Abakanowicz, John Ahearn, Ferdnand Botero, Doug Hyde, Iraqi Abu Temple sculptures, Luis Jimenez, Edward Kienholz, "King Mycerinus and Queen Chamernebty," Marisol Escobar, Michael Naranjo, Polykleitos, Alison Saar, George Segal, Rigoberto Torres, Manuel Neri, and "Winged Victory of Samothrace."
Collage and text	Luis Cruz Azaceta, Jean-Michel Basquiat, Georges Braque, Romare Bearden, Epoxy Art Group, Richard Hamilton, Edgar Heap-of-Birds, Jenny Holzer, Mary Kelly, Barbara Kruger, Henri Matisse, Catalina Parra, Howardena Pindell, Richard Prince, Robert Raushenberg, Kurt Schwitters, and Alexis Smith.
Clay pots and containers	Korean Koryo period, ancient Greek vases and jars, Chinese Ming, Pueblo and pre-Columbia pottery, Japanese Jomon ceramics, Thai Sukothai pe-

Suggested Art Project	Correlative Art Appreciation
Clay pots and containers (*cont'd*)	riod, Lydia Buzio, Peter Voulkos, and Shoji Hamada.
Clay figure modeling	Clay figures of Greek Tanagra style; Japanese Haniwa period; Chinese Tang period; Hohokan pottery of Arizona; Mexican, Peruvian, and Guatemalan pre-Columbian ceramic sculpture.

Cast bronze plaque, 1550–1650 AD, Kingdom of Benin, Nigeria. The University Museum, University of Pennsylvania. Photo Malcolm Varon, NYC © 1989, Malcolm Varon.

The artistic power of this African chief sculpture is magnified by the surrounding figures and their objects. Seen are his two lieutenants, his secretary, assistant with the spiral cone, his children, and the maces, shields, clothing, and headdresses of authority. Further power and richness are produced by symmetry and repetition. Patterns of dots, zig zags, circles, and interlocked forms add beauty.

Chapter 19

Teaching Art Criticism and Aesthetics

Conducting Art Criticism Discussions

Two other ways of building students' artistic awareness are through discussions in art criticism and aesthetics. In art criticism, a major goal is the students' ability to point to evidence in the work to support their interpretations. During the primary grades, encourage the children to ask questions about visual phenomena, list special eye-catching items in the picture, and decide what they like. During the upper grades, have students discuss criteria for judgment (realism and accepted methods for representation) and determine categories of works. Have them hypothesize about how else a picture might have been made or what alternate messages it might have conveyed. Encourage them to bring out questions about social significance.

A highly condensed summary of the sequence of children's development from grades 1 to 8 is:

Personal preference → Realism → Expressive aspects

While visits to art galleries and museums are ideal, it often is more practical to bring art to the students. If possible, use original art; if not, use colorful reproductions, color slides, and book illustrations.

The purpose of art criticism in schools is to develop appreciation and understanding in the students. This purpose should not be confused with art criticism as it might occur in a college studio-art course, where the professor's objective is to judge and improve the students' artwork. Another helpful distinction for students to be aware of is the difference between portrayal criticism and persuasive criticism. *Portrayal criticism* helps the viewer to slow down and see what the work includes. It suggests there is no one "right way" to see an artwork but rather several. In contrast, *persuasive criticism* (like some newspaper reviews) is judgmental and argues the worth of the work.

Three different approaches to art criticism and aesthetics used in schools are: art elements, themes, and cultures. The teacher's willingness to help students look at their own and each other's culture is very important; some exemplars should reflect the community and cultural background of the class. Local artists and craftspeople can be invited to visit classes, demonstrate skills, and discuss what it is like to be an artist. Acknowledge the neglect that non-Western cultures have received. Cultures such as the African, Asian, and Native American have different ways of responding to art that are nonacademic and not part of the European tradition, and people who have different cultural backgrounds can share their approaches with the class.

A Sequential Approach to Art Criticism

In schools, art criticism usually is done by having students study the features of an artwork in a sequential way, by answering specific questions in order. The steps and questions listed below often are used. Both the teacher and students may not know precise answers, but what is important is that they go about searching for answers in a scholarly way, through inquiry. Even if the teacher knows little about a work—its medium, who made it, or when or where it was made—learning can occur as long as an attitude of inquiry prevails. When the minds of the students and teacher are applied as if in solving a mystery, successful analysis will occur.

A Sequence for Art Criticism

1. Identifying the content or subject matter of the art	What things do you see in this picture?
2. Recognizing the technique or art medium	What art materials did the artist use and how were they used?

Cirque, plate II, *Jazz*, 1947 (color stencil in gouache), Henri Matisse, (1864–1954). National Gallery of Art. Washington, D.C. Gift of Mr. and Mrs. Andrew S. Keck.

Wheelchair-bound for the last 13 years of his life, the French artist Henri Matisse was unable to paint and was prepared for his death. Instead, he returned to making paper cutouts, a technique he had used decades earlier for stage decorations, and created some of the world's most life-affirming artwork. What do you see in this picture? How did the artist arrange colors and shapes to make a beautiful design?

3. Identifying the compositional or design factors in the art, and recognizing their importance

How did the artist tie the picture together?

4. Recognizing the unique, individual style of the artist

Why do we think this other picture might be made by the same artist?

5. Searching for the meaning of the art, and inquiring into the artist's intent

What does the picture say to you?

6. Identifying the context

What do you think might have been going on in the world at this time?

Saturday Classes. Frank Wachowiak, Athens, GA. Bicentennial High School. Courtesy of Mary E. Swanson, Nashua, NH.

Having studied Matisse's cutouts, students can use cutouts in collage to gain an awareness of the power of positive and negative shape. Figures drawn in contour line and cutout depict a street fight at night. The abstractness of the collage medium makes it an excellent choice for such emotional themes.

Identifying the Content

Category 1—*identifying the content or subject matter of the art*—sets the stage for understanding a work of art. What does the viewer see: a woman, child, dog, house, tree, vase of flowers? What event is being depicted: a wedding, riot, sports event, fair, family reunion, rite of passage? Enthusiastic student participation usually develops when the subject matter is real or recognizable. Try to complete the inventory of what is perceived before going on to interpretation.

Identifying the Medium

Category 2—*recognizing the technique or art medium*—often is challenging. There are so many new directions in contemporary visual expression other than painting *per se*. These include collage, montage, assemblage, etching, lithograph, collograph, mobile, light sculpture, site sculpture, or earthwork. Actual studio involvement by children with the media, techniques, and artist's materials helps them to appreciate the artist's solutions.

Identifying Design Features

Category 3—*identifying the compositional or design factors in the art and recognizing their importance*—is one of the most enlightening tasks in the whole process. Detect the basic line structure, the main thrusts, the avenues into the composition, and the dominating and subordinating themes. Find the rhythms, balances, and contrasts of line, shape, value, color, pattern, and texture, and pinpoint those that unify the picture. All this can develop into a fascinating game of search and self-discovery, an art adventure wherein both students and teacher learn that the whole is indeed greater than the sum of its parts.

Identifying the Artist's Style

Category 4—*recognizing the unique, individual style of the artist*—is another intriguing and rewarding aspect of learning through art appreciation. When students, guided by a knowledgeable and imaginative teacher, achieve the critical and perceptual skills to identify the work of

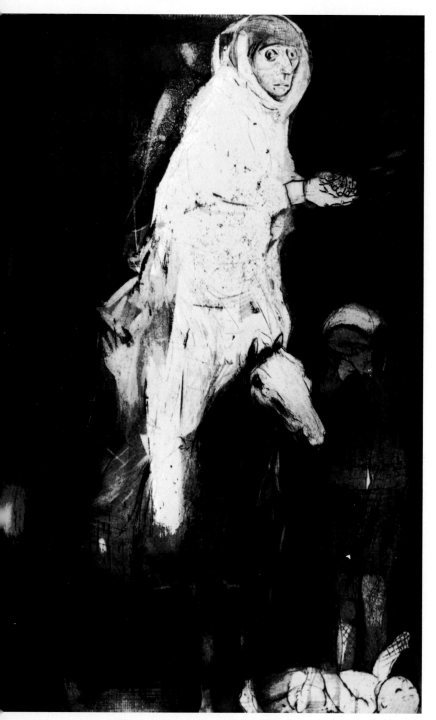

Michelangelo, Rembrandt van Rijn, Pablo Picasso, Louise Nevelson, Jacob Lawrence, and Joseph Beuys by recognizing their individual styles, they are on their way to a richer understanding and enjoyment of art's world of treasures.

Interpreting Intent

Category 5—*the search for the meaning of the art and thinking about the artist's intent*—is no doubt the most subjective phase of the cycle. There are many opportunities to influence and/or convince the students with the teacher's own judgments and prejudices about the meaning. If students merely parrot the teacher's views of art, children may not be able to relate the artwork to the aesthetic dimensions of their own lives. Avoid telling the students what *you* see in the art, what *you* feel about it, until they have had a chance to tell you what *they* see and feel. Children will spontaneously put forth their explanations of the artwork's meaning. While you may not agree with their analysis and judgment, do not force your opinions on them. The meaning that a student finds may not be the artist's intent, but that does not invalidate the student's interpretive process.

As in the inductive method of science, let the students form hypotheses based on evidence they assemble. Allow the artists, craftspeople, and architects to speak for themselves through their art and their journals. For example, in a critique of the work of Vincent van Gogh, introduce the letters the artist wrote to his brother Theo. Help the students to gain a deeper understanding of how van Gogh's painting related to his creative highs and his frustrating, disappointing lows. The general classroom teacher, who is charged with teaching interpretive writing, creative writing, and expressive writing, is in an even better position than the art specialist to have students write about artworks using metaphoric, expressive writing. What could be a better subject for such correlative writing than the most interesting visual objects on earth—artworks?

Espana, 1959 (color intaglio), Mauricio Lasansky (32 × 21″). Collection of Frank Wachowiak, Athens, GA.

A good way to begin thinking about a picture is to have students first describe what is seen. Seated on a tiny white-faced horse is a large human figure. Its hands are anxiously cupped together, its eyes open very wide, and its lips tightly drawn. It wears an unusual white costume. Also seen is an adjacent figure, probably a woman, in a skirt and with a scarf on head, with head in hands and perhaps weeping. At their feet is a 1-year-old baby, with two upraised hands, and lying on the ground.

Discussing how the art medium is used is one way of understanding art. Students can compare how the theme of an animal is carried out in a variety of subtractive sculpture media. Clockwise, from top right, are a wood-pod monkey from Malaya; a cryptomeria rooster from Japan; an ivory elephant from India; a boxwood bird from Indonesia; a wood elephant from Africa; an ivory horse from China; and in the center, a wooden frog from Mexico. Discuss how the carver achieved form. Did the medium present limitations, perhaps in the grain? How much detail is desirable or possible? Describe the main form from which the piece was carved ("like a barrel, like a rectangle with extra ears attached"). Also discuss how shapes are repeated and varied to present a unified and charming representation. Also discuss its context, where was it made, and what that animal might mean in that society.

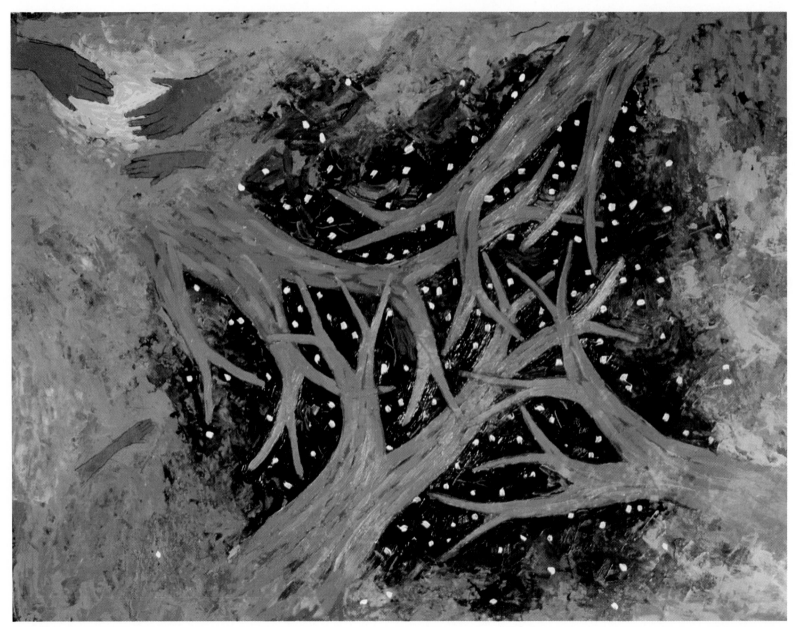

Untitled (36 × 24 inches). Private collection.

Wonder comes into one's mind contemplating the tornado-tossed trees against a starry night. Also, what could be the meaning of the red hands against a sun? This painting is by New York neo-expressionist painter Louisa Chase.

Understanding the Context

Along with the personal interpretation, examine the *context* (category 6) in which the work was made. What did the artist do to make a living? What forces were dominant in the world at that time? What was the social, religious, and economic nature of the artist's world? The teacher can supply significant information, or at this point, students might use materials in an art-learning center or the library. A new emphasis on cultural relevance and an openness to many different interpretations recently has come about, in part through developments in feminist art criticism and contemporary theories of art.

Conducting Discussions of Aesthetics

Discussing aesthetics is the third way of learning about art in discipline-based art education. As teachers, we want our students to think about what makes objects and phenomena artistic; this is what constitutes aesthetics. Children love to ask "why" questions, and the questions "Why?" and "How do you know that?" are central to aesthetics. The most important teaching strategy in leading discussions of aesthetics is to encourage questioning. Essential to success is the ability to admit there are things that we do not know. Most important, teachers must believe that students can gain something through being encouraged to question and to wonder about art ideas. Thomas Ewens (1990) said:

> Wonder is something which comes upon us, overwhelms us and suggests a kind of transcendence, out of the ordinary, the wonder-full, the extra-ordinary. It is a combination of the intellectual, the emotional, and the sensuous. It is the not-taken-for-granted. Our task is to protect the wonder of the young. The disciplines of thinking and artmaking grow out of and are nourished by this soil. Their roots are in wonder.

Some goals that many teachers want their students to achieve are the ability to:

- Speculate
- See implications
- Handle abstract ideas
- Use language for clear thinking about art
- Raise questions and make statements about aesthetics
- Present reasons supporting their positions and thus justify their judgments
- Listen to others' points of view, and ask questions about the other students' ideas

Photo courtesy Deborah Lackey, Atlanta, GA.

Some questions in aesthetics can be "How important is originality to a work of art? Is it OK to copy somebody else's artwork? Is it valuable?"

Furthermore, aesthetics is not just about knowledge; it also is about feelings. Instructional objectives concerned with feelings, or affect, are that the students will be able to tolerate uncertainty, value questioning, be curious, and respect thoughtful disagreement.

Because aesthetics is so much a part of ordinary conversation, it can easily go unnoticed. Listen for questions and comments such as

Private Collection.

Questions can be raised as to whether, in showing the figure, correct proportions and shading should be used to depict muscles. The direct expression of the African-American folk artist Mose Tolliver is shown here. His painting Black Jesus (20- × 12-inches) defies certain "expected" artistic conventions. Is realism always better? Is a balance between naiveté and realism desirable?

"Why is that weird thing supposed to be art?" and "Ugh, gross." Naturally occurring instances of art criticism need to be encouraged so that they can be transformed into significant discussions of aesthetics. On hearing students ask such questions and make such responses, we must learn to bite our tongues. We must not immediately answer, "Because the paint is so wonderfully thick, because it shows deep emotion, because it's in the Museum." Instead, ask questions back to the students. Let your interest in their comments guide the students to think more deeply.

Say to them, "What makes you say that?" "Does everyone agree?" Model for the students the use of strategies in good reasoning. Help them to learn how to think logically about their statements. Logical extension is one way: "If that is true, then how can [cave art] be explained?" Another way is through counterargument: "Is this always the case? Can anyone think of an instance when this isn't true?" The teacher's role is not to indoctrinate students with one "right" view or to inundate our students with information. This would defeat the purpose of aesthetic inquiry, its concern with contested issues. Our challenge is to promote critical thinking.

Aesthetics and art criticism tend to blend together, but a helpful distinction to keep in mind is that aesthetics focuses on the ideas behind the artwork and not on the artwork itself (which is the subject of art criticism). For starting aesthetic discussions, however, it is useful to have some art reproductions around the room or displayed over the chalkboard that can be used as references. Ask the students if any picture in particular has raised questions in their minds. The most obvious beginning is the open question, "What do you think about this picture?" Another good way to begin a discussion of aesthetics is by asking, "What's wrong with this picture?" because this presumes disputed ideas about right and wrong. Still another way of generating discussion is for students to select shocking or ugly art—anything out of the ordinary—and then to defend their selections. Topics and questions such as those in the following table can be brought up matter-of-factly when they arise as a part of an ongoing classroom discussion.

Topic	Aesthetic Question
Accident in design	Can a picture that looks like the artist just threw paint around be called good art?
Advertising art	Should art be used to make people want to buy things they do not really need?

Topic	Aesthetic Question
Anatomical accuracy	Is art better when figures depict muscles rather than sausage-looking arms? Are cave paintings with stick figures any good?
Art's role in life	Is art work or play?
Artist's intention	If someone gets a different idea or meaning from your picture, does that mean that your art is not as good? Is is better if the person knows exactly what you wanted to say?
Artist's involvement	Can art be made by just calling up a factory and saying "make me a red metal cube 6 feet square?" Must the artist have hands-on involvement in making it?
Art critics	If experts say something is good or bad, must we accept this evaluation as our own?
Art institutions	Does putting something into a museum make it art? If an artwork is not in a museum, does that mean it is not art?
Art support by government	Should our government give money for art that some people think is bad?
Clarity and metaphor	When you see an artwork and you cannot put into words exactly what the artist was saying, does that make it better or worse?
Commercial design	Can objects like bicycles, t-shirts, fancy dress gowns be called art?
Disabilities	If a person is color-blind, uses colors nonrealistically, and makes a good piece of art, can it still be called art even though the person could not see it right?
Economic validity	Because someone spends a lot of money for a piece of art, does that mean it is always good art? If no one spends any money for a piece of art, does that mean it is not art?
Education	Are artists born or made? Does art that looks like little kids made it mean that it is not good art? Do people who go to school a long time

Photo courtesy of Frank Wachowiak.

Discussions of aesthetics might concern whether the medium that is used should look like itself or whether it should look like things. Can beauty in painting be created by using tools other than paint brushes? Is beauty always desired? What is beauty? If realism is not most important, what is? Here, James Herbert, a professor of painting at the University of Georgia, employs rubberglove-encased hands to apply paint to his mural-sized canvas.

Topic	Aesthetic Question
Education	usually make better art than people who do not go to school much?
Function	What good is art, after all? If art is used for bad purposes, is it still good art?

Topic	Aesthetic Question
Gender	Why aren't there more famous women artists? Why are women usually represented as helpers and as just waiting around?
Human art	Can monkeys make art?
Human endeavor	Why do people bother to make art when they could just relax and enjoy life instead of working so hard to make something that most people probably will not like much anyway?
Individual authorship	Is it really art if several people make it instead of just one person?
Judgment	Does an artwork mean whatever anyone says it means, or are there absolutely right and wrong answers?
Mental and emotional functioning	Can people who have mental or emotional problems make good art even if it shows an upset world? Do people have to be sort of crazy to make art that has a special, weird quality?
Quality and intent	Can you name some things that are bad art? What is the difference between things that are bad art and things that are not supposed to be art at all?
Realism	Can a piece of art still be called good art even if the objects in it are not drawn so that they look like they are in realistic three dimensions?
Realistic depiction of nature	Can a picture be good if the sky does not touch the ground?
Scale	Are buildings or pictures that are big usually better art than those that are little?
Source and object	Are real rainbows art? Are wasps' nests art?
Spontaneity	Are pictures that took a long time to make usually better than pictures that were done very fast?
Technology	Can art made with machines be called art? If a camera or computer makes an artwork, can it be called art?

Topic	Aesthetic Question
Text	Can art be just some words on a piece of paper, canvas, or a light-emitting screen? Why or why not?
Time and effort	Can junky, carelessly made stuff that looks like someone just brought in a bunch of junk be called art?
Ugliness	Is art supposed to be only about beauty? Can it also be about ugliness?

Remember that discussions of aesthetics can use the students' everyday language. Students need not use special terminology. Discussion of aesthetics is not something foreign to art teaching; rather it is central to it. Good teachers of art have always have done it.

Art Criticism at Home

Parents may be at a loss concerning what to do with their child's artwork when it is brought home. Some parents feel compelled to criticize their child's art: "You're just like me—can't even draw a straight line." Of course, negative assessment is not the kind of art criticism that we wish to promote. A brief letter to parents sent home with the first artworks of the year can suggest ways for talking with their child about those works. It can describe what will be taught in art history, art criticism, and aesthetics. This is a good way to connect the student's art production and art criticism abilities. Suggest ways to build confidence through displaying the works. Suggest ways that the child's art can serve as a vehicle for generating family dinner-table discussions and ways that the child's opinions about aesthetics issues can lead to the family's discussing such ideas. Let the parents know what your art-program goals are so that they can help to build their child's interest in art. Here is a sample letter:

Dear Parents and Guardians:

This letter is being sent home, along with one of your child's first art pieces done this year, to tell you something about our art program.

This year we will be discussing what makes a good artwork. We will talk about whether looking real is the only thing that makes a picture good and how friends and neighbors make art. We will be studying art history masterpieces, especially Egyptian art. A major way you can help to foster your child's interest is through visits to museums and helping your child to participate in enrichment classes. Weekend art museum hours at the Quinlan

Art Center (548–2314) are Saturdays, 9–3, and Sundays, 1–5, and it has Family Art Days four times a year. The Recreation Department at Lyndon House Art Center (546–9968) has children's art classes on weekdays, 3:30 to 5:00 PM.

Research has shown that it is helpful for the child to have a place for art materials at home and a quiet place in which to make art. Collections, artwork, and posters artistically arranged in a child's bedroom stimulates interest in art. When adults have their own artistic and cultural hobbies, involving the child spurs his or her interest.

During the course of the year, we will be sending home with your child about eight art projects, including a still life, a group of figures in motion, a portrait of a classmate, an oil pastel of a farm scene, a computer art design, and a clay castle.

If you want to talk with me about your child's growth in art, or if you have access to human resources or art materials that could be used in our school art program, please call me at 546-9987 between 2:00 and 4:00 PM or at home at 543-7654. I hope that I will meet you soon at a PTO meeting (the last Wednesday of each month, 7:00 to 8:00 PM), where you will have the chance to see more of our class' artwork.

Students might sort art reproductions into chronological order or match those of similar cultures and describe similarities and differences among them. **Top:** *Ashura, Buddhist deity, eighth century, dry lacquer, Kofukuji Temple, Nara, Japan.* **Bottom:** *The Calfbearer, ca. 560 BC, Greek, stone.*

Part 4

Teaching Art Production

Photo A: Iowa City Elementary Laboratory School, courtesy of Frank Wachowiak and David Hodge; Photos B-L: Saturday Children's Classes, courtesy of Frank Wachowiak, Athens, GA, and Mary Sayer Hammond, Fairfax, VA.

Previous page: Row 1, left to right (A to D): A. *Very large figure consisting of geometric shapes, grade 1. B. Tempera painting: a still life of flowers outdoors. C. Painting pattern in a forest scene. D. A very large collage animal facilitates incorporating detail.* **Row 2, left to right (E to H):** *E. Students seated close around several still-life arrangements. F. Crayon engraving. G. Filling areas between chalk lines with oil pastel. H. Crayon resist.* **Row 3, left to right (I to L):** *I. Shapes flow around the edges of a box sculpture J. Tissue collage over marker still-life drawing. K. Tempera painting: a carnival. L. Hollow clay slab animal.*

Chapter 20

Drawing

Overview of Art Production

Mounting evidence, exemplified and corroborated by contemporary child-art creations such as those illustrated in this book, suggests that we have been underestimating children's capabilities. In many instances, we have not even begun to tap their true potential for "thinking" and "problem solving" through art media. The ensuing pages describe a host of art projects and techniques in both two and three dimensions that are recommended for a qualitative art program in elementary and middle schools.

These chapters should prove to be most helpful to those classroom teachers who themselves may be untaught in the basic art disciplines of drawing, painting, printmaking, collage, and sculpture. The lessons described also will help art specialists who are searching for new dimensions and challenges in school art programming. Both the projects and their documentation resulted from many years of in-depth teaching by dedicated and knowledgeable instructors of both elementary and middle school art. This has entailed continuing motivational experimentation, media exploration, process and product evaluation, and research in qualitative art practices in schools around the world.

The art program should be planned at all levels for in-depth involvement and sequential growth. An in-depth method may not be as popular as a smorgasbord of quick, unrelated projects, but in the long run, it will produce greater gains as students come up with their own ideas and create art of the highest quality.

The following descriptions of art projects include motivational possibilities, clarify complex art techniques, offer solutions for organizational and supply problems, and suggest evaluational criteria. In no instance is the implication intended, nor is the reader to assume, that the projects and processes described are the only possible choices. The best lessons, of course, are those that come from the teacher's heart and soul.

Informed by the needs of the class and in combination with recommended art education practices, this deep belief results in the best lessons. The projects described in the following chapters, however, have been tried and found to be highly successful in situations typical of today's elementary and middle schools—in classrooms filled with eager, bright, boisterous, fidgety, dreamy, energetic, inquisitive, and sometimes apathetic students.

Three Kinds of Drawing

Elementary school children should draw every day. A drawing curriculum should address not just one way of drawing but all three families of the world of visual art objects: depictions, patterns, and maps. This chapter will mainly address the first, realistic depictions that usually are thought of as "children's art"—the creation of drawings and paintings from nature and life.

The second family—patterns and design—consists of creative play with shapes and spacing. This usually is thought of as design rather than drawing. Design receives more emphasis in later sections of this book: architecture, mosaics, printmaking, clay, and sculpture. Designing and creating patterns, however, also are important in making drawings and paintings. The doodles that one makes while on the telephone represent this kind of play with shapes and spacing. A design approach using shapes, lines, and blocks was central in the Froebel kindergarten method, which influenced Frank Lloyd Wright's architecture so profoundly. It also was central in the teaching at a famous German design school, the Bauhaus. Because design is based on intuitive balance and measure, it lends itself well to correlational activities with mathematics, architecture, and engineering.

The third family in the world of visual objects consists of maps, which are visual representations of what one knows rather than what

1 & 2, by Samantha Libman, 3 & 4 by Adam Levy, 5 & 6 by Staci Gruen, 7 by Jon Birnberg, and 8 by Elizabeth Siegel. Courtesy of Baiba Kuntz, Glencoe, IL.

One design approach using shapes is this wonderful block printing lesson for 7th and 8th graders. Students plan their blocks with two opposite corners being B & D, and the other two opposite corners A and C. Then, the block can repeatedly be printed side by side and turned to make different arrangements, as these two alternative printing arrangements of the designs show.

one sees. Conception, not perception, is the focus. The problem of communicating an idea through a map is not governed by the criteria of photographic realism. Assignments can be to map the events of one's daily life, how a pumpkin grows, how one's insides function, or where the food we eat comes from. Children can make a map of their neighborhood or show the cycle of evaporation and rain. Mapping helps students to conceptualize relationships among the ideas they have in their minds. ("Using the international travel signs and symbols, show how you get home from school.") Students use graphic equivalents to represent objects and functions, and mapping lends itself to correlation with science. This type of "visual thinking" is embodied in such conceptual artworks as Alice Aycock's piece on cloud dispersion and Maria Merz's artwork based on Fibonacci series. Some other drawing activities that promote flexible visual thinking are drawing something from a nonhuman point of view, such as an ant's-eye or a bird's-eye view.

When preschool-age children draw their families, those drawings are like maps in that they draw what they know, not what they see. Similar visual representations of knowledge are found in works by folk artists as well as naive artists, who do not feel so constrained by demands for realism. This kind of drawing unfortunately is too often discouraged, however, by some teachers who establish perceptual realism as a standard for artistic excellence. One example of a young child's "thought representation" not meeting a teacher's criteria for perceptual realism occurred when the sculptor Henry Moore was in primary school. He felt crushed when his teacher criticized him for drawing feet pointing downward rather than realistically pointing sideways. The solution is not for teachers to be laissez-faire, but instead for teachers, especially of young children, to foster both ways of representation; perceptual and conceptual. In a class, some will draw what they know, others will draw what they see, and most will use a combination.

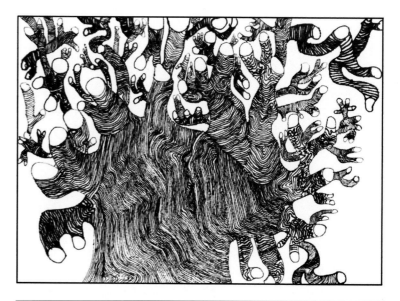

Encourage both ways of representation: what is conceived in the mind and how it appears. This beautifully detailed drawing of a tree was created by a second-grade youngster from Saga Prefecture, Japan.

Figure Drawing

Which skills and techniques in figure drawing should be introduced and developed in elementary and middle school art programs? What should teachers say to the child regarding delineation of the figure? When, if ever, should the relative proportions of the human figure be identified and emphasized? The strategy most often proposed, unfortunately, is a laissez-faire placebo of "Let the children alone. They will find their own solutions." This injunction admittedly provides the teacher with a face-saving excuse if results are less than satisfactory; however, it is hardly the kind of advice given by teachers of subject areas such as math, reading, and language. Through lack of guidance, students fail to meet their potential in drawing and painting the human figure. Instant art and gimmicky shortcuts, such as cutting and pasting photographs, keep students from developing the basic skills of creative self-expression.

If teachers want students to grow in their representation of the human figure, they must provide learning experiences and practice sessions for such growth. Direct the students' attention to details. Extend the child's frame of reference with statements such as, "Show us how your face looked when you were in the dentist's chair." Children want to be able to draw well. Students of all ages feel that the level of realis-

tic representation is the most important criterion in determining the quality of each other's artworks.

Fortunately, there are some avenues a teacher can pursue to help children develop confidence in life drawing. Teachers can ensure a more intense awareness of the human figure and its characteristics by using posed models at every grade. The delineation of the figure in even the youngest child's drawings does not spring forth from a vacuum. It results from the varied encounters the learner has had in perceiving and conceptualizing the human figure, both in and out of school, through books, comics, television, and peers' art. Sadly, the drawings of most nonartistic and artistically untaught adults are no better than those of preadolescents. They first draw a large head and then ill-defined facial features. Hands and feet often are not visible, the body is segmented, and the picture shows an overall lack of organization. Too many students graduate from school with a sense of inferiority about how they draw. Teachers can help them to acquire or maintain confidence in their drawing ability.

Before the students actually begin drawing, a warm-up session is recommended. Motivating, leading questions should be proposed.

Courtesy of David Hodge, Oshkosh, WI.

The contour-line technique is perhaps the most viable and successful drawing method for upper-elementary and middle school youngsters. Suggest that students draw slowly and deliberately with a soft-lead pencil. Urge them to look intently at the object they are drawing. This figure is by a middle school student.

What action is the model performing? What is the model wearing? What portion of the model do you see from your drawing station? How large is the model's head in comparison with the body? How big are the hands? Ask students to place one hand over their own faces to realize its size. How large are the feet? They must be big enough to keep the model balanced. Where is the model's arm the biggest—at the shoulders, elbows, or wrists? Where is the model's leg the biggest—at the ankle, knee, or hips? Where does the body, neck, leg, and arm bend? How wide can the feet stretch apart? How high can the arms reach above the head? How far can the body turn around while standing in one position? How far does the arm reach when held at the side?

As the students draw, encourage them to look at the model constantly, carefully, and intently. Tell them to get their eyes full! Caution them against rushing through their drawing, scribbling, or making any hasty, random, meaningless lines. Always remind them to look first and then draw. Encourage them to make the figure large, to fill the page with it, then there will be space to enrich it with many details and individual characteristics. In general, it is helpful for children to begin their drawing of a figure with the head at the top of the page.

In drawing figures, the size of the head generally determines the size of the figure. If the students draw the head too small, the body will not fill the page. If they draw the head too large, they will not be able to fit the whole body on the page. Children in the primary grades often draw a three-heads-high figure, like the *Peanuts* cartoon character Charlie Brown, and minimize the rest of the body to fit it on the page. Others will draw tiny heads and stretch the legs to reach the bottom of the page. In both cases, the results should not be discouraged, because the drawings capture the child's development at a moment of special charm.

Because many teachers believe they lack the expertise to guide children in drawing figures, they settle for what the students can accomplish on their own. Students need instruction, but the wrong kind of direction is not the answer. Formulas such as stick or sausage figures and face proportions measured by rulers can create a stultifying dependence on stereotypes. The best instruction emphasizes heightened observation.

Adult artists pay careful attention to contours and how planes are implied. While you teach your class, you can point out these features to your students. As children learn to draw, they first use outlines that do not suggest form. This is followed by strong interior contour lines that overlap each other. Later, there is some implying of form through planes, and still later, children begin to join interior lines with outlines.

Courtesy of David Hodge, Oshkosh, WI.

A middle school life drawing class in action. Notice that tables were arranged to make a unified drawing area where the model can be viewed easily by all the students. Paper size for sketching was 18 × 24 inches. Tools for drawing included sharpened dowel sticks and twigs dipped in India ink containers. If several drawings are planned, the model, as well as the position of the model, should be changed so that students are afforded a variety of views.

In upper grades, teach contour-line drawing by discussing how the line of an interior edge becomes visible and then joins the exterior silhouette. As it rounds the form, it becomes hidden. In the upper grades, talk about planes—the plane of the front of the body, the plane of the head, or the plane of a box. Show how the plane is revealed by its edges. Then, you will be pleased at how well some of your students can suggest planes in space.

Figure drawing, like all drawing from life, teaches students to observe in many ways. Those who are perceptually aware very quickly will notice and draw the rich embellishing details, such as belts, ribbons, shoelaces, buttons, necklaces, earrings, bracelets, wristwatches, pockets, collars, cuffs, wrinkles, zippers, pleats, eyeglasses, teeth braces, hair combs, and clothing patterns such as stripes, checks, florals, and plaids.

An alternative approach to figure drawing does not use a model but instead relies on the representational devices of comics and TV cartoons. Some young people's interest in drawing is triggered by comic-book-illustration techniques: scenes in a series, thought balloons, speed lines, star-and-lightning-bolt symbols of violence, and strongly contrasting effects of light on muscles.

When children draw their classmates, be prepared for the occasional self-conscious titter or embarrassed laughter. Emphasize how we are all learning to see. Provide examples such as Jean Dubuffet's *art brut* drawings to show that realism is not the sole criterion of art. Be understanding when a student does not want to model for the class (perhaps because of embarrassment about appearance or clothing), because there are always other volunteers.

Students, especially in the upper grades, can later use their linear figure drawings in a painting, collage, print, or mural. The line drawings themselves, however, often have a validity, presence, and charm of their own. Subject-matter themes such as playing ball, riding a bike, flying a kite, brushing teeth, holding a pet, playing a musical instrument, holding a bouquet, cheerleading, skipping rope, ballet dancing, football, basketball, tennis, playing on the swing, setting the table, twirling a Hula Hoop, and lifting barbells lend themselves to space-filling compositions. Some other figure-drawing strategies are:

A motorcycle was brought to the middle school art room to make the drawing more true to life. Following the making of a careful line drawing, vibrant colors of oil pastel were skillfully employed to enhance the composition.

Pose a student in a colorful costume (clown, cowboy, dancer) or sports uniform. So that everyone has a clear view, pose the model on a table or a counter top.

Pose the model in the center of a circle of sketching classmates, affording each child a different view. For an overlapping, multifigure composition, change both the action and direction of the model in later poses.

Introduce new drawing and sketching tools. Try free-flowing felt-tip markers, small watercolor brushes, Q-tips, eyedroppers, turkey feathers, twigs and balsa woodsticks sharpened at one end as ink applicators, as well as charcoal and conté crayon.

Pose the student model against a sheet of cardboard, plywood, or Masonite approximately 4 × 8 feet—in any case, slightly larger than the model. This will help the students to relate the posed figure to the boundaries of their paper. For additional interest, decorate the board with drapery, fishnet, or colorful posters.

Consider having the model wear items of an ethnic costume and placing ethnic patterned cloths in the background, thus opening up opportunities for social-studies integration.

Demonstrate new techniques and directions for drawing the figure: contour, gesture, scribble, and mass methods. Following Henri Matisse's example in his famous paper cutouts, have students cut the figure from construction paper without making a preliminary drawing.

Use a pose with more than one student taking part. The figures might be socially interacting, such as one handing something to the other or helping another put on a coat. Stage the models in a related still-life and background.

Challenge the students to use their imaginations. Let the action or stance of the model trigger a fantastic or legendary figure who they can capture in line. Fill in the background with ideas from the imagination and remembered experiences.

Assign different class members to take 5- or 10-minute turns posing in various sports actions. Urge the students to overlap the figures as they draw them on their paper.

Vary the paper size and dimensions. Try a 9- × 18-inch or a 12- × 24-inch sheet for a standing figure, or use a long, wide paper for a group of figures. Challenge them to fill the page.

If your room has sufficient space, have the students use 24- × 36-inch paper with wide felt-nib markers, giant chunk crayons, or big brushes.

Introduce a variety of papers: plain newsprint, cream or gray manila, recycled papers, assorted-color construction paper, computer-print-

Courtesy of Suzy McNiel, Iowa City, IA.

How marvelously observed are the details, such as eyelets, wristbands and folds in clothing and cheekbones. See how the pattern changes in the falling socks. A first-grade child did this! Have high expectations and your students will rise to meet those expectations.

Courtesy of David Hodge, Oshkosh, WI.

Rich visual stimulation is extremely important for students to create quality artwork. Many teachers build an ever-changing still-life environment in their classrooms as a challenging and continuing motivational resource. Here, a young adolescent is attired in goggles, snowflake patterned sweater, striped pants, and high boots while modeling against intriguing antique Americana artifacts.

out pages, and newspaper classified-ad pages. Newspapers may donate the ends of newspaper rolls, which are useful for large drawings. Older students might benefit from using resources such as a real skeleton, department-store mannequin, or life-size medical chart of the body's muscle structure.

For action or gesture drawing that requires a loose and free approach, students should hold the crayon, pen, pencil, charcoal, or chalk horizontally as they sketch rather than in the tight, upright manner used in writing.

Inexpensive, lightweight drawing boards that are excellent for field trips can be constructed out of heavyweight chipboard, hardboard, or Masonite, about 18 × 24 inches, with the edges protected with masking tape. During the drawing sessions, these boards can be propped against a table or desk, thus affording the students a better working position from which to capture details.

Portrait and Self-Portrait Drawings

The self-portrait or portrait of a classmate should be on the agenda of every school art program. What more effective and immediate subjects are there for expressive drawings in all grades than the children themselves? Children of all ages like to draw the figure. Only a few 6-year-olds can draw reasonably correct proportions, but this increases to over half by 14 years of age. A small number of 12-year-olds can draw true to appearance.

If possible, discourage students from doing the typical portrait stereotype: the symmetrical frontal pose with arms stiffly at the side. Instead, create contrasting directions of the arms and hands in unusual positions. Add interest and relevance with uniforms, costumes, a variety of headware, and assorted objects to hold. Encourage three-quarter or full-profile views. Some suggested poses are:

- Arms folded above the head or akimbo
- Straddling a chair with head resting on folded arms
- Holding a musical instrument, sports equipment, open umbrella, bouquet of flowers, or pet
- Putting on a hat, combing or brushing hair, applying make-up, or using a hand mirror

The background adds immeasurably to the composition—a foliage arrangement, a multipaned window, a giant travel poster, a folding screen. Encourage the students to add elements in the background that are drawn from memory and imagination, such as "my interests" or "animals I care about."

Stereotyped portraiture usually results from hasty, superficial observation. Urge students to look intently at the model, whether it be their own image in a mirror or classmates posing for them, and to pay close attention to unique characteristics. To encourage self-acceptance in self-portraiture, show portraits of famous women and men, and discuss their widely dissimilar, far-from-perfect features and the different shapes of their heads. Call attention to the hairline, and how the hair follows the contour of the head. No thoughtless scribbles for hair should be allowed! Discuss the shape of the ears (tell them to feel their own ears) and their junction to the head. Discuss ways of delineating the nose, and show drawings by Pablo Picasso and Ben Shahn. Use a rich motivation of color slides or reproductions showing different portraiture styles from a variety of times and cultures. Show how to draw the lips as two subtly differing forms and the eyelids' structure as complementary features to the eyes. Bring out the astonishing fact that no two faces—or even two sides of the same person's face—are alike.

In upper elementary and middle school, *blind contour drawing* is a good way for students to capture the spirit of the subject rather than strive for absolute realism. In blind contour drawing, students look intently at the subject—but not at their paper as they draw. If the students become concerned that their drawing does not look like the posed model, tell them that the aim of expressive portraiture is not to achieve a photographic likeness. Remind them that the same model drawn by various artists will look different in each rendition.

Drawing the Landscape or Cityscape

Although very young children in the primary grades enjoy drawing simple themes and single objects, such as a butterfly, bird, pet, themselves, a classmate, or a house, maturing students will respond to the challenge of complex composition: the still life, the landscape, and the cityscape. In the upper elementary grades and middle school, they are interested in outdoor sketching and the excitement of field trips. The busy and infinitely varied world beckons and unfolds at their doorsteps. These students are fascinated by:

- Nearby building construction
- The colorful and crowded street of shops
- The county fair or park bandstand
- The boat marina or harbor with its ships

Bottom: Courtesy of David Hodge, Oshkosh, WI.

Top: *In the center of the room, a standing girl and seated boy pose on a table. The table contains objects to break up space.* **Bottom:** *With stiff boards to back the drawing paper, peers draw each other in small groups.*

- The highway interchange
- The factories and foundries
- The bus, train, and airport terminals
- The challenging perspective down an alleyway
- The giant city skyscrapers

Drawings of classmates by eighth graders show virtuosic handling of the hair and blouse by Jennifer Buntman, magnificent patterning of the shirt by Ashley Milne, varied weights of blouse lines by Kasey Passen, and a self-portrait with recalled imagery by fifth grader Lauren Conway.

- The cluster of farm buildings on a country road
- The community's elaborate architecture
- The view from a bedroom or classroom window

These sites, as well as imagined cities of the future, can be the inspiration for sketches, compositions, paintings, prints, and col-

Courtesy of Baiba Kuntz, Glencoe, IL.

lages. A variety of media can be used for field-trip sketching. These include pencil, chalk (school chalk is recommended for sketches and preliminary drawings on colored construction-paper backgrounds), charcoal, crayon, felt-nib or nylon-tip marker, conté crayon, and even a stick dipped in ink (depending on the maturity of the students).

Most children on a field trip draw with enthusiasm and confidence; however, some who are perplexed will besiege the teacher with questions such as: What should I draw first? Where should I start on the paper? Must I put everything in my picture? The complex view may overwhelm them, and the spatial and perspective problems often confuse them. Remind the students that they will be creating an entirely new

The most important and architecturally distinguished building in town makes a good subject. It is valuable both for the study of drawing and architecture, as in this Colombian 13-year-old's drawing.

aesthetic unity out of the vast conglomeration of visual stimuli. One recommendation for successful landscape and cityscape drawing is to use a light pencil or chalk sketch to establish the basic shapes and general outline. Values and details can be added later.

Another strategy, and one that is especially recommended for the complex view, is to have the students begin by drawing the shape in the center of the site (a doorway, window, telephone pole, tree) as completely as they can. Then, have them proceed to draw the shape to the

Left: *Because going on field trips can pose difficulties, the teacher may need to locate sketching sites from a school window or on the school grounds.*

Right: *A motorcycle parked in the school lot will pique the imagination of students and afford lots of details to draw.*

Brush, ink, and watercolors on white drawing paper, actual size. Grade 9, Dubuque, IA.

How sensitively observed, drawn, and delineated is this charmingly complex neighbor-hood scene viewed from a school window. Notice how the free-form preliminary washes tie the composition together and how the overlapping trees create a subtle depth in space. Notice, too, the variety employed in the lines, shapes, and positions of the buildings, windows, and roofs. Observe how the houses and trees terminating at the paper's edge create avenues leading the viewer into the composition.

right and left of it, above and below it, and so on, until they fill their paper to the border. They will find and discover that incomplete shapes touching the paper's edge will create line avenues leading into their compositions. Encourage them to enrich their drawings with details, patterns, and textural effects.

Problems that students have defining distance in space often can be clarified by an understanding and use of the following guidelines. Objects or shapes in the foreground plane (those closer to the observer) usually are drawn larger, lower on the page, and in more detail. Objects farther away from the viewer (in the background plane) usually are

Courtesy of Frank Wachowiak, Athens, GA.

drawn smaller, higher on the page, and with less observable detail. Effective space is subtly created by overlapping shapes and elements in the composition, such as a fence, tree, or telephone pole against a building.

Simple perspective principles based on employing the horizon line, vanishing points, and converging lines should be introduced when the students indicate a need for them. Some students in grades 7 and 8 will want to take up this challenge. Simple exercises in perspective may appeal to them, but remind them that mastery of perspective rules does not ensure that they will achieve compositional success.

Sketching field trips should be undertaken only with adequate preparation by both the teacher and students. The teacher should scout out exciting subject matter beforehand. Avoid the barren view or monotonous vista that provides little opportunity for a varied breakup of compositional space. Permission to be away from school must be cleared with the principal's office and, when necessary, signed permission slips obtained from parents. Arrangements for using the school bus should be made well in advance.

A class discussion with visuals before the field trip should emphasize specific challenges. Tell the students to look for the architecturally significant character of the buildings, to see the value contrasts of windows in daylight, the foreground space allowed for steps and porches, and the receding of roads, sidewalks, and fences. Bring in aesthetic concepts. ("Will we see and depict nature as it is dominated and controlled by humans, or nature gaining control?")

On the day of the field trip, the teacher should review rules of behavior and caution students to respect private property in the sketching vicinity. Directions for proceeding to and returning from the sketching site should be made clear, especially if it is within walking distance of the school. Keep the class in a line or group, bringing up stragglers when necessary. If roads are to be crossed, stop signs that are held by the teacher or monitors to warn and halt traffic are recommended.

Drawing landscapes or cityscapes directly at the site is recommended for upper elementary and middle school children. Sometimes however, conditions make it inadvisable, and the center and bottom illustrations show what can be accomplished when youngsters draw from a sequence of projected color slides. First, slides of towers, steeples, and chimneys were drawn high on the page. Then, storefront facades and signs were projected for the middle plane. Finally, street furniture, lamps, telephone poles, hydrants, traffic lights and signs, parked cars, motorcycles, and trucks were projected to complete the foreground.

In most instances, supplies for drawing should be distributed to the students before they leave the classroom. In some cases, the teacher may want to carry the drawing tools until the site is reached; at the end of the field trip, gather them up again. If students walk to the site, they can carry their own drawing boards. If a bus is used, class monitors can bring the materials, drawing tools, sketchboards, extra paper, and thumbtacks to distribute on arrival.

At the sketching site, discourage students from sitting too closely together. Many a field trip can end up as a time-wasting social hour.

Remind the students that while drawing, they may use the artist's prerogatives of changing, adding, deleting, or simplifying what they see. Explain that the criterion is not necessarily photographic reality or rigidly measured perspective. Students may add more trees, fences, telephone poles, fire escapes, air vents, chimneys, or windows. They may change a roof line or the cast of a shadow. They may delete a parked car or a trash dumpster. In the sky, they may add helicopters, birds, clouds, and fantasy creations. Each decision they make, however, should embody the dynamic rules of art: variety, unity, balance, emphasis, contrast, and repetition.

The most important responsibility of the teacher at the sketching site is to guide the students in a self-evaluation of their drawings, employing the perennial principles of composition and design. In the final analysis, if all the teachers have done is to bring the students to see something they have not really seen before, to notice something they have never noticed until that moment—a molding or cornice on a door or window frame, the shadow of a tree against a wall, the overlapping of shingles, the variety in tree bark, or the texture of a brick wall—then they have succeeded in enriching the lives of their students a thousand-fold. The teacher may have started them on an exciting quest for shapes, patterns, textures, and color—on an endless journey of visual discovery.

Drawing the Still Life

Whether as inspiration for drawing, painting, print, or collage, the still-life arrangement fosters an appreciation of commonly observed, every-

Top: Courtesy of Frank Wachowiak, Athens, GA. *Middle:* Photo courtesy of W. Robert Nix, Athens, GA. *Bottom:* Courtesy of Joyce Vroon, Trinity School, Atlanta, GA.

Do you know someone who would be willing to loan your classes interesting taxidermic specimens or antique objects? Perhaps the florist will donate flowers past their selling peak time.

Dolls, fancy chairs, musical instruments, and lunch boxes make good still life material. Bottom by fourth-grade student Elizabeth Thackston.

day objects. It encourages keen observation and sensitivity to shapes, contours, and overlapping. From the third grade on, children can be guided to see the limitless design possibilities in still-life compositions. When acquiring objects for still lifes, scavenge at secondhand stores, flea markets, attics, basements, and garage sales. Avoid trite objects

such as miniature figurines or bud vases. Plant life is popular and can trigger nature discussions about why plant leaves have developed in shape and texture the way that they have. Also popular is clothing such as ballroom gowns, costumes borrowed from theater programs, athletic uniforms, and military uniforms as well as apparatus from army surplus stores. Objects from outdoor life and camping, taxidermic specimens, as well as targets and bull's-eyes from shooting ranges also will interest some students. Large art reproductions, posters from athletic wear stores and automobile dealerships, and unused billboard sheets make interesting backgrounds.

The placement of the various objects is critical to the success of the composition or design. Have the students participate. Make construction of the still life a motivating, adventurous part of the lesson. For example, arrange the objects on an antique table, old sewing machine, rocker, stepladder, window ledge, desk top, or table in the middle of the room so that students can be seated in a circle around the still life as they draw. Employ a variety of heights and levels (use cardboard cartons as well as plastic or wooden crates or storage units as supports). Create space through placing some objects behind others. Work for an informal rather than a formal balance in the arrangement. Use assorted fabrics, colorful beach towels, flags, banners, fishnets, bedspreads, quilts, or tablecloths to unify the separate elements and create visual movement.

In most cases, the more objects that are used in the still-life group, the more opportunities students will have for selection and rejection. Indeed, the more objects the students include in their compositions, the more likely they are to achieve design success.

There are several ways to begin drawing. One successful strategy is to have students begin by drawing the central object in the still life, as seen from their point of view, in the middle of their paper. They continue by drawing the objects next to it, left and right, above and below, until they have either filled the page or completed the still-life arrangement. Thus, the more varied and abundant the still life is, the more the students' compositions will have filled the space.

Another tactic is to have students select items from a general store of still-life material, choosing one object at a time to sketch at their desks or tables. They will build their compositions gradually, employing the principles of variety in size and shape of objects, overlapping, repetition, avenues into the composition, and informal balance. Talk with the children about how shapes are described by their edges and an object's interior lines and outlines join together.

Some teachers suggest to their students that they make a light, tentative sketch in pencil, charcoal, or chalk to indicate the general, overall arrangement. This preliminary drawing then is developed stage by stage, employing value (light and dark) and texture effects, pattern, shading, detail, and linear emphasis.

Drawing Animals

Most children respond enthusiastically to drawing pets and other animals. Students in the upper elementary and middle school often are especially interested in drawing horses. If the drawing of animals is to become a significant experience for the students, however, then have them observe live animals at zoos, aquariums, natural history museums, pet shops, farms, parks, and animal shelters whenever possible. Pets brought to class provide a stimulating and immediate source of drawing inspiration.

Skill in drawing realistic animals develops slowly. Nearly all first graders draw "just an animal"; by sixth grade, a third of students still do so. "Horselike" animals are drawn by 20 percent of second graders and perhaps 50 percent of sixth graders. Even by seventh grade, only 5 percent of students are able to make drawings that can be classified as "true to appearance."

Before an animal-drawing field trip, let the students look at celebrated animal drawings. Include Rembrandt van Rijn's lion and elephant; Rosa Bonheur's horses and those by Chinese Han- and Sung-period artists; Albrecht Dürer's hare, squirrel, and rhinoceros; and Andrew Wyeth's birds. Discuss the animals' special characteristics: the textural pattern of the rhino's skin; the repeated yet ever varied spots of the leopard, the rhythmic rings of the armadillo's protective shell, the beautiful op-art variations of the zebra's stripes, the gracefully curved horns of the antelope, and the wrinkled and leathery face of the orangutan.

Discuss the animals' sociological and cultural significance, such as sacred tigers and cows, imperial dogs, and royal lions, their strength symbolically representing the emperor. Encourage the students to think of similarities between people and animals in resting, eating, running,

Visually appealing desserts might be donated by a caterer, for a lesson tied to Wayne Thibaud's dessert still-life paintings. Notice how third-grade students Sarah Nix and Ginny Gay used overlapping in the compositions. Also note the tables arranged around the still life, and the egg boxes and trays used for mixing the many tints and shades of tempera paint.

Courtesy of Joyce Vroon, Trinity School, Atlanta, GA.

Top: Courtesy of Michael F. O'Brien, American Military Dependents School, Seoul, Korea. *Bottom:* Courtesy of David Hodge, Oshkosh, WI.

Drawing of rabbits by a first-grade child, Japan.

bathing, grooming, and caring for their young. As John Dewey wrote, "The roots of art and beauty are in the basic vital functions, the biological commonplaces man shares with birds and beasts" (Dewey, 1934).

To stimulate kinesthetic awareness, students can dramatically reenact the animal's poses and actions using their own bodies. Older students can be challenged to capture the animal's peculiar stance, the swinging rhythm of the chimpanzee, the arching stretch of the giraffe, or the sway of the elephant's trunk.

Careful observation and sensitive variation of line are required in drawing animals. As the students draw, remind them to fill the page.

Facing page: Still-life arrangements need not be limited to the usual floral arrangements; they are all around us. Consider the bicycles, Jeeps, campers, and station wagons parked behind the school. Consider the open car trunk, the tool shed, cupboard, or closet. How about the piled-up desk, cluttered kitchen sink, box of playground equipment, and table set for dinner? **Right:** The animal world has always interested child artists. **Top:** Rembrandt's use of wrinkle lines in the elephant's baggy skin indicate form and can give children ideas for their drawings. **Middle:** This first-grade student has drawn his elephant large to fill the space, and is now completing the filing in of the background. **Bottom:** A sixth-grade Iowa City youngster used oil pastel for this ant-eating aardvark at a natural history museum.

Top and Middle: Ann Arbor Schools; *Emphasis Art,* Second Edition. Bottom: Courtesy of Ted Ramsay.

African-American folk artist Nellie Mae Rowe's family plowed many hours with a mule. She brought this knowledge to her rich colored-pencil drawing. In the background, imaginative patterns of checkerboards and circular, floral, and overlapping scallop designs create a thrilling feast for the eyes.

The larger the drawing, the more opportunities the child will have to define special details, patterns, and textures. Pencils, sticks cut to a point and dipped in ink, and felt-nib or nylon-tipped pens are good for small sketches. Charcoal, conté crayon, chalk, crayon, oil pastel, Q-tips, eyedroppers filled with ink, and large-size blunt or square-tipped ink markers can be used for large works.

Limit the drawing activity to a single animal developed in depth rather than cursory attempts to draw several. Students also might be encouraged to draw detailed studies of an animal's eye, ear, snout, or horns. Because textural nuances can be added later when the students return to class, on-the-site drawings might be limited to capturing significant form. It might be a sketch showing the animal's spirit rather than an attempt to make a completed, detailed study.

Sketching from live animal or taxidermic specimen is best. When this cannot be done, the color slides, films, filmstrips, and opaque projections of illustrations can provide supplemental motivation. In the primary grades, the visual material might be discussed and then posted for reference on the bulletin board. Photos and slides fulfill a definite need, but they should serve as an inspirational and informational reference only and are not to be traced or rigidly copied.

Remind the students to consider the entire composition. In too many instances, the animal is isolated in the middle of the paper, floating in space without a hint of complementary foreground or background atmosphere. Add compositional elements such as trees, shrubs, grasses, rocks, bushes, vines, hills, cliffs, clouds, and companion animals in the foreground or background. Follow the example of Henri Rousseau, who used his own house plants as models to create his jungles. Use plants, dried foliage, roots, rocks, and twigs from the immediate school vicinity drawn giant size to become ledges, mountains, and jungle trees for the animals' imagined habitats. Students should be provided with continuing opportunities to become aware of nature as an endless source of design inspiration.

Chapter 21

Crayon and Oil Pastels

Crayon

At the turn of the century, crayons began to be manufactured for use in schools. Artists such as Henri de Toulouse-Lautrec, Georges Seurat,

Courtesy of Shirley Lucas, Oshkosh, WI.

Crayon was richly used in this drawing of eight animals. Notice how the grassy terrain was outlined in a series of analogous colors.

Tunceli, Turkey. Courtesy of the International Collection of Child Art, Illinois State University, Normal, IL.

Crayon alone was used to create the glowing rich colors in this 11-year-old Turkish student's illustration of the fable, "The Old Man, His Son, and Their Donkey." Four scenes are shown simultaneously, and a handsome texture is achieved in in the straw-colored area by scrathing in a texture.

Henri Matisse, and Kaethe Kollwitz have used them. Today, they are available in over 64 colors. Resourceful teachers often combine crayon with other media to provide renewed student interest in its exciting potential. Some of these innovative techniques, which are described in the following pages, include crayon resist, crayon encaustic, crayon engraving, and multicrayon engraving.

Unfortunately, the rich possibilities of the wax crayon with its own singular merits as an expressive coloring agent, often are investigated

Saturday Children's Classes. Courtesy of Frank Wachowiak, Athens, GA, and Mary Sayer Hammond, Fairfax, VA.

These crayon drawings of memories of a tree house began with a series of questions, such as "How will you climb into it? Who will come into it?" A preliminary drawing with white chalk was made on 18- × 24-inch colored construction paper, which gives each drawing a suffused overall tone. Breaking up the background shape into varied colors adds interest.

not fully. Typical classroom projects in crayon usually are weak in color intensity, value contrast, and texture quality. In most instances, crayon is employed as a pallid, sketchy coloring agent instead of the glowing, vibrant, and excitingly expressive medium that it can and should be. If children are expected to grow in crayoning skills, the crayon's rich possibilities must be taught beginning from the first grade.

Whenever possible, request that the students or school supply agent obtain the large 48- or 64-color crayon boxes, with their beautiful range of tints and shades and their wide selection of neutralized hues. To bring out the deepest, richest color, prompt the students to apply the crayon with heavy pressure. ("Who can make the color sing?" "Who can make it shout?" as opposed to "Who is making it mumble?") Have students use a lot of newspaper padding under the paper to be crayoned. Point out the effects of using contrasting colors and of juxtaposing dark next to light colors, neutral next to high-intensity colors.

Challenge the students to create patterns of stripes, checks, plaids, diamonds, stars, spirals, and dots. Use paintings by artists such as Vuillard, Bonnard, Ida Kohlmyer, Mariam Shapiro, van Gogh, and Gauguin as exemplars of vibrant color, and show them Picasso's crayon drawings.

The entire mood of crayon work changes when the crayon is applied to varicolored or varitextured surfaces. Work on backgrounds other than the commonly used cream manila or white drawing paper. Pleasing results come about when crayon is employed richly on pink, red, orange, purple, blue, green, and even black construction paper. Have the students allow some of the background to show between objects; the background paper color will unify their compositions. Color changes its appearance on different color papers. Yellow changes to dull green on black construction paper, and all of the warm colors are slightly neutralized when they are applied to green paper but shimmer vibrantly when applied to red, pink, and orange surfaces.

Wax-crayon still lifes created by university students. College students hopefully will discover in their teacher training classes the luminous beauty inherent in the common, *everyday wax crayon. Then, they will be more motivated and qualified to help children in their classes bring forth the rich potential of the crayon medium used by itself.*

Preliminary sketches for crayon pictures on colored paper may be made with school chalk or a light-colored crayon. Do not let students use a pencil, because they grow frustrated when they try to manipulate a blunt crayon to color in a pencil-sketch's tiny details. Encourage bold use of the crayon. Urge color repetition throughout the composition to achieve unity. Completed crayon pictures may be given a sheen by rubbing them with a facial tissue or a folded paper towel.

Some issues of aesthetics to discuss include: What does color add to a picture? Why should colors be intense? Should all colors be intense? Why should we push a medium to its limit?

One vexing problem that the teacher of art faces is children who rush through their crayoning, who quickly color in a few shapes and then claim that they are finished. Some suggestions for dealing with this are given in Chapters 10 and 13. As always, the most successful strategies involve a teacher's well-planned, resourceful motivation that taps the students' concerns. This leads to a richly detailed drawing, which sets the stage for the crayon's expressive coloring.

Crayon Resist

For students of all ages, an exciting, creative art experience is the combination of vibrant, glowing wax crayon with translucent, flowing watercolors. For this technique, subjects that are rich in pattern and allover design, such as fish, birds, reptiles, insects, and butterflies, are recommended. Students genuinely are excited by the variety of insects in their environment, and the teacher can stimulate further interest by having them collect specimens to share with classmates. Illustrated books, wildlife periodicals, color slides, and films will broaden the students' awareness of nature's adaptational variety. Studying the design of insects' bodies increases general knowledge of design. For example, help them to see and draw the filigree pattern of insects' wings, the rhythmlike segments of a grasshopper's abdomen, the symmetrical balance of a ladybug's body, and the grace of a praying mantis's legs.

The pattern, details, and designs of the subject are of utmost importance in the crayon-resist technique, adding as they do to the sparkling effect of the finished painting. Whatever the theme, the more detail that is incorporated and the more overlapping of shapes that is achieved, the richer the design becomes. When the design is rich and complex, the negative areas evolve into varied shapes as well. Background embellishment—adding flowers, weeds, trees, vines, webs, and rock and cloud formations—will tie the composition together.

A successful crayon resist requires the following:

The crayon must be applied with heavy pressure, so that it will resist the watercolor (or water-diluted tempera) in the final stage. A

Iowa City Elementary Laboratory School, Iowa City, IA. Courtesy of Frank Wachowiak, Athens, GA.

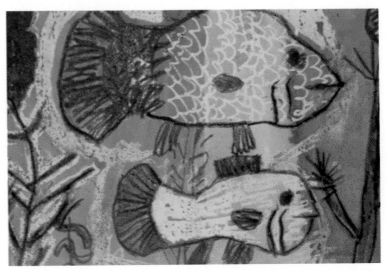

Courtesy of Frank Wachowiak, Athens, GA.

Underwater themes are particularly good for crayon-resist paintings. Here, the predominant use of a blue wash has one area of a highly effective contrast: the child chose a contrasting and off-center vertical band of pink water-diluted tempera going across both fish and background.

demonstration by the teacher of the results of light and heavy crayoning will make the point of how hard the students must press.

Putting several layers of newspaper padding under the paper facilitates heavy crayoning.

Leave some of the paper uncrayoned, such as between two solid shapes, two colors, and object and background color.

Negative space can be enriched with a pattern of radiating lines. These might include effects such as those formed around a pebble

Steps in a crayon-resist painting. Using white paper for the background, make a preliminary drawing in the first class session, using a light-colored crayon rather than a pencil. A second class period is for adding the crayon patterns, background details, and selected solid crayon areas. The children must be guided to apply the crayons with a strong pressure so that the wax will resist the subsequent watercolor. The watercoloring itself requires a final art class. Remind students to keep the watercolors transparent by adding sufficient water so that the paint does not obliterate the crayon design.

dropped in water together with dots, spirals, circles, hatching, and cross-hatching.

Encourage students to be imaginative in their choice of color. Reliance on natural or realistic colors should be minimized. Show the paintings of Raoul Dufy as examples of fantasy choices and use of washes. White crayon can be especially effective in this technique, providing a happy, magical surprise when the paint is applied. If a final black tempera wash is not planned, black crayon provides strong contrast.

When the crayoning is completed and the student is given the teacher's go-ahead, two techniques of resist may be employed: the wet-paper process, or dry-paper process. In the dry-paper method, students paint directly on their completed crayon work using watercolors or tempera. If tempera is being used, the teacher must first adjust the tempera's viscosity on a sample. Students may limit themselves to one color in painting the background or employ a variety of watercolors, as exemplified in the multileaf composition illustrated in this section. If the crayon has been applied heavily, paint can be applied directly over the crayoned area, producing an attractive texture.

Courtesy of Joyce Vroon, Trinity School, Atlanta, GA.

Second-grade student Emily Sharbaugh paints with different areas of color around the crayoned forms, being careful that the colors of wash do not run together.

Courtesy of Donna Cummins, Brookview Elementary School, Atlanta, GA.

A heavy coat of crayon will resist the dark wash, which here has beaded up on the surface to create a texture enriching the crayon radiating flower design.

In the wet-paper method, the desks or tables first should be covered with newspapers. Because the paper is fragile when wet, students should put their piece on a solid surface such as a Masonite board and, at the sink, immerse both paper and board in water until soaked. Students then transport their pieces (still on the board) to the painting station and lift them off carefully. Students then should load their brushes with watercolor or diluted tempera and drop or float the paint onto the un-crayoned areas. They also may direct the paint-laden brush around the

Saturday Children's Classes. Courtesy of Frank Wachowiak, Athens, GA.

Crayon engraving is used boldly and directly to make a statement about flowers and insects. Children express their ideas in direct, inimitable ways. In the foreground butterfly and in the huge, right-hand flower, the child's intuitive use of positive and nega- *tive pattern is brilliant. What youngsters depict so honestly and naively can be awe-inspiring.*

Courtesy of Frank Wachowiak, Athens, GA, and Mary Sayer Hammond, Fairfax, VA.

A youngster applies a heavy crayon undercoat for his crayon engraving.

edges of the crayoned shapes and let the color flow freely. They may use one watercolor wash (blue or blue-green is a favorite) or a variety of hues. They must be careful, however, that several bright colors do not flow together to make a dull, neutralized color. The wet-resist method is especially suited for undersea, aviary, and flying-insect themes. To add to the picture's charm, leave some white areas of the paper unpainted. For a large class, the teacher might prepare in advance several containers of water-diluted tempera. A large table or counter space near the sink can be designated as a painting area and students can take turns applying the wash over their crayon composition while the rest of the class is still crayoning or otherwise engaged.

In addition to the subject ideas mentioned earlier, the following themes are recommended for crayon-resist projects: a flower garden, fireworks display, the circus, the fair, umbrellas in the rain, a Halloween parade, falling autumn leaves, kites in the sky, in the swimming pool, underwater explorers, and jungle birds with plumage.

Crayon Engraving

Crayon engraving, which is sometimes referred to as "crayon etching," is a fascinating technique. It involves the use of sturdy, white drawing paper or manila file folders, wax crayons, black tempera paint, soap, brush, and engraving tools. It is a standard and popular school project, although its

many possibilities seldom are carried to maximum expressiveness. If teachers allow students to be satisfied with quick, superficial scribble designs and later with random scratches, students will never discover the new worlds of pattern and color overlay or the rich enhancement that results when crayon engraving is combined with other media, such as oil pastel.

Crayon engraving uses a linear approach. Therefore, materials that are rich in line, pattern, detail, and texture are ideal subject matter, and the natural sciences are a rich source. Some examples are animals such as the porcupine, anteater, armadillo, zebra, leopard, tiger, and rhino. Birds, especially those with exotic plumage, are good subjects, as are reptiles such as turtles, iguanas, and horned toads and insects such as dragonflies, praying mantises, butterflies, grasshoppers, and beetles. Also of interest are crustaceans, such as crabs and crayfish; fish, shells, and coral of many species; and all varieties of plant life.

The preliminary drawing for a crayon engraving should be made in pencil on a separate piece of newsprint or manila paper that is the same size as the sturdy paper to be used for the final work. Because crayon engraving is a labor-intensive process, students with limited stick-to-itiveness may come to appreciate using paper of a small size. Keeping sizes constant will prove to be beneficial for students retracing their drawings with dressmaker's white transfer paper.

The first step in a crayon engraving is to apply varied colors of crayon solidly to the sturdy paper's surface. The crayon should be applied evenly and with a strong pressure so that no part of the paper background shows. Coloring in two overlapping directions may help to ensure a rich coat of crayon, as will newspaper padding under the paper. The children may begin the crayoning phase by first making scribble designs in a light-colored crayon all over the paper and then filling in the resulting shapes solidly with a variety of bright colors. Alternatively, they may apply swatches or patches of color or have their crayoned areas coincide with their compositions. Avoid black and metallic crayons; use the most brilliant colors.

After the crayoning has been completed, the surface crayon flecks should be brushed off with a cloth or paper towel. *Caution:* Be sure that students put their names on the backs of their crayoned sheets *before* the paint is applied. The black tempera paint should be about the consistency of thin cream. To make it adhere to the waxy, crayoned surface, it must in most cases have liquid soap or detergent added; approximately 1 tablespoon per pint of tempera is needed. Alternatively, the brush filled with tempera can be rubbed over a bar of soap before it is applied to the crayoned surface. The teacher should make a test swatch and, when it is dry, determine its engravability. If the paint is too thick, it will chip off during the engraving.

Top left and right: Fish by middle school students. Courtesy of David Hodge, Oshkosh, WI. *Bottom:* Insects by a third-grade student. Saturday Children's Classes, courtesy of Frank Wachowiak, Athens, GA, and Mary Sayer Hammond, Fairfax, VA.

When the paint is thoroughly dry (overnight or longer), transfer the preliminary line drawing as follows:

Coat the drawing's reverse side with white crayon or chalk, or use dressmaker's white transfer paper.

Paper-clip the drawing (white crayon–surface down) to the black tempera–coated side of the sturdy paper, and with a pencil or ballpoint pen, make the transfer.

Engrave the lines through the tempera coating down to the crayon surface using a nail, scissors point, compass, or similar tool. (*Note:* Newspapers on the working surface are required, because the engraving phase can be messy.)

After the lines are engraved, add textures, patterns, and details with nut picks, forks, and pieces of old combs.

High contrast can be achieved by scraping away some solid-shape areas down to the crayon surface using a plastic, picnic-type disposable knife. A recommended tool, if the school budget permits, is the Sloyd or Hyde knife. This sturdy, short-bladed knife can engrave a fine line with its point or scrape away a large surface with its flat edge.

After completing the engraving, students may enrich their compositions by applying oil pastel colors back over some of the black tempera surfaces. Finally, the composition may be further enhanced by engraving details and texture through the newly oil-pasteled areas.

Crayon engraving is a challenging mixed-media technique. It opens up new avenues of discovery in line, color, contrast, pattern, and texture, especially for students at the upper elementary level and above. (See page 232.)

Crayon Encaustic

Crayon encaustic is a challenging painting medium to add to the upper elementary and middle school art repertoire. Many museums contain ancient Egyptian Fayumic mummy portraits that still glow with the inner light of wax. The Greeks used encaustic on marble, and early Christians mixed little glass pieces, called *tesserae*, into it. The encaustic

Facing page: In these three crayon engravings, students wisely preserved certain dark areas intact to contrast with the light-colored areas from which they scraped away the crayon. Approximately half of the areas are light and half of the areas are dark. The dark areas are either plain black or remain dark even after having been gone over with crayon.

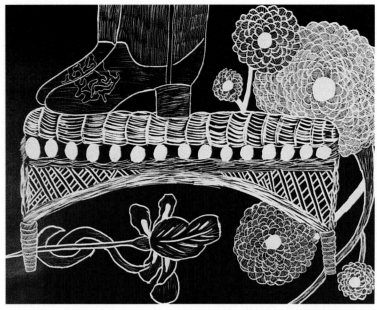

Eighth-grade. Courtesy of Baiba Kuntz, Glencoe, IL.

A related technique that might be considered a variation of crayon engraving and is superb for capturing textures is scratchboard. Notice the shades of grey achieved in the radiating scalloped pattern of the chrysanthemum heads.

process is the kind of creative adventure that is reserved for those teachers who are brave in spirit, eager to try something new, and persevering enough to collect a year's supply of broken crayons. Some teachers make encaustic painting an annual late-spring event, which the students eagerly anticipate. One teacher times the activity with the blossoming of colorful anemones, which become the visual motivation for the project.

The steps are as follows: Remove paper wrappings from the crayons, break the crayons into small pieces, and put them in glass babyfood jars or similar containers (not made of plastic or paper) or metal muffin tins. Each jar or compartment should contain a different color. If a muffin tin is used, make sure that it fits into a deeper and slightly larger baking tin. This slightly larger cake tin containing water, making a double-boiler arrangement to heat the containers of wax, is required to prevent fires. Because of space limitations, the number of colors may need to be limited to the primary and secondary colors plus white, black, and a few tints.

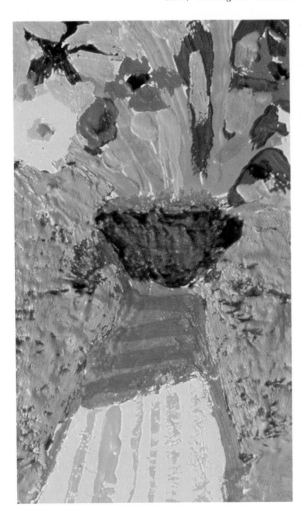

Grade 3, Athens Academy. Courtesy Mary McCutheon, Athens, GA.

These charming paintings were created by employing the melted crayon or encaustic method. The size of the cardboard is approximately 8 × 12 inches. Color reproductions of flower paintings by artists such as Odilon Redon, Vincent van Gogh, Paul Cézanne, and Paul Gauguin were displayed and discussed during the project. A bouquet of freshly picked, multihued anemones provided the immediate visual motivation.

The most functional working station for encaustic painting is a large, sturdy, newspaper-covered table. Place one end of the table against a wall near an electrical outlet. Place one or two electric hot plates in the middle of the table. Put the crayon-filled containers or muffin tins in a 2- or 3-inch-deep metal baking pan. Fill the pan two-thirds full of water, and place it on the hot plate. When the crayons have melted, reduce the heat and place one or more Q-tips or water-color brushes into each crayon container. These brushes should be old and reserved for this encaustic project only. Keep the water at the temperature of the melted crayon to maintain a consistent flow of crayon.

White or colored cardboard approximately 9 × 12 or 12 × 12 inches is recommended for the painting surface. Scrap mat board, chip-board, gift-box covers, and grocery carton cardboard coated with latex are other possibilities.

A preliminary sketch for a crayon-encaustic painting is recommended, unless the theme is purely nonobjective, in the manner of Jackson Pollock, Helen Frankenthaler, and Hans Hoffman. Subject-matter possibilities include a flower bouquet, butterflies, an exotic bird in foliage, a fantastic fish among shells and seaweed, an imaginary monster, and a clown.

The teacher must supervise encaustic painting carefully. Never crowd the working station. The group must be limited to four to six students depending on the size of the table. To prevent wax fires, the water must never be permitted to boil out of the pan. The electrical current may need to be turned off and on periodically so that the melted crayon does not cool off. Additional pieces of crayon will need to be placed in the containers. Remind students that brushes or crayon applicators should *not* be switched from container to container; students must wait their turn for a color. *Caution:* The crayon containers are filled with molten wax and must not be taken out of the heated pan during painting.

This project cannot be rushed; sometimes, the beauty of encaustic does not materialize until several layers of melted crayon have been applied. If layers are built up, the finished work will take on an exciting, thick impasto quality. When one color is applied over another, there is the possibility of further embellishment. This can be done by incising lines with a nail through the top coat to reveal the crayon color underneath. To solve the problem of an insufficient number of old crayons when a large area must be covered, powdered tempera can be mixed with melted paraffin. Crayon encaustic produces paintings with color richness and glow that are unsurpassed. (See also page 236.)

Oil Pastel

The introduction of oil pastels in their rich and exciting array of hues has opened a whole new world of color exploration and expression in both elementary and middle schools. These glowing oil pastels generally are within most schools' budget range. The only caution is that because of their oil content, they may stain clothing.

The most attractive feature of oil pastels is the ease with which students can apply them to obtain shimmering, vivid, painterly color compositions. Thus, students can produce rich results without the pressure required for regular crayons. Oil pastels work especially well on deep-colored construction paper, in which the colored background serves as

Athens Academy. Courtesy Mary McCutheon, Athens, GA.

Note the floral fine-art reproductions displayed, the live anenome bouquet, the newspaper-covered table, and the jars of melted crayon in the double boiler-type pan within a pan over a hot plate.

Saturday Children's Classes, courtesy of Frank Wachowiak, Athens, GA, and Mary Sayer Hammond, Fairfax, VA.

a unifying or complementary factor. Young students should be encouraged in their first efforts to apply the pastels boldly in solid-color areas, pressing hard to achieve a glowing surface, and to use color contrasts. Because the intensity of the pastel hues is affected by the paper color, students should note the effects of small color swatches on their paper's reverse side.

Recommendations for oil-pastel projects, especially when colored construction paper is used for the background, are:

Make the preliminary drawing or sketch with white or light school chalk or crayon. Chalk is excellent, because it is easily erased. (Use a paper towel or facial tissue if the students want to make changes.)

Press for the richest effects. One suggestion for coloring in small or complex shapes is to apply the pastel in a line close to the chalk outline and then fill in the shape. Discourage haphazard, scribbled coloring.

Remind students that colors have many tints and shades, which are especially important for capturing leaves and grassy fields with their nuances of light and shade.

Black, white, and grey add to any color scheme.

Colors, both tints and shades, bright and dull, including the blacks and whites, should be repeated in different parts of the composition to create unity. This color repetition should employ differences of size, shape, and intensity. A hue that is repeated for unity should be differentiated in value so that the echo of the color is there without the monotony of pure repetition. This is especially true when the student is making a pattern such as bricks on a wall, tiles on a roof, or stones in a walk, where the repetition of the same color becomes static and lifeless unless sensitively varied.

Remember that contrasting values are stronger than contrasting hues.

When it is desired that the colored paper background show through in a complementing way, apply the pastel impressionistically in strokes, lines, or dots.

New colors can be created by applying pastel over pastel; however, a very light color cannot be totally darkened unless the light is first

Top: A collection of butterflies, as well as color photographs of butterflies in a garden, provided motivation. They inspired this oil pastel by an upper elementary grade youngster. Notice how large and small butterflies in different shapes create variety and beauty. A host of patterns was used for the background: circles, dots, and wiggly as well as rippling lines. **Middle:** *Astronauts in their spaceship was the theme for this third-grade oil pastel.* **Bottom:** *Oil pastel on black paper of birds in trees.*

A portrait was done in oil pastels on black paper following a study of Van Gogh and his Post-Impressionistic manner of applying colors in small directional strokes.

Steps in the process of oil-pastel resist. **Top:** *Preliminary drawing in school chalk on colored construction paper.* **Middle:** *Oil pastel applied in solids and patterns up to but not covering the chalk lines.* **Bottom:** *Slightly water-diluted black tempera applied lightly with a soft-bristle brush.*

Saturday Children's Classes, courtesy of Frank Wachowiak, Athens, GA, and Mary Sayer Hammond, Fairfax, VA.

Oil-pastel resist takes oil pastel a step further. The resist color of wash goes into the lines left empty to create a stained-glass effect and also adds texture on the plain areas. Here, many shapes of different sizes and types help create beauty.

scraped off. A dark color can be lightened somewhat by the application of white, and colors can be dulled through application of their complements, such as red over green, orange over blue. To alter a color, first use soft pressure with varidirectional strokes, and then increase pressure.

Oil-Pastel Resist

Oil pastels alone can be beautifully employed as a final step in many techniques, such as tempera paintings, crayon engravings, and vegetable or found-object prints. However, they also can be used in the oil pastel–resist process with stunning results.

Teachers and students who are familiar with the crayon-resist technique will welcome oil pastel as another resist medium. It does not require the time or intense exertion on the part of the students demanded by crayons.

The same steps as outlined for the crayon-resist technique should be followed:

- Make a preliminary drawing in chalk.
- Vary the width of the chalk line, and emphasize thicker lines.

- Apply the oil pastel heavily so that it will resist the final coat of black paint.
- Leave the chalk lines uncovered.
- Use the brightest, most intense pastel hues.
- Avoid black.

Before applying paint, evaluate the final oil-pastel composition for a variation of repeated colors. Also, look for a variety of patterns: dots, circles, overlapping wiggly lines, radiating lines in circles or rays, ripple-in-a-stream lines, hatch and cross-hatch lines, stars, asterisks, diamonds, and spirals.

Before applying paint, also gently brush off the chalk lines. Place the composition on a newspaper-protected surface and apply a coat of black tempera paint. Applied with a soft brush, the paint must be of exactly the right consistency—not too thin, not too thick. Because paint formulas change, always do a test first (some tempera paints now contain an adhesive and cannot be used). If the paint covers the areas of oil pastel, it is too thick. The resisting oil in the oil pastels will dry out soon after it is applied to the paper, so do not wait too long to apply the black paint. Finally, oil pastel–resist compositions may be given a protective coat of gloss polymer medium to enhance their beauty.

Chapter 22

Painting

Painting with Watercolors

While tempera is the most common and popular painting medium in elementary and middle school art programs, teachers in many instances use transparent watercolors. These come in semimoist cakes or tiny tubes packaged in metal or plastic containers, and they are available in primary and secondary colors plus black. Transparent watercolor painting demands special technical skills, and mature painters devote countless hours to its mastery. They employ a wide range of beautiful colors available in tube form and costly sablehair brushes.

The watercolor paintings on page 244 are by Japanese elementary school children. These children are provided with a spectrum of watercolors in tubes and painting palettes beginning in the first grade. Most of their watercolor paintings begin with a preliminary sketch in pencil or pen. In some cases, children moisten the paper before beginning the coloring. As these paintings reveal, many persevere to produce rich, space-filled compositions that exhibit transparent watercolors' characteristic spontaneity.

Teachers often employ the semimoist watercolors to teach about the color properties of hue, value, and intensity. Mixing primary colors will produce secondary colors, and mixing secondary colors will produce tertiarycolors. Diluting a color with water in gradual stages can produce a color-value chart. Color can be neutralized through mixing with complementary hues, and creating watercolor washes on moist paper achieves dark-to-light sky and water effects.

The following recommendations constitute a "primer" for watercolor projects:

White watercolor or construction paper is recommended.

Newspapers under paintings help to speed cleanup and also provide a practice surface.

Round, pointed, soft-bristle, camel-hair brushes are recommended. They should always be rinsed clean at the end of the period and stored either bristle-end-up or flat in a container.

Watercolor boxes containing the semimoist cakes of paint should be rinsed and wiped clean at the close of the period and then allowed to dry open.

Water containers should be changed when the water in them becomes muddy. Paper towels are handy for spills and blotting up excess paint on works in progress.

Preliminary sketches in pencil, felt-nib or nylon-tipped pen, or light watercolor applied with a small brush are recommended.

Areas that are to appear white or light in the final painting can be masked with masking tape before the paper is moistened or the painting begun. When the painting is completed and dry, the mask can be removed and a final touch-up made.

Watercolor washes of the same color in the same value applied over one another will darken the color. It is recommended that students begin a painting with light colors or values and build to darker colors for detail.

When painting is done on a wet surface, the paper may need to be remoistened by lightly sprinkling the surface with water from time to time.

Paintings appear vibrant and contrasting when moist but unfortunately lose their brilliance when dry. A second application of watercolor paint over a dried color may help.

While wet or moist, paintings should not be stored one on top of another. If no drying rack or counters are available, dry the paintings on the floor around the room's perimeter.

Some very successful watercolor projects are those in which watercolor is combined with colored crayons or oil pastels in a resist method (see Chapter 21).

This boldly direct and colorful painting of a watercolor box in use is by a talented teenager. Notice the thin and thick lines and the overall spontaneity, which is particularly desired in watercolors.

Study art history exemplars: watercolors by Winslow Homer and John Singer Sargent, and brush paintings from China and Japan.

One aesthetic issue to be considered is the importance in art (and in life) of spontaneity, verve, and assuredness—a vibrant, fresh appearance versus a labored, overworked, fussy, muddled appearance.

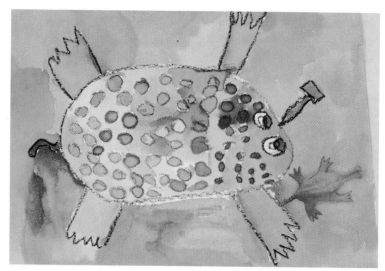

Courtesy of Melody Milbrandt, Valdosta, GA.

To illustrate a story, a kindergartner painted this frog, made delightful by multihued bumps and the breaking up of the body's form with a spectrum of colors.

Painting with Tempera

All children should have the opportunity to express their ideas in brush and paint. The best-quality tempera paints, whether in powder or liquid form, are rich in color and have excellent covering properties. Children who paint with tempera can apply color over color freely to achieve jewellike effects or repaint areas with which they are not pleased.

Although teachers are aware of the possibilities for colorful art expressions offered by tempera, they sometimes do not include it in their art programs because of its cost and the housekeeping chores involved. Tempera projects do require more preparation of materials, more careful storage, and more controlled cleanup procedures than watercolor or crayon projects; however, these factors should not prevent teachers from discovering how tempera painting can enrich children's art repertoire. Even when classes are large and facilities limited, there are expeditious, time-saving methods for incorporating tempera into the art program.

Cardboard soda-bottle containers and discarded glass-tumbler carryalls can be used as carrying cases. Discarded baby-food jars and half-pint milk cartons can be used as containers. To prevent the paint from

This delightfully entrancing watercolor, My Friend and Me, *is the work of a first-grade child in Japan. Notice the variety of lines in the hairy, toothy main figure. Opposite colors, yellow and purple, along with mixtures of each color give the work power.*

drying out between sesssions, the milk cartons can be resealed with spring clothespins.

Students can both perform a service and gain color knowledge by helping to prepare the tempera paint. They can mix various hues, tints, shades, and neutralized colors. For extra beauty in the paintings, consider restricting the color choices to, for example, just triadic colors, a narrow range of analogous colors, or all very light colors. For a class of 30 children, about 60 containers of varying colors should be prepared, with an additional six containers of white and four containers of black. Containers should only be filled partway to keep paint from covering the brush's metal ferrule and the students' fingers.

If class time is limited, the teacher may need to prepare the color assortment in advance. Those who object to this procedure because it does not give students the opportunity to learn about mixing colors should be reminded that professional artists usually have a wealth of colors, tints, shades, and neutrals at their disposal to create paintings. Children deserve the same advantage. When the class is limited to a few basic colors because there is not enough time to mix a variety, the expressive output of children suffers, and the joy in painting diminishes.

Individual containers of paint should be placed on a table or rolling cart that is accessible from all sides. It should be low enough so the various colors are visible. If possible, a separate brush should be available for every container. This procedure saves time, paint, and squabbles over brushes. The children take turns choosing a container of color, and when they have finished with it, they return it (with its brush inside) to the supply station. Children should use one color at a time— and use it thoroughly throughout the painting. Some teachers have used a timed swap of colors among all their students. To achieve unity and balance in their paintings, encourage students to repeat colors around the picture. While primarily aesthetic, this injunction has the practical advantage of minimizing traffic around the supply station.

Adequate time should be allotted for cleanup. Because brushes that are left standing for long periods of time in paint lose their elasticity, they should be taken out of the paint containers and any excess paint remaining in the brush squeezed back into the container. Then, they should be placed in a large basin of soapy water to soak overnight. The next morning, they can be rinsed in clear water and stored either

---

Painting with tempera on large paper surfaces gives children a real opportunity to express their ideas in paint. This bold portrait by a primary-grade student is on 24 × 36-inch paper. Newspapers covered the floor, and the child painted freely.

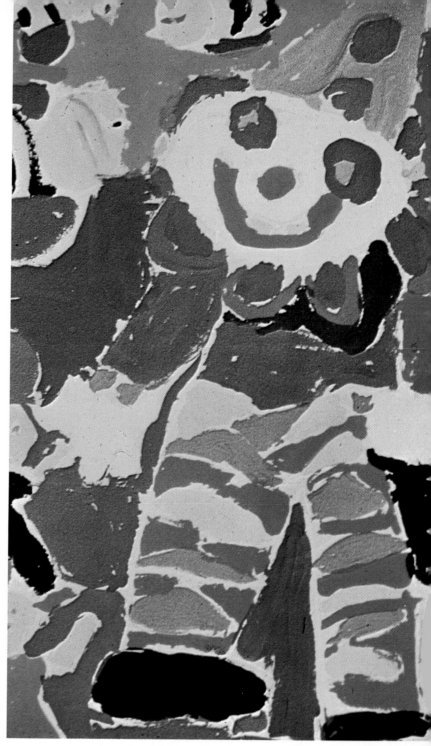

Courtesy of Frank Wachowiak and Ted Ramsay, University Elementary School, Iowa City, IA. *Emphasis Art*, First Edition.

Courtesy of Joyce Vroon, Trinity School, Atlanta, GA.

Paint the large background shapes first. Then when the color is dry or another day, add other colors to create patterns and textures, as third-grade student Christine Bunyan did in this clown painting. "Pass the Paint" was used; on the teacher's signal, students switched paint containers.

Courtesy of Joyce Vroon, Trinity School, Atlanta, GA.

Neutralized tints and shades in both warm and cool colors were derived from a fabric design and applied to the student's subject matter of a scene.

bristle-end-up or flat in a box. Brushes with wood handles must be washed and stored to dry immediately lest the wooden handle be damaged. Unless the baby-food jars of paint can be covered, store the jars in an airtight cupboard or drawer, or put the containers on a tray and seal the tray in a giant plastic bag. To prevent the lips and edges of containers from sticking, they should occasionally be wiped clean or waxed.

Some teachers use plastic egg cartons or ice-cube trays as tempera paint containers. In this method, each student has a brush, and the brush is washed clean each time another color is chosen. Preventing drying of leftover paint is more difficult with this method, but the cartons or trays can be sealed in plastic bags. To help prevent the unpleasant odor of aging tempera, a drop of wintergreen can be added to the big jars of tempera.

Semimoist cakes of opaque paint are now available in tubs or tins, and some teachers claim that these save time in cleanup and storage procedures. Others, however say they inhibit the free-flowing style that liquid tempera encourages in children.

During the primary grades, tempera painting is a natural for children. The very young child especially enjoys making bold, splashy designs in paint and needs only the materials and invitation to start. Themes such as explosion in a paint factory, Fourth of July fireworks, butterflies in a flower garden, bunny rabbit's Easter party, a kite fight, and planets in outer space fire the imagination. Colored construction paper, including black, provides an excellent surface, because the color of the paper can unify the composition. Also consider adventurous choices like wallpaper samples and newspaper classified pages.

The following strategies have proved to be helpful in tempera painting projects:

Students should be encouraged to make preliminary sketches on their paper in chalk or using a brush and light-colored paint.

Minimize cleanup by using protective newspapers on paint supply stations and individual painting areas. Have moist towels available for accidental paint spills and use protective plastic on the carpet.

Develop preventive strategies for those likely to make spills—for example, a minimal amount of paint in the containers, or special holders and containers.

Encourage children to wear protective clothing, such as an old shirt.

Remind students to wipe excess paint from their brushes back into the containers.

Lest the colors run together, caution children about painting next to a painted area that still is wet.

When making a color change, urge students to wait until a color is completely dry before painting over it.

If brushes must be cleaned during the painting session, tell students to squeeze out the excess water thoroughly before using the brush to

Courtesy of Melody Milbrandt, Valdosta, GA.

Tempera paints mixed ahead of time in attractive tones can produce handsome paintings, as in this primary grade student's painting of reading a book about a cat named Gregory.

paint again. If not, the paint in the individual containers will become water-diluted and less intense.

During upper elementary and middle school, students can design with paint on moist, colored construction paper. They can use the dry-brush or pointillistic approach to achieve texture. They can explore mixed-media techniques, combining tempera and crayon, tempera and pastel, and tempera and India ink in a semibatik process. Encourage older students to mix a greater variety of tints, shades, and neutralized hues to achieve a more individual and personal style. They can use discarded pie tins, TV-dinner trays, and plastic cafeteria trays for their palettes. They must be cautioned, however, to be economical and not mix more paint than they need. For tints, they should add the hue a little at a time to the white paint rather than vice versa. Paint tins always should be rinsed out at the end of class.

Wearing painting smocks of old white shirts to protect their clothing, second-grade students paint a large palette by mixing their own colors in little paint trays.

Students cannot rush through a tempera painting project any more than they can hurry through any qualitative creative endeavor; therefore, sufficient time must be allotted for all phases of the undertaking. First comes the motivational time, then the preliminary sketching session. These are followed by the studio work, which involves choices of colors and then achievement of contrast, pattern, and detail. Throughout the studio activity, there should be evaluation of the work in its several stages. Finally, the completed paintings are exhibited. Tempera painting should be included in every school art program!

Tempera Resist

For middle school students who have had many elementary school experiences painting with tempera per se, try tempera resist. Tempera resist employs both a liquid tempera underpainting, followed by a final coating of India ink. It is a challenging technique replete with hidden surprises. Although highly recommended as an exciting project in painting, it presents some materials problems, the high cost of India ink among them.

Fifth-grade student Sarah Billington paints in the areas of her marker drawing of a bird. She chose an assortment of low value colors to create a dramatic night effect.

The black resist line varies in width amongst the variety in the painting of the trees and the different background colors.

Saturday Children's Classes. Courtesy of Frank Wachowiak, Athens, GA, and Mary Sayer Hammond, Fairfax, VA.

Bits of black attached to the solid-paint areas add interest to this painting of a dozen different flowers and a spider in its web.

Burney Harris Middle School, Courtesy of Nancy Elliott, Athens, GA.

Tempera-resist painting by a middle school student shows a beautiful flowing divisions of shapes and a sophisticated series of analogous colors.

The tempera paint that is employed should be a good quality liquid tempera and applied heavily. Powdered tempera is not recommended, although some teachers claim that powdered tempera works when it is mixed with a small amount of liquid glue. Whether liquid or powder, the paint must be of a thick, creamy consistency, and not watery. Watery paint will absorb the final ink coating rather than resist it.

Bright, intense hues of tempera should be employed for the highest contrast of black ink against color. Discourage the use of dark blue, dark purple, and brown, which will not show up. Subtle, lightly greyed hues, such as sienna, ochre, light umber, and light grey are effective. White

Saturday Children's Classes. Courtesy of Frank Wachowiak, Athens, GA.

may be employed with discrimination but generally should be repeated, because a solitary white area often detracts from the rest of the composition. Recommended papers are construction paper in white or light colors and cardboard from store cartons.

Considerable time is needed for the various steps in the process: the preliminary drawing, the tempera painting, the inking, the rinsing, and the optional coating with gloss polymer. The sketch or preliminary drawing should be made in chalk. Encourage students to vary the pressure of the chalk lines, making lines from thick to thin. The importance of this will be revealed in the second phase, when the ink is applied and soaks into the space left by the chalked lines. A relevant aesthetic consideration for this project is that the more the students break large shapes into small shapes, the more beautiful the finished result will be. As students paint with the tempera, urge them to paint up to, but not over, the chalked lines, leaving a gap from $\frac{1}{16}$ to $\frac{3}{16}$ of an inch wide. The more varied the chalk lines or the paper surface remaining between painted areas, the more successfully contrasting the composition will be. Remind students not to paint the shapes, areas, and details they want to be black in the completed painting.

Caution students that a tempera color painted over another dry tempera area will wash off in the final rinse; therefore, they must plan their color scheme in advance. Patterns painted into wet tempera areas can be effective, however. Encourage students to be expressive in their color usage—for example, to employ varied kinds of green for grass and trees, or many values and intensities of blue for skies. After all of the desired colored areas are painted, the work should be stored to dry completely.

For the India inking phase, cover a working surface with newspapers. With a tissue, wipe off the chalk remaining in the lines. Place the painting on newspapers, and paint with the India ink in random, circular strokes. Totally cover the painting, and store overnight to dry completely.

Wet paintings tear easily. For the final rinsing phase, put the painting onto a protective backing, such as a Masonite board or old

---

Top: *Steps in creating a tempera-India ink resist. The preliminary drawing is made in school chalk on white or light-colored construction paper.* **Middle:** *Paint is applied up to the chalk outline but not covering it, and allowed to dry completely.* **Bottom:** *Then, undiluted India ink is applied generously over the tempera surface, allowed to dry thoroughly, and rinsed off at the sink.*

cafeteria tray, and then put them into the sink and rinse with cold water or take them outdoors and rinse gently with a hose. Begin rinsing in the center of the work and move outward. Do not direct the water toward the same area too long, or too much paint will wash off or, even worse, the paper will disintegrate. A moist sponge or finger run may bring out the color where the ink stubbornly sticks. After rinsing, very carefully lift the painting onto a counter or the floor, and blot it with paper towels. When the tempera-resist painting is completely dry, give it a protective and enhancing coat of liquid wax or glossy polymer medium.

Mural Making

Mural projects help students to acquire not only art knowledge but also another kind of knowledge; what it means to plan and carry out a project through working together. Collaborative art builds self-esteem and diminishes alienation. Memorable experiences are achieved through group involvement in projects of large scale and scope—for example, decorating the classroom for a celebration, or presenting a series of works on a central theme. With the teacher acting as facilitator, students as a group can generate ideas. Educational goals can be organized according to objectives, and strategies for assessing the project's effectiveness in solving problems in social settings can be developed.

Some subjects have almost universal appeal to particular age groups, and certain themes are especially appropriate. For very young children, suggested topics are a butterfly dance, land of make-believe, fish in the sea, Noah's ark, and a flower garden. Intermediate and elementary school children respond to the farm, birds in a tree, animals at the zoo or in the jungle, fun on the playground, when dragons roamed the world, and fun at the beach. Upper elementary and middle school students react positively to astronauts in space, a kite-flying contest, aquanauts exploring the sea, rodeo, rock festival, block party, state fair, three-ring circus, winter carnival, world of the future, and where and how young people in our community play and relax. (See Chapters 11 and 12 on integration with other subjects.)

Before the class begins a mural, the teacher who is interested in integrating social studies with the project can ask: "What is the purpose of a mural?" "Who painted the first murals?" Show cave paintings from Altamira and Fonte de Gaume. Are there any murals in your commu-

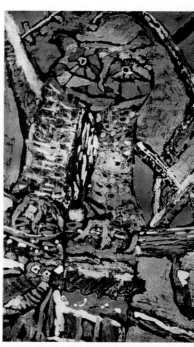

Courtesy of David Hodge, Oshkosh, WI.

Before and after results in a tempera and India ink resist project by a middle school youngster. For successful results, be sure that the tempera paint is a quality-brand liquid type and the India ink is used undiluted.

nity's buildings, post offices, and schools? What was their original social, political, or educational intent? Knowledge of art history can be developed through discussion of the artist who made the mural. Using art criticism methods, debate the relative merits of each mural. Discuss the aesthetic issues of realism and abstraction and of colors muddied by aging.

The great Mexican murals were made to promote both social consciousness and aesthetic awareness, and older students can be involved in decisions about how to include real community concerns and goals in a mural. When murals are made out in the community, a rich social setting comes into play and enriches the process. In mural-making projects, when aesthetic interests go along with other interests such as civic, commercial, health, or moral issues, the combination can make the experience doubly important to students.

An upper elementary grade youngster retouches the lines on the painted rhinoceros he contributed to a jungle-theme group mural. The preliminary drawings were made with school chalk on large cardboard sheets salvaged from mattress boxes. Then, chalk lines were gone over with brush and black tempera to provide unity of line quality through-out the mural. The children then colored up to, but did not cover, the black outlines. Finally, the murals were taken into the community to enliven a children's ward in a local hospital.

Taking advantage of transmitted light for a "stained glass window" effect, fourth- and fifth-grade students stand atop the shelving to paint their jungle mural.

University Elementary School, Iowa City, IA. Courtesy of Frank Wachowiak and Ted Ramsay, *Emphasis Art*, First Edition.

The group mural Fun at the Park *was painted by elementary school children on a 10- × 200-foot plywood construction barrier. The preliminary sketch on the previously primed barrier fence was made in chalk, then reinforced with black enamel applied with ½-and 1-inch-wide utility brushes. Parents donated leftover paints in a variety of colors for the project.*

Having settled on a theme, other questions follow: What medium or technique should be employed? How large should our mural be? Where can we work on it? Where will it be displayed when completed? How shall each student's contribution to the mural be decided?

If, for example, a collage-type pin-up mural is agreed on, the following procedure is recommended: When all students have completed their individual contributions to the total mural, the teacher and students should devote at least one art session to composing the mural. Discuss the merits of the placement and design. Here, the teacher's tact and gentle persuasion play an important role. Bring to the children's attention that a mural in one sense is like a giant painting and requires the same compositional treatment. Urge students to strive for varied sizes of objects or figures, varied heights, and varied breakup of space in both foreground and background. Encourage overlapping of shapes, grouping of objects to achieve unity, and quiet areas to balance busy or detailed ones. Have students use larger shapes or figures at the bottom and smaller ones at the top to create an illusion of distance.

Arts & Activities, photo courtesy of Virginia S. Robinson.

Hundreds of clay balls were flattened and stamped with designs. Some were stained. Then, they were arranged by middle school students into a mural of lasting beauty. See Virginia Smithwick Robinson and Robert Clements, "Mosaic Panels." May 1982.

Children who complete their assigned main segments early can enhance the compositions with space-filling elements, such as rainbows, clouds, and pets. Put in recreational and transportation equipment: balls, kites, cars, trucks, bicycles, motorcycles, frisbees, planes. Some can make street furniture: telephone poles, mailboxes, signs, fences, benches, and landscape elements of trees, bushes, and rocks.

When the separate segments finally are arranged in a composition that is pictorially unified, they are stapled or glued. If the mural is attached to a separate piece of plywood or heavy carton cardboard, display it in the school's entrance foyer, hallway, or lunchroom for everyone to enjoy; exhibit it in a building out in the community; or exhibit it first in the school and then in the community.

Take, for example, fun on the playground as the theme for a collage (cut-and-paste) mural. Ask the following questions: How many different kinds of games or sports should be included? (List them on the chalkboard.) How shall we decide which activity each student will select to portray? How many different areas of the playground will be included? What types of playground equipment will be included? Why should all children not be the same size? Will they all be dressed alike? (Make a list on the chalkboard of the different kinds of clothing and uniforms they might wear.) What patterns might be shown on their clothes? (Wallpaper samples or fabric remnants may be used). What else can be included? (Make a list on the chalkboard: trees, fences, airplanes, signs, and so on.)

Some other mural techniques and media also can be used. For freestyle, expressive murals that are painted directly on surfaces such as oaktag, cardboard, poster board, and hardboard, use tempera paint, enamels, or latex paint. Use a preliminary outline in black paint to give unity and spark the composition. From designs made by individuals or small groups, one may be chosen, or several effective designs may be incorporated into one design that will be painted by small groups who take turns painting.

Saturday Children's Classes. Courtesy of Frank Wachowiak, Athens, GA, and Mary Sayer Hammond, Fairfax, VA.

A collage-type pin-up mural was created from fourth-graders' oil pastel drawings of astronauts and spaceships. Students then cut them out and transformed them into an exciting group mural project.

DRAG'ON IN TO LAURENS PRIMARY

For a detailed description of this unusual project by Diane Turner, see the February 1983 issue of *School Arts* Magazine. Illustration courtesy of Davis Publications, Worcester, MA.

Billboard mural, 10 × 25 feet, designed and created by second-grade children in Laurens, South Carolina. The medium is wax crayons on billboard paper. The children made small sketches of dragons, from which a selection for the billboard was made. Several youngsters worked in tandem on each dragon, so that every child could contribute. Two donated billboards were on display in the community during the March Youth Art Month Celebration.

Chapter 23

Paper Projects in Two Dimensions

Collage

A popular form of visual expression in elementary and middle schools today is collage, with its related family of montage, decoupage, mosaic, collograph, and assemblage. Over 50 years ago, shocked dismay greeted the initial collages of Pablo Picasso, Georges Braque, Carlo Carra, and Kurt Schwitters, in which the artists dared to include cardboard and printed words. Today, their creations in paper, cardboard scraps, and paste (the word *collage* derives from the French *coller*, which means "to glue") appear relatively tame. The wellsprings from which contemporary artists such as Robert Rauschenberg and Alexis Smith now draw their materials are so bountiful that the technique is limitless in its possibilities.

The collage technique promotes design using overlapping of shapes and colors, positive and negative shapes, value contrast, pattern, and texture. Students have the unique opportunity of rearranging the elements in their work until they achieve a satisfying composition. Approaches to collage range from simple cutting, tearing, and pasting of paper to complex sewing, shearing, and gluing of fabric, plastics, posters, plywood, cardboard, Day-Glo paper, wallpaper and rug samples, paint chips, colored tissue paper, and colored magazine pages. (The artist Jean Dubuffet even used coffee grounds and butterfly wings!)

A preliminary sketch is recommended when the subject matter is a landscape, figure composition, or still-life arrangement. For themes from the imagination, for fantasy, or for purely nonobjective designs, direct cutting, tearing, and pasting are acceptable. In both processes, however, permanent adherence of the separate parts should be postponed until both student and teacher critique the work's strengths and weaknesses. Some other suggestions are:

Cut and arrange the large shapes or motifs first. If a colored background is being employed, include it in your design by allowing some of the background to show and unify the composition.

 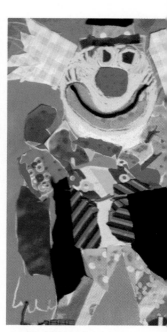

Saturday Children's Classes, courtesy of Frank Wachowiak, Athens, GA.

First a large drawing that bumps the edges is made with chalk on a piece of 12- × 18-inch colored paper. Then, the child cuts cloth scraps to fit the areas. Yarn, buttons, rickrack, and colored paper scraps also can be used. Here, oil pastels were added on the face and hands.

Small details and patterns can be pasted onto the large shapes before they are glued to the background surface. Overlapping of shapes is a major feature of collage making.

Eye-catching materials, such as aluminum foil, synthetic silver and gold foils, shiny plastic, and cellophane, fascinate children, who tend to overuse them. Guide the students to use such materials only as points of emphasis. Remove them if they detract from the whole.

Repetition of a color, shape, value, pattern, or texture adds unity to a collage; however, instead of repeating the element, color, or shape exactly, vary it somehow.

Recommend using an uneven rather than an even repetition of elements. For example, repeat a certain shape or color three times rather than twice.

Encourage the use of informal (asymmetrical) rather than formal (symmetrical) balance.

Avoid a lot of "sticky" problems by using discarded magazines as paste applying surfaces. When a clean pasting area is needed, turn to another page.

Ambitious teachers may want to enlist both parents and children in making cloth banners from the students' paper designs. Army units in ancient Rome each had their own decorated standard. Cloth banners were first used in the Middle Ages during the Crusades, when each force had its own insignia. Artists such as Miriam Shapiro, Jim Dine, Henri Matisse, and Richard Lindner have had banners of their collage designs made.

Tissue-Paper Collage

On the first day of a tissue paper–collage project, the teacher can surprise students by unfolding a package of tissue papers of assorted colors. Excitement grows as one color of tissue overlaps another on a white paper background or against the window. Students can tell the teacher which colors to overlap, and then they can invent a name for the resulting hue.

To encourage color awareness and exploration, a free-design, nonobjective, colored-tissue collage is recommended for children from the third grade up. Using a sheet of oaktag, white drawing paper, or construction paper approximately 12 × 18 inches as a background surface, cut or tear different sizes and shapes of tissue. Adhere them to the background using undiluted liquid laundry starch as the adhesive, and overlap the various shapes. A ½-inch utility brush or a large watercolor brush makes an excellent starch applicator. Because it is most difficult to change the value of a dark tissue by overlapping, begin with the lighter-colored tissues and proceed only gradually to darker values. Reserve the darker colors for the second phase of pasting.

First, apply a coating of starch to the area that is to be covered with tissue. Then, the tissue should be placed down carefully over the wet area and another coat of starch applied over it. If brushes pick up some

Recycle scraps of colored construction paper into collage projects such as these. Primary-grade youngsters arranged paper scraps in assorted sizes, shapes, and colors for their compositions. Supplemental details, patterns, and motifs were added with crayons, oil pastels, markers, paper punches, and brush and paint.

Saturday Children's Classes. Courtesy of Frank Wachowiak, Athens, GA.

Pieced and appliquéd cotton embroidered with plain and metallic yarns, 69 × 105 inches. Bequest of Maxim Karolik. Courtesy of the Museum of Fine Arts, Boston, MA.

What could have more power and charm than the collagelike quilts made by African-American Harriet Powers (1837–1911), a former slave from Athens, Georgia? Her artworks now hang in our nation's most important museums. You can give your artwork strength by using her ideas. A large checkerboard pattern gives unity. Color is restrained to mostly white and very dark. Tints and shades of essentially only two complementary colors, orange and blue, are used. The almost abstract figures create bold positive and negative shapes. Most important, the artwork is about deeply felt Biblical stories and combined with personal anecdotes in her own words, such as, for the lower left square, "Cold Thursday, 10 of Feb. 1895. A woman frozen while at prayer. A woman frozen at a gateway. A man with a sack of meal frozen. Icicles formed from the breath of a mule. All blue birds killed" Can you find the dead blue birds, woman praying, man with sack, and the mule with icicles?

Saturday Children's Classes. Courtesy of Frank Wachowiak and Ted Ramsay. Pictures 2 & 4, *Emphasis Art*, Second Edition.

The colored-tissue compositions illustrated here began as free-form collages. The youngsters cut or tore the tissue and they applied it on white construction paper in overlapping stages with liquid laundry starch. When it was dry, they used black and colored felt-nib markers to search for and outline recognizable shapes. Some children used crayons and others paint and brush. Suggest that students begin pasting light values of tissue first and then progress to darker values. This is because a dark-color tissue area is difficult to change to a light value. One solution is to paste a sheet of white paper over the area and start again.

of the color from the moistened tissue, rinse them. Be sure that all loose tissue edges are well glued down. Empty half-pint milk cartons are economical and practical starch containers. Because tissue is expensive and wrinkles and crumples very easily, storage boxes should be used to store the tissue, one box for each hue.

Although the abstract composition has an aesthetic validity of its own, it can be augmented as follows: After the students have filled their composition to the borders of the paper, challenge them to look for hidden shapes. These might be suggestive of animals, birds, insects, fish, or fantasy creatures. Once a form emerges, students can glue on additional torn pieces or strips of tissue in deeper colors to represent appendages, which give the shape character and individuality. Avoid outlining the revealed figure so boldly that it is isolated from the rest of the composition. Employ a variety of dark-colored tis-

Presbyterian Church School, Athens, GA. Frank Wachowiak. Saturday Classes.

This beautifully composed colored-tissue-paper collage by a talented middle school student from Athens, Georgia. Photographs and color slides of matadors, toreadors, and "brave bulls" provided the visual stimulation. The preliminary drawing was made with a felt-nib pen (permanent black-ink type) on white construction paper. Before application of the colored tissue, the student chose certain shapes—matador's trousers, jacket, and so on—for a patterned embellishment and pasted colored sections from magazines onto those parts. The tissue was applied by first coating an area with liquid laundry starch and then placing the tissue over it. Then, the area was coated again with the starch, making sure that all edges were smoothly secured. Light-colored tissue was applied first, progressing to the darker colors. Caution was employed in the final stages so that dark-value tissue did not obliterate the important, form-defining ink lines.

sues for this step rather than a single hue. Black tissue can be used, but only in a most restrained way. Similarly, if students outline only one figure with a black felt-nib marker, that one figure will be isolated, but if all emerging figures are outlined in black, a unity will be achieved.

In addition to black markers, students can use crayons, colored markers, and tempera paint in white, grey, or black to delineate desired shapes, such as bark on a tree, scales on a fish, feathers on a bird, and veins in a wing or leaf. Wait until the tissue surface is dry, especially if using water-soluble markers.

The free-design approach using colored tissue described earlier is only one of many avenues for creating with such tissue. Another uses a preliminary drawing made with black or dark-colored crayons on light-colored, heavy paper. After the drawing is completed, the cut or torn tissue paper is applied; as in the previous method, begin with the lighter hues. Cut or tear the tissue sheet slightly larger than the shapes that are drawn. Drawn lines sometimes are obscured by dark tissue overlays, but when the tissue layer is dry, these lines can be redrawn for emphasis. Using lettering from printed publications in conjunction with colored tissue adds a new dimension to the tissue collage, and this is one way to incorporate text concerning social issues into the artwork—an important consideration in contemporary art expression.

Mosaics

The multifaceted technique of mosaic art, with its colored pieces called *tesserae,* is a welcome, albeit challenging technique for children's art expression. It requires a generous time allotment, supplemental storage, and above all, students with both patience and persistence. Standard art materials (colored construction paper, paste, and scissors) are used. Creating mosaics, a pleasantly repetitive and creative project, calls for much small-muscle, tactile activity. It teaches that wholes are made of parts, which is an important concept in mathematics, science, and social studies.

A drawing with permanent marker of a seated boy with bird and bicycle wheel was made on 18- × 24-inch white paper. Then, a tissue shape was cut or torn and an area selected for it. Next, laundry starch was applied to that area and the shape firmly pasted down. For extra interest, tissue shapes do not follow the figure's form.

Courtesy of David Hodge, Oshkosh, WI.

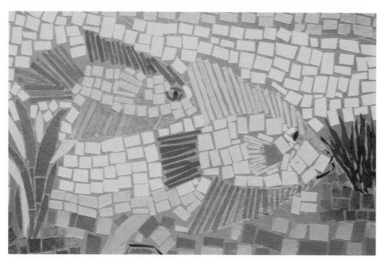

Courtesy of David Hodge, Oshkosh, WI.

Motivation for the project might include visits to mosaics in the community. If available, show color films and slides of mosaic art, both past and present. This can include San Vitale in Rome, Gaudi's Cathedral in Barcelona, Simon Rodia's Watts Towers in Los Angeles, and the mosaic-paved avenues of Rio de Janeiro. Subject matter for paper mosaics that is manageable yet exciting includes birds, fish, and animals in their habitats; flower bouquets; butterflies in a garden; dragons; and clowns.

In mosaic design, as with most two-dimensional art expression, an important initial step is the preliminary sketch. Make it from life and nature, from visits to museums, or from references to photographs and color slides. The preliminary sketches then are developed into a linear composition the size of the actual mosaic that is desired. The background surface may be colored construction paper, chip-board, or salvaged gift-box container.

Critical to the project's success is an adequate supply of tesserae. Cut narrow strips of colored construction paper, not necessarily the same width, and store them according to color in shoe boxes. Students then cut these strips as needed into individual tesserae. They need not cut all of the strips into perfect squares; some can be rectangular or triangular. Some adventurous teachers have used vinyl, tile scraps, linoleum, and even colored glass (with caution) instead of construction paper.

During a mosaic project, students should take turns selecting the desired color strips or tesserae from the supply-table boxes. Apply school paste or white glue to the background paper, and press the tesserae firmly into the adhesive. Usually, it is best to begin on the outer edge of a shape and work inward toward the center. To achieve the mosaic effect, tesserae should not touch or overlap each other. The students should be reminded that in professional mosaic work, a grout is mortared between tesserae. Avoid a rigid, bricklaying technique—the minute, open spaces between tesserae should vary somewhat for best effects.

Students may create excitement with their mosaic compositions through a contrast of colors in specified areas. Contrast the wing of a

Underwater themes are especially effective for mosaics, because of the variety of shapes, details, and patterns that are found in fish, shells, coral, and seaweed. These beautifully space-filled compositions are by upper elementary grade youngsters, who used a variety of sizes and shapes of the tesserae.

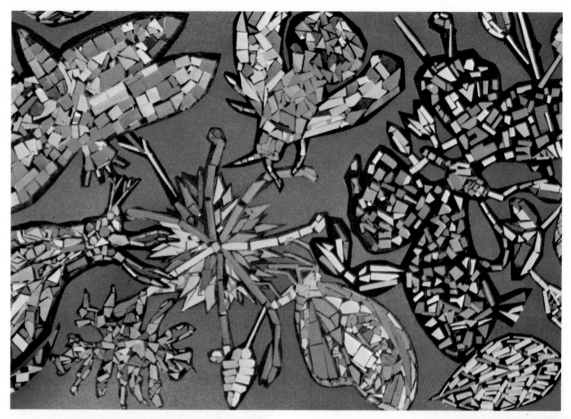

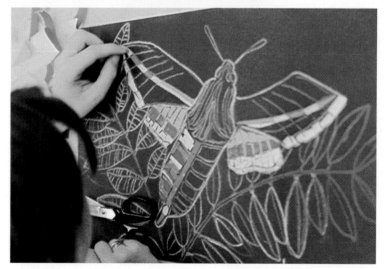

Saturday Children's Classes, courtesy of Frank Wachowiak, Athens, GA, and Mary Sayer Hammond, Fairfax, VA.

A group mural in which each student's mosaic insect on black paper was cut out, with border preserved, and then mounted onto a large piece of brown cardboard.

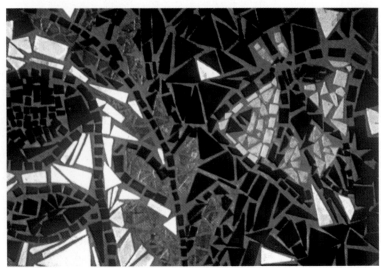

Both courtesy of Frank Wachowiak and Ted Ramsay, Iowa City Elementary Laboratory School, Iowa City, IA. *Emphasis Art*, First Edition.

Left: *Recommended background surfaces for paper mosaic projects include construction paper in assorted colors, railroad board, chip-board, oaktag, or discarded gift-box covers. Suggested adhesives include school paste, white glue, or glue sticks. The bird mosaic employed vinyl and linoleum tesserae glued to Masonite board with color-tinted grout as a filler. Grade 6.* **Above:** *An attractive colored-construction-paper mosaic of an angelfish and seaweed by an upper-elementary-grade student.*

bird against the body, the stamen against a flower petal, an insect against a leaf. One important strategy in achieving expressive mosaic quality is to employ several values of a color in the larger areas: For example, use two or three values of blue in the sky, and two or three values of green in the grass and leaves. Use several kinds of brown ochre, umber, and sienna colors for earth and tree trunks. The brightest, most intense colors may be reserved for sharp contrast or emphasis—on the beak or claws of a bird, the eyes of a tiger, the stamen of a lily, or the horns of a bull.

Chapter 24

Printmaking

Printmaking with Found Objects

Printmaking projects should range from simple processes during the primary grades to complex techniques in upper elementary and middle school. Some of the most colorful and successful prints can be made by very young children employing vegetables and fruit. Found objects, such as buttons, flat or round wooden clothespins, wooden spools, bottle caps, mailing tubes, corks, sponges, and erasers, also can be used. Cord can be glued to the smooth metal top of a condiment container in a free design to produce a printing stamp.

A science-correlated study of nature's form and function can use assorted vegetables (okra, cabbage, mushrooms, peppers, carrots, artichokes) that are cut in half or in pieces, painted, and printed. The excitement quickens when students gain awareness of the hidden design in these natural forms. The halved or quartered vegetables are painted on the cut side with colored tempera of a creamy consistency, or they are pressed on a tempera-coated, folded paper towel. Water-soluble printing ink also can be used. Then, they are printed repeatedly on colored construction paper or tissue paper to form an allover or repeat design.

For best results, the vegetables must be fresh, crisp, and solid. They should be kept refrigerated between printmaking sessions. The most popular vegetable for this project is the potato. Cut in half, its flat, open surface is incised to create a relief. Children must be reminded to exercise caution when using sharp tools, however. Recommended tools include small scissors, fingernail files, nut picks, dental tools, and assorted nails. Melon-ball scoops are excellent for creating circular designs. In upper elementary and middle school, paring knives, Sloyd knives, or Hyde knives may be employed if they are used with extreme care.

Students should strive for a simple, bold breakup of space in their cutout or incised designs. Suggest the use of cross-cuts, wedges as in a pie, assorted-size holes, and star, asterisk, cogwheel, sunburst, and spi-

der's web effects. Students can use large potatoes to print monogram motifs, but letters must be reversed to print correctly. Students should make a preliminary drawing on paper of the shape of the cut potato to guide them in their cutting. It is possible to reverse the design at the window and then copy it onto the potato surface.

Construction paper in assorted colors is perhaps the most popular and serviceable surface for vegetable printing, although colored tissue, wallpaper, and fabrics have been used. Generous newspaper padding should be placed under the paper to be printed to ensure a good impression. Standing up helps students to exert firm pressure, and wedges cut out of the holding end of the potato can improve the grasp.

A few practice applications of the vegetable stamp on scrap paper are recommended. Students might be encouraged to develop a repeat pattern in several places on their paper (this does not have to be a measured, mathematical repeat), thus allowing some prints to go off the page to create an allover effect. Discourage restamping without reinking and rushing to finish, which result in sloppy printing. Often, however, the imperfection of a child's effort lends a fresh, spontaneous quality to the product. By sharing their stamps, children can produce exciting variations.

For a project correlated with writing, have the students use vegetable and found-object prints as covers for their creative-writing notebooks. The prints also can be used for pencil containers (glue the printed paper to a discarded box or can). In both cases, students can coat the surface with gloss polymer medium.

Vegetable and found-object prints, which are artistic in their simplest form, also can be embellished for added richness. One or more crayon or oil-pastel colors can be added in the negative spaces between the printed shapes. For unity, let some of the background surface between the pasteled or crayoned areas and the printed motifs remain uncolored.

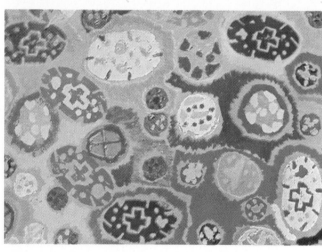

Saturday Children's Classes, courtesy of Frank Wachowiak, Athens, GA, and Mary Sayer Hammond, Fairfax, VA.

Top right: *A potato, with the pattern cut into it, is inked or painted before making the print. Do not insist on a measured, rigidly controlled design. Since caution must be exercised in cutting the designs, use nails, plastic knives, and melon scoops for this process.* **Top left:** *Vegetable prints are enhanced by the application of oil pastels. A youngster applies the pastel colors between the printed motifs, allowing some of the background paper to show.* **Middle left:** *Notice in this example how the light blue pastel complements the yellow-orange paper color.* **Bottom left:** *Notice how the jagged edges of the oil pastel areas adds a contrasting element against the round forms of the potatoes.* **Bottom right:** *Vegetable-print, allover repeat designs make excellent covers for notebooks, pencil holders (recycle a soup or coffee can), and household dispensers. To protect the surface and make it shine, apply a coat of gloss polymer medium.*

Courtesy of David Hodge, Oshkosh, WI.

Glue-line relief print by a sixth-grade student based on a drawing from a posed model. Because of the pressure applied by the soft-rubber brayer, the printing ink covers parts of the background as well as the glue lines.

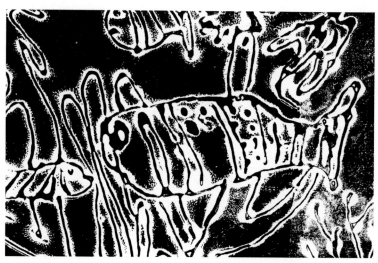

Saturday Children's Classes. Courtesy of Frank Wachowiak, Athens, GA.

Beauty is achieved through the flowing parallel lines and clarity of forms.

Glue Line–Relief Prints

A printmaking process that is remarkably successful with students in all grades is the glue-line-on-cardboard print. It is a relatively simple technique, but it requires at least two class sessions. Time is needed both for the glue to dry overnight before printing and because students must take turns at the inking stations.

In addition to pencils, other required materials are:

- Printing plates—use a smooth-surfaced cardboard (discarded, glossy-surfaced gift-box covers are excellent) or tagboard; recommended plate sizes are 9 × 9, 9 × 12, 12 × 12, or 12 × 18 inches
- Small plastic containers with a nozzle of white liquid glue or, even better, the new thick line variety
- Water-soluble printing ink (black is recommended)
- A soft rubber brayer or roller for inking
- An inking surface, such as a discarded cafeteria tray or metal cookie sheet.
- Protective newspapers
- Newsprint, tissue paper, or classified-ad pages on which to print

Appealing subject-matter choices for young children are butterflies, birds, fish, flowers, and animals. Students in upper elementary and

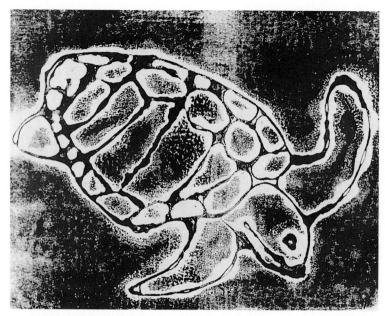

The flowing glue-line technique adapts well to portraying the swimming of this determined sea turtle.

middle school may choose more complex themes: historical legends, space and science explorations, still life, cityscape compositions, portraits, and figure studies.

A preliminary drawing definitely is recommended. Because intricate details will blend together in the glue line and get lost, make the initial drawing with chalk for boldness and simplicity. Limit the composition to one large motif (bird, insect, fish, animal) with its complementary foliage or seaweed rather than using several smaller motifs. With only one large figure, there will be room to clearly delineate details, such as eye, beak, whiskers, antenna, claw, feather, and fish scales. Evaluate the compositions with the student for space-filling design, shape variation, and pattern.

The cardboard plate with its linear composition now is ready for the glue application. Gently squeeze the container, trailing the glue over the drawn line. A linear variety is achieved naturally, because it is difficult to manage an even, steady flow of glue. Dots of glue will produce sunburst effects in the final printing. The glue must be allowed to dry thoroughly overnight before inking; when dry, the glue will be transparent and free of white ridges and welts.

See the later section in this chapter on printing for specific recommendations. The most successful prints are those that capture both the raised glue lines as well as the background inked areas. This will require pressure with palm and fingers into the smaller background areas. Uninked areas between glue lines and background provide the necessary light and dark contrast. For the demonstration, the teacher might use white tissue so that students can actually see the ink absorbing into the paper and detect areas requiring more pressure. Several prints can be made from the same plate. Trim borders, if necessary, and mount the print on colored construction paper for an exciting display.

Collographs

Students in intermediate and upper elementary as well as in middle school are interested in and challenged by more complex approaches to printmaking. Cardboard prints sometimes are referred to as *collographs* (a word combination of *collage* and *graph*), and collographs can be created with commonly available materials and nonhazardous tools. The final results, however, often are comparable to those of woodblocks and lino prints. An especially welcome advantage of this technique is the flexibility it allows in rearranging or deleting compositional elements before the final gluing.

The following tools and materials are required: a sheet of sturdy cardboard (such as the lid or bottom of a gift box), chip-board, discarded scraps of illustration board (tagboard is not recommended), glue, scissors, assorted-weight papers (smooth or textured), assorted-size paper punches, soft-rubber brayer, water-soluble printing ink in black or dark colors, newsprint, gloss polymer medium, a utility brush, and lots of protective newspapers.

The animal world is a favorite theme for collographs. A strong, lively design is desired. Especially important is using a variety of cut-out shapes to fill the space. While helpful, an overall preliminary drawing is not required. Separate motifs or shapes may be drawn first before cutting. Large printing plates may create a management problem in crowded classrooms; therefore, a recommended plate size for students in the intermediate and upper-elementary grades is a sheet 9×9, 9×12, or 12×12 inches.

Students draw and cut out the separate, individual shapes from tagboard (oaktag), construction paper, brown wrapping tape, and other assorted-weight papers. Then, they create open patterns in some of these

The Jungle, 18 × 36 inches. Group project collograph by intermediate elementary grade children. A paper punch created pattern in the leopard and on the bushes. Pinking shears were used to cut the palm tree leaves. Additional cutout holes as *well as little squares and triangles of paper also were pasted down onto the cardboard plate. See especially the gorilla's exciting background at left. The plate was then printed.*

shapes, employing paper punches and utility knives, and arrange these elements on the background cardboard until a satisfactory composition is achieved. Some shapes may overlap for unity, spatial effects, and interest. Students can add a variety of found materials to create textural qualities, using gummed reinforcements, textured wallpaper samples, masking tape, fabric, string, yarn, confetti, liquid glue, and flat, found objects. If the relief is too high, however, such as from thick cord or buttons, the print will not be successful. When the students, with the teacher's guidance, achieve a satisfying, space-filling design, they carefully glue down the pieces. Use a discarded magazine as a gluing surface, and turn to a clean page for each application. All edges must be glued securely.

The whole composition then is sealed with a coat of polymer medium to further prevent the separate pieces from coming loose during the printing and cleaning phases. A separate table or counter that is protected by newspapers should be designated as the sealing area. Allow the plates to dry overnight before inking. (See the section in this chapter on inking and printing.) Collograph plates need not be washed between printing sessions. Finished prints can be attractively mounted for display, and students may want to exchange prints. The plate itself can be painted and mounted. It also can be covered with heavy-duty aluminum foil and further embellished, as described in the later section in this chapter on aluminum-foil relief.

Iowa City Elementary Laboratory School, IA. Courtesy of Frank Wachowiak and Ted Ramsay, *Emphasis Art*, Second Edition.

Steps in making a collograph print. **Top left:** *Gluing down the paper-punched birds.* Caution: *If water-based printing ink is employed, the teacher must give the plate a protective, water-resistant coating.* **Left middle:** *Inking the collograph.* **Top right:** *A middle school student peels back the print from the plate while checking that areas have been sufficiently inked and pressed.* **Bottom left:** *The finished print with very attractive tree shapes.*

Linoleum Prints

A technically demanding form of expression recommended for students in the upper elementary and middle school is linoleum ("lino") block printing. Students are challenged by using diverse tools and by manipulating, if available, a heavy roller press. Because of these built-in attractions, teachers will have little trouble introducing lino prints into the art program.

The unmounted, grey, pliable "battleship" linoleum suggested for this project may be obtained from art-supply companies. Cut the linoleum plates large enough to give the students ample opportunity for a rich composition. A minimum size of 9 × 9, 9 × 12, or 12 × 12 inches is recommended. The basic materials and tools that are needed include sets of lino-cutting gouges for the students to share, rubber brayers, inking surfaces of cookie tins or old cafeteria trays, and water-soluble printing ink.

Iowa City Elementary Laboratory School, Iowa City, IA. Courtesy of Frank Wachowiak, Athens, GA, and Ted Ramsay, Ann Arbor, MI.

Linoleum prints with bold designs by fourth- and fifth-grade children. The left picture of monkeys uses a series of monkeys—big, small, and smallest—to set up a rhythm. The right kangaroo picture has an interesting feature, a positive and negative cactus.

Subject-matter themes for lino prints are almost unlimited, but the most effective promise a strong light- and dark-value composition, with a variety of shapes, pattern, and detail. Some possibilities are birds, jungle animals and their young, insects, fish, shells, old houses, legendary or mythological figures, portraits, and still-life arrangements composed of musical instruments, antiques, plants, household utensils, and sports equipment. A field trip to a natural-history museum will provide a wealth of motivational material.

A preliminary drawing on paper with black crayon, felt-nib pen, brush and ink, or white crayon on black paper is an important requisite for a successful lino-print project. It usually determines the final composition and establishes the dark and light pattern, variety of textural exploitation, points of emphasis, and lines of motion. Letters and numerals must be reversed in the sketch.

After preliminary drawings have been made and evaluated for design potential, the students may use them as a reference for their drawing on the lino plate. Another way is to transfer them to the lino plate with carbon paper or dressmaker's white transfer paper. If the lino surface is dark and no white transfer paper available, paint the block with white tempera paint first. To reverse a sketch before transferring it to the block, hold it against the window, and trace lines on the back of the sheet. Another solution is to transfer the design by placing the drawing pencil-side down onto the block, taping it down securely, and rubbing over it with a metal spoon.

This fifth-grade student's linoleum print began with a sketching trip drawing animals at the natural history museum. Notice how the left-over linoleum lines in the sky were *cut in an attractive movement to give a feeling of unity to the composition. Note how some birds in the sky were black on white and others white on black.*

After the drawing has been made but before the cutting begins, check that there are enough sharpened gouges in various sizes for the entire class. Students should be introduced to the potential of the many gouges through a teacher demonstration emphasizing the correct way to hold and manipulate the gouge. Never put a supporting hand in front of a cutting tool. To make lino cutting safer, a wooden bench hook can be anchored against the table edge to provide a supportive ridge to hold the block. Each lino gouge makes its own particular cut, and although gouges are not as easily controlled as pencils or pens, they often produce lines that are more dynamic. The richest print effects are achieved by

using a range of gouges, from veiners to scoops and shovels. Number 1 and 2 veiners or V-shaped gouges are suggested for making the initial outlines. Another approach is to use the scoop or shovel gouges, working from inside the shapes and thus minimizing tightly outlined compositions.

To prevent mistakes in cutting, students can mark an "X" on those areas to be gouged out. Use directional gouge cuts to follow the object's contours, like ripples around a pebble tossed in a stream. Students should be instructed not to make their cuts too deep into the lino, because the low ridges that remain will produce an attractive texture. If students have difficulty cutting because the linoleum is too hard, heat it on a cookie tin over an electrical hot plate turned to a low setting. (See following section on inking and printing.)

Wooden scraps are an alternative to using linoleum. Such scraps often can be secured from building sites or lumber yards. Especially with small blocks, a bench hook is required for safety. Before inking, seal the wood's porous surface with diluted white glue.

Proofing, Inking, and Printing

This section applies to glue line, collograph, linoleum, and aluminum-foil relief prints. Proofs of the work-in-progress can be made by placing paper over the design and with the side of a black crayon or oil pastel, rubbing over the paper with a steady and even pressure. The resulting proof will reveal to the students how the print design is progressing. To save time spent giving individual instructions, demonstrate the the inking, printing, and wet-print storage procedures step by step for the entire class at one time.

Inking and printing are very exciting, but without careful planning, this stage can develop into a chaotic bedlam. Designated inking and printing tables, covered with newspapers, should be positioned so that several students can stand and work comfortably. Several inking

These woodblock prints of a bird and its hungry babies, cows at milking time, and three hens are by Japanese children, grades 4 and 5. Notice how much was observed and recorded in these space-filled compositions. Printmaking that incorporates woodblock cutting tools is introduced in the third-grade in Japanese schools. Note in the top design the skillfully cut pattern of positive and negative shapes in the leaves and branches.

Actual size woodblock print. This seventh-grade student found and created strong patterns in the tree branches and feathers. The block was painted with colored tempera and printed in several stages to achieve the color overlays.

surfaces and soft-rubber brayers that are 3 or more inches wide (do not use the gelatin type) as well as black, water-soluble ink are needed. At the inking station, squeeze out a brayer-width ribbon of ink onto the inking surface. With the brayer, roll out the ink until it is tacky—you will hear a snapping, hissing sound—and then apply the ink to the plate in both directions. Standing up to get more pressure, evenly ink every part of the plate, especially its edges and corners. Then, carefully and quickly lift and carry the inked plate to the printing station.

Make the print immediately, because water-soluble ink dries rapidly. Use newsprint, brown wrapping paper, colored construction

A woodblock print by Käthe Kollwitz (1867–1945) was the motivation for the three self-portrait prints by upper-grade Japanese youngsters.

Iowa City Elementary Laboratory School Iowa City, IA. Courtesy of Frank Wachowiak, Athens, GA.

Two examples of linoleum blocks printed over colored-tissue collages. **Right:** white printing ink was employed over a dark tissue design. **Left:** black printing ink was used over a lighter-valued tissue underlay. Which of these middle school designs do you like better? Be sure that the tissue is glued down firmly, smoothly, and is thoroughly dry before pulling the print.

Busy upper elementary youngsters at work on a group project, a reduction linoleum print. Step One: In this variation of the regular lino print process, the students first cut away selected areas of the linoleum and pulled several prints using red printing ink. Step Two: While the prints were drying, the youngsters gouged out additional sections of the

block. Step Three: The cleaned plate was inked again in green and printed over the first red edition, with care being taken to "register" or match the second printing over the first. Step Four: While the two-color prints dried, students cut away the final selected areas. Then they used black ink for the third and last impression. The completed print is shown.

paper, colored tissue paper, wallpaper samples, fabric remnants, classified-ad pages, or colored pages from magazines. Carefully place the slightly larger-sized sheet of paper over the inked surface, and pat it down with the palm of hand. Begin in the center, and smooth out to the edges, being careful that the paper does not shift. Standing up, exert stronger pressure with a rubber brayer, heel of a hand, jar cover, spoon, or commercially available baren, and go over the entire surface, especially borders and corners and between the shapes. Where the print is to be darker, press harder. To check the impression, lift the paper partially off the block from various sides, and if not satisfied, apply more pressure.

Caution: Do not wait too long to carefully remove the newsprint from the plate. The water-soluble ink dries quickly, and it may cause the paper to stick to the plate. Therefore, pull the paper off the block carefully. So that all students can get a turn to print, the number of ini-

tial prints a student pulls must be limited. Additional prints always can be made later.

Aluminum-Foil Reliefs

The aluminum-foil relief over collograph plate, collage, or glue line–relief plate is an exciting and novel technique to which students in upper elementary and middle school will respond. The process is not technically a printmaking process; rather, it is a subsequent process that follows the making of a glue-line or a collograph print.

Materials needed include heavy-duty aluminum foil, blunt-point pencils, soft-rubber brayer or inking roller, white glue (check for consistency, glue should not be watery), gold patina, masking tape,

Saturday Children's Classes, student Cal Clements. Courtesy of Frank Wachowiak, Athens, GA, and Mary Sayer Hammond, Fairfax, VA.

The final richness of the aluminum-foil relief transcends the readily available materials from which it was made: household heavy-duty foil instead of expensive copper sheeting, cardboard, white glue, blunt pencils, and water-based printing ink. The glowing finished product makes a gift that is often preserved by families for decades.

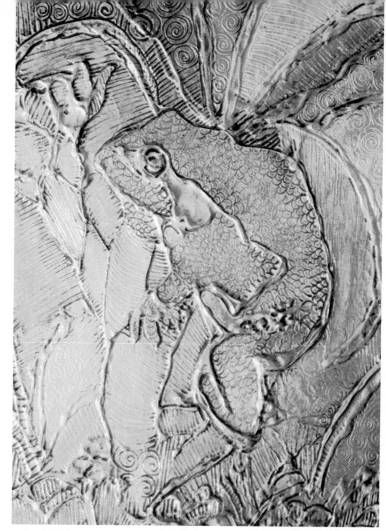

Saturday Children's Classes. Courtesy of Frank Wachowiak, Athens, GA, and Mary Sayer Hammond, Fairfax, VA.

Aluminum-foil relief is an exciting adventure in bas relief and embossing that has untold possibilities for exploration in the art program. Here, a frog looks this way and that, half-submerged in the pond and awaiting the next morsel. The project also affords an ideal medium for learning about ways to create texture and pattern.

water-soluble printing ink (black or dark hue), and protective newspapers.

If students have been pulling prints from a collograph or a glue-line plate, they can reink the plate and, while the ink is still sticky, cover it (shiny side up) with a sheet of foil slightly larger than the printing plate. Then, stretching the foil with the heel of a hand toward the edges of the plate, overlap the foil on the back of the plate. Secure the excess foil on the other side with masking tape. To keep the corners as flat as possible, carefully fold them.

On an uninked collage, be sure the pieces of the collage are secured. With glue-line prints, be sure the glue-relief lines are thoroughly dry. Then, give the plate a coat of white glue, and while wet, apply the foil.

Next, using a blunt-pointed pencil, press into the foil along both edges of the glue lines and also along the edges of collage shapes to emphasize the relief. Avoid puncturing the foil. Teacher and student both should check to see that all relief edges have been sufficiently emphasized. Then, enrich the relief by indenting the foil with the pencil point to create additional details, patterns, and textures. These can be leaves on a bush, veins in the leaves, grass, feathers on a bird, scales on a fish, bark on a tree, or ripples in a stream. Incorporate a variety of invented patterns, such as hatching and cross-hatching; dots, circles, and dots within circles; triangular and diamond shapes; wiggly, jigsaw, and radiating lines; asterisks; stars; and spirals. The more detail, pattern, and texture that are employed, the more effective the result.

To ink the aluminum plate, apply water-soluble, black printing ink to the surface with a soft-rubber brayer so that the whole plate is covered except for the deep pencil indentations. Some teachers recommend applying the ink with a dauber. To be sure that ink gets to all crevices, ink can be applied with a dauber, made by rolling several paper towels into a tight cylinder and taped together. See previous printing section for how to make a print.

After making a print, make the foil relief from the plate itself. While the ink is still moist on the plate, use newspapers to remove the excess. Press one sheet at a time over the moist plate with a hand or brayer. When no impression is visible, take a folded flat (never bunched or crushed), moistened paper towel and wipe the plate gently to remove excess ink from all areas except the indented ones. When one side of the towel gets inky, unfold and fold it again to provide a clean surface. When the moist towel no longer shows an ink residue, use folded, dry paper towels to burnish the plate, being careful to allow ink to remain in the indented lines. This can be the final stage of the project, or you can enrich the raised surfaces of the plate by the slightest application of gold patina. Aluminum-foil reliefs can be attractively mounted and displayed, and they make excellent gifts.

Chapter 25

Computer Art, Photography, and Video

Computer Art

There are a number of advantages to including computer-art activities in the overall art program:

Computers already have an established importance as central elements in education. Thus, use of computers in the art program can lend prestige to the program as a whole. In addition, art students and teachers can help the school through desktop-publishing programs to create school publications with top-quality design and graphics.

It sometimes is possible to obtain costly computer resources on a scale unheard of considering traditional art-teaching budgets.

Computer equipment now is available in a growing number of elementary and middle schools. Teachers of traditional academic subjects, however, may have grown frustrated in their efforts to integrate computer work into their curricula, and art teachers wishing to use computers may find they have the equipment virtually to themselves.

Early computer-art experiences can overcome students' fear of computers in general, and it can become a bridge to skills and experiences that will spur their interest in the "careers of tomorrow," many of which require high-level computer literacy.

If used imaginatively, interactive computer programs for the creation of graphics and page layout can be extremely flexible design tools.

The Computer as a Design Tool

Using the computer as a design tool enables learners to "see" design operations that involve repeating and varying images:

Courtesy of Carol Case, Argyle Elementary School, Smyrna, GA.

Second-grade student Erika Pshsniak's computer painting of water lilies show blending in the flowers and leaves and a textured paper effect in the background.

cut	paste	duplicate
shrink	mirror	enlarge
fragment	blur	trace edges
transparency	superimpose	magnification
distort	bilateral symmetry	four-way symmetry

Computers permit students to save progressive stages of a work and to create an infinite number of variations. They foster thinking

An elementary child created a marathon-race effect by multiplying images using the computer's cut and copy or drag functions.

in terms of scale—students can look at a work at normal size, then zoom in for close-up work. Sophisticated visual effects can be achieved by using a range of special tools—for example, putting one image one over another using different transparency functions, making forms grow according to predetermined patterns (fractalizing), or making forms appear as if they were in a reflecting orb (spherizing). Computers offer sophisticated ways to combine letter forms and words with graphic elements. Thus, they can perform a valuable educational role in integrating school art programs with writing programs.

Implementing a Computer-Art Program

One problem in implementing a computer-art program arises when there is not enough equipment to serve a whole class, or a portion thereof. When there are too few computers in the classroom, children seldom have individual time at the machine.

Fortunately, research indicates that students can learn computer skills as effectively in small groups as they can individually, and computer art can be taught to small groups of children, one group at a time. When this is done, however, it may be difficult for the teacher to keep students who are not at computers working on some other task. If the teacher focuses attention on those students who are en-

gaged in noncomputer activities, the problem then becomes one of providing effective instruction in the qualititative production of computer artwork.

One solution may be to have students do computer artwork only after they finish other assignments, or to have them come in either before or after class. Another is to have traditional methods of drawing and painting included as a part of computer-generated projects. For example, a group of students can begin a design on the computer and have a copy printed out for each student in the group. Then, those students can go to their desks to do the hand coloring, while another group of students, who have been generating design sketches by hand, render them on the computer.

Another way to deal with the problem of a shortage or absence of computers is to approach computer art as an activity in art criticism. Class discussion can focus on the computer-art imagery that students see daily—for example, in special effects during movies, in the animated images that open television programs, in newspaper graphic layouts, and in special lettering effects. Art criticism can be con-

Courtesy of Jackie Ellett, Fort Daniel Elementary School, Gwinnett County Schools, GA.

Fourth-grade student Malory Brock made these triangular tessellation patterns filled with colored circular motif and printed it on a dot matrix printer.

Courtesy of Bell South Advertising and Publishing Corporation, 1990.

Children learn computer skills as well in small groups as they do individually. This painting was made in a technique discussed earlier, tempera resist.

ducted on these mass communication images and analysis done both of their formal design and on how the design elements complement the idea content. A bulletin board in the room containing found examples of computer art can serve as a center for this collection and analysis.

Another way to develop interest in computer art during elementary school is to have students with computers at home bring their own computer designs to be mounted in an exhibit. Such an exhibit may spur school administrators to support a school computer-art program that would be available to all children. Those who have used computer-art programs at home then can use the school computers to teach those who have not had access to these machines.

The best solution, of course, is for the teacher to convince the school administration that computers should be an integral part of the program, that using computers for art expression is just as essential for students' educational development as using computers for programming, mathematical operations, and word processing.

Photography

The magic of the camera can become real to your students. Using photographic principles, they can capture that most ephemeral of all art elements—light! Blueprint paper acquired from a local blueprint company or light-sensitive photographic paper obtainable from a photo store can be used by elementary school children for beginning photographic experiences. Through this medium, they can create designs and learn concepts such as geometric, organic, sinusoidal, pierced, undulating, and lacy.

Before you begin, find a totally dark closet somewhere in the school building. Then, with your students, collect an array of opaque, translucent, and transparent objects of varying color values that have interesting shapes, patterns, and textures. Suitable items are fern leaves, grasses, confetti, flowers, ribbon, lace, torn paper shapes, tissue, acetate, window screen, crumpled plastic wrap, shapes of figures and animals cut from paper, checkers, shoelaces, paper doilies, drawings on acetate or translucent tracing paper, and three-dimensional objects, such as coins and keys.

Courtesy of Alisa Hyde, Savannah, GA.

When the rope ladder is pulled up, no girls would be able to come into this tree house.

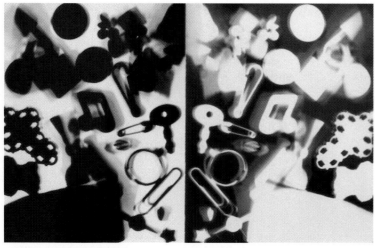

Courtesy of Nancy Elliott, Athens, GA.

These photograms are of objects as simple as keys, religious medals, pins, and paper clips. They helped teach middle school the students concepts of overall pattern and positive and negative shape.

Children first plan out their designs. They arrange an assortment of these objects on a stiff sheet of clear acrylic plastic, acetate, or overhead transparency plastic. Properly supervised older students can use a piece of glass with its edges taped. Emphasize consideration of the negative shapes (the empty spaces). Also, urge students to think about repetition, unity, and variation. While the children are waiting for their turn in the darkroom, have them write out a list of the objects they have collected and the design concepts they embody; this will build their art vocabulary.

For the printmaking stage, have a student monitor govern when the darkroom door may be opened. Students take turns carrying their designs into the darkroom. In the dark—by feel or with a red safelight on—they position their design on top of a same-size piece of blueprint paper. Then, the design of shapes *on the clear plastic on the blueprint paper is taken outside and exposed to sunlight for about 15 minutes (or until the yellow paper turns white).

Then, the print is developed. Use a teaspoon of household ammonia on some cotton in the bottom of a large jar with a fitted lid, such as a gallon mayonnaise jar from the school cafeteria. Roll the print tightly enough to fit it into the jar, insert it, and recap the jar. The ammonia

Exhibited at the School Art Symposium, Georgia Museum of Art, Athens, GA. Courtesy of Molly Chase and teacher George Mitchell, Atlanta, GA.

Student Molly Chase of Atlanta, Georgia, studying photography at school, captured a special moment of children at the neighborhood store. Probably only a young photographer could elicit the charming expressions of these children caring for children. The photograph is given structure by the geometry, repetition, and perspective in the mammoth shortening display.

Courtesy of Nancy Elliott, Athens, GA.

Middle school students constructed pinhole cameras. Then, they went into the school-yard to capture light on the forms of sports cars, gravel, walkways, and buildings.

fumes will turn the paper blue in a few minutes, and the process is complete.

If light-sensitive photo paper is available, the design transfer can be done in a darkroom, using a flashlight to expose the film, and then developed as you would a photograph. With either method, after the print is made, the designs may be left as they are or worked back into with oil pastels and markers to add color. Another variation of this lesson, and one that is especially suitable following a contour line–drawing lesson, is to have the students go into the darkroom, and using a tiny pocket penlight, draw the figure as they remember it on the light-sensitive photo paper. Picasso's drawings with this technique may be studied. Another variation is for students to draw on a sheet of translucent paper with a black marker and then make a reverse print in the darkroom; the results will be similar to the cliché verre process used by Corot.

Class discussion afterward should build art vocabulary through listing on the chalkboard names for the shapes, patterns, and textures that the children have created with light. Discuss similarities between their works and those of Fox Talbot and Man Ray. Students from the fifth grade up can use pin-hole cameras to make their own photographs. Load the camera in a darkroom with slow-emulsion, plastic resin–coated paper. Have the children go into the schoolyard and point the camera at what interests them—for example, a bicycle wheel, a friend's face, a tree silhouetted against the sky, patterns of bicycle shadows on the ground. Tell them not to worry about composition or whether the subject moves. An impression is what is sought. Have the children develop the image inside the darkroom, and a negative image can be contact-printed back for a positive. This lesson can be correlated with a study of such artists as Corot, Delacroix, Courbet, the impressionists, and the futurists, who were fascinated by photography. Discuss what kind of day and light were captured. Was the light direct, soft, or diffuse? Look at the shadows, and describe them.

Still another approach is to use Polaroid or 35-mm print film in a camera. One roll of 36 pictures will let each child make one picture. Slides are the least expensive. A language arts–correlated lesson is to have the children make up a story using the slides, then put on a slide show complete with narration and sound effects and the children playing the roles. A local photo lab may donate out-of-date film. If the supply of film is limited, have the children work in pairs to plan out the subject of their photo and take the picture. Some other topics to document might include activities on the playground, friends, an architecture field trip, the class garden, and a diorama on almost any subject. The children's photos then can serve as visual complements to art projects using traditional media and methods.

Teach children the vocabulary of photography. Terms and concepts about light include: light and shadow, direct light and reflected

Courtesy of Joyce Vroon, Trinity School, Atlanta, GA.

Surreal wave reflections, mountain ridges, and a bold value pattern characterize this photo by sixth-grade student Mandy Freel.

Courtesy of Joyce Vroon, Trinity School, Atlanta, GA.

After studying David Hockney's photo collages, a sixth-grade student made this photo collage of the construction at his home.

light, contrast, value, low contrast, high contrast, direction of light, high-key delicate lighting containing nothing darker than middle grey, low-key somber lighting containing nothing lighter than middle grey, sharp and diffuse shadows, point of view, low angle, distant shot, foreground, near ground, middle ground, and background. Terms about the technical process include: positive, negative, camera, shutter, lens, diaphragm, f stop, focus, film speed (ISO), stop bath, and fixer. Historical terms include: daguerreotype, Talbot-type or Calotype, ambrotype, tintype, and cartes de visite (visiting cards with a photograph).

A study of Edward S. Curtis's photos of Native Americans and Matthew Brady's of the Civil War can be correlated to social-studies units. The lesson also can be integrated with a unit on the science of light and art history, replicating the 1830s sun drawings of Henry Fox Talbot. Photos of scientific phenomena, close-up microscopic views, and macrocosmic views of outer space can be studied as works of art using the photographic vocabulary described earlier. Art criticism can be taught using a collection of photographic masterpieces. For example, cut photographs from an issue of *Life* magazine on the history of photography; with these photos, students can engage in some of the educational gamelike activities discussed in Chapter 17.

Video

Video—the art medium of our time—is transforming the nature of art and of our lives. The famous video artist Nam June Paik said, "In-

formation has to be recognized as an alternative energy source. Information changes our life style" (1987). Video's power to capture the affect in human interactions, its accessibility, its spontaneity, and the ease with which it is disseminated are awesome. Unfortunately, and perhaps because of a fear of technology, too much video equip-

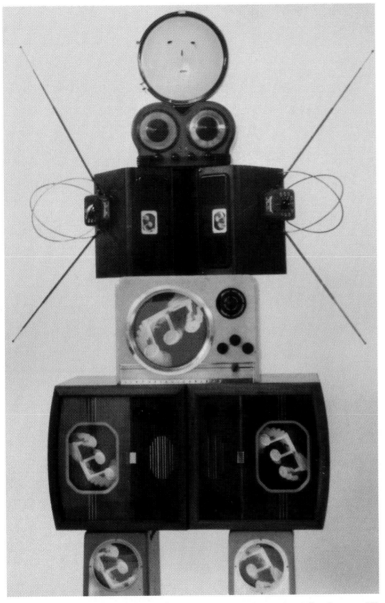

Family of Robot: Aunt, 1986 (video sculpture, 86 ½- × 21-inches). Courtesy of Carl Solway Gallery, Cincinnati, OH.

Pioneering video artist Nam June Paik (born in Korea in 1932) uses hundreds of tele-vision monitors to create video walls of information. He wants them to humanize and demystify television technology, as does the figurative piece shown here that is con-structed from TV sets.

ment stays locked in school closets, gathering dust and becoming ob-solete.

Video can provide valuable educational experiences to students. Most homes now have videocassette recorders (VCRs), and families with cameras shoot their own home videos. Teachers of art should put this technology into the hands of our students. Video can be used to document events in the classroom, school, and community. Art con-cepts of light, space, movement, and time become real to the students as they make films, watch, and analyze videos and films.

Some instructional objectives for a video program are as follows: In the area of art creation, the students will be able to use the video cam-era to apply spatial concepts involving the use of close-ups and long shots and to manage the art elements of light and space. In the area of art criticism, students will analyze techniques used in art-history videos as well as those made by famous artists. Students will learn the vocabu-lary of motion film. They will identify instances of backlighting, soft fo-cus, freeze frame, establishing zoom shots, slow disclosure shots, low-an-gle shots, long shots, and panning shots.

Students will describe how artists have humanized technology—for example, the installations and performances of Nam June Paik and Lau-rie Anderson. Students can carry home the videos they make and view them on their home VCR. With their families, they can discuss how they made their shots and how they used light, space, and action. Videos of students creating in another art media can be used as a tool to help them critique their performance in achieving the video-related art objectives.

Art displays in elementary school hallways can be videotaped as a way of documenting the quality of the work. This video can be shared with the students whose work is depicted as a way to give them feedback. It also can be shared with future classes when they embark on the same kind of project. Videos documenting the com-munity's artists can be used as part of an art history/social studies cur-riculum. Videos of senior citizens sharing their arts and crafts her-itage become historical records of knowledge that can be passed on to future generations.

A student can video his or her classmates making art, then take the videotape home and write a critique of the result. Students depicted in the video can take the tape home and watch it, then write a review of their art-making process, telling what they would like to do better or differently. If the museum permits, videos can document your students' museum field trips; this visual documentation then can be used to re-view the experience and give the students the opportunity to share their responses. All of these videos can provide valuable documenta-

An elementary school child videotapes a guest speaker discussing his passion, raising horses. Children also can video field trips to sketching sites and peers in the process of making art.

tion of a program's effectiveness that can be shared with evaluators as well as at parent–teacher meetings and programs.

Students who have received training in camera use can document school functions, game days, and seasonal festivities. These can be played in the school hall or in classes to provide feedback to the participants. Art-club members can videotape the musical, dramatic, and dance performances of the other arts programs. In many middle schools, where art competes with orchestra, band, and chorus for enrollment, videos of the art program in action can be used as a way of recruiting students and building a program of quality.

Video can bring the art program out into the community. School-produced videos can be shown at the local library as part of a humanities program. Documenting the historical contributions of groups in the community is a way to gain valuable community support for your art-education program. Videos can document your students' reactions to social and political events in the community, such as older siblings going off to war and the impact of that event on younger siblings at home. Videos documenting community life can be shown at town festivals; for example, a video of making sorghum syrup might be shown at a local fall festival. For social studies projects, students might make a video in a nearby senior citizens' center, documenting their memories of fires, riots, wars, and floods. Teachers are amazed at the time and energy that children put into their involvement in video projects. This medium gives students a way to create their own reality.

Courtesy of Melody Milbrandt, Valdosta, GA.

A student gives a video-recorded demonstration in the classroom while another student does the recording.

Chapter 26

Three-Dimensional Design: Additive and Subtractive Sculpture

University Elementary School, Iowa City, IA. Courtesy of Frank Wachowiak and Ted Ramsay, *Emphasis Art*, First Edition.

In box sculpture, allow the shape of the box itself to trigger the student's imagination. Square and rectangular boxes are much easier for young children to assemble.

Many challenging sculptural techniques, both additive and subtractive, await those upper elementary and middle school students and their teachers who are ready and willing to make a serious, time-consuming commitment to a painstaking yet adventurous task. Too often, sculpture in the elementary school has been presented as a therapeutic activity, with minor emphasis on its expressive potential. If sufficient time cannot be allotted for students to become thoroughly involved in the sculptural process, postpone it until the middle school years, when more time is budgeted for art and the students' perseverance and constructive skills are more developed, because young adolescents definitely enjoy chiseling and carving in substances. If the elementary school teacher of art understands the sculptural media and can motivate the students to carry projects through to culmination, however, the sculpture experience can be one of the most fulfilling in the upper-elementary grades' art program.

The major consideration often is not so much of motivation as of material resources, preliminary planning, special techniques, cleanup, and storage. A class of 25 or more students working on additive or subtractive sculpture poses several organizational problems. Teachers must decide beforehand whether they want the entire class to use the same medium or to allow students to work with materials of their choosing. Skilled instructors may be able to control a large class in which some students are working on toothpick or balsa-wood construction, some on plaster block carving, and some on wire or metal sculpture. The resulting products, however, must show evidence of the students' growth in sculptural design. If, as often is the case, the teacher becomes merely the dispenser of various materials and tools and has little time to evaluate work in progress with the students, it is much wiser to limit the offering and have the entire class use only one sculptural medium. In such instances, the teacher can organize the materials, tools, and storage space more effectively. A rich motivational

Excitement and hope light the eyes of first-grade student Cal Clements as he constructs a sculpture from wood scraps.

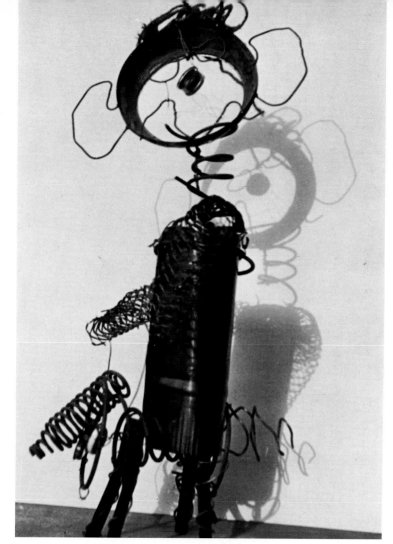

Iowa City Elementary Laboratory School, Iowa City, IA. Courtesy of Frank Wachowiak, Athens, GA, and Ted Ramsay, Ann Arbor, MI.

In view of today's widespread ecological concerns about our planet's vanishing resources, sculptures from recycled materials take on added significance. Some soldering skills were necessary for this metal construction by a middle school student. It is another example of the adage "The whole is greater than the sum of its parts."

plan and evaluation plan can be developed over the several days necessary for the project.

This chapter will first discuss box sculpture and constructions in space, then masks, and finally, subtractive sculpture in plaster.

Box Sculpture and Constructions in Space

Older and more mature children often need a change of pace. New challenges, materials, and techniques can spark them to maintain a growing interest in art. Using cardboard boxes, mailing tubes, and assorted found objects gives upper elementary and middle school students a rare opportunity to express their individual ideas in a unique, three-

Saturday Children's Classes. Courtesy of Frank Wachowiak, Athens, GA.

After the boxes have been taped together, the sculpture is allowed to dry and become sturdy. Then, the sculpture can be painted.

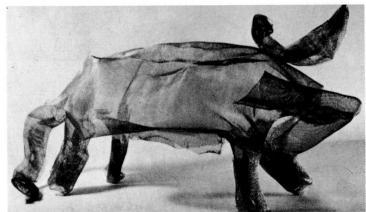

dimensional form. They find value in recycling discarded materials at the same time they struggle with a complex construction problem. They realize in a creative way the adage that "the whole is greater than the sum of its parts."

An exciting new world of additive sculpture has opened up with the burgeoning exploitation of found materials. These include applicator sticks, drinking straws, thin dowels, assorted toothpicks, reeds, discarded game parts (for example, Tinkertoy pieces), pick-up sticks, scrap lumber, and plastic packing materials. The resulting constructions have many labels: stabiles, mobiles, space modulators, combine art, scrap sculpture, or assemblage. Constructions definitely will add an adventurous dimension to art programs and hold the interest of today's students.

Wood scraps, rope and yarn remnants, dried corn husks, discarded metal screen, and spools from thread can be recycled in today's school art programs. This lion, elephant, and grasshopper are successful examples. Let the youngsters' imaginations soar.

Iowa City Elementary Laboratory School, Iowa City, IA. Courtesy of Frank Wachowiak, Athens, GA.

In many instances, students will be eager to create nonobjective, abstract, and geometrically oriented constructions, allowing the materials to dictate the form. This is particularly true when straws, applicator sticks, toothpicks, and reeds are the building elements. The design grows stick by stick, straw by straw, dowel by dowel. Unless the construction itself is stable, an auxiliary support or separate base of wood, plywood, or Masonite is needed. Determine the placement of supports that are required, then drill or hammer holes into the base at these points. Begin the structure by securely inserting and gluing the initial supports into these holes.

A host of materials can embellish stick or straw constructions. Experiment, for example, with bottle corks, thread spools, beads, cord, Ping-Pong balls, small rubber balls, pegboard pegs, construction paper, mailing tubes, colored cardboard, cardboard spools from tape dispensers, miniature cardboard boxes, plastic pieces, wood or plastic buttons, and tiny film canisters. Outdoors, the teacher can give completed constructions a coat of black or white spray paint, which contributes to a striking unifying visual impact.

Additive sculpture also can be made using more challenging materials and techniques. Wire can be combined with found metal pieces. Toothpick and applicator-stick constructions can be dipped into melted crayon, wet plaster, or liquid metal. Corrugated cardboard can be cut into various shapes and then slotted, joined, and glued together into a stabile. Cardboard mailing tubes can be cut into multi-sized cylinders and rings, then assembled into animals, insects, and figures. Exacto knives, Sloyd knives, or utility knives are necessary to cut cardboard boxes, but they must be used only under a teacher's strict supervision. A coping saw or little vibrating-table jigsaw is useful for cutting heavy cardboard, chipboard, Masonite, and heavyweight cardboard tubes.

At least 2 to 4 weeks before the project begins, students should start collecting discarded cardboard boxes. A letter to the parents listing materials that are needed will help to build a necessary store of discards, scraps, and remnants. This early, personal involvement on the

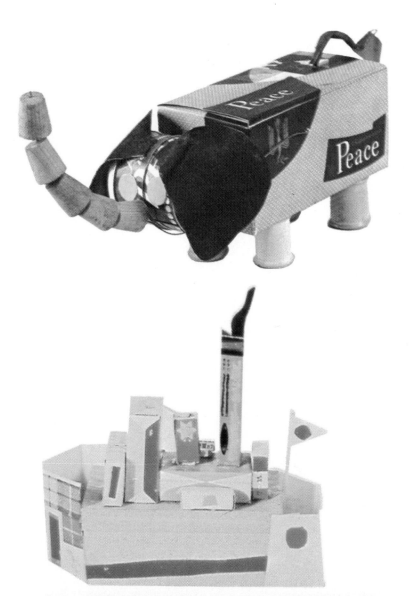

Iowa City Elementary Laboratory School, IA. *Top and middle:* Courtesy of Frank Wachowiak, Athens, GA. *Bottom:* Courtesy of Frank Wachowiak and Ted Ramsay, *Emphasis Art*, First Edition.

Top: *As is the case with this elephant, it is not always necessary to paint box sculpture. Some boxes already have colorful printed designs.* **Middle:** *This cruise ship ingeniously employs box sculptural forms.* **Bottom:** *This construction of reeds and construction paper by a sixth-grade student shows a good use of restraint. It employs only triangular shapes, which create a unified design.*

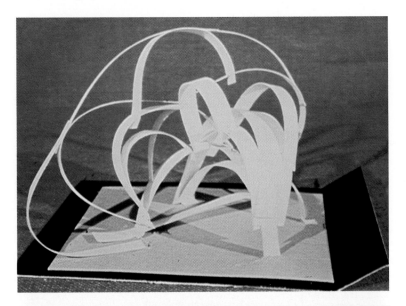

Courtesy of Barbara Thomas, Whit Davis School, Athens, GA.

Using a piece of ³/₄-inch Styrofoam insulation for a base, the structure grows with shish-kebab skewers, Popsicle sticks, and golf tees.

Top: Milwaukee, WI. Bottom: *Three-Fold Manifestation II* (steel painted white, 32-feet high). Alice Aycock. Storm King Art Center, Mountainville, NY. Gift of the artist. Photo: Jerry L. Thompson.

Top: *A sixth-grade student created this space modulator with construction paper strips and school paste.* **Bottom:** *Perhaps such a project will inspire one of your students to become a sculptor and to create pieces, not 30- inches high, but rather 30- feet high. In any event, because of the school experience that you provide, all students will be able to appreciate more intensely the rhythm, repetition, and construction in such works as Alice Aycock's 1987 sculpture.*

part of the students builds interest in the expressive adventure ahead. Store the accumulated boxes and objects until needed in a giant cardboard carton, or students can store their personal collections in their own grocery sack.

Useful fastening materials include straight pins, masking tape, paper-clips, string, double-faced tape, rubber bands, gummed tape, white liquid glue, school paste, scissors, paper punch, nails, and wire. Plan ahead so there are adequate storage facilities for the found objects, for the supply of fastening devices and materials, and for the constructions in progress.

Imaginative box-sculpture themes are almost limitless: astronauts, spaceships, space stations, robots, creatures from another planet, engines, planes, toys, rockets, homes, vehicles and computers of the future, fantastic designs for playground equipment, masks, nonobjective space modulators, and imaginative animals, bugs, birds, and fish.

One way to start the project is to invite students to select three or four different-size boxes and a set of cardboard mailing tubes (for small constructions, use toilet-tissue tubes), then juxtapose these in various configurations until an idea is triggered. Another approach is to have a theme in mind and select boxes to form this preconception. After students decide on a basic shape for their creations, making sketches will help them to plan. The excitement builds as students see the creation grow. Sometimes, an unusual box turns up that is just right for the head of a monster and triggers the design for the rest of the construction. Often, a box can be partially opened and hinged to become the mouth and jaws of a voracious, mythical lion or dragon. What began as a dream car might easily emerge in the final stages as a space station.

The most difficult part is fastening the separate boxes together and securing the appendages. The recommended method includes first gluing and then tying, pinning, paper-clipping, and/or taping the boxes together until the glue dries overnight. Finding an adhesive with ideal properties can be problematic, because many adhesives have some, but not all, of the desired properties. For example, white glue (such as Elmer's glue) is safe, available in most schools, and reasonably effective, although its tackiness and drying time are not ideal. A new product, Elmer's Tacky Glue, has more tackiness and therefore is superior for box and wood-scrap sculptures. Glues such as airplane glue and Duco Cement should not be used in classrooms, because they contain the harmful solvents xylene or toluene. A hot-melt glue gun might be used by the teacher for difficult attachments.

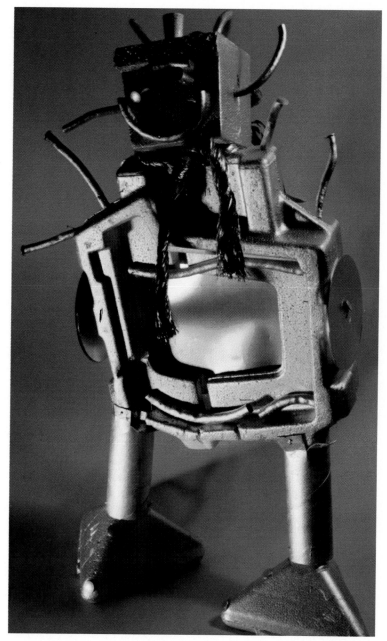

Courtesy of Ted Ramsay, Ann Arbor, MI.

A sixth-grade student combined plastic discards to produce this imaginatively constructed robot. Then, after working surfaces had been protected with newspapers, the entire sculpture was sprayed with metal paint. Only the teacher, not the students, should use spray paint; even then, spray out of doors in good ventilation.

Courtesy of Julie Daniell Phlegar, Upper Tammany County Elementary School, Slidell, LA.

This second-grade student loved making his dramatic mask headdress of blue waves and four patterned water snakes. From tagboard, the bottom 6 inches of the paper are cut in partway to form a headband, and the lower three inches cut away even more to leave just a mask, which was colored with markers.

Working on a stiff base, such as a 1-foot-square piece of cardboard or Masonite, gives increased stability to the piece-in-progress and facilitates its rotating so that all sides can be studied. In constructing standing figures, students must decide how to make the figure stand upright. If necessary, a stabilizing third leg or support can be created. A tail can be added, or the figure can hold gear, such as a spear or banner standard, that touches the ground. Heightened interest, decoration, and texture can be added by using egg cartons, corrugated and embossed cardboard, paper drinking straws, plastic packing noodles, clothespins, toothpicks, paste sticks, dowels, corks, pipe cleaners, reeds, beads, Tinkertoy pieces, Ping-Pong balls, and game parts.

Sometimes, the containers themselves with their printed designs and logos are so exciting that painting them would only mask their bold design qualities. Rather than painting boxes that already contain graphics or lettering, another possibility is to camouflage them with colored paper, comic-book and magazine pages, tissue paper, wallpaper samples, cloth, or gift-wrapping papers. If the sculpture is to be painted,

the features that give it individuality must be emphasized, especially the eyes, mouth, nose, ears, and horns. If the boxes' glossy surfaces resist water-based paint, make it adhere by adding soap to the paint. Spray paints are not considered to be safe for student use, and any spray painting must be done by the teacher and conducted outdoors. Silver, copper, or gold paint may be employed for a robot, knight in armor, or astronaut. There are endless possibilities in box and found-object sculpture. The teacher and students who are resourceful, persistent, and patient enough to try this project have a real art adventure awaiting them.

Masks

Multicultural education certainly will include the study of masks. Rather than tying mask making to overworked Halloween motifs, the activity is on a firmer academic base when integrated with a social-studies cultural unit: In Africa, likenesses of departed chiefs are used in memorial services. Native Americans use masks in rain-making and

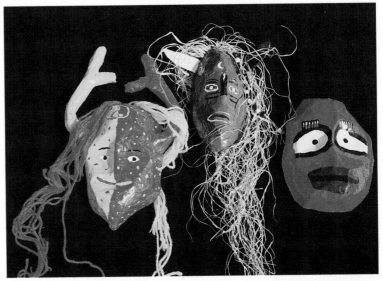

Courtesy of Nancy Eliott, Burney-Harris Middle School, Athens, GA.

Middle school students made these papier-maché masks, and decorated them imaginatively with straw and fiber hair, one with a half-yellow, half-red face with antlers and a dark mask with white and black horns.

agricultural ceremonies. Judges in New Guinea wear masks to heighten their authority. The masks worn by medieval mummers might signify one of the seven deadly sins, biblical characters, or forces of nature. In China, Burma, and Ceylon, masks were worn to prevent illness and cure diseases. Thieves wear them to conceal their identity. Police officers, firefighters, hospital personnel, and football players wear masks for personal protection.

Always a popular undertaking, mask making in the elementary and middle schools has, unfortunately, been one in which design considerations seldom have been effectively implemented. Too often, basic compositional factors have been minimized and raw colors applied in a random, slap-dash, form-negating manner. On occasion, very young children can create colorful, expressively naive masks when richly motivated. Because of the cultural and symbolic connotations of mask making and the often complex techniques required for implementation, however, mask making is best postponed until students reach upper elementary and middle school.

The most inspired and evocative masks of past centuries and cultures almost always have been based on an abstract, stylized concept rather than on natural appearance. To emphasize certain features, mask makers often abstracted the face, whether human or animal, into combinations of ovals, squares, and circles. A study of masks such as those

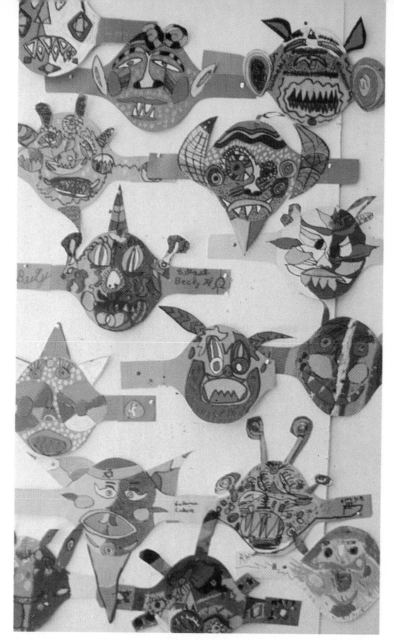

Iowa City Elementary Laboratory School, Iowa City, IA. Courtesy of Frank Wachowiak, Athens, GA.

Observe the highly imaginative and free features which these upper elementary children invented for their bulletin board full of colored-construction-paper masks. The teacher and students discussed different ways to draw mouths, eyes, and noses. Everyone came up with a unique way to depict each feature; no two are alike. Marker drawings then were enriched with oil pastel and pattern, both used in equally unique ways.

Kindergarten children created their own Halloween costumes by recycling paper garment bags. If such bags are not available, fasten together with glue or masking tape two large-size grocery bags, one with the bottom cut off.

University Elementary School, Iowa City, IA. Courtesy of Frank Wachowiak and Ted Ramsay. *Emphasis Art*, First Edition.

Colored-construction-paper masks. A three-dimensional effect was achieved by cutting short slits into the borders of a square or rectangular sheet of paper and then overlapping the resulting tabs and stapling them together. Masks make highly decorative artifacts to brighten up the classroom.

Courtesy of Frank Wachowiak, Athens, GA.

Posing on the jungle gym with their scary outstretched claw-like hands, first-grade students loved making these giant colored-construction-paper masks and scaring each other with them.

by tribal Africans and Native Americans reveals recurring aspects. Whereas facial features that capture the mood or spirit usually are exaggerated, they seldom are distorted to the extent that they appear to be something so alien and trite as star-shaped eyes. The most expressive masks are imbued with the essence and vitality of a particular mood or emotion: astonishment, serenity, power, anger, dignity, joy, fury, frenzy, benevolence, or wonder. Another recurring characteristic is continuity

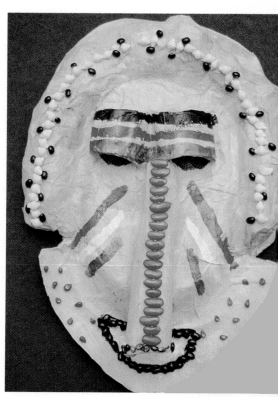

Right: Courtesy of Barbara Thomas, Whit Davis School, Athens, GA. *Others:* Courtesy of Frank Wachowiak, Athens, GA.

Varied approaches to mask making. **Far left:** *Boxes, spools, paper cups, and yarn create a face by varying conical forms.* **Center:** *Construction paper is bent into a canoelike shape and raffia added. Feathers could also be incorporated.* **Right:** *Beth Pearson used red, white, and black beans to create repeated patterns and lines. Basic mask forms also may be achieved by applying newspaper strips with wheat paste or liquid starch over a balloon or mixing bowl.*

of facial forms and features, as exemplified by the linear flow of the nose structure into the eyebrow contour.

Decoration is used to heighten the mask's visual appeal. Taking a cue from mask makers of the past, students should use lines or shapes to reinforce and emphasize the dominant features. They should create pattern and texture on the face, delineate hair and beard, and emphasize eyes by using highly contrasting colors and values. Color must be used judiciously, however, lest it jeopardize the mask's impact or appeal. Color must be integrated with the features, not superficially applied, and it must complement rather than detract. Subtle, limited color har-monies should be encouraged and primary colors used with discretion (generally only to provide a necessary contrast).

Papier-maché over a clay foundation still is the most popular and effectively controlled technique, allowing for highly individualized interpretations and detailed facial modeling. Also recommended is papier-maché or plaster-impregnated gauze applied over a mixing or salad bowl, small dishpan, balloon, or beach ball. As the pasted form develops, it can be embellished with additional pieces of plastic foam, bent cardboard, and found objects to create nose, eyes, mouth, and ear shapes. String, yarn, raffia, and plastic packing material may be used for

Courtesy of Frank Wachowiak, Iowa City Elementary Laboratory School, Iowa City, IA.

Masks created for a totem-pole project. Colored construction paper, 12 × 18 inches, and oil pastels were used. Noses, teeth, ears, and cheeks were made by cutting slits in the mask. These portions then were bent out to create three-dimensional forms. Completed masks were secured to discarded food tins from the school cafeteria.

hair, beard, and other textures. These details are covered with a final layer of gauze or glue-moistened paper toweling. When dry, the mask can be painted.

A popular mask-making technique is the paper- or cardboard-construction process. This generally requires intricate cutting and scoring of the paper to achieve an effective, three-dimensional quality. It has many possibilities, however, and because of the availability of materials and tools, it can be pursued in the ordinary classroom. Unlike papier-

maché projects that involve a lengthy cleanup period and abundant storage space, paper-sculpture masks are simpler to manage and store. For children in the primary grades, creation of a paper-plate, paper-sack, or plastic meat-tray mask is the most practical and successful technique, because it does not involve a complex, three-dimensional process.

Totem Poles

A study of early Pacific Coast Native-American life provides rich motivation for several art projects, including the group construction of a totem pole; however, the culture of the Northwest Native Americans must be genuinely examined. Cross-cultural comparisons can be made about the role of art in their culture and their beliefs about nature, death, religion, and the roles of men, women, and children. For the Native-American carvers, art is empty when it omits the spiritual dimension of life. As was the custom of the totem carvers, encourage students to identify with some other living entity or with an animal or bird school symbol.

Use a sheet of colored construction paper 12 × 18 inches as the background for each totem mask. With the paper placed horizontally on the desk and the 18-inch border at the bottom, students draw with chalk the outline of their mask in the center of the paper. The top and bottom of their mask should touch the edge of the paper. The larger they draw it, the better, but they should leave some of the paper plain at each side to wrap around the pole. When the drawing is complete, the mask may be painted with tempera paint or colored with crayon or oil pastels. Students should be encouraged to exploit unusual color combinations in their masks, including the use of black and white; to repeat colors for unity; to create contrast by juxtaposing light and dark colors; and to emphasize important parts of their masks through a selection of vivid, dominant colors.

*Facing page: Totems usually are made in conjunction with a study of Native-American culture. **Top right:** In a second-grade class, each child selected an animal thought to have special powers and made a northwest Native-American totem dedicated to it. **Bottom right:** Northwest Haida women's hats were made and the women's stories told. **Top left:** Cylindrical forms were made by a column of school cafeteria cans being stacked and taped together. **Bottom left:** A tree was used for the vertical column, and masks by upper-elementary school children attached to the column.*

Top left: Iowa City Elementary Laboratory School, courtesy of Frank Wachowiak, Athens, GA. *Bottom left:* Barrow Elementary School, Athens, GA. Others courtesy of Alice Ballard Munn, Anchorage, AL, and Diane Rives, Athens, GA.

Subtractive sculptures. **Top left:** *Sandcore, a by-product from metal casting, and porous firebrick can be carved. Notice how cleverly this child has solved the problem of thin legs breaking off by keeping a central band intact between the legs.* **Top right and bottom left and right:** *Teachers usually add vermiculite to plaster of Paris so it can be carved more easily. The vermiculite also gives a rough texture. Observe in this bear, mountain goat, and rhinoceros how these sixth-grade artists have solved the problem of delicate parts breaking off by using volumetric compact forms.*

After the mask is colored, make parts of it three-dimensional by cutting slits with scissors around an ear or nose and either folding these pieces outward from the main mask or bending them back. A backing sheet of a contrasting color, 12 × 18 inches, may be added when assembling the several masks into the totem form. Students also may add supplementary shapes of multicolored construction paper for teeth, fangs, horns, ears, earrings, and eyebrows.

There are several ways to construct totem poles from the separate masks. One way is to get a gallon food tin from the school cafeteria for a base foundation, and weight it down with sand or clay. Then, wrap a 24 × 36-inch sheet of tagboard around the can, and secure it with masking tape, creating a 36-inch-tall cylinder. Build another cylinder above the first, if desired. Secure it again with tape, and with the tagboard cylinder as a steady foundation, fasten the masks around it with glue, masking tape, or staple-gun tacker. Another type of pole can be made from a cardboard cylinder from a carpet showroom.

Once the basic totem pole is sturdily constructed, embellish it with supplemental wings, feet, and arms made of cardboard. Display the completed totem poles at a cultural celebration or in the school foyer as a way of sharing the multicultural learning experience with the school at large.

Subtractive Sculpture in Plaster

Subtractive sculpture (carving) has appealed to artists of all cultures throughout history. Wood probably has been the most popular medium for sculptors, but exquisite creations have been carved in a host of materials, including jade, ivory, bone, marble, soapstone, and alabaster. Many of these art materials are, of course, unsuitable for the usual art class. They may be banned (such as ivory), too costly (such as jade), or too dangerous (such as soapstone, which may contain asbestos). For school use, ideal materials must be safe, economical, relatively easy to carve, and allow easy cleanup. Recommended and readily obtainable materials for subtractive sculpture include plaster-of-Paris, leather-hard clay, balsa wood, porous firebrick, and large bars of soap. A metal-casting byproduct, sand core, which consists of sand held together with binders, may be available free from a local metal foundry.

Plaster usually is the material chosen for subtractive sculpture in school programs, because it is cheap and easy to get. Plaster should be mixed with additives such as white sand or fine-grain zonolite to give it a texture and make it easier to carve. Approximately one-part additive to one-part dry plaster will produce a fairly porous and workable carving block. A half-gallon or quart-size milk or juice carton made of waxed cardboard makes a sturdy, leak-proof container.

Subjects that students can handle successfully include fish, nesting birds, animals (especially those in repose, to prevent thin legs from breaking off), and portrait heads. Organic or nonobjective free forms can be developed from motifs based on rocks, shells, nuts, pods, and other natural or biomorphic forms.

Often plaster is used both additively and subtractively on the same sculpture. Shown here is how a sturdy interior form called an armature can be constructed and covered with plaster. For larger projects, bend and weld reinforcing bars together. Then fill out the form with thinner wire, mesh, string, wood, and paper. Finally, add plaster and carve away the excess.

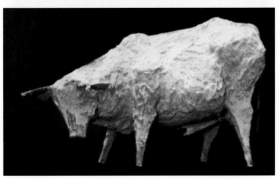

Students begin by making preliminary front-, side-, and back-view sketches for their sculptures on paper, cut to the size of their plaster block. While the class is sketching, the teacher can help two or three students at a time to make their plaster molds. All necessary materials and tools should be on a newspaper-protected table or counter and near a water source (if possible). Have ready the molding plaster, vermiculite or sand, scoops or cups, milk cartons opened wide at the top, water, small-size rubber or plastic dishpan, wood stock or paddle, dry tempera colors (if desired), and lots of newspapers to line the nearby wastebaskets and both cover and recover the counter and floor around the plaster-mixing area.

Fill a milk carton three-fourths full with water, and pour the water into the dishpan. Sift plaster into the water slowly, using a hand, cup, or scoop. When islands of plaster appear above the water, add zonolite or sand. Stir the mix gently yet swiftly by hand, squeezing out the lumps until thoroughly mixed. As the mixture thickens very quickly, be ready to pour it immediately into the milk carton. After pouring it into the carton, tap the carton on the table to remove trapped bubbles, or stir it quickly with a stick or paddle. *Caution: Never pour plaster down the sink, or even rinse plaster-coated tools there. Instead, scrape excess plaster left in the dishpan, on hands, and on tools into the newspaper-lined wastebasket. Then, rinse hands and tools in another pail of water, but do not pour this rinsing water down the sink either.* Allow the plaster mold or block to dry overnight. If color is desired in the plaster block, mix tempera powder into the dry plaster before it is mixed with water. Neutral colors such as umber, ochre, sienna, and earth-green are recommended.

Students may transfer preliminary pencil sketches to the block using carbon paper, or using their sketches as a reference, they may draw directly on the block with a pencil or ink marker. The sculpture should make fullest use of the block. Remind students that no amount of texture, detail, or pattern will redeem the work if the basic form is weak. Students should be cautioned against choosing a subject that is too intricate and complex or that might be expressed more easily in wood, wire, metal, or clay.

The recommended tools for the carving process are a Sloyd or Hyde knife with a 2-inch blade, a utility knife (a knife with a metal handle encasing a replaceable blade), or a small plaster rasp. Then, they cut, file, rasp, or chisel away the excess plaster to delineate the dominant profile or outline view. Next, they may refer to their top, front, and rear sketches and carve away to define those contours. They should proceed cautiously as they remove the plaster, turning the block around to define all forms consistently. As they carve, encourage them to think about how each part flows freely and naturally into the next.

Tables and floors in the working areas should be covered with newspapers or plastic dropcloths to expedite cleanup. Cleanup also may be minimized by having the students hold the plaster block inside a large, shallow cardboard box as they carve. In fair weather, minimize mess by having the class carve outdoors, working on dropclothes away from high-public-visibility areas such as building entrances.

When sculpting animals, heads, or human figures, keep the bottom part undefined during most of the carving process. This way, the piece does not become top-heavy, topple over, and break. Teachers should help the students to evaluate their in-process sculpture: to be aware of large masses contrasting with small forms; to capture the characteristic stance or action; to emphasize a feature, such as the beak or claws of a bird; and to enrich the surface of their creation through texture and pattern. Delicate appendages such as hands, ears, horns, tusks, beaks, tails, and other jutting forms should be kept undefined until the basic shape is well established. During the final stages, carve textural and decorative details with nails, discarded dental tools, or nut picks.

The finished sculpture may be stained, glazed, waxed, or metalized. To provide a sealed undercoat for the stain or patina, coat the sculpture with slightly diluted white glue, and allow it to dry thoroughly. A paint stain in subtle shades can be applied freely and allowed to penetrate into the incised areas. After letting the stain set briefly, judiciously wipe the raised areas to bring out highlights. A complementary sculpture base of driftwood, stained blocks of wood, and sections of tree trunks with the bark left intact can help to give the carving distinction.

Both courtesy of Lawrence Stuek, *The Design of Learning Environments*, Ph.D dissertation, 1991, University of Georgia, Athens, GA.

Chapter 27

Architecture

Architecture has been called the mother of the arts, because it contains all other art forms. Architectural education conducted in elementary school can do much to sensitize future citizens not only to the delights from the study of architecture but also to the importance of wise community design decisions. Unfortunately, architecture has not been a well-established component in elementary school art programs. Nevertheless, architecture is an art form so readily apprehended and essential to the character of our communities that such education is essential.

One recommended activity is to construct a model of architecturally interesting buildings in the town. Elementary classroom teachers have correlated this activity to the study of social science and careers and included math and writing skills connected with the various occupations. Some instructional objectives are:

- Students will create a model of an existing building incorporating the design qualities of repetition, pattern, and texture.
- Students will discuss the reasons why particular buildings have architectural character.
- Students will arrange their model buildings to replicate an actual section of a town.

Design sources can be photographs, slides, or drawings of the actual buildings. Small boxes, such as hand-appliance, cereal, shoe, and drugstore gift boxes, can be used for the basic structure. These can be cov-

Top: Children can gain awareness of architectural form by helping to build a playscape. *Bottom: Fourth-grade children converted their classroom into a model city. They designed and constructed their own buildings: a bank, court, post office, newspaper building, etc. Subjects were taught through an integrated curriculum.*

Courtesy of Joyce Vroon, Trinity School, Atlanta, GA.

A series of house facades drawn on accordion-folded tagboard comprise Josephine Allen's street-front scene.

Courtesy of Baiba Kuntz, Glencoe, IL.

Courtesy of Baiba Kuntz, Glencoe, IL.

Top right: Fifth-grade student Lisa Molinaro's sketch of an imaginary house shows arched second story windows in groups of two and four. **Bottom right:** Good clay working tools are essential for the careful work entailed in making a clay house bas-relief. **Above:** Lisa's finished house showing the series of arched windows, a bay window and arched front door, along with landscaping.

Courtesy of Baiba Kuntz, Glencoe, IL.

ered with construction paper, or they can be painted. Signs and architectural features can be cut from paper, decorated, and attached. Temporarily arrange the buildings onto a large piece of cardboard, such as from a major appliance. Then, the streets and grounds can be sketched in, the background painted, and models of vehicles, street signs, and street furniture, such as benches and stop signs, added. The project might be given a public display, and publicity, at the meeting of a community development group, such as at the Chamber of Commerce or downtown development authority.

Models of local architecture can be constructed in other media as well. Designs of individual building facades can be rendered in clay and labeled. Then, these can be attached with construction adhesive to plywood to make a mural for long-term educational display and appreciation. Three-dimensional clay models of historic buildings may become prize community possessions. Pen-and-ink drawings of buildings can be assembled for a community calendar, or a cloth quilt based on historic community buildings can be made for public display.

Sketching fantasy houses is another architecture lesson. Sketches of one's dream house might include exotic architectural features, such as moats, drawbridges, and crenelated towers. Students of a more practical mindset may want to design something for actual use, such as a design for the interior of their bedroom or a corner of a garden. Students enjoy expressing their personalities through the choice of artwork, interior design, furniture arrangements, color schemes, plants, and bushes. A scrapbook of components can be put together from department-store newspaper advertising sections, home and garden design magazines, and postcards and photocopies of historical exemplars, and the collection can be used by students as the basis for a colored, overall design plan. A follow-up activity is to have students take before and after photos of places where aspects of their designs actually were implemented.

Young primary-level children can enrich their architectural imaginings about castles and fortresses through use of a sandbox. Using their bodies, they can enact architectural forms, such as arches, tunnels, and tiny spaces, and imagine what it feels like to be a building. With string or rope, several students in a group can make geometric shapes. Students can experience one aspect of architecture by developing design criteria and temporarily rearranging the classroom seats and cabinets.

On a walk around the school, have the students sketch the elements they see—for example, triangular pediments, quoins at corners, columns, arches, fan windows, foyers, and courtyards. In art criticism and art history, teams of students can critique their classroom, school, and community buildings: How do the parts work together? What mes-

Courtesy of Joyce Vroon, Trinity School, Atlanta, GA.

Ceramic low-fire underglaze colors and clear glass glaze enhance the finished quality of sixth-grade student Whitney Brown's clay house bas relief.

sages about society are conveyed by the forms? How do you feel about the different spatial arrangements in our school building? How does it show its functions? How would you characterize it, as heavy, serene, or lively? If we could redo it, how would we change it?

The architecture of Antonio Gaudi and other fantastic architecture can be shown to children to motivate their construction of imaginative structures, such as these sea cas- *tles by young Japanese schoolchildren. In most instances constructions like this are assigned as group table projects.*

A local architect can be invited to share building plans with a class, and students can do sketches for the visitor to critique. During a follow-up group discussion, students can share their reasons for preferring modern or traditional styles, classical or romantic designs. Students can go on a sketching tour of their community's most illustrious buildings and list their architectural features.

Informed citizens should be able to interpret architectural plans before buildings are actually constructed. As one way to develop such a skill, students can analyze and critique plans that were used for existing structures or areas, such as their school or a nearby recreation center, park, neighborhood, or subdivision. They can judge whether design strengths and shortcomings found in the built structures were foreshadowed in the plans.

Nelson Goodman believed that a building is a work of art only insofar as it signifies, means, refers, or symbolizes in some way. Students can discuss the "meanings" of buildings, the messages that buildings send out. Some other aesthetic issues might be addressed by asking such questions as: How does the visual complexity of patterns affect the "interest quotient" of a building? Can a building have too much regularity? Do size and cost determine the quality of a building?

Students can debate what qualities should be considered when ranking buildings ("What is more important, complexity or orderliness?"), and then do a class poll to determine whether preference relates to personality. Because architecture is so public an art form and so open to community response, aesthetics and art criticism activities are especially appropriate to the study of architecture.

The world of the future as illustrated in pen and ink by upper elementary youngsters from Saga, Japan.

Courtesy of Faye Brassie, Athens, GA.

A drawing of a local historic home by a middle school student.

Saturday Children's Classes, courtesy of Frank Wachowiak, Athens, GA, and Mary Sayer Hammond, Fairfax, VA.

Children who are challenged to be aware of their environment and encouraged to be "noticers" draw their homes in a personal, individual way. They emphasize those features that make each house unique. Third-grade student David Nix worked 2 hours on his felt-nib pen drawing.

Courtesy of the National Building Museum, Photo Jack Boucher, HABS.

The National Building Museum, Washington, DC was established by Congress in 1980 to encourage the nation's aesthetic sensitivity to architecture. It is in the National Pension Building, built in 1881 in the Italian Renaissance style. Its Great Hall, shown here, is considered to be one of America's most architecturally thrilling interior spaces. Outstanding architectural education materials for school children are available there.

Chapter 28

Crafts

Crafts is a very broad area. Some materials and techniques that it almost always includes (and examples of which will be shown in this chapter) are works in cloth and fiber, as well as jewelry and metalwork. Also, other crafts are mentioned elsewhere in this book; for example, cloth banners and quilts are described under collage. The aluminum-foil relief process (described under printmaking) is a variation of repoussé metalwork. Also usually considered as crafts are ceramics and sculpture. Sculpture was covered in the preceding chapter, and ceramics is covered in the final chapter.

Whereas the initial designing may take only a short time or be done as the project is made, most crafts require considerable labor-intensive handwork during the execution phase. This results from the repetitive, cumulative nature of many craft activities and handicrafts, such as spool weaving, bead work, shag pillows, and metal work. Teachers often decry students' avoiding activities requiring focused, long-term attention and their seeking seemingly instantaneous rewards. The rewards that come from attending to criteria over a considerable period of time to produce something of significance is a valuable lesson—and one that crafts can teach. This attending to goals and applying principles over a period of time is at the heart of the qualitative method espoused in this book. Also central to the qualitative method is the student's receiving expert guidance and evaluation, which points out both the student's accomplishments and areas in which he or she could profit by additional effort. Craft activities can help to promote in the student both the habits and rewards of careful craftsmanship. Students will develop the taste for and love of things well executed.

This effort and response between the craftsperson and the material that one works on is central to the African concept of "Mana," which means being sensitive to the spirit within the object one is making. For example, the Hausa people urge those making their subtractive embroidered robes to have "an ear for what the cloth wants to say." To

Saturday Children's Classes, courtesy of Frank Wachowiak, Athens, GA, and Mary Sayer Hammond, Fairfax, VA.

Metal repoussé can begin with preliminary drawings on paper taped to a sheet of copper or aluminum of a limited size such as 6 × 9 or 9 × 12 inches. Transfer the design through the paper to the metal using a blunt pencil. Then work directly on the metal, adding details. To show off the embossing further, black shoe polish can be applied and then wiped off.

Courtesy of David Hodge, Oshkosh, WI.

With his macramé frame taped to his desk and his lengths of yarn in neat pull-out bows, this student can clearly see which yarns go over and under.

Courtesy of Claire Clements, Athens, GA.

Courtesy of Claire Clements, Athens, GA.

Hooking is done with a crotchet hook through burlap. A shagrug technique is used for a wall hanging of a yellow and black bee.

Macramé is made with square knots and double half-hitches. Used by sailors and ancient Egyptians, the variety of knots in macramé make it a challenging craft and one that produces a beautiful and sophisticated product.

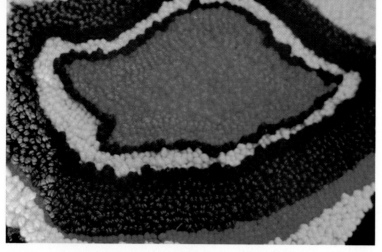

Courtesy of Claire Clements, Athens, GA.

Rug hooking makes an excellent group project, or for individuals, burlap pillow covers or wall hangings can be made. Here, an attractive, island-like design with radiating surrounding forms will be used for a pillow cover.

Africans, shaping material with one's hands involves both a giving out and a taking in; it entails sensing the reciprocating spiritual force between the hand of the maker and the material being made.

Because crafts often require a special love and special skill, as well as specialized tools, it is desirable that a teacher with real interest in the activity conduct it. Let the activity be that teacher's forte, something for students to look forward to as they proceed through the years; let it be a quality, in-depth experience driven by the motivation from within the teacher's heart.

Techniques must be taught. The teacher must create the vessel in which self-expression can occur. The initial work almost always requires specific directions made quite clear. Consider Frederich Froebel's instructional pattern: from structured activities to semi-structured and on to free activity. This conceptual model for craft technical instruc-

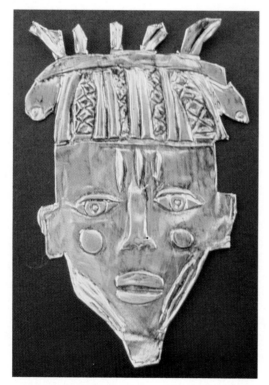

Courtesy of Sharon Burns-Knutson, Cedar Rapids, IA.

Metalwork repoussé can be done with heavy gold embossing foil and related to the study of African masks.

Charming yarn pictures can be stitched by children who take the time to solidly fill in areas with color. Notice the variety in the directions of the stitching of this red-headed figure.

Children love to make porcelain medallions using their initials and hang them from their own macraméd necklaces.

In this elementary student's stitchery, the columns of pink stitching seem akin to the folds on the face of a heavy-set person.

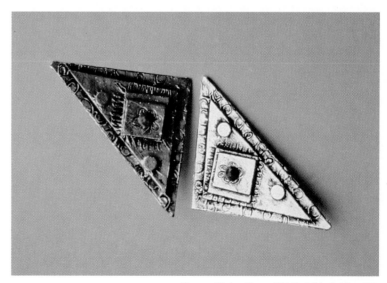

Earrings can be made by building up layers of thin cardboard and using an aluminum foil repoussé process.

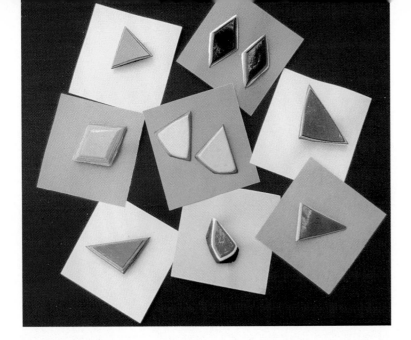

Gluing together several layers of colored papers and cardboard, and then sanding the edges to reveal a series of colored parallel lines surrounding the shape, is a way to make attractive earrings.

Bracelets can be made by gluing cut-out shapes and holes punched from thin cardboard to a strip of oak tag, then gluing the strip into a circular bracelet shape, wrapping with aluminum foil, and engraving with a pencil.

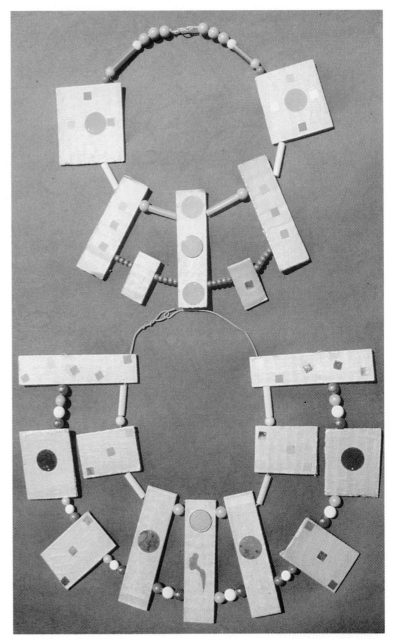

All jewelry photos courtesy of Barbara Thomas, Whit Davis School, Athens, GA.

Third-grade students made these Egyptian-style necklaces from rectangular shapes of cardboard, gummed stick-ons, beads, and telephone wire.

Courtesy of Howie Oakes, Athens, GA.

Use people in your community for resources. Here, Gary Carroll, a computer sales-
man, shows his hobby. He practices the Western Ukrainian art of the Hutzel people
called pysanki—*eggs decorated with colors and symbols. First, either hard boil or*
blow out the eggs.

Courtesy of Athens Academy, GA.

Mexican Huichol Indians made nearikas—yarn art pictures by pressing bits of scrap
yarn into softened wax. Here, third-grade students used the technique, using white
glue instead of beeswax, to paste small scraps of yarn to a hard backing to make a jun-
gle mural of lions, elephants, giraffes, zebras, parrots, and monkeys.

tion offers a way to bring in both the structured beginning as well as the later, imaginative opportunity.

While the structured beginning is important, so is the last phase—the individually creative and personally meaningful ending. ("Does anyone have an idea how they can make it in their own unique way?") Always work to personalize and give added meaning to the project. ("Who will you give it to?" "What colors do you associate with that person, maybe the yellow and red of a campfire you sat around together?") Urge students to come up with their own meanings for their designs. Help them to learn to think symbolically as a way of giving depth to personal experiences and developing abstract thinking skills.

A class of students totally involved in a craft activity is a joy to behold; eyes, brains, and hands are in synchronicity with each other, producing an aesthetic experience. Crafts also are excellent for students who come to school early or have idle time around lunch or recess. Some crafts can even be done while riding the bus to and from school. Some students with special needs may find crafts to be an especially sat-

isfying avenue for achievement, perhaps because of the calming, repetitive activity.

There also will be certain special-needs students, however, who will require additional help in the psychomotor operations. Team up these students ahead of time with those who can perform the operations easily. Using peer teaching can prevent students' frustration as well as afford the other child an opportunity to teach. Also, the teacher can avoid frustration—for example, being asked to tie knots for 30 students in a brief time. For gifted students, have craft examples by more mature artists available to motivate and extend the gifted students' efforts and abilities.

Involve the community's craft practitioners with your instructional unit. Through a display of a community craftspeoples' work in the school, give students a vision of the craft form carried out at a more elaborate and mature level. Conversely, have the students' productions exhibited in the adult members' venues, such as at a fibercrafts guild meeting, or display their crafts at a community art fair. Seek the involvement of industries in the community. For example, a carpet mill might donate yarn for shag rugs, or a store's drapery department might donate discontinued sample books to use for banners.

Crafts can readily be integrated with other academic areas. Develop a social-studies unit on how famous individuals have related to the craft form. For example, Paul Revere and his silversmithing might be tied to a repoussé lesson on aluminum-foil relief. In social studies, examine how the economy and governmental policies interfaced with the craft—for example, nontraceceable purchases of indigenous Southeast ceramic jugs during Prohibition. For history, point out how the technique has been used in other cultures and for other purposes, perhaps for utilitarian, secular, and governmental articles of apparel and display. Reading can be brought in through stories about people practicing the craft—for example, *Silas Marner* and weaving. Mathematics can be integrated through studying the units of measurement required—for example, lengths of yarn required for fiber crafts. Bring in economics by discussing how entire cultures flourished through trade in certain crafts, such as Oriental silks during the sixteenth and seventeenth centuries.

Weaving

Weaving is the interlacing and crossing of threads to form cloth. The warp threads run lengthwise and form the skeleton of the fabric.

Comer Elementary School. Courtesy of Claire Clements and Jo Nan Tanner, Athens, GA.

Elementary students did these weavings on cardboard box looms, made from a box such as a sturdy shoe box cut diagonally on its two long sides and the upper material removed, along with the one short end. The top and bottom cardboard edges the are measured at one half inch intervals and cut one half inch deep and then the warp threads put on; then, the horizontal weaving of the colorful weft begins.

Courtesy of David Hodge, Oshkosh, WI.

A primary grade girl weaves on a cardboard loom. Notice how her black marker drawing on the cardboard beneath guides her as she fills in the areas with her weaving.

Courtesy of Deborah Lackey, Fulton County Schools, Atlanta, GA.

In this well-equipped art classroom, a boy works on his woven hanging using a floor loom that alternates his warp threads up and down to facilitate his weaving through of the weft threads.

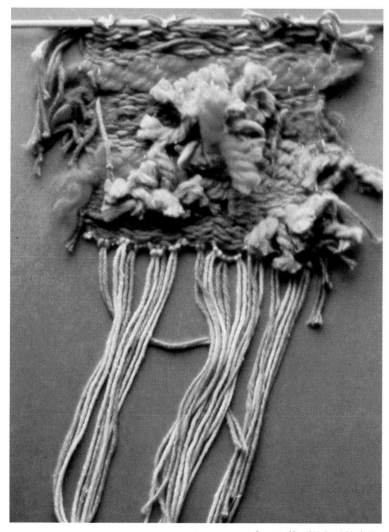

A weaving by a primary-grade child, using a variety of yarns of different sizes and with some cut loops extending forward.

Putting the warp threads on the loom is called *warping the loom*. The weft threads run at right angles and bind them together. The weaver alternates threads, lifting alternate ones up and going underneath the others. To simplify the task, there are any varieties of heddles, or devices for lifting alternating rows of threads. Other variations of weaving

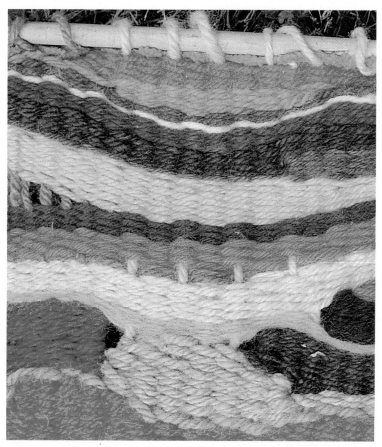

The primary-grade child who made this weaving showed an intuitive mastery of color and undulating shapes.

include plaiting or braiding as well as looping, which includes knitting and crotcheting.

One way to introduce weaving to kindergartners is having several students stand in a row, side by side, in front of the room. Then, have the first student take the end of a long piece of rope and go in front of the first student, behind the second, and so on, then at the end come back again. This is a good way to refresh their concepts of "in front of," "behind," "over," and "under" as they relate to weaving. Early weaving activities usually include paper weaving, in which the warp is cut on a

Using a cardboard-box loom, this first-grade student wove her placemat from sticks, reeds, and straws.

The thin black warp threads are woven partially together in discrete areas of heavy yarn, and areas are filled in with sticks to create a distinctive wallhanging. The heavy stick across the top gives structure to the hanging, and the grouping of the top warp threads into two clusters makes a unique method of hanging.

folded piece of paper (but not so far as to cut through the edge). Pre-cut lengths of rug yarn and regular yarn, along with lengths of natural fibers such as weeds, often are woven through these papers, along with strips cut from colorful photos and foils.

Weaving's rhythm of over and under also can be taught through the ever-popular *Ojo de Dios*, (Eye of God). Crossed sticks, or tonque

depressors, are used for the warp structure of decorative weavings made in Central American countries and hung above doorways to protect and bring good luck. (See page 145 for an illustration of a magnificent display made of several classes' *Ojo de Dios*.)

A really easy and convenient loom is made from plastic soda straws. They can be used full length or cut in half for little hands.

Four or six is about the limit that one can hold between thumb and forefinger. A little half-inch slit is made in the top of each straw, the lengths of warp yarn are sucked through the straw, and the top is firmly taped in the slit. Then, holding the pack in one's left hand, the over and under wrapping proceeds, always adding the new row on the top. Eventually the weaving fills up the straws, causing the weaving to be pushed off onto the loose warp threads. Varicolored yarn can be used, or just tie on a different yarn when a change in color or texture is desired.

Cardboard purse looms are a good early weaving activity. The top and bottom of a stiff piece of cardboard are slit at half-inch intervals and a half-inch deep, and the warp thread is wrapped around the cardboard. For a cylindrical variation rather than a rectangular shape, weaving can be done on an oatmeal box. A cardboard-box loom can be easily made from a sturdy shoe box or other sturdy cardboard box cut diagonally on its two long sides and the upper material removed along with the one short end. Then, the top and bottom cardboard edges are measured off in half-inch intervals, cut a half-inch deep, and then the warp threads put in place. The horizontal weaving of the colorful weft then begins. The advantage of this diagonally cut box is that a large,

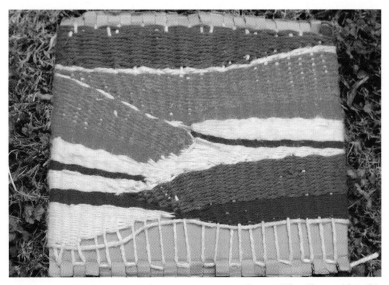

Courtesy of Claire Clements, Athens, GA.

Here, a purse is shown still on the cardboard loom. Notice how the student has made landscapelike forms by weaving in irregular shaped areas.

Courtesy of Claire Clements, Athens, GA.

These purses seem to be just the right size for these proud first-grade boys to use to hold their valuables.

open area beneath the weaving is provided for manipulating the over and under threading. Simple wood-strip looms also can be made. Just drive finishing nails at half-inch intervals slanted outward on the top and bottom boards, and then string or "warp" the loom. Alternately, old picture frames or unused stretcher strips can be used.

Finger weaving (really knitting) using a skein of varicolored yarn is a pleasant introductory activity guaranteed to keep any active child occu-

Courtesy of Claire Clements, Athens, GA.

Some purses made by a class of elementary children.

Courtesy of Claire Clements, Athens, GA.

This batik in a radiating design was dyed in successive yellow, red, and brown dyes. Before each successive dyeing, a larger area of the cloth was masked out and the cloth crinkled to create an attractive network of fine lines. For natural dyeing, boiled onion skins will give a gold color, and sumac berries will give an orange-brown.

Courtesy of David Hodge, Oshkosh, WI.

Students can weave on stretcher strip frames, such as those used for canvas paintings.

Courtesy of Joyce Vroon, Trinity School, Atlanta, GA.

Colorful wax batiks hang outside on the line to dry.

Courtesy of Joyce Vroon, Trinity School, Atlanta, GA.

Here, children use rubber gloves and tongs to make certain that dye reaches all areas of the cloths.

and then cast what is now the new lower course once again over the top. Eventually, a long knitted rope will fall off the back of the hand. A similar knitting activity uses an empty spool and fine metal wire. On a large, empty spool from the sewing box, five tiny headless brads can be pounded around the hole and fine metal wire woven around them and then cast off, with a pointed object such a large nail, down the hole in the middle. These cords then can be used to make jewelry.

From time to time, embroidered jackets and jeans become a fad which sweeps a school and are seen by the students as ways to celebrate and comment upon one's own culture. This interest can affford a good opportunity for the teacher to develop a unit on embroidery and to bring out its design constraints and opportunities for expressing in fresh ways the values of the young people. Exploring ways to decorate wearing apparel can also be chances to bring in related fibercraft methods, such as batik, appliqué, and molas. One strong feature of applique, and related techniques, is that it is an activity for all ages and one which costs practically nothing.

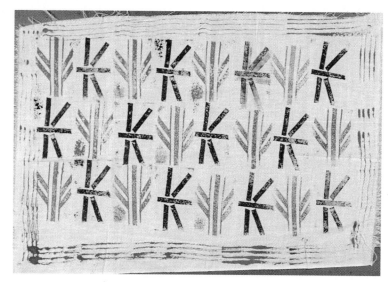

Courtesy of Jackie Ellett, Fort Daniel Elementary School, Gwinnett County Schools, GA.

Adinkira is a patterned fabric made by the Ashantis from the African Ivory Coast and is used for their togas. It is made by stamping designs on the cloth's surface with calabash (potatolike) prints combined with lines made with a wooden comb dipped in dye. Here, a fourth-grade student used rubber-stamp designs, made from strips of rubber inner tube glued to blocks of wood and printed in rows and columns for his adinkira design.

pied. Wrap yarn over and under around the fingers of one's left hand (assuming one is right-handed) and then back again, then use the fingers of the right hand to pick up the bottom layers and cast them over the top. Proceed to wrap the fingers with another course of yarn, over and under,

Courtesy of Sharon Burns-Knutson, Cedar Rapids, IA.

Fifth-grade student Phyliss Helwig's weaving shows a judicious use of greys which make the red, white and black stand out.

Starch-Resist Batik

Batik originated in ancient Egypt and is very popular in modern India and Java. For cloth batik, first wash the cloth to remove sizing. The process can be as easy as making a simple paste of flour and cold water.

Courtesy of Sharon Burns-Knutson, Cedar Rapids, IA.

Sixth-grade student T. J. Meyerholtz made his weaving after studying bold geometric Native-American designs. Among the Hopi Indians, it is the men who weave; among the Navajo, it is women.

Over one cup of flour is gradually added to one cup of water, and this is brushed on or squeezed through a plastic condiment bottle and/or spread with a fork or stick. Dry overnight, and then, rather than dipping, brush or sponge on the dye color.

For a higher-quality recipe, follow the "adire eleko" starch-resist paste cloth pattern design technique of the Yoruba people of Nigeria. They used cassava tubers, and the cloth was subsequently dyed with indigo (which grows in the southern United States). The starch paste first was tinted with rust to make it easier to see and then applied with a chicken feather. A paste is made of $\frac{3}{4}$ cup pearl tapioca and water, cooked in a double-boiler pot until smooth. Dissolve in a $\frac{1}{2}$ cup of cold water, 6 tablespoons of gluten flour and cornstarch, and blend into the tapioca mixture in $\frac{1}{2}$-cup portions. Cook uncovered in a double boiler until thickened, add $\frac{1}{2}$ teaspoon of alum, and refrigerate. For best results in using the paste, spread the starch on thickly with a tongue depressor, and scratch lines in it before it dries. After the starch is thoroughly dry, dye the cloth, and then remove the starch by peeling, scraping, or soaking. The Yoruba women used indigo and avocado leaves, which they chopped and boiled for their blues and rust colors of dye. In our elementary schools, starch resist avoids the hazards of hot wax.

Fibercrafts are particularly appropriate to integrate with the study of other cultures, because a culture's clothing and other fiber articles may be quite distinctive. For example, the Crow Indians of the American Plains had distinctive parfleches (leather-storage bags adorned with geometric designs). The Inca people of South America's west coast are famous for their patterned tapestry weaving and feather work. The artistic designs used in Panamanian appliqués and the molas of the Cuna Indians convey to us something of the values and unique traditions of their civilizations.

Chapter 29

Clay Modeling

All children, both in elementary and middle school, should have the opportunity to create and express their ideas in clay. Clay is a hands-on wonder—sensuous, malleable, unpredictable, and on occasion, messy. Some students respond to clay more enthusiastically than others, but all children benefit from the unique challenges provided by this gift from Mother Earth.

Clay in the Primary Grades

Young children work with clay in several ways. Most add clay pieces to the basic form. A few will pat clay into a pancake and draw into it, and a very few will pull out features from a ball or lump of clay.

The teacher's main responsibility in the early stage is to provide the children with an adequate supply of workable clay. Check the plasticity of the clay at least a day or two before the project takes place. If the clay is too dry, poke holes in it and moisten it; if it is too wet, put it on bats or on newspapers to dry it out. A ball of clay the size of a grapefruit is recommended for each child. Use newspapers or plastic sheeting to protect desk or tabletops, and introduce just enough stimulating subject-matter motivation, such as animals and their young, to get the class started.

A period of experimentation with the clay should precede every project. Before students can express a particular idea, they first need to acquire the feel of the clay. During these orientation sessions, call the students' attention to the desired plasticity. Discuss keeping excess clay moist by rolling the pieces and crumbs into a single ball, and explain the mechanics of cleanup.

Emphasize how touch experiences help to give shape to objects. One way of introducing students to the exciting tactile potential of clay is to play the clay-in-a-paper-sack game. The students put a ball of clay about the size of a grapefruit or orange into a sturdy paper sack and, without looking, manipulate it until it has an interesting form. Encourage them to think with their hands, to stretch the clay, squeeze it, and poke it. Above all, they must not peek. When completed, the finished pieces are displayed. Ask the students if anyone sees a real form hidden in the clay creations—an animal, a bird, a fish? What did they learn about clay?

The animal kingdom provides a wealth of inspiration for the young clay manipulator. Four-legged mammals, such as cows, horses, pigs, hippos, elephants, rhinos, and bears, are especially suitable, because the child can model sturdy legs to make them stand. Other popular animals are cats, dogs, rabbits, turtles, frogs, squirrels, whales, porpoises, and alligators. Group projects, such as Noah's ark, a three-ring circus, the zoo, the farm, and the jungle, are very popular with young children as well. Standing human figures can be difficult, however, and children must be guided to provide additional supports or model thick, sturdy legs and bases to hold the figure erect.

Primary school children especially love clay's plastic changeability as they poke, squeeze, pound, stretch, and roll it. They may describe a sequence of action with one figure, such as a clown or an acrobat, manipulating it to create various postures—standing on its head, bending backward and forward, and falling down. Clay manipulating and modeling may fulfill a therapeutic and a storytelling need.

Some students will pat and pound their clay into a flat, cookie shape. More advanced students will hold the clay ball in their hands to model their animal's body in three dimensions. They will pull out or add legs,

Courtesy of *London Sunday Mirror*, London, England.

Facing page: *Terra-cotta clay sculpture by a middle school adolescent, London, England. Notice how the textural quality of the clay has been retained to give the work a spontaneous naturalness.*

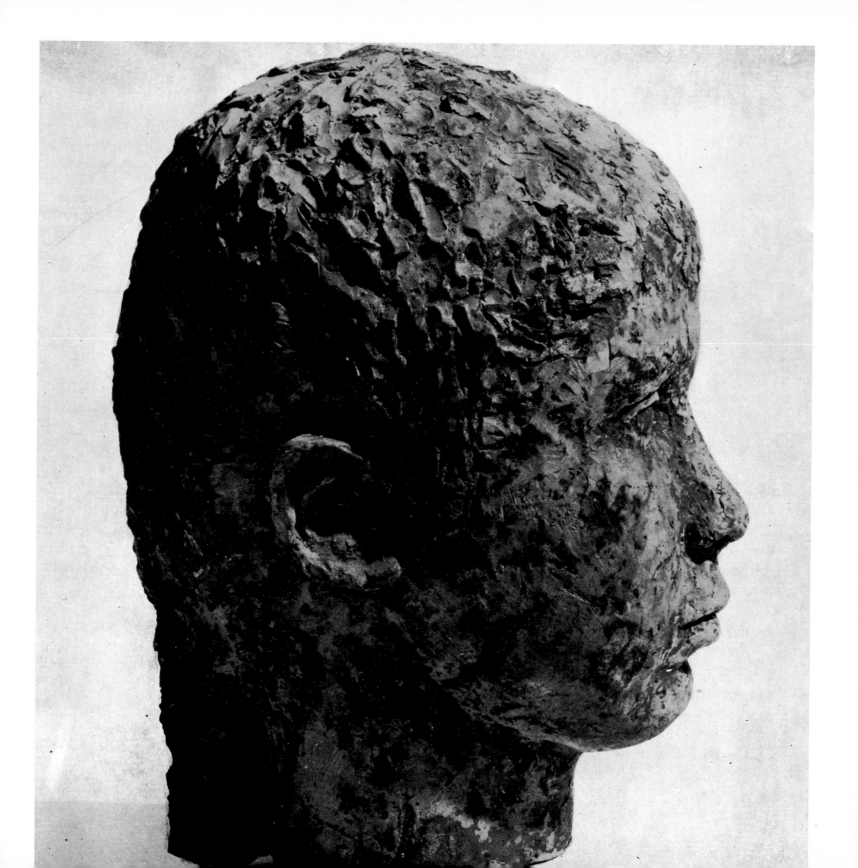

Japan

tails, trunks, horns, beaks, and wings. Because figures made in pieces often come apart during drying and firing, many teachers strongly advocate that students be taught to pull out appendages from the body rather than to add them on. Encourage students who insist on adding the appendages to make holes in the body with a stick or fingers and then insert the appendages into those holes to strengthen the joint. Older students can learn to score and join clay with slip (a paste made of clay and water). To prevent the sagging of a form, use temporary clay or cardboard supports, such as a "fifth leg" under the animal's body, until the clay is leather-hard. Always emphasize the importance of a sturdy basic form.

Although many children in the primary grades are not concerned with detailing, some will enjoy experimenting with textures and pattern on their creations. A collection of found objects (which should be washed at the close of the project) such as plastic forks, popsicle sticks, bottle caps, nails, screws, toothbrushes, dowels, and wire mesh will spark their interest.

Children enjoy making small figures not only of clay but also from a variety of other moldable, plastic materials. Such homemade mixtures contain varying proportions of material, binder, and water. Here are few "formulas" for such mixtures:

- Everyone is familiar with mixing flour and water in equal parts to make modeling mixtures for relief maps. A firmer mixture can be used to model objects.
- Also easy is salt ceramic, made from 1 cup of salt, $\frac{1}{2}$ cup of cornstarch, and $\frac{3}{4}$ cup of water.
- Another popular mixture, often used for seasonal ornaments, is baker's clay, for which 4 cups of flour, 1 cup of salt, and $1\frac{1}{2}$ cups of water are mixed, shaped, and then baked at 350 degrees for 1 hour until hard.
- For a sawdust–wheat paste mixture, use 2 parts sawdust, 1 part flour or wheat paste, and hot water. (Optionally, $\frac{1}{2}$ part of plaster can be added.) This is good for tennis ball–size puppet heads. For the puppet's neck, roll a cylinder of oaktag paper around one's index finger,

Japan

Left: This elephant's head, neck, ears, and front legs were pulled out from the clay rather than added onto; encourage children to hold the clay in their hands when modeling small sculptural pieces, especially in the beginning stages. This promotes sturdiness. Michelangelo said that a good sculpture should be capable of being rolled down a hill without parts breaking off. *Right:* The kangaroo's large tail provides support to the burden of the adolescent contentedly sitting in its pouch. The theme of an animal and its young is a surefire hit, one that all children can identify with.

Top: Three stages in the construction of a clay hippopotamus are illustrated. First, basic body with legs and tail added. Second, a tongue depressor may be used to create the open mouth. Third, addition of characteristic details: ears, eyes, teeth. *Bottom:* The directness of clay manipulation holds a universal fascination for children. The delightful clay figure illustrated at right possesses a mobility that only the clay medium captures so well. Youngsters can first take a variety of poses themselves and feel the kinesthetic awareness in their own bodies before making a figure in clay perform similar action-packed feats. Children might strut, twist, dance, juggle, bend, and even stand on their heads.

tape the tube together, and for sturdiness, tear or cut and flare out the tube's top edge to facilitate its embedment into the mixture, which then is packed around the tube to make the head.

Clay in the Upper Grades

Older students are more successful in mastering the complexities of advanced clay modeling, but they may ask for help with specific problems.

This sturdily constructed clay elephant was made by pulling out forms. Then the elephant was decorated with pattern and texture. Youngsters can employ objects such as tubes, pencil erasers, bottle caps, bark, wire mesh, and pinecones to add imaginative texture and pattern to their clay creations.

For example, figures and appendages may sag or come apart, and students may need help with balance and proportion or the intricate delineation of eyes, mouth, nose, and ears.

At this stage, effective motivations include: field trips to sketch animals at a farm, zoo, animal shelter, pet shop, or natural-history museum; family pets brought to class to model; as well as photographs and art reproductions. As a subject, prehistoric creatures fire students' imaginations. Dinosaurs are uniquely adapted to interpretation in clay. Their ponderous mass, armor-encrusted body, and wrinkled, scaly skin evoke the quality of the ancient earth itself.

Emphasize structural elements that can give the piece character. Talk about the sway of the body, stance of the legs, swing of the tail, tilt of the head, action of the jaws, flow of the mane, or flare of the wings. An imaginatively expressive creature also may combine the characteristics of several different animals. In upper elementary and middle school, a preliminary drawing of figures to be modeled in clay often helps students to clarify their ideas.

Extra clay may be needed, especially for reinforcing junctures. To prevent cracking and exploding when the clay is dried and fired, avoid using armatures, such as sticks, inside the structure. To develop the form three-dimensionally, the sculpture should be viewed from all sides. Use a 12- or 16-inch-square Masonite sheet or a turntable as a working base to facilitate rotation.

Whether on a clay pot, figure, animal, or tile, there are almost no limits to clay-relief pattern and textural exploitation. To make scaly, armorlike dinosaur hide, students might roll out balls, coils, and ribbons of clay, then apply them to the body of the creature. Slip can be used as an adhesive to secure the pellets and coils of clay to the main surface. Discarded broken saw blades and combs can be used for linear effects. Squeezing moist clay through window screen produces masses of clay strings for manes or tails.

Construction Techniques

Hand Building

In overcrowded middle school classes, the beleaguered art teacher would find it difficult, if not impossible, to instruct everyone in the sophisticated, highly technical, and time-consuming craft of throwing pottery on a wheel. Do not frustrate a majority of students by demanding skills that college ceramics majors work long hours to attain. Instead, concentrate on hand-building techniques all students can master.

Students must be guided to avoid trite bud vases and ashtrays. Show films and photos of contemporary ceramic and hand-building techniques. Introduce students to the exciting work of contemporary potters, such as Mary Engel, Andy Nassisse, and Shoji Hamada, and to the beautiful, functional clay vessels of the pre-Columbian craftspeople of Mexico, Gautamala, Colombia, and Peru. Encourage students to collect an assortment of stones, shells, seedpods, nuts, and driftwood to trigger ideas.

The basic form must be the first critical concern. No amount of additional embellishment or decoration can redeem a piece that is weak in formal concept or structure. Critiques of clay work-in-progress should be standard procedure during every studio session, and students should share their discoveries with their classmates.

Variety in the basic sculptural form should be emphasized. Because students are accustomed to symmetrically styled ceramics, the teacher must guide them to see the beauty of asymmetry. Variety can be achieved through contrasting the forms of the appendages, spouts, necks, and feet. It also can be achieved through exploitation of the positive and negative spaces created by the vessel's openings, by its handles and lids, and by its delineation of incised and relief areas to create dark and light pattern.

Unity also is vital to the total impact of the clay structure. There should be a natural flow from one plane or contour to another. Ap-

Courtesy of David Hodge, Oshkosh, WI.

The handsome branch pots, made by seventh-graders, started as basic coil, slab, and pinch-pot forms. Through the addition of complementary clay and feet and the elegant decoration of surface forms, they emerged as distinctive, one-of-a-kind ceramic containers. Decoration enhances rather than disguises or destroys the fundamental ce- *ramic form. After staining, if the stains appear to be too intense, earth can be rubbed into the surface to subdue the effect. Further embellishment can be achieved by inscribing designs through stained surfaces, and liquid wax can provide a subtle sheen as well as a protective surface.*

pendages should grow naturally from the basic body structure and be in scale with it; they should complement, not detract from, the whole. The same is true of decorations: designs should go with the form, not compete with it or ignore it.

Clay-Slab Construction

Slabs of approximately $12 \times 18 \times \frac{1}{2}$ inch should be prepared in advance. Moist clay, a rolling pin, a burlap- or linen-covered board, guiding strips of wood $\frac{1}{2}$-inch thick, and plastic covering to keep slabs moist during storage also are needed. Additional slabs can be made as the project progresses. Impress fired clay-relief stamps and found objects into the moist slab to enrich the surface before begin-

ning construction of the container. Divide the large slab into the number of slabs that will be needed for the sides and bottom (and sometimes top) of the container. The junctures where two slabs are to be joined should be scored (roughened) and covered with water or slip before attaching the slabs. When slabs are joined, use a wooden paddle to secure them and form the container's shape. Two or more clay-slab constructions in different sizes may be joined to make a larger, more complex structure.

Pinch-Pot Sculpture

For pinch-pot sculpture, approximately 5 pounds of moist clay per student is recommended. First, a large portion of the clay is shaped into a

Right: Courtesy of Baiba Kuntz, Glencoe, IL.

Students concentrate as they create their clay projects. **Left:** *A boy studying ancient cultures constructs a model of a cliff dweller's home.* **Right:** *This tall pot is being constructed from coils. The coils are then smoothed together for strength. Rows of bold balls and loops give contrast.*

tional decoration may be done by using stamped, incised, and bas-relief motifs.

For unusual effects, students may apply clay pellets, straight and undulating clay ribbons or snakes, and clay coils to the surface. Be sure the surface clay is sufficiently moist for the adhesion of any additions. If not, moisten it, or use slip. Feet, handles, bases, legs, animal necks, and heads may be added, but to preserve strength, the sealed ball should not be opened until the whole container is complete. Once opened, spouts and vase necks may be added. Many exciting forms result when students combine two or more pinch-pot balls of various sizes and shapes into one unified structure.

large ball and cut in half. Then, each half is formed into a pinch-pot shape, keeping the walls fairly thick and each pot similar in size. Students then join together the two pinch pots (scoring and moistening the junctures) and pinch the seams tightly to form a hollow ball. Holding the hollow ball of clay in one hand, the student paddles it until the pinched seams disappear. To create a decorative surface effect, use a piece of wood, approximately $1 \times 2 \times 15$ inches and wrapped at one end generously with cord. Students must rotate the clay ball as they paddle so that the entire ball will be paddled evenly. This action packs the clay and seals in enough air to support the walls. During paddling, students can change the shape of the ball to resemble a pod, nut, or gourd. Although a cord-wrapped paddle produces an attractive texture, addi-

Collection of Frank Wachowiak, Athens, GA.

An ancient ceramic Haniwa horse from the pre-Jomon period, Japan. Hollow clay cylinders form the animal's basic shape. Notice how clay coils were flattened to add characteristic reins and saddle.

Ceramics can play a role in a multidisciplinary approach correlating art with science and social studies. **Left:** *Intermediate-elementary children studying ocean life made clay fish. They cut fish shapes out of clay slabs and attached them to the ocean-floor bases. The pieces then were bisque-fired and painted with acrylic paint. The two fish on the left are kissing; the top left fish is dining on another fish.* **Right:** *Second-grade children studied the role of monsters in medieval culture and saw how cathedrals used grotesque gargoyle waterspouts. The children then made these clay monster plaques painted with simulated-stone spatter paint.*

Drying, Firing, Glazing, and Staining

If a kiln is available, clay sculptures should be allowed to dry evenly and slowly in a cabinet or under a sheet of plastic before firing. When leather-hard, solid forms over 1-inch thick should have holes or hollows made in their understructures. Another way of allowing air to escape during firing is to poke pin holes in the leather-hard piece. Trapped air can cause an explosion, and one exploding piece can destroy a kilnful of other pieces. Some other precautions are proper wedging of the clay to remove air bubbles, and adding grog to increase the clay's strength. Another precaution is to keep the kiln lid cracked open for 1 hour or more when firing begins and then raise the temperature very slowly. Pieces even 2-inches thick can survive firing if the heat is raised *very slowly* over a period of days.

It is relatively easy to fire greenware. Raw-clay pieces may be stacked closely inside of or on top of one another, rest against one another in the kiln, and even rest against the kiln's sides (taking care they

Face mugs allow a study of caricature and create memorable objects. Students have adorned their face mug characters with features such as mustaches, beards, and a monocle.

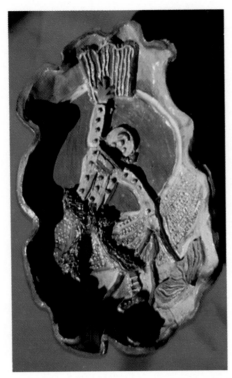

Ceramic glazes add beauty to this ceramic slab dish. The piece's undulating sides make the piece unique.

do not touch the heating elements). Engobe-decorated pieces, in which the clay slip is applied before firing and scratched through for graffito designs, can be fired in a similar manner. Do not let the clay get too dry before applying slip decoration, however, lest peeling and cracking occur during firing.

Glaze firing requires more care. Kiln glazing of bisque-fired clay pieces (those that already have been fired once) is a way for ambitious teachers to bring the ceramic process to a rich culmination. Children create beautiful pieces, which frequently become family treasures. (Because old glazes sometimes contained dangerous elements, such as lead and arsenic, use only glazes certified as being safe, especially for food containers.) The glazed pieces must be stacked carefully so that no piece touches another or the wall of the firing chamber. Because

molten glaze will adhere the piece to the kiln's floor, a protective kiln wash is useful. The bottom and lower $\frac{1}{4}$- to $\frac{1}{2}$-inch of the piece should be wiped free of glaze, or supports such as stilts or pins should be used. Weeks of firing may be necessary, especially if the students have created large clay structures. The large student populations of elementary schools, limited budgets, and limited kiln size frequently make it impractical to glaze large pieces.

An alternate way to beautify fired clay is to rub neutral colors of pigment, moist dirt, or soil of another shade into the incised areas. Before the dirt or applied stain dries, the raised surfaces may be partially wiped with a moist rag to create contrasting effects. In most cases in which staining or coloring (try gluing on torn pieces of colored tissue paper) is applied to bisque-fired clay, adding a final coat of liquid wax or clear gloss polymer is advised. Other clay projects are shown on pages 41, 60, and 63.

Clay Plaster Reliefs

Students in upper elementary and middle school often are self-critical concerning their drawing ability and need the satisfaction and challenge of creating in an art medium more dependent on design skills. Creating plaster reliefs, which involves manipulative skills with special tools, materials, and surprise effects, is one such challenging adventure. (Other art projects in this general category are metal repoussé, ceramics, papier-maché, stitchery, weaving, and mobiles.)

For a plaster-relief project, you will need moist clay, plaster, a plastic or rubber dishpan, and a container for the clay mold (shoe box, cigar box, or half-gallon or gallon waxed-cardboard milk carton). Also needed are an assortment of found objects (spools, nails, wire, cogwheels, lath, screws, keys, clothespins, buckles, rope, bolts, cord, reed, dowel sticks, bottle caps, jar lids, coins, printer's letters, combs, plastic forks and spoons, and natural objects, such as twigs, pinecones, acorns, nuts, seashells, and bark). To finish the piece, you will need a plaster-sealing medium, such as white glue or polymer medium, a 1- or 2-inch utility brush, and stains.

The first step is to reinforce the box sides with masking or strapping tape. Use the lid under the box to reinforce the bottom, and line the inside of the box with wax paper. Milk cartons requiring no protective lining can be cut in half lengthwise and the open end resealed. If the separate reliefs are to be assembled later into one large, group mural design, uniformity of sizes may be desirable. A free-form relief shape can be made by using a sheet of tempered Masonite as the working surface and building a clay wall around the slab of clay.

Two attractive plaster reliefs by middle school youngsters. Notice especially how composition fills the space and the metal patina brings out the relief highlights. "Animals and their young" is a popular theme chosen by many students for this challenging, *three-dimensional project. Suggest that students limit the stains to neutral colors at first to achieve unity. Be sure to apply one or two coats of white glue to the plaster relief before staining it. Allow the stain to flow into incised lines.*

There are two methods for making the basic slab of clay. The simplest is to roll out the clay into a slab approximately ½- to 1-inch thick, cut the slab to the size of the box, and place the slab in the bottom of the box, ready for the next stage of the process. In the second method, the clay is placed pellet by pellet into the box until the bottom is filled with a clay layer ½- to 1-inch thick. If a very flat surface is desired, the clay may be stamped down with the end of a 2- to 4-inch woodblock.

Before students begin their relief designs, incisions, and textural impressions in the clay slab, they should practice on a sample slab. Demonstrate that impressions made in the clay will be reversed in the plaster cast. Designs that are pressed or incised in the clay will bulge out in the plaster version. Show students examples of relief sculpture throughout art history. For example, the Greek Parthenon frieze, coin designs, and sculptures by the modern artist Marino Marini can be used in discussions about the beauty of high and low relief. Letters and numbers must be imprinted backward in the clay to read correctly in the final product. Once the teacher has made these basic principles clear, students are free to be expressive and innovative.

There are several ways to model in the slab. A very free and natural approach involves the use of hands and fingers. Commercial ceramic tools also may be employed. Coils, pellets, and ribbons of clay cut from a thin slab may be applied with water or slip.

With younger children, it might be wise to limit designs to those that can be achieved by pressing into the clay, because it is more difficult to dig lines out of the clay. (In addition, the digging approach often produces sharp, hazardous edges in the final plaster cast.) For straight lines, use applicator sticks, popsicle holders, or the edge of a thick piece of cardboard. For curved lines, use bent reed, cord, or the edges of round containers.

Recommended subject-matter themes for plaster reliefs include: birds with plumage, fish, insects (butterflies), animals in their habitat, flowers, theater or clown faces, heraldic devices, personal insignia, monograms, and nonobjective designs. By combining individual efforts into one large "mural" composition, a project of significant scope can be achieved.

When the impressed and incised designs are completed, liquid plaster-of-Paris is poured over the clay to a ½- to 1-inch thickness. (Plaster-

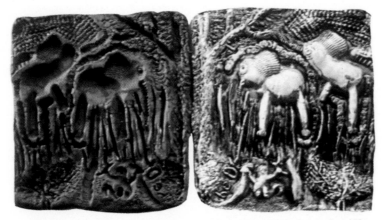

A clay negative mold and the completed plaster relief. Letters and numerals must be impressed backward into the clay mold to read correctly in the final relief; shapes pressed into the clay bulge out in the plaster version. A seashell was used to make the elephant's ears. Other effective imprinting objects include beads and discarded costume jewelry, plastic forks and spoons, crumpled heavy-duty aluminum foil, heavy cord, reed, and wire.

mixing procedures are described in Chapter 26 in the section on subtractive sculpture.) Before the plaster sets, insert wire, twisted at the ends, for a hanger. The hardening capabilities of plaster vary widely; semi-hard pieces are easily broken, and the teacher should allow time for the plaster to harden. Hardening takes at least 1 to 2 hours; plaster should be allowed to set overnight.

If your class does a sand-plaster project at a beach, care must be taken to form the mold far enough up the beach so that the plaster will not be affected by dampness at the water's edge. If there is too much moisture in the sand, the plaster will not harden. If you are at a salt-water beach, use fresh water, because salt can weaken the plaster's strength. Sand will not hold nearly as much detail as clay, so the outer edges of sand-plaster reliefs usually form the shape of the object. Sand-plaster reliefs often require coat hangers, wire, or sticks added quickly after the plaster is poured for added strength.

When the plaster is quite hard, the student pries open the cardboard container and separates the plaster from the clay. If the separation is done carefully, most of the moist clay in the mold can be salvaged for a future project. (*Note:* If the clay contains bits of plaster, do

not re-use it for a clay project that is to be fired; the plaster may cause the clay to explode.)

To prepare the plaster relief for staining, students should file or sandpaper away the excess edges and any sharp, abrasive points. The relief then should be washed with water, using a discarded toothbrush or nail to clean away the clay from narrow recesses. Before staining, give it a generous coat of slightly water-diluted white glue, and allow it to dry thoroughly. Then, apply stain, and wipe the raised areas to bring out highlights.

Plaster reliefs are a good project for upper elementary and middle school teachers and students looking for a different three-dimensional experience. Plaster reliefs are not so dependent on drawing skill, yet they have a sophisticated, finished appearance.

In this clay/plaster bas relief pond scene by a sixth-grade student, frogs, a toad, and flowers teem with life.

Art Materials and Facilities

Materials and Supplies

To develop the confidence that will help them to teach art successfully, teachers must be familiar with the art materials and equipment that are available for their classes. They should discover the art potential of these materials through actual involvement with them. The following art materials and tools usually are found in elementary and middle schools today and are furnished either by the school or the students. Teachers should learn to use them creatively, know the available sources, order them in economy lots and sizes, and store them properly.

Expendable Materials

Pencils	Clay
Wax crayons	Manila paper
Oil pastels, craypas	Newsprint
Colored chalk	Construction paper
School chalk	White drawing paper
Fingerpaint	Oaktag (tagboard)
Tempera paint	Fingerpaint paper
Watercolors	White liquid glue
School paste	

Nonexpendable Supplies and Equipment

Art slides and slide projector	Paper cutter
Art reproductions	Overhead projector, slide projector, and projection screen
Scissors	
Watercolor brushes	Rulers, compasses
Easel brushes	Hammer, saw, stapler

Generous Budget Supplies and Equipment

TV, art videos, and VCR	Computers, Art history CD-ROMS
Felt-nib or nylon-tip pens	Art gum erasers
Printing inks (water, oil base)	Felt-nib watercolor markers
India ink	Linoleum and tools for block cutting
Brayers (rubber rollers for printmaking)	
	Clay glazes
Clay kiln	Tissue paper (assorted colors)
Poster board (for mats)	Gloss polymer medium

Toxic Materials and Inhalants

Toxic art materials are particularly harmful to children, whose nervous systems, internal organs, and reproductive systems are more at risk because the cells are still dividing. In 1990, Congress passed a law requiring that all toxic art materials have labels warning of their toxicity. Many toxic materials still do not have such labels, however, and old materials purchased before the law went into effect still may be on the shelves. These materials should be discarded. School shelves may hold pigments containing lead (lead white or flake white), cadmium, mercury, chromates, manganese, and cobalt. All of these are toxic. The main risk is ingestion through eating and nail biting while working.

One in six U.S. children, or 3.5 million youths, have harmful levels of lead in their blood. An elevated blood lead is linked to learning disabilities, lower IQ, and higher dropout rates. Toxic ceramic glaze chemicals may be especially dangerous if they are used on ceramics that will be used for food or drink. Wheat paste contains toxic preservatives, yet it is used in over half the schools. All toxic materials should be banned in elementary schools.

Other health hazards are:

Carbon monoxide and often sulphur dioxide and nitrogen oxide from unvented kilns. School kilns should be vented through a canopy hood.

Turpentine and other solvents. Over a 3-hour period, one-fourth to one-half of a small cup of turpentine can evaporate. Inhaling high concentrations of fumes from turpentine or mineral spirits can cause narcosis, dizziness, nausea, fatigue, and respiratory irritation. (Odorless mineral spirits are less hazardous.) Prolonged exposure to all solvents containing aromatic hydrocarbons can cause skin allergies, and ingestion of benzene, toluene, and xylene can be fatal. For this reason, references to varnish and shellac, which require mineral spirits, turpentine, and alcohol as solvents, have been deleted from this book. Teachers are urged to use gloss polymer medium when a sealant or a high sheen is desired. At this time, alternatives to mineral spirits that are akin to baby and vegetable oils, are in the developmental stage.

Adhesives. Building supply adhesives and household cements, such as model cement and Duco cement, contain hydrocarbons, which are harmful when inhaled.

Markers. Permanent felt-tip markers contain aromatic hydrocarbons, can be very toxic, and never should be used in elementary classrooms.

Aerosol spray paint contains chemical compounds that can be extremely harmful when inhaled by students who use this "legal drug" for a cheap, brief, and intense high. The student first sprays paint into a plastic bag. Then, the student blows the bag up the rest of the way, and puts the narrow opening to his or her mouth, and inhales. Some students spray paint into a soda can and then innocently appear to be drinking. Some children paint their nails with typewriter correction fluid repeatedly throughout the day.

Inhalants are particularly prevalent in the eighth, ninth, and tenth grades. Paradoxically, as drug use has been declining nationally, inhalant use has been increasing. Telltale signs are a loss of interest in appearance, food, and family activities. "Spaced-out" behavior, lack of coordination, sores on the nose and mouth, frequent coughing, dried spray paint on clothes, and empty aerosol cans (from hair spray to Scotchguard to Reddi Whip) may be indications. Long-term effects of sniffing are mood swings, depression, hallucinations, memory loss, and impaired judgment. Brain, kidney, and liver damage, as well as damage to the central nervous system and heart failure, also may result.

Practical Suggestions

Practical suggestions for the art teacher include:

Keep all tools and materials in order. Store them in cigar boxes, shoe boxes, freezer containers, coffee or vegetable-shortening tins, and commercially available tote trays. Label the containers, and paint tool handles with an identifying color.

Keep all tools clean. Do not let metal tools get rusty. Wipe them dry if they get wet, and oil them if they are to be stored. Do not use scissors for clay or plaster projects, and never pour plaster in any form down the sink.

Mount motivational resource photographs on oaktag (tagboard). Store them in labeled accordion folders or flat drawers, or put them in plastic, looseleaf protectors and keep them in notebook binders.

Wash brushes clean (use detergent if necessary) and store them bristle-end-up in a jar or tall coffee can. Be sure that students rinse and clean watercolor tins. Leave them open, and stack them to dry overnight. Order semi-moist cakes of watercolor in bulk to refill empty tins.

Store scrap construction and tissue paper flat in drawers or discarded blanket cartons to prevent the paper from being crushed.

When placing orders for tempera paint, always order more white paint, because a great deal is used to mix tints of colors. You also can order crayons or oil pastels in bulk.

Hardboard in 4- × 8-foot pieces of ¼-inch thickness is excellent for drawing boards and working surfaces on desks or tables. For drawing boards, have the lumber dealer cut the hardboard for you into either 18- × 24-inch or 12- × 18-inch rectangles, depending on which size works best in your situation. For longer wear, mask the edges of the boards with tape.

Yarn purchased on skeins should be rewound on balls or spools for ready use. A closed cardboard carton with holes punched in it for the yarn to pass through may be used as a dispenser.

Keep school paste in jars until needed, then dispense it on small squares of cardboard. Scrape the unused paste back into the jar at the close of class. Moisten it slightly with a few drops of water, and cap tightly.

When crayons break and do not easily fit into the original carton, store them in discarded cigar boxes, coffee or vegetable-shortening tins, or freezer containers.

Powder tempera is much easier to store than the liquid kind, but liquid tempera has definite advantages. It always is ready to use if sealed

Courtesy of David Harvell, Fourth Street Elementary School, Athens, GA.

Left: *Organized materials not only make things go better but also teach children that order facilitates learning. The wall has adjustable shelves, and matched boxes have been attractively covered in wallpaper and labeled. The colored-paper display dispenser facilitates putting up bulletin-board displays.* **Above:** *Open bins make collecting, sorting, and distributing tools and supplies easy. Bins hold fine and broad markers, crayons, bottles of white glue, and palettes.*

properly, and it usually has a smoother texture. The most vexing problem in tempera projects is what to do with the liquid tempera that remains in multicompartment muffin tins, plastic egg cartons, or ice-cube trays. It cannot be poured back into the original containers; this is why paint should be doled out a little at a time, with refills as needed. To minimize the chance of spills, the teacher should be in charge of paint distribution (if possible). Before closing tempera jars, check the plasticity of the paint. If the paint is too dry, add a little water to ensure moistness, and then cap the jar tightly. To prevent liquid tempera lids from becoming difficult to open, wipe the jar rim before closing, or put a little petroleum jelly on the rim. To prevent liquid tempera from becoming sour, add a few drops of wintergreen or oil of cloves to each container.

Recycling Materials

Recycled materials not only enrich artworks, their use conveys a valuable lesson about conservation of Earth's limited resources. In America's productive and wasteful society, there are vast resources that teachers of art can tap for nontraditional art materials. Using imagination and skill, discarded items, empty containers, scraps, and remnants that ordinarily are thought of as worthless can be recycled into artworks. Care must be taken, however, to keep students from regarding the use of interesting materials as an end in itself. The artwork must transcend the materials, becoming a whole that truly is more than the sum of its parts.

Interesting sizes of cut-off paper can be secured for free from printing companies, and newsroll ends often are donated by newspapers. Other sources of paper are computer printouts from institutions and businesses, cardboard boxes from appliance stores, and unused printed billboard papers from outdoor advertising companies. Virtually every company that produces objects has some discarded materials that may be useful in sculptures, collage, weavings, and so on. A company might even underwrite an exhibition crediting their contribution. Most art teachers are not shy about requesting materials for such a societally worthy cause as children's art expression. Children and their parents can help to build a store of materials such as:

Acorns	Blades (saw, broken)
Baby-food jars	Blinds (matchstick, plastic)
Balls (rubber, polystyrene, Ping-Pong)	Blotters
	Bolts and nuts
Bark (tree)	Bones
Beads	Bottle caps

Japan

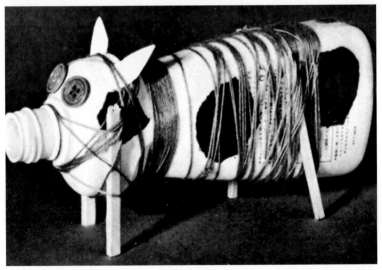

Japan

Recycling material conveys an important ecological lesson. Wood scraps, which usually would be carelessly burned or buried, can be made into imaginative animal sculptures. Care must be exercised when cutting into plastic. It may be prudent to reserve such constructions for upper elementary and middle school. Plastic containers, yarn, sticks, and old buttons usually end up in landfills; instead, such materials can gain a reprieve as animal sculptures and serve a higher purpose, to build the minds and imaginations of tomorrow's creative, adaptive, inventive leaders.

Bottles
Boxes
Bracelets
Buckles
Burlap remnants
Buttons
Cardboard
Carpet samples
Cartons
Cellophane
Celotex
Checkers
Clock parts
Clothespins
Coat hangers
Confetti
Cord
Corks
Cotton
Dowels
Driftwood
Earrings
Fabric remnants
Feathers
Felt
Foam rubber (scraps)
Foil (aluminum)
Greeting cards
Gourds
Leather remnants
Linoleum scraps
Magazines
Marbles
Masonite scraps
Meat trays (plastic foam)
Mirrors
Nails
Necklaces

Newspapers
Nuts
Paper bags
Paper cups and plates
Paper tubes (toilet tissue, mailing)
Paper towels
Paper (shelf, gift wrap, crepe, tissue, plain, colored)
Pebbles
Pie plates
Pinecones
Pins
Pipe cleaners
Polish (shoe)
Q-tips
Reed
Ribbon
Rope
Rubber (inner tube)
Rubber bands
Sand
Sandpaper
Sawdust
Screen
Screws
Seashells
Shades (window)
Spools
Sticks (applicator)
Straws
String
Tile (acoustic, vinyl)
Tongue depressors
Toothpicks
TV-dinner trays
Wallpaper samples
Wood scraps
Yarn remnants

Special Materials and Tools

Special materials and tools include:

Hardboard—For drawing or sketching board, as protective coverage for desks or worktables, and for mural projects.

Brayer (rubber roller)—For inking plate in printmaking. Get the sturdy, soft, black rubber kind (not the gelatin type) for longer wear.

Celluclay—Commercially available dry mixture for use in papier-mâché projects.

Dextrin (powdered)—Add to dry or moist clay (5 to 10 percent) to harden completed work without firing.

Drywall joint cement—For creating relief effects on a two-dimensional surface; can be painted when dry.

Firebrick (porous, insulation type)—For upper elementary and middle school three-dimensional and relief-carving projects.

Grog—Aggregate for plaster molds, clay conditioner.

Masonite (tempered)—For clay modeling board, inking surface in printmaking projects, and rinsing board in tempera or crayon resists; also practical as a portable sketching board.

Pariscraft—Plaster-impregnated gauze in varied widths for additive sculpture projects.

Plaster-of-Paris (molding plaster)—For plaster sculpture and reliefs.

Polystyrene—For printmaking plates, collage and craft projects, and printmaking stamps.

Posterboard (railroad board)—For multicrayon engraving projects; available in several colors.

Sloyd knife (Hyde knife is similar)—All-purpose utility knife with a semisharp blade; excellent for carving in plaster and for delineating details and pattern in crayon engraving projects.

Dressmaker's transfer paper—A white carbon paper useful in crayon engraving projects.

X-acto knife—Craft knife with sharp, interchangeable blades for paper and cardboard sculpture. *Caution:* To be used by the teacher only.

Planning Facilities for Art

The elementary classroom or art room can be the child's first and often most enduring art lesson. There, through exciting displays and eye-catching exhibits, teachers can provide the example for good design through creative, inspiring, and stimulating surroundings. Students should be involved in projects to make the classroom attractive and colorfully stimulating. Bulletin boards and displays should be changed regularly and often to provide evaluative and appreciatory opportuni-

Saturday Children's Classes, courtesy of Frank Wachowiak, Athens, GA.

Collages such as this fantasy environment can be made from wallpaper sample books, and patterned paper.

of 55-square-feet per student is recommended; there also should be a vented kiln, separate storage area, and a sink. The self-contained classroom should provide adequate space at the rear and along one or two walls for storage, a cleanup (sink) facility, and counter working space. There should be sufficient room at the rear for one or two large, sturdy tables that are suitable for craft activities and group projects.

Tables and desks should be easily movable for special projects. Counter surfaces of nonglare, waterproof, and scratch-resistant materials are recommended. Light-colored, laminated-plastic working surfaces must be protected during projects involving linoleum or wood-block cutting, carving in semi-hard substances, or sawing and hammering on wood constructions. In the special art room, stools that can be recessed under tables during cleanup can ease traffic problems. In the primary grades, free-standing easels can effectively augment limited desk space.

Sufficient storage for art supplies, tools, visual aids, work in progress, and completed art projects held over for future display is helpful. Adjustable shelves and tote trays are helpful for various-size art papers and materials. Yarn, wood scraps, and found materials can be stored in large cardboard cartons painted in bright colors. Sturdy galvanized or plastic waste containers, water-tight and air-tight, are necessary for clay and also can be used for plaster, zonolite, and sand.

A cabinet or movable cart with shelves and pegboard panels is suggested for the storage of small tools. Pegboard secured to a wall and the accompanying hardware can alleviate the most pressing tool-storage problems. Painting an identifying shape or outline of each tool on the pegboard expedites storage and inventory. A hollow box made of Masonite with holes drilled in the top provides an excellent scissors container and inventory device.

Because so much of children's art revolves around painting, there should be adequate horizontal storage spaces for paintings in progress. This is especially true in the special art room, where one class quickly follows another. A clothesline and spring clothespins can be used as a drying facility for prints—but not for tempera paintings, which will drip.

To minimize traffic problems, sinks should not be located in a closet or a corner. They should be large enough to allow use by two or three persons at once. They should be low enough that children can reach faucets with ease; if not, students should be provided with step-up platforms.

ties for completed projects and to whet student's interest in further art endeavors. Still-life arrangements should be on view for sketching, and students should be encouraged to contribute to the store of found objects and nature's treasures on display.

Most elementary art projects take place in the self-contained classroom. A few schools boast a multipurpose art room. To make rooms function better for art teaching, changes that need to be made are in the strategic areas of storage, display, and cleanup. If a multipurpose art room is planned, it should be on the first or ground floor, adjacent to the stage of the auditorium or cafeteria, and near a service entrance. An outdoor court, easily accessible from the art room, can provide excellent auxiliary space for sketching, mural making, ceramics, and plaster sculpture in favorable weather.

Sufficient space should be provided to allow students to work on individual projects with some flexibility of movement. Easy rearrangement of furniture for group projects should be planned, and an easy flow of student traffic to the teacher's desk, storage, cleanup areas or stations also is desirable. In the elementary art room, a space

Generous amounts of space should be allotted for display purposes and instructional bulletin boards. Display-panel backgrounds should be neutral in color; subtle and nonglare whites, greys, umbers, and blacks are recommended. In most instances, surfaces, should be matte finish in cork or Celotex; this affords easy pinning, stapling, or tacking of artwork. Acoustic tile can be glued directly to wall surfaces, Masonite, or hardboard panels to provide a display facility, and Cork-surfaced doors on cupboards, closet doors, and storage cabinets also will augment display space.

Floors should be of nonskid materials, hard yet resilient, and easily cleaned. Ceilings should be acoustically treated and provide maximum light reflection. Room-darkening shades or blinds are required for the projection of color slides, videos, and films, and a permanent projection screen should be installed.

Electrical outlets should be provided at frequent intervals around the room. For a ceramic kiln, 220-voltage wiring usually is required. Electrical outlets should not be near sink areas. The ventilator fan in the hood also requires wiring.

Special furniture and equipment can promote a qualitative program. The following items are recommended: clay bin or cart, vibrating jigsaw, color slide projector, projection screen, workbench with vises, large-size paper cutter, electric heating plate, utility cart, ceramic kiln, drying rack for flat work in progress, gun tacker, stapler, large scissors, yardstick, and several wastebaskets or large-size trash containers.

Courtesy of Ted Ramsay and Frank Wachowiak, *Emphasis Art*, Second Edition.

Illustrations on this page show easily constructed, plywood storage facilities for both two- and three-dimensional art projects. Notice in the background of the left picture the rack for art magazines and books and the file cabinets for storage of motivational reproductions. At right, sturdy plastic trays, available commercially, slide in and out on wooden runners tacked to the sides of the cubby holes. Ceramics and reed sculptures with wooden bases are attractively displayed on a background of varied colored papers.

A Brief Chronology of Art Education in the United States

1870—To train artists for industry, the Industrial Drawing Act passed by the Massachusetts legislature required that drawing be taught to all students over 15 years of age in communities of over 20,000.
The Oswego Movement emphasized the study of geometric solids in kindergartens.

1871—The Metropolitan Museum of Art in New York City was established.

1873—The Massachusetts Normal Art School, the first training school for the preparation of teachers of industrial drawing in the country, was established. Walter Smith was the founder and first principal. As the Boston schools' art instructor, he wrote *Teachers' Manual of Free-hand Drawing Designing*. Later, he organized the Massachusetts Art Teachers Association, the first professional art-teachers group, and published a series of graded art lessons to teach geometric drawing. Copying was encouraged to train the eye and hand.

1875—The Art Students' League, New York City, was founded. William Merritt Chase was one of the first instructors.

1876—Thomas Eakins began teaching at the Pennsylvania Academy of Arts, Philadelphia. He relied little on cast models and instead stressed anatomical studies.

1883—The Department of Art Education was established as an integral part of the National Education Association.

1896—John Dewey started the University of Chicago Laboratory School.

1898—Arthur Wesley Dow became art instructor at Teachers College, Columbia University, New York City. Dow subsequently wrote the textbook *Composition*, which stressed design and influenced many art teachers.

1901—First publication of *The Applied Arts Book*, which later became *School Arts*, with H. T. Bailey as editor. The book employed picture-study units that emphasized the storytelling aspects of paintings and the design content.

1904—John Dewey, author of *Art as Experience*, joined the faculty of Columbia University.
Franz Cizek, called the Father of Child Art, began his influential children's art classes (*Künstgewerbeschule*) in Vienna, which emphasized drawing from memory rather than from life.

1912—Paintings by children were exhibited in Steiglitz Gallery, New York City.

1913—A. H. Munsell introduced *A Color Notation*, which established a structure by which color theories can be taught. It provided the color wheel, color terminology, and color harmonies.
Armory Show opened in New York City, introducing the paintings of the fauvists ("wild beasts"), futurists, cubists, and postimpressionists to the United States art community.
Clive Bell wrote *Art*, a treatise that emphasized formal elements.

1919—The Western Arts Association, the largest of the regional art-education associations, was founded. Drawings from nature sources were emphasized.

1920—Pedro J. Lemos, who served as editor of *School Arts Magazine,* wrote *Applied Art*, emphasizing multicultural contributions.

1923—Robert Henri wrote *The Art Spirit*.

1924—Margaret Mathias, an art teacher in Cleveland, Ohio, wrote *The Beginning of Art in the Public Schools*.
Belle Boas wrote *Art in the School*.
From 1900 to 1930, the progressive education movement emphasized the child's process of learning, stressed the importance of subjects' correlation, and decried copying.

1928—Leon L. Winslow wrote *Organization and Teaching of Art*.
Sallie Tannahill wrote *Fine Arts for Public School Administrators*.

During the twenties, the picture-study movement was responsible for bringing art reproductions, especially those emphasizing patriotic and family values, into the schools.

1933—With the Carnegie Corporation as sponsor and Edwin Ziegfeld as director, the Owatonna, Minnesota, Community Home Art Project began, emphasizing the role of art in daily life. The project continued through 1938.

Joseph Albers, author of *Interaction of Color*, introduced the German Bauhaus design philosophy and techniques at Black Mountain College, North Carolina.

1934—The Works Progress Administration (WPA) provided employment for many artists. Scores of murals in state and federal buildings resulted.

John Dewey wrote *Art as Experience*.

1938—Leon L. Winslow wrote *The Integrated School Art Program*.

1940—Natalie R. Cole wrote the inspirational book *The Arts in the Classroom*. It describes how painting, drawing, printmaking, and lettering were creatively taught by an elementary classroom teacher. Art for personal adjustment, emotional release, and leisure-time activity were especially emphasized during this period.

The Progressive Education Association, chaired by Victor D'Amico, published *The Visual Arts in General Education*.

1941—Kimon Nicolaides wrote *The Natural Way to Draw*, which emphasized contour and gesture drawing.

Ray Faulkner, Edwin Ziegfeld, and Gerald Hill wrote *Art Today*, an art appreciation textbook emphasizing art and design in daily life—for example, furniture design.

1942—Victor D'Amico, educational director at the Museum of Modern Art, New York City, wrote *Creative Teaching in Art*.

Wilhelm Viola wrote *Child Art*, documenting the teaching methods of Franz Cizek.

During the war years, art for social responsibility and individual freedom received special emphasis.

1943—Herbert Read wrote *Education through Art*.

The National Committee on Art Education was formed, with Victor D'Amico as chairperson. The committee urged teachers to seek closer ties with practicing artists.

1947—Viktor Lowenfeld, professor at Pennsylvania State University, wrote *Creative and Mental Growth*, which emphasized art for self-expression and creativity.

Rose H. Alschuler and LaBerta Hattwick wrote *Painting and Personality*, a psychological approach to understanding the visual expressions of young children.

1948—The National Art Education Association (NAEA) was established and gradually assumed the administrative functions previously held by the four regional art associations.

Henry Schaefer-Simmern wrote *The Unfolding of Artistic Creativity*, which emphasized matching the individual's stage of conceptualization and documented the role of art in helping people with disabilities.

1951—Florence Cane wrote *The Artist in Each of Us*.

Herbert Read helped to found the International Society for Education through the Arts (INSEA).

1952—Charles and Margaret Gaitskell of Ontario, Canada, wrote *Art Education in the Kindergarten*.

Olive L. Riley wrote *Your Art Heritage*, an art-appreciation text for secondary schools.

1955—Rudolph Arnheim wrote *Art and Visual Perception*.

1957—The National Endowment for the Arts and Humanities established.

1958—Charles D. Gaitskell wrote *Children and Their Art: Methods for the Elementary School*.

Italo DeFrancesco wrote *Art Education: Its Means and Ends*.

1961—Louis F. Hoover wrote *Art Activities for the Very Young*.

June King McFee wrote *Preparation for Art*, giving new emphasis to perceptual, sociological, and environmental issues in art education.

1965—Title V of the Elementary and Secondary Education Act (ESEA) was enacted. Federal funds strengthened state departments of education and made it possible for 36 states to hire a state art director.

The Pennsylvania State University Seminar for Research in Art Education became one of the first federally supported conferences to bring together experts from many fields to discuss content in art education.

Essentialism emphasized the intrinsic value of art study as a discipline itself.

Frank Wachowiak and Theodore Ramsay, both teaching at the University of Iowa, wrote *Emphasis Art: A Qualitative Program for the Elementary School*.

During this period, a movement called "visual literacy" emphasized drawing for perceptual and cognitive development. Newer media, such as film and TV, began to be studied.

1969—As part of an assessment of the quality of education in many subjects, the U.S. Office of Education funded a National Assessment Program in Art, directed by Brent Wilson.

The National Endowment for the Arts established Artists in the Schools programs.

1970—Edmund B. Feldman, professor of art at the University of Georgia, wrote *Becoming Human through Art: Aesthetic Experience in the School.*

Frank Wachowiak, University of Georgia, and David Hodge, University of Wisconsin, wrote *Art in Depth: A Qualitative Program of Art for the Young Adolescent.*

1972—The Central Midwest Regional Educational Laboratory, directed by Stanley Madeja, developed multiarts aesthetic educational materials.

1975—Public Law 94-142 mandated that students with disabilities were to receive the full range of educational services.

1976—Art educators of New Jersey wrote *Insights, Art in Special Education, Educating the Handicapped through Art.*

The NAEA begins sponsoring a National Art Honor Society for 12,000 students.

1978—Francis Anderson wrote *Art for All the Children: A Creative Source-book for the Impaired Child.*

Rawley Silver wrote *Developing Cognitive and Creative Skills through Art.*

Multicultural emphases brought an awareness of sociology, along with popular, folk, and commercial arts into classrooms.

1982—The Getty Center for Education in the Arts, directed by Lani Lattin Duke, was established. The center supported establishment of discipline-based art-education programs in schools.

Museum education was increasingly seen as a supplement to classroom instruction.

1984—Claire and Robert Clements wrote *Art and Mainstreaming: Art Instruction for Exceptional Children in Regular School Classes.*

1987—Michael Parsons wrote *How We Understand Art: A Cognitive Development Account of Aesthetic Experience.*

1988—The National Endowment for the Arts published *Toward Civilization: A Report on Arts Education* (first draft written by Brent Wilson).

Ros Ragans wrote *Art Talk,* a student text incorporating art criticism with studio activities.

1989—The NAEA began sponsoring a National Junior Art Honor Society.

1990—The National Governors Council adopts the National Education Goals.

1992—Claire Golomb wrote *The Child's Creation of a Pictorial World.*

1993—Getty Center publishes *Discipline-Based Art Education and Cultural Diversity.*

1994— Congress enacts the Goals 2000: Educate America Act, containing National Visual Arts Standards.

David Perkins wrote *The Intelligent Eye: Learning to Think by Looking At Art.*

1995—ARTSEDNET@GETTY.EDU, an electronic on-line service over the Internet for K-12 art teachers, classroom teachers, academics, and advocates, was established by the Getty Center for Education in the Arts.

The NAEA establishes an Electronic Media Interest Group.

National Endowment for the Arts and National Endowment for the Humanities programs were cut and restructured.

National Art Education Association develops a five-point plan based on the Goals 2000: Educate America Act for the National Visual Arts Standards and a Professional Development Initiative.

Abrahamson, Roy E. 1980. "The Teaching Approach of Henry Schaefer-Simmern." *Studies in Art Education* 22(1):42–50.

Alexander, Kay, and Michael Day (eds.). 1991. *Discipline-Based Art Education: A Curriculum Sampler.* Los Angeles: Getty Center for Education in the Arts.

Anderson, Tom. 1988. "A Structure for Pedagogical Art Criticism." *Studies in Art Education* 30(1):28–38.

—.1995. "Toward a Cross-Cultural Approach to Art Criticism." *Studies in Art Education* 36(4):198–209.

Armstrong, Carmen. 1993. "Effect of Training in an Art Production Questioning Method on Teacher Questioning and Student Responses." *Studies in Art Education* 34(4):209–221.

—. 1994. *Designing Assessment in Art.* Reston, VA: National Art Education Association.

Arnheim, Rudolf. 1966. *Art and Visual Perception: A Psychology of the Creative Eye.* Berkeley: University of California Press.

Baker, David W. 1990. "Git Real: On Art Education and Community Needs." *Art Education* 43(6):41–49.

Barrett, Terry. 1994. *Criticizing Art: Understanding the Contemporary.* Mountain View, CA: Mayfield Publishing Co.

Batain, Margaret. 1994. "Cases for Kids: Using Puzzles to Teach Aesthetics to Children." *Journal of Aesthetic Education* 28(3):89–104.

Beittel, Kenneth R., et al. 1961. "The Effect of a 'Depth' vs. a 'Breadth' Method of Art Instruction at the Ninth Grade Level." *Studies in Art Education* 3(1):75–87.

Berrson, Ron. 1983. "For Cultural Democracy: A Critique of Elitism in Art Education." *Art Education* 39(4):41–45.

Bickley-Green, Cynthia. 1995. "Mathematics and Art Curriculum Integration: A Postmodern Foundation." *Studies in Art Education* 37(1):6–18.

Billings, Mary-Michael. 1995. "Issues vs. Trends: Two Approaches to a Multicultural Art Curriculum." *Art Education* 48(1):21–24, 53–56.

Blandy, Doug. 1988. "A Multicultural Symposium on Appreciating and Understanding Art." *Art Education* 41:20–24.

—. 1994. "Assuming Responsibility: Disability Rights and the Preparation of Art Educators." *Studies in Art Education* 35(3):179–187.

Blandy, Doug, and Kristin Congdon. 1990. *Culture and Democracy.* New York: Teachers College Press.

—. 1991. *Pluralistic Approaches to Art Criticism.* Bowling Green, OH: Bowling Green University Press.

Blandy, Doug, E. Pancsofar, and Tom Mockensturm. 1988. "Guidelines for Teaching Art to Children and Youth Experiencing Significant Mental/Physical Challenges." *Art Education* 41(1):60–67.

Bloom, Benjamin S. 1984. *Taxonomy of Educational Objectives: The Classification of Educational Goals.* New York: Longmans.

Bowers, C. A. 1990. "Implications of Gregory Bateson's Ideas for a Semiotic of Art Education." *Studies in Art Education* 31(2):66–77.

Brouch, Virginia, and Fanchon Funk (eds.). 1987. *Appleseeds.* Reston, VA: National Art Education Association.

Broudy, Harry S. 1972. *Enlightened Cherishing: An Essay on Aesthetic Education.* Urbana, IL: University of Illinois Press.

Brown, Eleese V. 1984. "Developmental Characteristics of Clay Figure Modeling by Children: 1970–1981." *Studies in Art Education* 26(1):56–60.

Chandra, Jacqueline. 1993. "A Theoretical Basis for Non-Western Art Historical Instruction." *Journal of Aesthetic Education* 27(3):73–84.

Chapman, Laura H. 1982. *Instant Art, Instant Culture: The Unspoken Policy for American Schools.* New York: Teachers College Press.

Chijiiwa, Hideaki. 1987. *Color Harmony: A Guide to Creative Color Combinations.* Rockport, MA: Rockport.

Churchill, Angiola. 1970. *Art for Preadolescents*. New York: McGraw-Hill.

Clahassey, Patricia. 1986. "Modernism, Post Modernism, and Art Education." *Art Education* **39**(2):44–48.

Clark, Gil, Michael Day, and Dwaine Greer. 1987. "Discipline-Based Art Education: Becoming Students of Art." *Journal of Aesthetic Education* **21**(2):130–193.

Clark, Gil, and Enid Zimmerman. 1987. *Educating Artistically Talented Students*. Syracuse, NY: Syracuse University Press.

Clements, Claire, and Robert Clements. 1984. *Art and Mainstreaming: Art Instruction for Exceptional Children in Regular School Classes*. Springfield, IL: Charles C. Thomas.

Clements, Robert D. 1975. "A Case for Art Education: The Influence of Froebel Training on Frank Lloyd Wright." *Art Education* **28**(3):2–7.

—. 1975. "Instructional Objectives or Objectionable Instructions." *Journal of Aesthetic Education* **10**:107–118.

—. 1978. "Art Teacher Appeals: A Way to Motivate and Discipline." *Art Education* **31**(7):15–17.

—. 1979. "The Inductive Method of Teaching Visual Art Criticism." *Journal of Aesthetic Education* **13**(3):67–78.

Cohen, Elaine, and Ruth S. Gainer. 1984. *Art: Another Language for Learning*. New York: Schocken.

Clements, Robert D. and Stueck, Lawrence E. 1984. "Earthworks: A Two-Hundred-Ton Art Educational Media," *Art Education* **36**(4):19–21.

Colbert, Cynthia, and M. Taunton. 1987. "Problems of Representation: Preschool and Third Grade Children's Observational Drawings of a Three Dimensional Model." *Studies in Art Education* **29**(2):103–114.

Cole, Natalie R. 1940. *The Arts in the Classroom*. New York: John Day.

Collins, Georgia, and Rene Sandell. *Women, Art, and Education*. Reston, VA: National Art Education Association.

Congdon, Kristin. "Multicultural Approaches to Art Education." *Studies in Art Education* **30**(3):176–184.

Corwin, Sylvia, and Ruth Perlin. 1995. "A Videodisc Resource for Interdisciplinary Learning: American Art from the National Gallery of Art." *Art Education* **48**(3):17–24.

Cromer, Jim. 1991. *History, Theory, and Practice of Art Criticism*. Reston, VA: National Art Education Association.

Dalton, Kimberly and David Burton. 1995. "Children's Use of Baselines: Influence of A Circular Format." *Studies in Art Education* **36**(4): 105–113.

Davis, Don Jack. 1990. *Behavioral Emphasis in Art Education*. Reston, VA: National Art Education Association.

Degge, Rogena M. 1985. "A Model for Aesthetic Inquiry in Television." *Journal of Aesthetic Education* **19**(4):85–102.

Delacruz, Elizabeth. 1995. "Multiculturalism and Art Education: Myth, Misconceptions, and Misdirections." *Art Education* **48**(3):57–61.

Dewey, John. 1934. *Art as Experience*. New York: Minton Balch.

DiBlasio, Margaret. 1987. "Reflections on the Theory of Discipline-Based Art Education." *Studies in Art Education*. **28**(4):221–226.

Dissanayake, Ellen. 1988. *What Is Art For?* Seattle: University of Washington Press.

Dobbs, Stephen. 1992. *The DBAE Handbook: An Overview of Discipline-Based Art Education*. Los Angeles: Getty Trust.

Douglas, Nancy, and Julia B. Schwartz. 1967. "Increasing Awareness of Art Ideas of Young Children through Guided Experiences with Ceramics." *Studies in Art Education* **8**(2):2–9.

Dunn, Phil. 1988. *Promoting School Art: A Practical Approach*. Reston, VA: National Art Education Association.

Eaton, Marcia. 1994. "Philosophical Aesthetics: A Way of Knowing and Its Limits." *Journal of Aesthetic Education* **28**(3):19–32.

Edwards, Betty. 1979. *Drawing from the Right Side of the Brain*. Los Angeles: J. Tarcher.

Efland, Arthur. 1990. *A History of Art Education: Intellectual and Social Currents in Teaching the Visual Arts*. New York: Teachers College Press.

Eisner, Elliot. 1979. *The Educational Imagination: On the Design and Evaluation of School Programs*. New York: Macmillan.

—. 1987. *The Role of Discipline Based Education in America's Schools*. Los Angeles: The Getty Center for Education in the Arts.

Erickson, Erik. 1963. *Childhood and Society*. New York: Norton.

—. 1968. *Youth, Identity, and Crisis*. New York: Norton.

Erickson, Mary. 1988. "Teaching Aesthetics K–12." In Steven Dobbs (ed.). *Research Readings for Discipline-Based Art Education*. Reston, VA: National Art Education Association.

—. 1995. "A Sequence of Developing Art Historical Understandings: Merging Teaching, Service, Research, and Curriculum Development." *Art Education* **48**(6):23–24, 33–37.

—. 1995. "Second Grade Student's Developing Art Historical Understanding." *Visual Arts Research* **21**(1):15–24.

Ewens, Thomas. 1990. "Flawed Understandings: On Getty, Eisner, and DBAE." In London, Peter, Judith Burton, and Arlene Linderman (eds) *Beyond DBAE: The Case for Multiple Visions of Art Education*. North Dartmouth, MA: Southern Massachusetts University.

—. 1990. "On Discipline: Its Roots in Wonder." *Art Education* **43**(1):6–11.

—. 1994. "Rethinking the Question of Quality in Art." *Arts Education Policy Review* **96**(2):2–15.

Feldman, David H. 1986. *Nature's Gambit*. New York: Basic Books.

—. 1987. "Developmental Psychology and Art Education: Two Fields at the Crossroads." *Journal of Aesthetic Education* **21**(2):243–259.

Feldman, Edmund. 1970. *Becoming Human Through Art*. New York: Prentice-Hall.

—. 1993. "Best Advice and Counsel to Art Teachers." *Art Education* **46**(5):58–59.

—. 1996. *Philosophy of Art Education*. Upper Saddle River, NJ: Prentice-Hall.

Fitzpatrick, Virginia. 1992. *Art History: A Contextual Inquiry Course*. Reston, VA: National Art Education Association.

Flannery, Merle. 1986. "Art as a Neotenizing Influence on Human Development." *Visual Arts Research* **12**(2):34–40.

Freeman, Kerry. 1994. "Interpreting Gender and Visual Culture in Art Classrooms." *Studies in Art Education* **35**(3): 157–170.

Freeman, Nancy. 1980. *Strategies of Children's Drawings*. New York: Academic.

Freeman, Nancy H., and M. V. Cox (eds.). 1985. *Visual Order*. Cambridge, England: Cambridge University Press.

Funk, Farley, and Ron Neperud. 1988. *The Foundations of Aesthetics, Art, and Art Education*. Westport, CT: Greenwood.

Gagné, Robert. 1975. *Essentials of Learning*. New York: Dryden.

Garber, Elizabeth. 1995. "Teaching Art in the Context of Culture: A Study in Borderlands." *Studies in Art Education* **36**(4):218–232.

Gardner, Howard. 1973. *The Arts and Human Development*. New York: Wiley.

—. 1980. *Artful Scribbles: The Significance of Children's Drawings*. New York: Basic Books.

—. 1982. *Art, Mind, and Brain: A Cognitive Approach to Creating*. New York: Basic Books.

—. 1983. *Frames of Mind*. New York: Basic Books.

—. 1989. "Arts Propel." *Studies in Art Education* **30**(2):71–83.

—. 1990. *Art Education and Human Development*. Los Angeles: The Getty Center for Education in the Arts.

Gardner, Howard, Ellen Winner, and M. Kirchner. 1975. "Children's Conceptions About the Arts." *Journal of Aesthetic Education* **9**:60–77.

Gates, Eugene. 1988. "The Female Voice." *Journal of Aesthetic Education* **22**(4):59–68.

Geahigan, George. 1983. "Art Criticism: An Analysis of the Concept." *Visual Arts Research* **9**(1):10–22.

Getty Center for Education in the Arts. 1986. *Beyond Creating: The Place for Art in America's Schools*. Los Angeles: The Getty Center for Education in the Arts.

Getty Center for Education in the Arts. 1993. *Discipline-Based Art Education and Cultural Diversity*. Los Angeles: The Getty Center for Education in the Arts.

Getzels, Jacob, and Mihalyi Csikszentmihalyi. 1976. *The Creative Vision: A Longitudinal Study of Problem Finding in Art*. New York: Wiley.

Goldsmith, Lynn T., and David H. Feldman. 1988. "Aesthetic Judgment: Changes in People and Changes in Domains." *Journal of Aesthetic Education* **22**(4):83–93.

Goldstein, Ernest, Theodore Katz, Jo D. Kowalchuk, and Robert Saunders. 1986. *Understanding and Creating Art*. Dallas: Garrard.

Golomb, Claire. 1974. *Young Children's Sculpture and Drawing: A Study in Representational Development*. Cambridge, MA: Harvard University Press.

—. 1992. *The Child's Creation of a Pictorial World*. Los Angeles: University of California Press.

Golomb, Claire, and D. Farmer. 1983. "Children's Graphic Planning Strategies and Early Principles of Spatial Organization in Drawing." *Studies in Art Education* **24**(2):86–100.

Golomb, Claire and Maureen McCormick. 1995. "Sculpture: The Development of Three-Dimensional Representation in Clay." *Visual Arts Research* **21**(1):35–50.

Goodlad, John. 1984. *A Place Called School: Promise for the Future*. New York: McGraw-Hill.

Goodwin, MacArthur. 1993. *Design Standards for School Art Facilities*. Reston, VA: National Art Education Association.

Greene, Maxine. 1987. "Creating, Experiencing, Sensemaking: Art Worlds in Schools." *Journal of Aesthetic Education* **21**(4):22.

—. 1994. "The Arts and National Standards." *Educational Forum* **58**(4): 391–400.

—. 1995. "Art and Imagination: Reclaiming the Sense of Possiblity." *Phi Delta Kappan* **76**(5): 378–382.

Guay, Doris. 1994. "Students with Disabilities in the Art Classroom: How Prepared Are We?" *Studies in Art Education* **36**(1):44–56.

Guhin, Paula. 1995. "Photograms, Compliments of the Sun." *Arts and Activities* **118**(5):28–29.

Hamblen, Karen. 1984. "An Art Criticism Questioning Strategy within the Framework of Bloom's Taxonomy." *Studies in Art Education* **26**(1):41–50.

—. 1984. "'Don't You Think Some Brighter Colors Would Improve Your Painting?' Or Constructing Questions for Art Dialogues." *Art Education* 37(1):12–14.

—. 1985. "Developing Aesthetic Literacy Through Contested Concepts." *Art Education* 38(5):19–24.

—. 1986. "Artistic Commonalities and Differences: Educational Occasions for Universal-Relative Dialectics." *Visual Arts Research* 12:2.

—. 1986. "Exploring Contested Concepts for Aesthetic Literacy." *Journal of Aesthetic Education* 20(2):67–76.

—. 1987. "Approaches to Aesthetics in Art Education: A Critical Theory Perspective." *Studies in Art Education* 29(2):81–90.

—. 1989. "An Elaboration on Meanings and Motives, Negative Aspects of DBAE." *Art Education* 42(4):6–7.

—. 1991. "In the Quest for Art Criticism Equity: A Tentative Model." *Studies in Art Education* 17(1):33.

—. 1993. "The Emergence of Neo-DBAE." Paper presented at the American Educational Research Association Conference in Atlanta.

Hamblen, Karen, and Camille Galanes. 1991. "Instructional Options for Aesthetics: Exploring the Possibilities." *Art Education* 44(6):12–25.

Harris, Dale. 1963. *Children's Drawings as Measurements of Intellectual Maturity*. New York: Harcourt, Brace and World.

Hausman, Jerome. 1990. "Editorial: Art Education and 'All that Jazz.'" *Art Education* 43(5):4–6.

—. 1990. "Unity and Diversity in Art Education." In London, Peter, Judith Burton, and Arlene Linderman (eds). *Beyond DBAE: The Case for Multiple Visions of Art Education*. North Dartmouth, MA: Southern Massachusetts University.

Haynes, Deborah. 1995. "Teaching Postmodernism." *Art Education* 48(5):23–24, 45–50.

Heberholz, Donald, and Barbara Heberholz. 1990. *Developing Artistic and Perceptual Awareness*. Dubuque, IA: Wm. C. Brown.

Henry, Carole. 1995. "Migrant Mother." *Art Education* 48(3):25–28, 37–40.

—. 1995. "Parallels between Student Responses to Works of Art and Existing Aesthetic Theory." *Studies in Art Education* 37(1):47–54.

Hewett, G. C., and Jean C. Rush. "Finding Buried Treasures: Aesthetic Scanning with Children." *Art Education* 40(1):41–43.

Holmes Group Executive Board. 1986. *Tomorrow's Teachers: A Report of the Holmes Group*. East Lansing, MI: ?.

Holt, David. 1990. "Post Modernism vs. High Modernism: Relationship to D.B.A.E. and Its Critics." *Art Education* 43(2):42–46.

—. 1995. "Postmodernism: Anomaly in Art-Critical Theory." *Journal of Aesthetic Education* 29(1):85–94.

Hurwitz, Al. 1983. *The Gifted and Talented in Art: A Guide to Program Planning*. Worcester, MA: Davis.

—. 1993. *Collaboration in Art Education*. Reston, VA: National Art Education Association.

Hurwitz, Al, and Michael Day. *Children and Their Art*. New York: Harcourt Brace Jovanovich.

Hurwitz, Al, and Stanley Madeja. 1977. *The Joyous Vision: A Source Book for Elementary Art Appreciation*. Englewood Cliffs, NJ: Prentice-Hall.

Johnson, Andra. 1992. *Elementary Art Education Anthology*. Reston, VA: National Art Education Association.

Kaelin, Eugene. 1989. *An Aesthetics for Art Educators*. New York: Teachers College Press.

—. 1990. "The Construction of a Syllabus for Aesthetics in Art Education." *Art Education* 43(2):22–34.

Katter, Eldon. 1995. "Multicultural Connections: Craft Community." *Art Education* 48(1):8–13.

Kauppinen, Heta, and Diket Read (eds.). *Trends in Art Education from Diverse Cultures*. Reston, VA: National Art Education Association.

Kellogg, Rhoda. 1970. *Analyzing Children's Art*. Palo Alto, CA: National Press.

Kinder, A. 1987. "A Review of Rationales for Integrated Arts Programs." *Studies in Art Education* 29(1):52–60.

Krathwohl, David, Benjamin Bloom, and Bertram Masia. 1984. *Taxonomy of Educational Objectives. Handbook 2: The Affective Domain*. New York: New Directions.

LaLiberte, Norman, and Shirley McIlhany. 1966. *Banners and Hangings: Design and Construction*. New York: Reinhold.

LaLiberte, Norman, and Alex Mogelon. 1967. *Painting with Crayons: History and Modern Techniques*. New York: Reinhold.

—. 1966. *Masks, Face Coverings, and Headgear*. New York: Reinhold.

Lark-Horowitz, Betty, Hilda Lewis, and Mark Luca. 1973. *Understanding Children's Art for Better Teaching*. Columbus, OH: Merrill.

Linderman, Marlene. 1990. *Art in the Elementary School: Drawing, Painting, and Creativity for the Classroom*. Dubuque, IA: Wm. C. Brown.

Lippard, Lucy. 1984. *Get the Message? A Decade of Art for Social Change*. New York: Dutton.

Lommel, Andreas. 1981. *Masks: Their Meanings and Function*. London: Ferndale.

London, Peter, Judith Burton, and Arlene Linderman (eds.). 1990. *Beyond DBAE: The Case for Multiple Visions of Art Education*. North Dartmouth, MA: Southeastern Massachusetts University.

Lowenfeld, Viktor. 1947. *Creative and Mental Growth*. New York: Macmillan.

Mager, Robert F. 1975. *Preparing Instructional Objectives*. Belmont, CA: Fearon.

Markowitz, Sally. 1994. "The Distinction between Art and Craft." *Journal of Aesthetic Education* **28**(1):55–70.

Mattil, Edward, and Betty Marzan. 1981. *Meaning in Children's Art: Projects for Teachers*. New York: Prentice-Hall.

McCann, Michael. 1985. *Health Hazards Manual for Artists*. New York: Nick Lyons Books.

—. 1991. "Oil Painting Hazards in Classrooms." *Art Hazards News* **14**:2.

McFee, June K. 1988. "Art and Society." In Getty Foundation for Education in the Arts. *Issues in Discipline-Based Art Education: Strengthening the Stance, Extending the Horizons*. Los Angeles: The Getty Center for Education in the Arts.

McFee, June, and Rogena Degge. *Art, Culture, and Environment: A Catalyst for Teaching*. Belmont, CA: Wadsworth.

Michael, John. 1983. *Art and Adolescence, Teaching Art at the Secondary Level*. New York: Teachers College Press.

Moody, Larrie. 1992. "An Analysis of Drawing Programs for Early Adolescents." *Studies in Art Education* **34**(1):39–47.

Moore, Michael. 1995. "Towards a New Liberal Learning in Art." *Art Education* **48**(6):6–13.

Morman, Jean. 1989. *One-Two-Three Murals: Simple Murals to Make Using Children's Open Ended Art*. Warren Publishing House.

National Art Education Association. *Position Paper: The Essentials of a Quality School Art Program*. Reston, VA: National Art Education Association.

National Commission on Excellence in Education. 1983. *A Nation at Risk*. Washington, DC: Government Printing Office.

National Endowment for the Arts. 1988. "Overview, Toward Civilization." *NAEA News* **30**(3):3–7.

Nicolaides, Kimon. 1941. *The Natural Way to Draw*. Boston: Houghton.

O'Brien, Bernadette C. 1978. *Tapestry: Interrelationship of the Arts in Reading and Language Development*. New York: New York City Board of Education.

Oliver, Teddy J. and Robert Clements, 1983 "Expression in Middle School Students' art," *School arts* **83**(1):24–27.

Perkins, David. 1994. *The Intelligent Eye: Learning to Think by Looking at Art*. Champaign, IL: University of Illinois Press.

Paik, Nam June, 1990. Cited in Beverly J. Jones. "Toward Democratic Direction of Technology." In Blandy and Congdon. *Culture and Democracy*, New York: Teachers College Press, pp. 64–73.

Pariser, David. 1995. "Not under the Lamppost: Piagetian and Non-Piagetian Research in the Arts: A Review and Critique." *Journal of Aesthetic Education* **29**(3):93–108.

Parsons, Michael, and Blocker, H. Gene. 1993. *Aesthetics and Education*. Urbana and Champaign, IL: University of Illinois Press.

Parsons, Michael. 1987. *How We Understand Art: A Cognitive Development Account of Aesthetic Experience*. Cambridge, England: Cambridge University Press.

—. 1994. "Can Children Do Aesthetics? A Developmental Account." *Journal of Aesthetic Education* **28**(3):33–46.

Peterson, Charles R. "Visual Art and the Physically Challenged Person." Videotape. Bloomington, IN: Agency for Instructional Technology.

Qualley, Charles A. 1986. *Safety in the Artroom*. Worcester, MA: Davis.

Read, Herbert. 1955. *Icon and Idea: The Function of Art in the Development of Human Consciousness*. Cambridge, MA: Harvard University Press.

—. 1973. *Education Through Art*. 3d ed. New York: Pantheon.

Reiff, J. 1991. *Learning Styles*. Reston, VA: National Art Education Association.

Rossol, Monona. 1990. *The Artist's Complete Health and Safety Guide*. New York: Allworth.

Rottger, Ernst. 1961. *Surfaces in Creative Design*. London: Batsford.

—. 1963. *Creative Clay Design*. New York: Reinhold.

—. 1969. *Creative Wood Design*. New York: Reinhold.

—. 1970. *Creative Paper Design*. New York: Reinhold.

Rush, Jean C. 1984. "Bridging the Gap Between Developmental Psychology and Art Education: The View from an Artist's Perspective." *Visual Arts Research* **10**(2):9–14.

Russell, R. L. 1991. "Teaching Students to Inquire About Art Philosophically." *Studies in Art Education* **32**(2):94–104.

Sacca, Elizabeth J. 1989. "Invisible Women: Questioning Recognition and Status in Art Education." *Studies in Art Education* **30**(1):122–127.

Sarason, Seymour. 1991. *The Challenge of Art to Psychology*. New Haven, CT: Yale University Press.

Saunders, Robert J. 1977. *Relating Art and Humanities to the Classroom*. Dubuque, IA: Wm. C. Brown.

—. 1982. "The Lowenfeld Motivation." *Art Education* **35**(6):30.

Schaefer-Simmern, Henry. 1948. *The Unfolding of Artistic Activity*. Berkeley: University of California Press.

Schapiro, Meyer. 1953. "Style." In A. L. Kroeber (ed.). *Anthropology Today*. Chicago: University of Chicago Press.

Schiller, Marjorie. 1995. "The Importance of Conversations about Art with Young Children." *Visual Arts Research* **21**(1):25–34.

Sharff, Stefan. 1982. *The Elements of Cinema.* New York: Columbia University Press.

Smith, Nancy R. 1982. *Experience and Art: Teaching Children to Paint.* New York: Teachers College Press.

Smith, Nancy, and C. Fucigna. 1988. "Drawing Systems in Children's Pictures: Contour and Form." *Visual Arts Research* **14**(1):66–76.

Smith, Ralph A. (ed.). 1986. *Excellence in Art Education.* Reston, VA: National Art Education Association.

Smith, Ralph, and W. Levi. 1991. *Art Education: A Critical Necessity.* Urbana, IL: University of Illinois Press.

Sorri, Mari. 1994. "The Body Has Reasons: Tacit Knowing in Thinking and Making." *Journal of Aesthetic Education* **28**(2):15–26.

Stokrocki, Mary. 1990. "A Cross Site Analysis: Problems in Teaching Art to Preadolescents." *Studies in Art Education* **31**(2):106–107.

Strommen, Erik. 1988. "A Century of Children Drawing: The Evolution of Theory and Research Concerning the Drawings of Children." *Visual Arts Research* **14**:13–24.

"Symposium: Blocker on 'Primitive' Art." 1995. *Journal of Aesthetic Education* **29**(3).

"Symposium: On Marcia Eaton's Philosophy of Art." 1995. *Journal of Aesthetic Education* **29**(2).

"Symposium: On the Child's Pictorial World." 1994. *Journal of Aesthetic Education* **28**(2):51–70.

Szekely, George. 1988. *Encouraging Creativity in Art Lessons.* New York: Teachers College Press.

—. 1995. "Circus." *Art Education* **48**(4):44–50.

Thorne, J. H. 1990. "Mainstreaming Procedures: Support Services and Training." *NAEA Advisory.*

Tolley, Kimberly. 1994. *The Art and Science Connection.* Reading, PA: Addison-Wesley.

Torrance, E. Paul. 1966. "Torrance Test of Creative Thinking." Bensenville, IL: Scholastic Testing Service.

Vallance, Elizabeth. 1988. "Art Criticism as Subject Matter in Schools and Art Museums." *Journal of Aesthetic Education* **22**(4):69–82.

Wasson, Stuhr, and L. Petrovich-Mwaniki. 1990. "Teaching Art in the Multi-cultural Classroom: Six Position Statements." *Studies in Art Education* **31**(4):234–246.

Wilson, Brent, and Harlan Hoffa (eds.). 1988. *History of Art Education: Proceedings from the Penn State Conference.* Reston, VA: National Art Education Association.

Wilson, Brent, Al Hurwitz, and Marjorie Wilson. 1987. *Teaching Drawing from Art.* Worcester, MA: Davis Publications.

Wilson, Brent, and Marjorie Wilson. 1981. "The Use and Uselessness of Developmental Stages." *Art Education* **34**(5):4–5.

—. 1982. *Teaching Children to Draw.* Englewood Cliffs, NJ: Prentice-Hall.

Winfrey, Anita. 1995. "Adinkra Prints." *Arts and Activities* **118**(3):24.

Winner, Ellie. 1982. *Invented Worlds: The Psychology of the Arts.* Cambridge, MA: Harvard University Press.

Wolf, Dennie, and M. D. Perry. 1988. "From Endpoints to Repertoires: New Conclusions About Drawing Development." *Journal of Aesthetic Education* **29**(3):13–35.

Wygant, Foster. 1993. *School Art in American Culture.* Cincinnati: Interwood Press.

Young, Bernard. 1991. *Art, Culture, and Ethnicity.* Reston, VA: National Art Education Association.

Zakia, Richard. 1993. "Photography and Visual Perception." *Journal of Aesthetic Education* **27**(4): 67–82.

Zimmerman, Enid. 1990. "Issues Related to Teaching Art from a Feminist Point of View." *Visual Arts Research* **16**(2):1–9.

—. 1990. "Questions About My Culture and Art Education or 'I'll Never Forget the Day M'Blawi Stumbled on the Work of the Post Impressionists.'" *Art Education* **43**(6):8–24.

Zurmuehlen, Marilyn. 1989. "Serious Pursuit of Cultural Trivialization." *Art Education* **42**(6):46–49.

—. 1990. *Studio Art, Praxis, Symbol, Presence.* Reston, VA: National Art Education Association.

Addresses of Professional Associations, Art Material Suppliers, Audiovisual Sources, Computer Webpages, and Electronic Lesson Plan Databases

These lists are by no means complete, but they can serve as starting points to obtain further information.

Professional Art Education Associations

National Art Education Association, 1916 Association Drive, Reston, VA 22091

>   Also, each state has a state art education association.

International Society for Education Through Art, c/o Prof. Kit Grauer, University of British Columbia, Dept. of Art Education, Vancouver, B.C. V6T 1Z5 Canada

United States Society for Education through Art (USSEA), c/o Dr. Mary Stokrocki, School of Art, Arizona State University, Tempe, AZ 85287

Art and Craft Material Suppliers

A few addresses of representative arts and crafts suppliers. Many also have regional distribution headquarters throughout the county.

Dick Blick Art Materials, P.O. Box 1267, Galesburg, IL 61402-1267

Nasco Arts and Crafts, 901 Janesville Ave., P.O. Box 901, Fort Atkinson, WI 53538-0901 (1-800-558-9595)

Pyramid Art Supply, 923 Hickory Lane, Mansfield, OH 44901-8104

R. B. Walter Art and Craft Materials, P.O. Box 62331, Arlington, TX 76005

Sax Arts and Crafts, P.O. Box 51710, New Berlin, WI 53151

Triarco Arts and Crafts, 14650 28th Avenue North, Plymouth, MN 55447

Sources for Audiovisuals: Reproductions, Slides, Cassettes, and Viseodiscs

American Library Color Slide Co., 222 West 23rd Street, New York, NY 10011

Art Education, Inc., Blauveldt, NY 10913

BFA Educational Media, 11559 Santa Monica Boulevard, Los Angeles, CA 90025

Communacad, The Communications Academy, Box 541, Wilton, CT 06897

Crystal Productions, Box 2159, Glenview, IL 60025. (1-800-255-8629; fax, 1-800-657-8149)

Encyclopaedia Britannica Films, 425 North Michigan Avenue, Chicago, IL 60604

Films for the Humanities and Sciences, P.O. Box 2053, Princeton, NJ 08543-2053 (1-800-257-5126)

Films Incorporated Video, 5547 Ravenswood Avenue, Chicago, IL 60640-1199

Gould Media, 44 Parkway West, Mt. Vernon, NY 10552

International Film Bureau, 332 South Michigan Avenue, Chicago, IL 60604

Media for the Arts, P.O. Box 1011, Newport, RI 02840

Reinhold Publishing Co., 600 Summer Street, Stamford, CT 06901

Shorewood Reproductions, Inc., 475 Tenth Avenue, New York, NY 10018

Society for Visual Education, 1345 Diversey Parkway, Chicago, IL 60614

The Roland Collection, 22-D Hollywood Avenue Ho-Ho-Kus, NJ 07423 (1-800 59 ROLAND)

Universal Color Slide, 8450 South Tamiami Trail, Sarasota, FL 34238

Van Nostrand Reinhold, 450 West 33rd Street, New York, NY 10001

Art reproductions and slides can also be acquired inexpensively from most art museums; a few addresses are:

Metropolitan Museum of Art, Fifth Avenue and 82nd Street, New York, NY 10028

Museum of Modern Art, 11 West 53rd Street, New York, NY 10019

National Gallery of Art, Constitution Avenue and 6th Street NW, Washington, DC 20001

Computer Webpages and Electronic Lesson Plan Databases

The Getty Center for Education in the Arts has established ArtsEdNe@GETTY.EDU, an electronic on-line information resource over the Internet for K–12 arts teachers, classroom teachers, academics, and advocates. Marlin Murdock (MMurdock@Getty.edu) directs the URL website at http:/www.artsednet@getty.edu.

The National Art Education Association has officially started an Electronic Media Interest Group. Address e-mail to LIST-SERVER@LISTS.ACS.OHIO State.EDU. To subscribe: NAEA-EMIG<your name>.

ArtsEdge, at http://kennedy center.org, is a collaboration between the John F. Kennedy Center for Performing Arts, the Dept. of Education, and the National Endowment for the Arts.

ARTS USA is created by the American Council for the Arts.

The Southeast Center for Education in the Arts provides teaching resources in art, music, and theater for K–12.

ARTnet is sponsored by the Nebraska Department of Education.

Several states have gateways; these include the Florida Institute for Art Education, the Minnesota Center for Arts Education, the North Texas Institute for Educators in the Visual Arts, and the Ohio Partnership for the Visual Arts.

Abstract in art, objects or figures that are depicted in a simplified or stylized way (in which nonessential aspects are discarded) yet remain recognizable

Aesthetic dealing with art theory or issues of appreciation in art; the beautiful as related or contrasted to the good, the true, or the useful.

Affective present or remembered emotions that may stimulate, or be stimulated by, an artwork.

Appliqué a decorative design made by cutting pieces of one fabric and applying them by gluing or stitching onto the surface of another fabric.

Armature a framework (of wood, wire, and so on) employed to support constructions of clay, papier-mâché, or plaster.

Balance a principle in art; may be formal or informal, symmetrical or asymmetrical.

Balsa a strong, lightweight wood used for model building and stabiles.

Baren a device made of cardboard and bamboo leaf that is used as a hand press in taking a print (of Japanese derivation).

Bas relief in sculpture, when the objects or figures remain attached to the background plane or project only slightly from it.

Bat a plaster block used to hasten drying of moist clay.

Batik a method of designing on fabric by sealing with melted wax those areas not to be dyed.

Bench hook a wood device secured to a desk or table to stabilize a linoleum block during the gouging process.

Bisque clay in its fired or baked state (unglazed).

Brayer a rubber roller used for inking in printmaking processes.

Burnish to make smooth or glossy by a rubbing or polishing action.

Calligraphy the art of fine writing, usually done with a brush or pen.

Ceramic a word used to describe clay constructions and products thereof.

Charcoal a drawing stick or pencil made from charred wood.

Chip-board sturdy cardboard, usually grey, of varying thicknesses; used for collage, collograph, sketching boards, and in construction projects.

Clay a natural, moist earth substance used in making bricks, tile, pottery, and ceramic sculpture.

Collage a composition or design made by arranging and gluing materials to a background surface.

Collograph a print made from a collage; relief plate created with an assortment of pasted or glued items, such as pieces of paper, cardboard, cord, string, and other found objects.

Color an element of art; also referred to as *hue*.

Color, analogous closely related color; neighbors on the color wheel, such as green, blue-green, and yellow-green.

Color, monochromatic all of the tints and shades of a single color plus its neutralized possibilities.

Colors, complementary colors found opposite one another on the color wheel, such as red and green.

Colors, primary red, yellow, blue; three basic hues.

Colors, secondary green, orange, violet; achieved by mixing primary colors.

Computer art a creator uses a computer with a program such as Kidpix, Dabbler, Photoshop, Painter, or Clarisworks Draw and Paint for expressive, artistic intent.

Construction paper a strong, absorbent, semitextured paper available in a wealth of colors and used for drawings, paintings in tempera, crayon, oil pastel, printmaking, collage, and paper sculpture.

Contour drawing a line drawing delineating the outer and inner contours of a posed model, still life, landscape, or other selected subject matter.

Correlation of subjects an educational term that has been replaced by the term *integration*.

Creativity an emphasis on originality, fluency, and flexibility as often found in artistic endeavor.

Domination a principle in art; opposite term is *subordination*. The two complement each other.

Easel a wood or metal frame to support an artist's canvas during painting; a simpler version is found in many kindergartens for use in tempera painting.

Embossing creating a raised or relief design on metal or leather by tooling or indenting the surface.

Emphasis a principle in art; important elements in a composition are emphasized.

Encaustic a painting process employing hot beeswax mixed with color pigment; sometimes used to describe melted-crayon creations.

Engobe clay slip, colored or white; used to decorate greenware before firing.

Engraving a process of incising or scratching a hard surface to produce a printed image, as in copper or crayon engraving.

Expressionistic a style of art, originally central European and early twentieth century, that emphasizes psychological and emotional conditions, often through use of high contrast and clashing color.

Expressive artwork that seems to spring directly and honestly from the artist's feelings.

Findings metal clasps, hooks, loops, and so on used in jewelry making.

Firing in ceramics, the baking of clay in a kiln or an outdoor banked fire; also see *Raku*.

Found objects discards, remnants, samples, leftovers, and throwaways that are exploited in collages, junk sculpture, assemblages, and as stamps in printmaking projects.

Frieze a decorated, horizontal band in paint or in relief along the upper part of a building or room.

Glaze a transparent or semitransparent coating of a color stain over a plain surface or another color; used in oil painting, plaster sculpture, or ceramicware.

Gradient a gradual shift from distinct to blended together, as in a textural gradient, or from one color to another, as in a color gradient (or graduated color blending).

Greenware unfired clay in the leather-hard stage, firm but not completely dry.

Grout a crevice filler, such as the conditioned plaster sealed between clay, glass, or vinyl tesserae in a mosaic.

Gum eraser a soft eraser used in drawing; available in cube or rectangle form.

Harmony a combination of objects or design motifs, which pleases an indivdual, contrasted to a clashing or unharmonious arrangement.

Hue another name for *color*.

Impressionistic an art technique, originally French and late nineteenth century, emplying thick, discontinuous strokes of color for representing fleeting effects of light on form.

India ink a waterproof ink made from lampblack; used for drawing, designing, and in tempera resists.

Integration of subjects when subject matter, methods, and sensibilities from different academic areas combine and catalyse a unique quality learning experience in both areas.

Intensity the level of richness or saturation or, conversely, dullness or subtlety of a color.

Kiln an oven used for drying, firing, and glazing clay creations.

Kinesthetic how the body's several senses and its movements can be used to enhance learning and esthetic response.

Kneaded eraser a grey eraser made of unvulcanized rubber that must be stretched and kneaded to be effective; most often used in charcoal drawing.

Line an element in art; the basic skeletal foundation of a design or composition.

Loom the supporting framework for the crisscrossing threads and yarn in weaving.

Macramé lacework made by tying, knotting, and weaving cord in a pattern.

Manila paper a general-purpose drawing or coloring paper; usually cream in color.

Masonite a pressed board made of wood fibers; used for clay-modeling boards, inking surfaces in printmaking, and rinsing boards in tempera and crayon resists.

Mat board a heavy poster board available in many colors and textures; used for mounting or matting artwork.

Mobile a free-moving hanging sculptural construction in space; Alexander Calder's gift to the art world.

Monoprint a one-of-a-kind print; usually made by incising or marking an inked glass plate and taking an impression.

Mosaic a design or composition made by arranging and gluing tesserae or geometric pieces of material next to, but not touching one another on a background surface.

Motif a recurring pattern (or figure, symbol, or artistic device) in an artwork.

Mouse a computer-art input device, along with keyboard, joystick, trackpad, touch pad, drawing tablet, and/or scanner.

Mural a monumental artwork on the inside or outside walls of a building; executed in paint, mosaic, metal repoussé, or a combination of materials.

Newsprint newspaper stock used for sketches, preliminary drawings, and prints.

Nonobjective art without objects, wholly nonrepresentational of anything in objective reality; sometimes confused with *abstract*.

Oil pastel a popular coloring medium consisting of a combination of chalk and oil; available in a host of exciting colors.

Papier-mâché name given to paper crafts that use newspaper moistened with wallpaper paste or laundry starch; also called *paper pulp constructions*.

Patina originally, the color produced by corrosion on metal (the antique sheen of old age), now artificially obtained through use of patinalike wax pastes.

Pattern design made by repeating a motif or symbol (allover pattern).

Perspective creation of a three-dimensional space illusion on a two-dimensional surface by means of vanishing points, converging lines, and diminishing sizes of objects.

Photogram design made on light-sensitive paper (with objects in areas blocking the light) made without a lens or camera.

Plaster a white, powdery substance that forms a quick-setting molding or casting material when mixed with water; sometimes referred to as *plaster-of-Paris*.

Portfolio often a collection of two-dimensional artworks and/or written materials, sometimes on a common theme or done by one student over a period of time, that may be used for assessment.

Positive–negative Positive shapes in a composition are the solid objects—the people, trees, animals, buildings; negative shapes are the unoccupied, empty spaces between positive shapes. Atmosphere, sky, and earth, which are considered to be negative space, sometimes are designated as *foreground* and *background* space.

Psychomotor often used in regard to educational activity that emphasizes how the mind, the body, and its movement interact.

Radiation lines, shapes, or colors emanating from a central core, such as sun rays, fan leaf, ripples around a pebble thrown into a stream.

Raku a ceramic firing process using a primitive kiln and producing smoky and iridescent effects.

Representational resembling in appearance the known likenesses of objects in nature.

Relief a projection from a surface; low relief as in a coin is called *bas relief*.

Repetition (rhythm) a principle of art; repetition of lines, shapes, colors, and values in a composition creates unity.

Repoussé a design technique in metal art wherein tooling and hammering are employed to achieve relief effects.

Resist an art technique wherein a material such as wax or starch is used to mask out areas that are to remain temporarily of a different color or value.

Rhythm the way that repeating, varying, and spacing elements create the equivalent of notes and pauses in music.

Scoring (clay) to make rough indentations in clay with a nail or similar tool as a step in cementing two pieces of clay together; also used to describe the guiding indentation in paper-sculpture curved-line folding

Selvedge the edge of a fabric where the weft returns to weave its way to the opposite edge.

Shade refers to the darker values of a color or hue. Maroon is a shade of red; navy blue is a shade of blue.

Sketch usually a preliminary drawing made with pencil, pen, crayon, charcoal, brush, pastel, or similar tool.

Slip clay diluted with water to a creamy consistency; used as a binder to join two pieces of clay in ceramic construction.

Space in art, the area and/or air occupied by, activated by, or implied to be in an artwork.

Stabile a sculptural construction in space resting on the ground, akin to a mobile that hangs.

Still life an arrangement of objects, usually on a table, as a subject for drawing, painting, collage, and so on.

Stipple for a pattern of closely spaced dots or small marks used in drawing and printmaking that may suggest modeling.

Style recognizable and recurring characteristics that can exemplify the work of an individual, group, or of a place and/or a period of time.

Subordination a principle of art; parts of the composition are subordinated so that others may dominate and be emphasized.

Tactile pertaining to the sense of touch, such as the use of textured materials and surfaces, often for an aesthetic purpose.

Tagboard a glossy-surfaced, pliable cardboard used in collage, collographs, glue-line prints, and paper constructions; sometimes referred to as *oaktag*.

Tempera paint an opaque, water-soluble paint available in liquid or powder form; also referred to as *showcard* or *poster paint*.

Tessera a small segment of paper, cardboard, vinyl, ceramic, and so on (usually in geometric shape) that is fitted and glued to a background surface to produce a mosaic (plural: *tesserae*).

Texture the actual or visual feel of a surface, such as bark on a tree, fur on an animal, sand on a beach.

Tint the lighter values of a color or hue. Pink is a tint of red.

Unity a principle of art; when everything in a composition falls into place through use of fundamental principles of art, unity is achieved.

Value in color terminology, the lightness or darkness of a hue.

Warp the thread or yarn that supports the weft in weaving.

Watercolors water-soluble colors, generally transparent or semitransparent; can be employed thickly to become opaque. Available in semimoist cakes or tubes.

Wedging a method of preparing moist clay by kneading and squeezing to expel the air pockets and make it more plastic.

Weft the thread that goes across the warp from side to side in weaving; also refers to the yarn used as weft.

Photo Credits

Index

In this index, topics and related illustrations usually appear on the same page or within a range of pages. For this type of situation, page numbers are given in regular type. When an illustration on a particular topic appears elsewhere in the text, and not on the same page with its related text topic, the page number is given in italic type: 478.